State and Society
in Medieval Europe

THE WILDER HOUSE SERIES IN POLITICS, HISTORY, AND CULTURE

The Wilder House Series is published in association with the Wilder House Board of Editors and the University of Chicago.

David Laitin, *Editor*
Leora Auslander, *Assistant Editor*
George Steinmetz, *Assistant Editor*

State and Society in Medieval Europe: Gwynedd and Languedoc under Outside Rule by James Given

State and Society
in Medieval Europe

Gwynedd and Languedoc under Outside Rule

JAMES GIVEN

Cornell University Press ITHACA AND LONDON

First published 1990 by Cornell University Press.

International Standard Book Number 0-8014-2439-9
Library of Congress Catalog Card Number 90-31274

Printed in the United States of America

Librarians: Library of Congress cataloging information appears on the last page of the book.

For my mother, Sara Buchanan Given

Contents

Acknowledgments

In the years that I have worked on this book, I have acquired many debts. My research trips to French and British archives were funded by an NEH Summer Stipend (FT-20646-81-1081) and a grant from the Harvard Graduate Society. The staffs of the Public Record Office, the Bibliothèque Nationale, and the departmental archives of the Tarn and the Ariège were unfailingly courteous and helpful in making available their resources. Thomas N. Bisson, Fredric L. Cheyette, Jonathan Dewald, Steven Epstein, Ralph A. Griffiths, Michael Johnson, Gavin I. Langmuir, Steven Ozment, Mark Poster, Steven Topik, Scott Waugh, William Weber, and R. Bin Wong kindly shared their opinions of earlier versions of this manuscript. Claire Ambroselli, Megan McLaughlin, and Robert and Margaret Shepard provided support and assistance in California and Paris. Jane, Leland, Bud, Oscar, Gamera, Grace, Rebel, Bruce, Tinker Bell, Hortense, Little Kitty, Black and White Cat, Kelly, Rita, and Aliz repeatedly reminded me that there was more to life than the study of medieval history. My wife, Ruth Given, provided me with acute criticism and a great deal of support during the course of a project that at times seemed to be without end.

Parts of Chapters 4 and 5 originally appeared in "The Economic Consequences of the English Conquest of Gwynedd," *Speculum* 64 (1989): 11–45, and are reprinted here with permission.

JAMES GIVEN

Long Beach, California

Abbreviations

AESC	*Annales: Economies, Sociétés, Civilisations*
AM	Archives Municipales
Ancient Laws	Great Britain, Record Commission, *Ancient Laws and Institutes*, London, 1841
Ann. Midi	*Annales du Midi*
ASV	Archivio Segreto Vaticano
BBCS	*Bulletin of the Board of Celtic Studies*
BEC	*Bibliothèque de l'Ecole des Chartes*
BN	Bibliothèque Nationale
BPR	Great Britain, Public Record Office, *Register of Edward the Black Prince*, 4 vols., London, 1930–33
Cal. Anc. Corr.	J. G. Edwards, ed., *Calendar of Ancient Correspondence*, Cardiff, 1935
Cal. Anc. Pets.	William Rees, ed., *Calendar of Ancient Petitions Relating to Wales*, Cardiff, 1975
Cal. Inq. Misc.	Great Britain, Public Record Office, *Calendar of Inquisitions Miscellaneous (Chancery)*, 7 vols., London, 1916–68
Cal. Var.	Great Britain, Public Record Office, *Calendar of Various Chancery Rolls*, London, 1912
CChR	Great Britain, Public Record Office, *Calendar of the Charter Rolls*, 6 vols., London, 1903–27
CCR	Great Britain, Public Record Office, *Calendar of the Close Rolls*, London

CF	*Cahiers de Fanjeaux*
CPR	Great Britain, Public Record Office, *Calendar of the Patent Rolls*, London
Doat	Bibliothèque Nationale, Collection Doat
HL	Claude Devic and Joseph Vaissète, *Histoire générale de Languedoc*, 16 vols., Toulouse, 1872–1904
Just. Itin.	Public Record Office, Justices Itinerant
Layettes	Alexander Teulet et al., eds., *Layettes du Trésor des Chartes*, 5 vols., Paris, 1863–1902
Littere	J. G. Edwards, ed., *Littere Wallie Preserved in Liber A*, Cardiff, 1940
PRO	Public Record Office
RC	Great Britain, Record Commission, *Registrum vulgariter nuncupatum 'The Record of Caernarvon,'* London, 1838
Regs.	Robert Fawtier et al., eds., *Registres du Trésor des Chartes*, 3 vols., Paris, 1958–78
RHF	*Recueil des historiens des Gaules et de la France*, 24 vols., Paris, 1738–1904
SC	Public Record Office, Special Collections
THSC	*Transactions of the Honourable Society of Cymmrodorion*
WHR	*Welsh History Review*
WTL	T. P. Ellis, *Welsh Tribal Law*, 2 vols., Oxford, 1926

State and Society
in Medieval Europe

Introduction

This book deals with the dialectical interaction of state and society in medieval Europe. It seeks to investigate the social constraints that shaped the nature of the states forming during the thirteenth and fourteenth centuries. It also tries to measure the impact these states could have had on the systems of social and economic relations that existed within western Europe.

This problem is addressed through a comparison of the way in which two local societies, Gwynedd in North Wales and Languedoc in the south of France, were incorporated into larger political organizations. Languedoc, although formally part of the kingdom of France, had before the thirteenth century been almost completely free of any direction from or control by the French monarchy. Beginning with the Albigensian crusades in the first decades of the 1200s, however, the region was gradually incorporated into the political system directed by the Capetian kings. Gwynedd had during the late twelfth and thirteenth centuries become the chief political force in the areas of Wales not already dominated by the English. But in two short wars in the 1270s and the 1280s, the English first broke the power of the dynasty that ruled Gwynedd and then destroyed the country's independence altogether. Although the empirical material for this study is drawn from the histories of Gwynedd and Languedoc, this is not a book "about" the history per se of either region. Instead the histories of these societies are used as devices with which to analyze the dynamics of the process of "state-building" in medieval Europe. I have been concerned, not so much with the particularities of the experiences of Languedoc and Gwynedd as with analyzing the social factors that either constrained or facilitated state action and with gauging the extent to which political activity could reshape social and economic behavior.

I have tried to produce a work that will be of use not only to medievalists but also to the larger scholarly world that is concerned with the problems of the "state" and political power. In recent years the "state," after an absence of several decades, has become once again a subject of intense discussion and debate among social scientists. This return of the state[1] follows a period between the 1950s and the mid-1970s when the state ceased to be a central concern of academic social science.[2] Before the 1950s the state had been one of the central organizing concepts of the discipline of political science. But in that decade many political scientists decided that the proper object of their study was not formal political institutions but political *behavior*. Much political behavior is, of course, concretized and canalized in institutions; much, however, is conducted outside of such institutions.[3] If one regards behavior, rather than institutions, as the proper subject for inquiry, then the concept of the state loses much of its analytical utility; indeed, its traditionally central position in the research agenda may seem a bar to proper understanding of the political system.

The decline of the state, at least in the United States, was also linked to the dominance within American political science of pluralist interpretations of the political process. These interpretive schemes emphasize problems of allocation rather than questions of coercion and control.[4] Members of the pluralist school conceive society as made up of a multitude of competing groups, whose memberships are fluid and whose interests often overlap. The state is neutral, an "empty slate," whose task consists of balancing the demands of these competing interest groups. Its role is, if we may use the language of the systems analysts, to translate the inputs and demands of interest groups into outputs that consist of authoritative allocations of scarce values. Pluralists direct their attention not to matters of control, coercion, and

1. See, for example, Peter B. Evans et al., *Bringing the State Back In.*
2. Krasner, "Approaches," p. 223.
3. Easton, *Political System*, p. 113.
4. Krasner, "Approaches," p. 226. See also Carnoy, *State*, pp. 33–39.

the power of the state, but to which groups and individuals have the most influence on the making of allocative policy.

Both of these tendencies helped make the state for many years a secondary item on scholars' research agenda. Indeed, some political scientists felt that the concept of the state had no useful place in the intellectual toolbag of the serious student. The state was not an analytic concept but a purely ideological one, the creation of nineteenth-century thinkers trying to grapple with the intellectual and moral crisis caused by the disintegration of social life and the growing untenability of the belief that the social order was either natural or divinely willed. Like all ideology, it was an effort to overcome the contradictions of social life through the manipulation of symbolic meaning. Henry Eckstein comments, "In the anomic, godless, unnatural world of modernity in the making, the State was necessary, and its Idea a needed, if somewhat pathetic, fiction."[5]

In the mid-1970s, however, the state returned with a vengeance as a major concern of political scientists and sociologists. Several factors contributed to this renewal of interest. First, there was the inescapable fact that states in the late twentieth century were taking on an ever more active role, intervening in virtually every aspect of their citizens' lives and playing a strategic part in the struggle for hegemony in the world economy. Second, there was the phenomenon of revolutionary movements in the peripheral and semiperipheral areas of the capitalist world-economy that sought to capture state power and use that power radically to reform civil society.

Third was the vigorous discussion among Western Marxists and neo-Marxists of the role of the state in late capitalism. These debates have been marked by a rejection of the temptations of those vulgar Marxisms that treated the economy as the "base," and such things as the state, politics, religion, and ideology as merely "superstructure," the totally determined and automatic effect of the underlying processes of economic production and distribution. Few Marxists would today agree with Marx and Engels that the capitalist state is but "a committee for managing the common affairs of the whole bourgeoisie."[6] Instead, they have come to see the complex of problems offered by the nature of the state—its relation to a society's econom-

5. Eckstein, "On the 'Science' of the State," p. 16.
6. Marx and Engels, "Manifesto of the Communist Party," p. 475.

ically dominant and subordinate classes, its role in capital accumulation, its relative autonomy and capacity for independent action, and its role in a worldwide system of states—as some of the most pressing issues awaiting their investigation.[7]

As yet, only faint echoes of this ferment in political science, sociology, and economics have been heard in the field of medieval studies. In general, the historians of medieval politics can be divided into three groups. First, there are the traditional narrative historians, whose primary concern is the telling of the story of politics, conceived of as the affairs of the medieval elite—that is, kings, princes, and prelates. Second, there are the administrative historians, who have devoted themselves to the production of thorough and often elegant studies of the machinery of medieval government. Finally, there are the Marxists, whose contributions in social and economic history have been very great but who have been content to treat the state, at least in its late-medieval guise, as primarily the instrument by which the feudal aristocracy sought to enforce and defend its dominant position within society.[8]

Of these three approaches, the dominant one, at least in the English-speaking world, has been administrative history. For many decades, the history of the state has been understood as the story of the process by which kings and princes equipped themselves with progressively more elaborate and professional organs of governance. Dissatisfaction with this limited interpretive scheme has begun to appear,[9] but as yet no new approach to the study of the medieval state has won general approval.

In the following pages I seek not to resolve each and every problem of the role of the state in medieval society but to begin to ask new questions about politics in medieval Europe, questions that are at least indirectly informed by the ongoing debates among contemporary political scientists and sociologists. I hope that in doing so I can enlarge, if only modestly, the inventory of intellectual tools medievalists use to understand politics. I also hope that what I have produced will be of some interest to political scientists and sociologists. With some notable exceptions, most social scientists interested in politics have restricted their attention to contemporary capitalist states, chiefly to

7. A good introduction to this body of literature is Carnoy, *State*.
8. See, for example, Brenner, "Agrarian Roots," pp. 236–40.
9. Wood, "Return of Medieval Politics," pp. 391–404.

those found in the world-economy's core areas, western Europe and North America. Relatively less attention has gone to the states in the peripheral areas of the capitalist economy and to socialist states. The empirical base on which political scientists ground their generalizations thus tends to be relatively narrow, limited in both its temporal and spatial dimensions. I hope that my study of some aspects of state-building in medieval Europe, with its noncapitalist economy and its less organized and coherent state structures, may thus offer them a novel perspective on some of their primary concerns.

I have tried, without reducing the state to the status of a mere epiphenomenon, to understand some of the social and economic constraints that shaped medieval state forms, and, without portraying the state and its directors as radically free to shape their environment as they please, to discover what impact medieval states could have on the societies that they endeavored to govern. To make my study manageable, I have not tried to write a total history of all aspects of the medieval state. Instead, I have chosen to look at only a single aspect of the relationship of state and society in medieval Europe: the incorporation of previously autonomous regions into the growing kingdoms of western Europe. Restricting the focus of my study to this single issue has, as I hope the reader will agree, allowed me to grasp in a particularly concrete and dramatic form some of the dynamics of the dialectical interaction between society and state in medieval Europe.

After all this talk of the state, the reader might reasonably expect me to offer a definition of it. Unfortunately, defining the "state" is no easy task. A distressingly large number of definitions have been offered (in the 1930s one political scientist counted close to 150),[10] but most are unsatisfactory in one way or another. Many definitions are little more than a list of traits of some modern states, often seemingly chosen in an arbitrary fashion, and hence of doubtful analytic value. Some useful definitions, however, can be found. Alfred Stepan provides one: "The state must be considered more than the 'government.' It is the continuous administrative, legal, bureaucratic and coercive systems that attempt not only to structure relationships *between* civil society and public authority in a polity but also to structure many crucial relationships within civil society as well."[11] This definition has the advantage of underlining the fact that the state is more than gov-

10. Titus, "Nomenclature," p. 45.
11. Stepan, *State and Society*, p. xii.

ernment and more than a mechanism that referees the allocation of values among competing interests. It is, however, somewhat time-bounded, taking as its reference point modern states where most ad-ministrative, legal, bureaucratic, and coercive systems are concen-trated in the hands of a clear-cut entity that can be labeled the "state." It is rather difficult to apply such a definition to a medieval political system, where no single entity monopolized the possession of such administrative and coercive systems.

Some Marxist efforts to define the state try to get around the tem-porally and culturally bounded nature of most definitions by empha-sizing the functional role of the state. The state is seen as a condition of class-divided societies, as the ensemble of coercive and ideological apparatuses that maintain the mechanisms by which the dominant classes extract surplus labor from the subordinated primary pro-ducers. Hence its nature varies from one mode of production to an-other, depending on the nature of the mechanisms of the appropria-tion of surplus labor.[12] This definition has the merit of treating the state not as a reified entity, possessed of certain invariant characteris-tics found in all societies, but as a variable, whose content and func-tion differs from one society to another. But, as the product of an analytical tradition whose merits are fiercely debated, it may not command universal assent. Perhaps the most innocuous thing we can say of the state is that it consists of those groups that make authorita-tive decisions that are binding most of the time on most of the people living within a particular polity.[13]

In studying modern societies, we usually do not have much trouble identifying what the state is. In the middle ages, the task is more dif-ficult. Many of the attributes and tasks that political scientists would argue constitute the state are widely diffused throughout society. Yet simply to label all forms of authority, ranging from that of kings and popes to that of village courts and family heads, as part of the state would seem to rob the term of any useful analytical content.

Moreover, as historians engaged in the concrete study of the past,

12. For one such definition, see Hindess and Hirst, *Pre-Capitalist Modes of Produc-tion*, pp. 28–41.

13. Although a systems analyst such as David Easton professes to find little use for the concept of the state, the makers of authoritative allocations of values, who play a pivotal role in his description of a political system, seem rather like what other people mean by the state. See Easton, *Systems Analysis*, pp. 29–33.

we need not an analytically elegant but an operationally sufficient definition. We need to be able to "operationalize" our concept of the state in such a way as to identify as a state some concrete set of institutions and social roles that we can measure and observe. Fortunately, in dealing with the history of northwestern Europe in the thirteenth and fourteenth centuries, we have available something that can function as our operational definition of the state. This is the government of kings.

After all the preceding discussion of states and political theory, this may seem a distressingly conventional, indeed timid, definition of the medieval state. But it does have some advantages. Royal governments can readily be identified and their activity measured. Moreover, royal governments in the thirteenth and fourteenth centuries do have features that accord with the more theoretical definitions of the state given above. Although they may not have had a monopoly of all of their societies' administrative, legal, bureaucratic, and coercive systems, they played a pivotal role in all these activities. Similarly, although they may not have constituted the total array of mechanisms that maintained the process of surplus extraction by the ruling classes, they were the final guarantors of the aristocracy's continued dominance of the class-divided societies of medieval Europe. And, within any particular kingdom, royal governments were those entities that made decisions that were binding on the largest number of people.

So we have an operational definition of the state, rather traditional, to be sure, but nevertheless serviceable. We should remember, however, that a state is not a universal and unchanging entity, a set of invariant institutions and functions to be found in every society. Instead it is a set of concrete relationships among people, a process more than a thing. It should be treated not as an unchanging constant but as a variable entity.[14] All class-divided societies may have states, but these vary widely from one society to another in their structure, their personnel, their spheres of activity, and their ability to affect their environment. In the pages that follow we will be endeavoring to discern, not the lineaments of some ubiquitous and unchanging medieval state, but some of the various forms that the state could take and some of the various roles it could play in medieval Europe.

14. See Nettl, "The State as a Conceptual Variable," pp. 559–92.

1 Problems and Methods

This book is concerned with certain aspects of the phenomenon of state-building in western Europe during the central middle ages. Before the twelfth century European society had been intensely local. With a few exceptions supraregional structures, whether political or economic, had either collapsed or atrophied in the centuries following the breakup of the Carolingian empire. For many generations the social and political horizon of the average inhabitant of western Europe was bounded by the structures of local life—the parish, the village, and the *seigneurie*.

In the twelfth and thirteenth centuries, however, all this began to change. As economic productivity grew, Europeans became involved in a network of commercial exchanges that tied them not only to one another but also to non-European civilizations. The church organized itself into a supraregional hierarchy extending from the papacy in Rome to the most remote rural parishes. And everywhere in Europe the inhabitants of the old local societies found themselves incorporated into the expanding kingdoms and principalities that were a prominent feature of the sociopolitical landscape of the late middle ages.

The process by which local communities were incorporated into larger polities was thus one of the major phenomena of European history in the twelfth and thirteenth centuries. It is also, I contend, a process that has been more often described than analyzed. The steps by which large-scale political organizations were built up in western Europe have often been recounted. Indeed, the expansion of kingdoms was one of the favorite subjects of an older school of medieval historians.[1]

This process, however, has often been treated as self-explanatory, indeed (in the hands of historians of a nationalistic bent), as natural and inevitable. But it is readily apparent that the construction of large-scale polities during the middle ages was a process that was neither simple in nature nor transparently comprehensible to the modern historian. Even a brief glance at the history of early modern Europe reveals that the directors of the much better integrated and coordinated political organizations of that era found it no easy task to control the affairs of the local communities over which they ruled.[2]

Understanding the process of state-building in the high middle ages is an even more difficult task. The state organizations that we encounter in the middle ages are, compared with those of modern or early modern Europe, far less organized and unified. Unlike their more modern counterparts, medieval states seldom possessed a monopoly of the legitimate use of force; mechanisms for the large-scale mobilization of their subjects' resources; and specialized governing institutions that were centralized, formally coordinated, and staffed by a self-conscious state elite enjoying a relatively large degree of autonomy vis-à-vis civil society. In medieval Europe powers of coercion and authoritative decision making were not concentrated in the hands of the agents of a unified state mechanism but instead were widely dispersed throughout society, residing in the hands of a multitude of lords and corporate organizations such as towns and villages. At the risk of sounding paradoxical, we could almost say that in this period we are observing state-building without the state. In our search to comprehend such a phenomenon it is obvious that the interpretive schemes devised to explicate the rise of the early modern and modern European state provide only approximate guideposts.

When medieval historians have concerned themselves with the problems involved in the incorporation of local communities into larger polities, they have tended to look at the issue from the perspective of the directors of the larger political organizations rather than from that of

1. See, for example, Longnon's *Formation de l'unité française*.
2. See, for example, Tilly, ed., *Formation*.

the local inhabitants.[3] As a result an important analytical opportunity has been overlooked. If we are interested in examining the dialectical relationship between state and society, in discovering the ways in which political and social structures shaped one another, we can find few other occasions where the issues are posed as clearly and as dramatically as when one previously independent region was brought under the control of an outside political organization.

These questions of how the structures of a local community interacted with those of the enlarged polities of which they became members have not been formulated very clearly by medievalists, but they have not been totally ignored. Judith Brown has tried to assess the effects on the Tuscan city of Pescia of its incorporation into the Florentine state. Much of R. I. Burns's work on the thirteenth-century kingdom of Valencia has explored how its Moslems fared under their new Christian masters. Lucien Musset has also discussed the effects on Normandy of its incorporation into the French royal domain.[4] But such studies are surprisingly few. It is safe to say that this problem has not received all the attention it deserves.

A glance through the available literature reveals that local communities could follow very different paths into larger political organizations. Pescia, for example, was allowed by Florence to keep its corporate identity and to retain many functions of self-government.[5] Normandy after its incorporation into the Capetian domain also kept its indigenous laws and governing institutions. However, since many of the most powerful Norman aristocrats remained loyal to the English king, thus forfeiting their estates, the province acquired an important new group of landowners whose origins lay in the old French royal domain around Paris.[6]

Valencia after its conquest by the Christians of Aragon and Catalonia retained its institutional identity, remaining a separate kingdom. Its social structure, however, was transformed as it was turned into a multi-ethnic, multireligious society. The importation of Christian immigrants produced a settlement pattern characterized by a

3. See, for example, Strayer, "Normandy and Languedoc," pp. 44–59, and Baldwin, *Government*, pp. 239–48.

4. Brown, *Shadow of Florence*; Burns, *Islam under the Crusaders* and *Medieval Colonialism*; Musset, "Quelques problèmes," pp. 291–307.

5. Brown, *Shadow of Florence*, pp. 19, 202.

6. Musset, "Quelques problèmes," pp. 295–304.

small number of cities which, although predominantly Christian, nevertheless contained Moslem ghettoes, a larger number of towns with mixed Christian and Moslem populations, and a multitude of Moslem villages. Within the framework of this new kingdom, many Moslems were guaranteed "religious, political, and legal survival as a self-contained community." Although the position of the Moslem ruling elite gradually eroded, the native population as a whole does not appear to have been exploited very harshly by its new masters.[7]

Political scientists might be tempted by the conclusions of these studies to advance the following as a working hypothesis: Given the fact that the state mechanisms of the period had not established a monopoly of all coercive authority over their territories and that other social organizations within those territories possessed important elements of political authority and jurisdiction, local communities, when incorporated into larger political organizations, would most likely retain most, if not all, of their indigenous political institutions. Outside rule, moreover, would not result in the imposition on local people of new norms governing the practice of political life; rather politics would continue to be practiced largely in accordance with traditional norms.

A Comparative Strategy

In the following pages I have sought to examine this hypothesis. In doing so I hope that I have cast some light on the pathways that local communities could follow on their road toward incorporation into larger political organizations. My strategy in trying to come to grips with this aspect of the state-building process in medieval Europe has been to adopt a comparative approach. I have studied the effects of rule by outsiders on the area of Wales known as Gwynedd and the region of modern France known as Languedoc.

Since comparative history has been more often praised than practiced by medievalists and because it presents some significant problems, the reader deserves some remarks on how I have conceived my project and why I have picked Gwynedd and Languedoc as my case

7. Burns, *Islam under the Crusaders*, pp. 21–24, 118–19, 352, 373, and *Medieval Colonialism*, pp. 21, 120. The quotation is from *Islam under the Crusaders*, p. 137.

studies. One virtue of a comparative approach is that it provides a partial corrective for the tunnel vision and problem blindness that can afflict even the most conscientious student of the history of a narrowly delimited region. The historian engaged in a tightly focused study faces two perils. One is the temptation to incorrectly posit causal connections between phenomena that are only coincidentally present in the social formation under examination. The other is to fail to perceive causal or functional linkages between certain aspects of the society he is examining.[8]

One can advance an even stronger argument in favor of comparative studies. We can say that only a comparative approach can allow us to seize the workings of medieval society as a whole. Human social formations are not examples of what Louis Althusser has termed "expressive totalities," in which each part of the system expresses the immanent essence of the whole.[9] Societies are not unified totalities but complex wholes, full of forces and processes that do not exactly mesh, but that pull in different, often conflicting directions. They are nevertheless organized, comprehensible systems that, although they may display much variability, nevertheless operate within specific parameters.

For a historian engaged in a comparative study, this is an important point. Some historians have assumed, a little naively, that the primary purpose of comparison is to find those uniformities characteristic of several different events and to demonstrate that every case under consideration follows a similar pattern in its historical development.[10] Although in clumsy hands this approach can result in crude reductionism, such a quest for what Charles Tilly has called "universalizing" comparisons is intellectually valid; but it is not the unique task of comparative history.

In this work, I will be making some "universalizing" generalizations, but I have directed most of my efforts to a search for "variation-finding" generalizations. A variation-finding comparative strategy looks for principles that explain why a particular phenomenon varies across two or more cases.[11] In my opinion it is through the under-

8. Köbben, "Comparativists," p. 593.
9. Althusser and Balibar, *Reading Capital*, p. 94.
10. See, for example, Brinton, *Anatomy*, pp. 6–7, 20–21.
11. See Tilly's discussion of the different forms of comparative studies in *Big Structures*, pp. 80–83.

standing of such concomitant variations that we can make real progress in trying to understand the medieval European social system as a whole. There was much variation in this system, but the number of variations was not infinite. The number of possible transformations that the social formations of medieval Europe could experience was limited. My purpose in using a comparative strategy has not been to engage in an illusory quest for a finite number of organizing factors that both explain and are expressed throughout all aspects of the medieval social system; rather I have sought to begin to uncover the limited number of transformations that could occur within the specific parameters of a social system. Only when we have discovered the nature of these possible transformations will the vast array of facts produced by research on the history of medieval society be truly accessible to our understanding.[12]

But while a comparative approach has advantages, it is not without difficulties. The most common objection to comparative studies is that they do violence to the living reality of concrete individuals by forcing them into the Procrustean bed of a predetermined analytic strategy. Comparing total societies is especially misleading. Societies, so the argument runs, are not mere congeries of temporally and geographically contiguous traits, which can simply be split off from the surrounding whole and compared. Instead they are organic wholes in which all the parts are systematically related. To take any trait out of the context that gives it meaning and to compare it with a superficially similar trait from another society is to engage in a meaningless enterprise.

To this one can object that all historical investigations, even the most narrow and tightly defined, do violence to the "living reality" of their subjects. Every scholar must impose order on the seeming chaos of the surviving data. Information must be selected, evaluated, and arranged into meaningful patterns. In doing this the researcher inevitably distorts in some fashion the reality of the past. But to refrain from any sorting or arranging would be to produce histories that are either mere jumbles of information or incomprehensible to anyone not so thoroughly steeped as their authors in the minutiae of the evidence.[13]

12. See Godelier, "Object," p. 108.
13. See Köbben, "Comparativists," pp. 589–93.

In summary, comparative and noncomparative history both have advantages and limitations. Ideally they should complement and complete one another. Without in-depth case studies, comparative history could not be written. And, one hopes, comparative studies may offer to the noncomparativist new perspectives and a more inclusive research agenda.

Even if one grants that comparative history is a worthwhile exercise, there still remain the questions of what can and what should be compared. On this subject one is assailed by a multitude of counsel. Anthropologists have devoted much thought to the problems of comparison and often use a functionalist interpretive framework. The goal of this work has been to identify what have been called the "laws of social statics," that is, to show how social functions are interdependent.[14] To do this, it has often been felt that the most appropriate strategy is to examine societies that are *isolated* from one another. Otherwise one encounters the classic dilemma known as Galton's problem: If one discovers correlations between cultural phenomena within neighboring societies, how can one tell if these correlations are the result of a real functional linkage or are the result of cultural diffusion?[15]

How medieval historians feel about the problems of comparative study is rather more difficult to discover. Marc Bloch in his essay on comparative history seems to express skepticism about the value of studying widely separated phenomena. He argues that the search for the sort of functional linkages which occupies many anthropologists and sociologists would produce conclusions that are too general to be of use to the historian. Such a "long-range" comparative method, he says, "postulates, and always reverts in conclusion to the fundamental unity of the human mind, or, alternatively, the monotony and astonishing poverty of the intellectual resources at man's disposal throughout the course of history." Bloch favors the "parallel study of societies that are at once neighbouring and contemporary, exercising a constant mutual influence, exposed throughout their development to the action of the same broad causes just because they are close and contemporaneous, and owing their existence in part at least to a common origin." Such a procedure would "reach conclusions of fact that are

14. Clignet, "Critical Evaluation," p. 610.
15. Naroll, "Some Thoughts," pp. 258–62.

less hypothetical and much more precise."[16] To this one might object that our goal is to produce useful and illuminating statements, not ones that although precise may be of limited analytical significance. Moreover, a comparison between two social formations that share many similarities might not be a particularly enlightening exercise.

The conclusion seems to be that there is no right or wrong way to conduct a comparative study. What one compares depends on what one wishes to learn. This has been the principle that has guided my choice of societies for comparison. In comparing the incorporation of two different areas into larger political organizations, we could say that we are constructing a model with at least two components. One component consists of the overarching, larger polities that are engaged in adding new areas to their territorial bases. In this study this component consists of the political systems directed by the French and English kings. The other component, that of the newly encapsulated regions, consists of Gwynedd in North Wales and Languedoc in the south of France. Although there were important differences between the French and English monarchies, they display some fundamental similarities in their structures and the social backgrounds out of which they had emerged. Languedoc and Gwynedd, however, differed markedly from one another in their social, economic, and political structures. By examining how these two regions were incorporated into the English and French kingdoms, we will see how the structures of these two regional social formations interacted with royal governments that were often similar in their structure and modes of operation. This strategy allows us both to understand the constraints put on political behavior by the preexisting structures of Welsh and Languedocian society and to grasp what capacity the political apparatuses of the outside rulers had to effect significant change in the regions they had brought under their political domination.

16. Bloch, "Contribution," pp. 46–48. What Bloch seems to be objecting to are the methods of a Sir James Frazer. As Ernest Gellner has described him, Frazer was "an evolutionist magpie, gathering a rich harvest of ethnographic tidbits from here, there, and everywhere. They were torn out of context, and used for the painting of a grand canvas of the evolution of the human mind." It was during Marc Bloch's lifetime that anthropologists such as Bronislaw Malinowski, in reaction against such procedures, were laying the foundations of modern anthropology by seeking "a form of explanation which related the data to one another within the unity of a single society or to human needs, rather than to some evolutionary sequence." The quotations are from Gellner, "Stakes," p. 18.

Two Feudal Monarchies

Although in the thirteenth century Gwynedd and Languedoc were areas with different traditions of political and social organization, the monarchies that extended their control over them display some similar features. Before discussing in detail how Languedoc and Gwynedd differed from one another, I first briefly sketch those factors that allow us to speak of the French and English monarchies as in some sense similar. I do not claim they were exactly alike, but they display enough parallels to allow us to use them in a rough-and-ready fashion as the constants in our model.

In both England and northern France monarchical institutions had developed in the context of a rural society dominated by a landowning aristocracy. In England a tiny group of a few thousand aristocratic families lorded it over a subject population of several million peasants. Within this aristocracy there was a marked disparity of power and wealth. A few magnates were masters of estate complexes numbering dozens of manors; the typical lord, however, owned perhaps no more than a single village.[17] In the north of France there was a similar asymmetric distribution of wealth and power, with a wealthy aristocracy dominating a subject peasantry.[18] The social and political scene was, however, complicated by the presence of numerous towns, whose inhabitants played a more autonomous role in the French kingdom than did their counterparts in England.

In both kingdoms the relationship of the king to these aristocrats was not that of a sovereign to his subjects. Instead, the king was tied to many of them by a personal, dyadic tie, that of lordship and vassalage, which carried with it promises of reciprocal services. The king's aristocratic vassals were, however, more than mere servitors. They were also lords, each possessing a measure of political power over his tenants and dependents, powers that they regarded as part and parcel of their family patrimonies. These aristocratic political powers were relatively restrained in England as compared to France, where the Capetians were slower to concentrate political authority in their hands. But even in the more unified English state, there were privileged enclaves,

17. Hilton, *Medieval Society*, p. 58. See also Given-Wilson, *English Nobility*, pp. 69–73.
18. Fossier, *Terre*, 2:673–87.

such as the palatinate of Durham or the lordships of the Welsh March, where royal authority was kept at arm's length.

The thirteenth-century kingdoms of France and England were, however, more than mere collections of fiefs recognizing their respective monarchs as feudal suzerains. In the twelfth and thirteenth centuries the kings of western Europe were developing old and creating new institutions of governance that transcended the feudal framework of their realms. By 1200 both the English and French kings were served by "central" administrations that were more professional and bureaucratized than they had been in previous generations. During the twelfth century, old arrangements—by which members of the king's entourage were delegated on an ad hoc basis to deal with administrative business as it arose—were displaced by permanent bodies of royal servitors specializing in particular aspects of royal administration. In 1200 the English kings were served by financial and auditing experts presiding over the court of Exchequer, by professional judges sitting in the king's courts, and by a bevy of clerks who were creating the chancery archives that make medieval England one of the best documented of medieval kingdoms. The Capetians tended to lag behind their English counterparts in the creation of centralized organs of governance. But, beginning with Philip Augustus's creation of a bureau of audit at Paris in 1190, the French kings embarked on a policy of institutional development that by the end of the thirteenth century saw them equipped with a set of governing organs almost on a par with those of the English.[19]

The French and English kings also developed a relatively dense network of local institutions of governance. The Norman conquerors of England had benefited from the fact that they took over the already developed system of Anglo-Saxon county government. Building on this solid basis, English kings during the following centuries created an ever more elaborate and effective local administrative network. To the traditional offices of sheriff and hundred bailiff there were added a host of new crown agents—coroners, escheators, constables, foresters and so forth.

In developing institutions of local government, the French once

19. See Baldwin, *Government*, pp. 137–52; Baldwin, "Decennie décisive," p. 326; Nortier and Baldwin, "Contributions," pp. 21–22; Lot and Fawtier, *Histoire*, 2:197–99, 2:334–36; and Hollister and Baldwin, "Rise," pp. 895–96.

again lagged behind. But by the reign of Philip Augustus a more complex form of local government had begun to take shape. To the old royal agents known as *prévôts* who collected royal dues there was added a new, superior official, the *bailli*. By the middle of the thirteenth century, territorially defined *bailliages* had taken definite shape. Throughout the thirteenth and fourteenth centuries, baillis acquired larger and more professional staffs to help them carry out their duties.[20]

Although the twelfth and thirteenth centuries saw important developments in royal governance in both France and England, one should not think of their governments, as bureaucratized and professionalized as they were becoming, as anything like modern state organs of government. The governing institutions of the French and English kings were, to use Max Weber's term, patrimonial in nature.[21] The king's government always remained, in a very real sense, his private affair. In both England and France the kings were expected to support the ordinary operations of their governments out of their own purses, which meant largely from the revenues of their own private estates. The officials who served the king were his personal agents. Their loyalty was to their master, not to an impersonal, overarching political order. Although royal servants were becoming more professional and were being organized into relatively specialized bureaus, they did not constitute a modern bureaucracy. They were recruited not so much on the basis of their technical aptitude, as on that of their personal and political serviceability to the monarch. They did not follow carefully delimited career paths, advancing only after careful examination and review by their bureaucratic superiors. And, finally, they were not imbued with any spirit of "bureaucratism," that is, by a desire to carry out their duties in accordance with abstract axioms and rules, treating everyone they dealt with in a formally equal fashion.

To be sure, the English and French monarchies were not exactly analogous. In the thirteenth century the governing institutions of the English monarchy were more developed than those of the French. In England royal institutions were also more central to the life of the kingdom's aristocracy than in France. English lords, whether great or small, were deeply involved in the day to day running of the royal

20. Lot and Fawtier, *Histoire*, 2:141–47.
21. Weber, *Economy and Society*, 2:1013–15, 1025–31.

administration on both the kingdom-wide and the local level.[22] By 1200 one can argue that the institutions of the monarchy had already become the primary political arena for the English aristocracy, who were deeply interested in the shaping of royal policy. Such an intimate involvement in royal institutions and passionate interest in the making of royal policy was less developed in France. It is important to note that when the English crown conquered Gwynedd, its governing institutions, whether local or central, had achieved a marked degree of development and maturity, some of them having a tradition of centuries behind them. In France, however, the acquisition of Languedoc and the development of Capetian royal administration were developments that took place at the same time. Gwynedd was thus joined to a relatively fully developed political organization, Languedoc to one that was still taking shape.

Although the French and the English monarchies in the thirteenth century do not constitute a perfect match, it is nevertheless unlikely that any other two monarchies in western Europe would be as good candidates for the constant component in our model.

Medieval Languedoc

For the other variable in the model, that of the incorporated communities, I wanted to examine social formations that were as different as possible. Fortunately, thirteenth-century Gwynedd and Languedoc were markedly dissimilar in their political, economic, and social organization.

Languedoc consists roughly of the region centered on the cities of Toulouse, Carcassonne, and Narbonne. In the middle ages it was a relatively rich and developed area. At the beginning of the fourteenth century its population was probably close to 1.5 million.[23] Within Languedoc there were, and are, a great variety of ecological systems. Among these are the lagoons of the Mediterranean coast, infested with malaria in the early modern period but perhaps healthier in the middle ages; the granite plateaus of the Cévennes; the fruitful plains of the Mediterranean hinterland and of the Garonne valley; the dry,

22. Holt, *Magna Carta*, pp. 40–42.
23. Wolff, ed., *Histoire du Languedoc*, p. 217.

barren plateaus, covered with a dense and nearly impenetrable shrubbery, known as *garrigues*; and the high mountain pastures of the Pyrenees. Whereas Gwynedd stood on the fringes of the medieval European world, Languedoc had long been part of the cultural, technological, and economic order that had grown up around the Mediterranean. Its agriculture, although perhaps not as productive as that of northern France, displayed the diversity typical of the Mediterranean, with rich grain producing fields, fruitful vineyards, and mountain pastures well stocked with sheep. Languedoc was also, by medieval standards, a relatively urbanized region, and in 1200 its merchants were involved in an expanding trade network.

In the decades immediately before the assertion of Capetian leadership, Languedocian political history was marked by much turbulence and war.[24] Languedoc possessed a number of immensely wealthy lords, both lay and ecclesiastical. But by the early thirteenth century no single aristocratic house had succeeded in integrating the region under its leadership. The counts of Toulouse were probably the most important political figures, but their leadership was contested by the counts of Barcelona and, after the counts inherited the crown of Aragon, by the kings of that Spanish realm.[25] Within Languedoc itself the ambitions of the Toulousan counts were contested by such powerful lords as the Trencavels, viscounts of Albi, Béziers, Carcassonne, and the Razès. On the fringes of the country the rulers of the Pyrenean lordships of Foix and Comminges were largely autonomous. The inability of the great lords to assert their effective political leadership over the region is illustrated by the spread in the late twelfth and early thirteenth centuries of voluntary associations sworn to uphold the

24. My discussion of sociopolitical arrangements in Languedoc before the Albigensian crusades has been hampered by the surprising lack of many detailed monographs on twelfth-century Languedocian society. The best available social history is Bourin-Derruau, *Villages*, but it deals only with the region around Béziers. Archibald R. Lewis, *Development*, and Magnou-Nortier, *Société*, do not concern themselves with the twelfth century. Pierre Bonnassie has produced in his *Catalogne* an excellent study of social and political arrangements in neighboring Catalonia. However, he confines his attention mainly to the tenth and eleventh centuries. It is also unclear how readily his findings can be applied to Languedoc. To an unfortunate degree I have found myself forced to rely on Auguste Molinier's rather old monograph, "Etude sur l'administration féodale."

25. On Catalan involvement in Languedoc, see the different views of Higounet, "Grand chapitre," pp. 313–32, and Abadal i de Vinyals, "A Propos," pp. 315–45. See also Cheyette, "Sale," pp. 826–54.

Peace of God. The oaths taken by those who joined these associations often required them not only to observe the peace, but to pay dues to support it, and if necessary to bear arms against those who violated it. In places, officials were appointed to superintend the peace. If T. N. Bisson is correct in his interpretation, these organizations may have provided an effective form of territorial political organization apart from, or in supplement to, the political structures being fashioned by the greater secular lords.[26]

Beneath the great episcopal and lay seigneurs there clustered a large number of lesser nobles. Although the greater of the local dynasties usually practiced primogeniture, these lesser lords did not. Although it was possible for a father to favor his eldest son, local inheritance customs tended to favor equal partition among male heirs.[27] To counteract the tendency toward progressive impoverishment that such inheritance customs posed, many of these lesser lords resorted to pooling their holdings in joint lordships, which were a common feature of the political landscape in Languedoc.[28]

Relations of domination and subordination among the local nobility were not as organized or rationalized as in certain other areas of Europe. Some nobles were vassals and held fiefs in return for various services, but these features were not as important in aristocratic life as they were in northern France. The obligations that vassals owed their lords were few and the authority exercised by lords over them correspondingly light.[29]

The relations of these lords with their peasants are unfortunately often obscure. The best guide to this subject is provided by Monique Bourin-Derruau's monograph on medieval villages in lower Languedoc. She confines herself to a discussion of the region around the

26. On peace associations, see Bisson, "Organized Peace," pp. 215–36, and Bisson, *Assemblies*, pp. 102–36. For a more skeptical view of the importance of peace associations, see Bonnaud-Delamare, "Légende," pp. 47–78.

27. Auguste Molinier, "Etude sur l'administration féodale," p. 151; Bourin-Derruau, *Villages*, 1:149–52.

28. Griffe, *Débuts*, p. 198; Griffe, *Languedoc cathare de 1190 à 1210*, pp. 114, 144.

29. On the relatively late appearance of "structures vassaliques" in Languedoc, see Giordanengo, "Féodalité," p. 191; Higounet, "Groupe aristocratique," pp. 569–71; and Ourliac, "Pays de la Selve," p. 582. See also Bisson's remarks on the nature of the feudal bond in "Mediterranean Territorial Power," p. 149. Bourin-Derruau, however, believes that by 1150 in the Béziers region the ruling elite "was completely penetrated by vassalage ties." (*Villages*, 1:266.)

city of Béziers, and it is unclear how well the patterns she discovers can be generalized to the rest of the large and complex region that was medieval Languedoc. The social changes she has discovered, however, show parallels to what is known elsewhere in the Mediterranean lands of Europe, such as Catalonia and Latium.

Until the early eleventh century, society in Béziers was marked by a continuation of the structures inherited from the Carolingian past. The habitat was relatively dispersed, with people living in small settlements referred to as *villae* in the texts. In the early eleventh century the political authority of the local viscounts disintegrated. It was usurped by lesser lords, who constructed small castles throughout the region, surrounded themselves with armed followers, and set about dominating the countryside. They imposed new and heavier demands on the peasants living near their fortresses; these dues included compulsory hospitality, known as *albergue* and various *corvées*. Peasant allodialists, that is, peasants who owned their land outright, became increasingly rare, and personal dependence on the nobility spread through the lower ranks of society. The erection of these *seigneuries banales* was accompanied by an important change in settlement patterns. In the twelfth century peasants increasingly grouped themselves into concentrated settlements, some around noble castles, others around monasteries; many of these settlements were ultimately surrounded by a girdle of walls. The inhabitants of these settlements were subject to their lord's justice, owed him corvée labor, and cash payments known as *tailles*, and they were saddled with various *banalités*. By 1200 the old, dispersed form of habitat had been largely replaced by these relatively large, fortified settlements, known as *castra*.[30]

Lordship had thus helped remake the social landscape of at least this region of Languedoc. It seems, however, that seigneurial control over the peasantry may have been less thorough in Languedoc than in certain other areas of western Europe. Not only in the Béziers region but throughout Languedoc, manorial organization, in the sense of a tight linking of tenants' estates with the working of the seigneurial demesne through compulsory labor services, does not seem to have been particularly developed.[31] Peasant tenants enjoyed a relatively large degree of control over their land, being able, on the payment of

30. Bourin-Derruau, *Villages*, 1:121–34, 228–37.
31. Magnou-Nortier, *Société*, pp. 141–42.

the proper dues, to alienate or subinfeudate it.[32] Serfdom was known in Languedoc, but it does not seem to have been particularly burdensome. It tended to be more "real" than personal, that is, a status incumbent on those who held particular pieces of property rather than a tie that bound one and one's descendants to a particular lord. If a serf gave up an unfree piece of land, he also gave up his unfree status. The dues owed by serfs to their lords, corvée labor and the *quête* (a type of taille, theoretically at the whim of the lord, but in actuality fixed in amount) were often similar to those of the free men of the castra. What really distinguished the status of the two groups was not so much their dues, but the fact that serfs performed homage to their masters.[33]

A final indication of the relatively privileged status of Languedocian peasants is the fact that in the late twelfth century many of the region's castra began to acquire the trappings of self-government. Increasingly leading citizens of the castra, known as *prud'hommes*, played an active role in guiding the religious and charitable life of their communities. In many places they came to have charge of the maintenance of the physical fabric of the local church; similarly, they administered the hospitals, leprosaria, and other charitable institutions that were established in many places. Ultimately, these men would fuse together with the prud'hommes who served the local lord, sitting in his court and collecting his dues, and form the nucleus of the self-governing consulates that began to spread through the region after 1200.[34]

One of the most striking features of Languedocian society in the late twelfth and early thirteenth centuries was the important role played by the local towns. During the Roman period Languedoc had experienced relatively extensive urbanization. The revival of commerce from the eleventh century on spurred the demographic and economic growth of these old cities. The coastal towns especially benefited from increasing trade in the western Mediterranean. Manufacturing also grew during this period, and by 1200 many towns were producing cloth, metal, and leather goods for export.

Many towns managed to win themselves an important measure of political autonomy. Of these the most powerful and successful was the

32. Partak, "Structures foncières," pp. 10–11.
33. Ibid., p. 12; Ourliac, "Servage," pp. 191–92; Ourliac, "Hommage servile," pp. 551–56; and Bourin-Derruau, *Villages*, 1:210–17.
34. Bourin-Derruau, *Villages*, 1:273–326.

city of Toulouse. Located at the intersection of several trade routes, its population grew dramatically in the twelfth century, making it by 1200 the largest city in the region. Toulouse's prosperity helped it win a significant degree of self-government from its master, the count. The Toulousains secured the right to manage their own affairs through an elected consulate and to exercise jurisdiction over most important legal matters concerning themselves. By the beginning of the thirteenth century they were expanding their power and influence beyond their walls. They compelled local nobles to abolish or curtail tolls on the city's commerce. Wealthy Toulousains also bought up lands and rights in rural areas. No other town in Languedoc acquired quite as much independence from its traditional lord or as much power over its surrounding countryside. Many, however, secured a measure of self-government, expressed in the institutional form of elected consulates.[35]

Although on the eve of the Albigensian crusades that were to end Languedocian independence authority was widely diffused, and no single leader had managed to integrate the entire region under his control, some of the leading aristocratic houses were beginning to develop more effective techniques of rule and coercion. By the late twelfth century specialized administrative officials had emerged in some seigneurial households. We know, for example, that Count Raimond V of Toulouse possessed chanceries in some of his lordships.[36]

Of the officials involved in the local administration of Languedocian lordships, the most important were perhaps the seneschals. In the areas entrusted to their care they exercised all of the authority of their master, whether military, judicial or financial.[37] The greater lords of the Midi also had other local administrative officials. The most important of these were the *viguiers*. Removable at the will of their employer, they exercised authority over areas more circumscribed than those supervised by seneschals. The actual administration of particular estates and revenue sources was entrusted to officers known as *bayles*, who often farmed their posts.[38]

35. Wolff, ed., *Histoire du Languedoc*, pp. 161–63.
36. Léonard, ed., *Catalogue*, pp. xli–lvi.
37. Boutaric, *Saint Louis*, pp. 141–42, and Molinier, "Etude sur l'administration féodale," p. 200.
38. Molinier, "Etude sur l'administration féodale," pp. 196–99.

In trying to mobilize the resources of their subjects, Languedocian lords collected many dues similar to those found in the north of France. In Languedoc seigneurs were, naturally, landlords and therefore collected rent, both in cash and kind, levied entry fines, and charged their tenants for permission to alienate their holdings. Various forced labor dues were also exacted.[39] Although many townsmen had managed to win for themselves a measure of self-government, they nevertheless had to disgorge some of their wealth for their masters. Most townsmen were liable for military service and were required to assess taxes on themselves for the repair of town fortifications. Monopolies were also a source of seigneurial profit. In some places lords exercised a monopoly over the sale of salt.[40] Many lords required their subjects to use their ovens, mills, forges, and winepresses, and to pay a fee in return for the services they received. Languedocian seigneurs also siphoned profits out of the local network of commercial exchanges. Merchants were saddled with tolls and payments for the policing of highways. Lords also used their judicial powers to ensure that markets and fairs provided them with revenue. The licensing of notaries, whose written instruments played a large role in Languedocian life, also brought in its share of profit to seigneurial coffers. The right to mint money, which many lords had acquired, was a steady source of income.[41]

Medieval Gwynedd

Languedoc, with its thriving towns, prosperous agriculture, and an aristocracy engaged in trying to create ordered territorial lordships at the beginning of the thirteenth century, presents a familiar picture to the historian of medieval Europe. The region fits nicely into the group of social formations that made up the core area of western Europe in the middle ages. To turn to Gwynedd, however, is to pass to what was, both geographically and socially, a fringe area of medieval

39. Bourin-Derruau, *Villages*, 1:128–32, 203; Molinier, "Etude sur l'administration féodale," pp. 156–57.

40. Molinier, "Etude sur l'administration féodale," pp. 164–65, 185; see also Dupont, "Exploitation," pp. 7–25.

41. Molinier, "Etude sur l'administration féodale," pp. 172–80, 186–90. See also Depeyrot, "Trésor," pp. 144–47; Castaing-Sicard, *Monnaies*, p. 9; and Dumas, "Monnaie," pp. 556–58.

Europe. Facing the Irish Sea and roughly coterminous with the nine-teenth-century British counties of Anglesey, Caernarfon, Merioneth, Denbigh, and Flint, this area constitutes a relatively tiny corner of Great Britain. Its geography is dominated by a core of low but rugged mountains. This mountain bastion is surrounded by a relatively nar-row coastal strip, which reaches it maximum extent in Anglesey and the Llŷn peninsula of Caernarfon.[42] With its often sharp relief, gener-ally poor soils, and damp climate, Gwynedd is not an area suitable for the development of an agrarian life based on the intensive cultivation of cereals. During the middle ages it was thus a relatively sparsely settled region, inhabited by a Celtic-speaking people practicing an agrarian economy that, although it gave ample attention to cereal production, had a very important pastoral component.[43] Although commerce and town life were not unknown, neither was as developed as in Languedoc, northern France, or England.

Welsh social arrangements in the middle ages presented such strong contrasts to those found in much of Europe that historians at the beginning of the twentieth century were tempted to regard them as "tribal" in nature. By this they seem to have meant that Wales pos-sessed a rural economy characterized by pastoral nomadism and that the parameters of social and political life were set by clan ties. This interpretation is no longer accepted by Welsh historians. If there had ever been a time when the Welsh were pastoral nomads, by the thir-teenth century they had become settled agriculturalists, although ani-mal husbandry played a large role in their domestic economy. Al-though unilineal descent groups were of great importance in the region's social life, territorially based forms of political and social organization also existed.[44]

Older historians may have erred in characterizing Welsh social structures as tribal, but they were correct in perceiving that social and political arrangements were often different from those commonly

42. E. G. Bowen, ed., *Wales*, pp. 19–20.
43. Estimating the size of the Welsh population in the central middle ages is almost impossible. The most firmly grounded guess is probably that of Williams-Jones, who puts the total population of all of Wales at the end of the thirteenth century at about 300,000; *Merioneth Lay Subsidy*, p. lix. Edward A. Lewis, "Contribution," p. 95, gives a lower figure of about 150,000 to 200,000 for the population of all of Wales. Although we can do little more than guess, we might say that the population of all of Gwynedd was probably not larger than 100,000 at the end of the thirteenth century.
44. See Glanville R. J. Jones's attack on "the so-called tribal system in Wales" in "Tribal System," pp. 111–32.

found elsewhere in western Europe. The political structures of England, northern France and Languedoc, despite some important differences, all show certain similarities—significant disparities in wealth and authority, political dominance by a landholding aristocracy, an important urban and mercantile population, and rapidly developing administrative mechanisms. In such company the unusual features of Welsh society stand out clearly.[45]

The people of Gwynedd were certainly not tribesmen living in an egalitarian society where kinship completely determined a person's social position. Wales knew marked differences in wealth, power, and status; ties of protection and dependence were widespread.[46] But it does seem that the distribution of wealth and power in this social formation was less asymmetric than in England, northern France, or Languedoc.[47] The country also lagged behind in the development of significant concentrations of coercive authority and the fashioning of specialized political institutions.

The absence of differences in wealth and authority as pronounced as elsewhere was probably due to the nature of the Welsh economy. Compared with the inhabitants of the other areas, the people of Wales devoted less effort to grain production and gave a heavier emphasis to pastoral pursuits. This meant that would-be political leaders found it difficult to expropriate and hoard whatever surplus the rather unproductive local economy generated. It is easier to store and preserve an agricultural surplus if it is in the stable and relatively imperishable form of grain. It is more difficult to care for and preserve a surplus made up primarily of animals. Welsh law, moreover, incorporated a number of mechanisms that inhibited the accumulation of landed property, thus making it difficult for anyone to create a permanent base of immovable wealth with which to support claims to a leadership role.[48]

45. The best discussion of social arrangements in *pura Wallia* is in R. R. Davies, *Conquest*, pp. 115–38.

46. Ibid., pp. 136–37. See also Wendy Davies, *Wales in the Early Middle Ages*, pp. 59–71.

47. According to Davies (*Conquest*, p. 69), twelfth-century Wales possessed among the free "a much less hierarchical and deferential society than that of contemporary England."

48. Welsh law called for the equal division of a man's land among his male heirs. Furthermore, under certain circumstances cousins and second cousins descended from a common possessor of "appropriated land" whose sons had partitioned his holdings could, after the death of the brothers, force a reallocation of the land; see Glanville R. J. Jones, "Post-Roman Wales," p. 321.

Solid evidence on the distribution of wealth in Wales before the English conquest is unfortunately lacking. The records of a lay subsidy imposed by the English on the county of Merioneth from 1292 to 1293, however, provide a hint as to what conditions might have been like. This document certainly reveals differences in wealth among the Welsh. The top 10 percent of taxpayers possessed 30.9 percent of all assessed taxable wealth while the bottom 10 percent had only 3.1 percent, a ratio of 10 to 1. Despite this asymmetric distribution of wealth, inequality does not seem to have been as pronounced as elsewhere in medieval Europe. In Merioneth the single largest accumulation of movable wealth held by a layman was £33.[49] By way of contrast, the fragmentary remains of the 1297 lay subsidy for the English county of Bedford reveals rather more inequality of wealth. The top 10 percent of the 1652 taxpayers listed possessed 42.8 percent of the assessed wealth; the bottom ten percent had 3.3 percent, a ratio of 13 to 1.[50] In Bedford the wealthiest 1 percent of taxpayers possessed 16.4 percent of all wealth assessed; in Merioneth the wealthiest 1 percent accounted for 7.5 percent of the county's wealth.[51]

Figures on the distribution of landed wealth would be useful but are very difficult to come by. Sheriff's accounts from 1307 indicate that parcels of land escheated to the crown averaged 26 acres in size, with a median of 4 acres.[52] Carr has observed that escheators' accounts for Anglesey for the period before 1350 record holdings ranging in size

49. Williams-Jones, ed., *Merioneth Lay Subsidy*, p. 69.

50. The figures for Merioneth are derived from Williams-Jones, ed., *Merioneth Lay Subsidy*; those for Bedford from Gaydon, ed., *Taxation of 1297*. Bedfordshire was chosen for purposes of comparison because of the ready accessibility of Gaydon's excellent edition of the 1297 lay subsidy roll. Although this roll is incomplete, some Bedfordshire hundreds being omitted, there is no reason to think that the social structure of those areas left out was so different that their inclusion would have radically altered the distribution revealed by the surviving portions of the roll. We can therefore treat the surviving portion of the roll as a reasonably reliable sample of the total population of the county. The omission of part of the county, however, probably makes the distribution of wealth in Bedford appear *more* equal than it actually was. The wealthiest taxpayers in Bedfordshire were those lords, both lay and ecclesiastical, who possessed several manors. By excluding parts of Bedfordshire, we are probably missing yet other manors possessed by these or other wealthy taxpayers, and thus minimizing the unequal distribution of wealth.

51. This means that in Bedfordshire the ratio of the wealth possessed by the wealthiest 1 percent of taxpayers to that possessed by the poorest 10 percent was 5 to 1; in Merioneth it was 2.4 to 1.

52. Colin Thomas, "Peasant Agriculture," p. 33.

from 2 to 60 acres. An early fourteenth century survey of the holdings of the bishop of Bangor in Anglesey reveals an average free holding of just under 5 acres. Finally, an escheator's account from Anglesey for 1408–9 reveals average arable holdings to be a little under 9 acres.[53] Even the local ecclesiastical corporations, in Gwynedd as elsewhere in Europe among the wealthiest of landowners, did not cut a very impressive figure. In the late thirteenth century the bishop of Bangor was master of forty settlements in the county of Anglesey. The revenues of these estates—including rents, mills, and the profits of justice—were valued, however, at only £42 15s. 2d. The Cistercian house of Aberconwy had perhaps the largest landed endowment of any monastery in Wales, its estates accounting for about 38,000 acres, but the revenues from these lands were reckoned at only £91 in the mid-fourteenth century.[54]

In England there was a much greater concentration of landed wealth. The 1279 Hundred Rolls from England, analyzed by E. A. Kosminsky, show that the average size of the 1,031 manors enumerated was 511 acres (with an average demesne size of 168 acres). Among the peasantry fully 38 percent of those listed had a quarter virgate or less (a virgate varied in size from 15 to 30 acres in the area Kosminsky studied, although he assumed that it tended to average about 30 acres).[55] It seems safe to assume that there was less disparity in landed wealth in Gwynedd than in England. This is not to say, of course, that there was *no* disparity whatsoever. My point is that although differences in wealth existed among the people of Gwynedd, there is some reason to think that they were probably not as pronounced as in the other three societies covered in this book. This small concentration of wealth probably contributed to the failure of the dominant classes in Gwynedd to concentrate political authority as successfully as the rulers of the other three social formations.

Within this society, which found the construction of enduring concentrations of political authority difficult, one of the most important institutions seems to have been the *gwely*, an extended male patrilineage.[56] In a sense ultimate legal title to the land belonged, not to an individual proprietor, but to the gwely as a whole. Only by virtue

53. Carr, *Medieval Anglesey*, pp. 172–74, 269.
54. Hays, *Aberconway*, pp. 19, 111.
55. Kosminsky, *Studies*, pp. 30 (n. 3), 35, 97, 100, 216.
56. On kinship among the Welsh, see Davies, *Conquest*, pp. 122–27.

of membership in such a kinship group could freemen (and, in many cases, the legally unfree bondmen) gain possession of land or access to the kindred's pastures. These kinship groups (in this case afforced by affines) also played an important role in the legal system, where the settling of offenses was in large part a matter of the negotiation of compensation between the kindreds of an assailant and his victim.

One might hypothesize that such patrilineal descent groups could have formed the basis for political organizations of some sort. The gwelyau of Gwynedd, however, possessed certain traits that did not make them promising for evolution into authoritarian political formations. First, rules of inheritance within the gwely called for the equal division of a man's property among all his male heirs, a device that tended to level out the distribution of wealth, thus inhibiting the concentration of authority. Gwelyau, although their memberships were well defined, did not possess compact tracts of land. Lands belonging to a single kindred, as well as to its individual members, were often scattered over very extensive areas. A single kinsman might hold land in several settlements, intermixed with lands claimed by members of other gwelyau. This too inhibited the development of clear lines of authority within the kindred.

Finally, gwelyau tended to lack clearly defined leadership roles. The Welsh legal treatises mention the existence of a head of the kin group, the *pencenedl*. How this individual was chosen, the nature of his authority, and how he exercised it are not well known.[57] Although the gwely was an important institution in the life of the free inhabitant of independent Gwynedd, it appears to have been, as a political action group, rather weak. Although the gwely may have constrained the social and economic life of freemen, it did not exert much political authority over them.

In Gwynedd the village community was also less developed and institutionalized than in England, northern France, or Languedoc. Village or manorial courts enforcing local bylaws do not seem to have existed in thirteenth-century Gwynedd. Although some rural commu-

---

57. Accession to this office probably involved a mixture of hereditary right combined with some form of recognition by the kindred as a whole. (See, for example, *Cal. Anc. Pets.*, pp. 84–85.) Ellis, however, in *WTL*, 1:29, is of the opinion that there was no hereditary succession to the office of pencenedl. Very little is known about the duties of the pencenedl. Indeed, it seems that many gwelyau did not even have a formal pencenedl. See *WTL*, 1:82–83, 456 (n. 5).

nities appointed a common shepherd and the demesne estates known as *maerdrefi* possessed figures analogous to English reeves, Welsh villages lacked the elaborate infrastructure of manorial officials we find in England or the elected consuls common in the castra of Languedoc.[58]

In the twelfth and thirteenth centuries northern Wales, like the rest of western Europe, saw efforts to create coherent territorial principalities. The most successful princes were members of the house of Llywelyn ab Iorwerth, whose ancient seat was at Aberffro on the island of Anglesey. In the thirteenth century they periodically dominated much of Gwynedd. At times they even exercised a form of hegemony over the other princes of mid and South Wales.

Princely authority was most effectively wielded over the bond element of the population. Those bondmen most thoroughly under the control of the prince were the inhabitants of his demesne agricultural settlements, the maerdrefi, of which there were twelve to fifteen in what were to become the counties of Anglesey and Caernarfon.[59] Typically one of these units included a *llys*, which was a princely palace or court with its out-buildings. Associated with this was an area of demesne land, the *tir bwrdd*. Nearby was a settlement inhabited by bondmen, the maerdref proper. Maerdrefi were what the Welsh knew as "reckoned land" (*tir cyfrif*) settlements. Each tenant had an equal share in the village's land. These allotments, however, were not heritable within a single family. Instead there was a periodic redistribution of land in equal portions among all the village's male inhabitants. The tenants were required to cultivate the prince's demesne and perform various other labor services under the supervision of the *maer y biswail* (literally "dung-hill reeve"), a bondman chosen by the prince.[60] Although the maerdrefi show similarities to contem-

58. I believe this to be true despite the importance that Davies attributes to the Welsh vill in *Conquest*, pp. 129–33. Much of the cooperation that he finds within Welsh villages took the form not of formal, institutionalized intervention by the village community in the affairs of its members, but of informal, ad hoc cooperation between neighbors. His examples of village communities acting together as collective entities come from the postconquest period, when English rule may have given the village community a more important and a more coercive role in Welsh social life.

59. Glanville R. J. Jones, "Rural Settlement in Ireland and Western Britain," p. 341. Lloyd, *History*, 1:231–40, lists a dozen of these settlements. In what eventually became the lordship of Denbigh there seem to have been two maerdrefi before the conquest; David Huw Owen, "Lordship," p. 209.

60. Pierce, "Caernarvonshire Manorial Borough," p. 139.

porary English manors, these Welsh estates were relatively tiny operations. The size of the demesne on the largest maerdrefi was often
below the *average* size of manorial demesnes in some areas of
England.[61]

Associated with the maerdrefi were other bond communities. Some
of these, but not many, were also reckoned land settlements.[62] Most
were instead characterized by what the Welsh called *tir gwelyog*. Although the obligations of the bondmen of these vills, especially labor
dues, were heavier than those of freemen, they were organized into
patrilineal descent groups similar to the gwelyau of freemen. The
inhabitants of most tir gwelyog villages seem at one time to have been
obliged to perform labor services on the prince's demesne estates. But
by the time the English surveyed the obligations of their new subjects
in the late thirteenth century, such labor obligations appear to have
been in retreat.[63]

It seems that in the course of the thirteenth century, with the rise of
the power of the princes of Aberffro and the leveling down of the
fortunes of many freemen by the unrestrained play of partible inheritance, the distinctions between freemen and bondmen were eroding.
In Gwynedd the services owed to the princes by freemen and bondmen were coming to be similar.[64] Even that most fundamental distinction between free and unfree, the right of the free to take their place in

61. In 1284 the English surveyed the maerdref of Abergwyngregin in Caernarfonshire. Its demesne was about 200 acres. Resident in the township there were only
twenty-four bond households and eleven families of cottagers. Abergwyngregin was
one of the largest maerdrefi in Gwynedd. Elsewhere on the mainland of Gwynedd
most maerdrefi were inhabited by only a handful of bondmen; Pierce, "Aber Gwyn
Gregin," pp. 37–41. At Aberffro in Anglesey, the traditional seat of the princes of
Gwynedd, the maerdref contained about 240 acres of demesne. (For a description of
Aberffro, see Glanville R. J. Jones, "Rural Settlement in Anglesey," p. 212.) By way
of contrast, in eleven of the thirty-three English counties examined by Kosminsky,
average demesne size was *greater* than 250 acres; Kosminsky, *Studies*, p. 290.

62. In Anglesey there seem to have been only thirteen of these; Pierce, "Medieval
Settlement," p. 276. In Caernarfonshire there were fifteen. *WTL* seems confused on
the number of tir cyfrif vills in Anglesey, giving a figure of twelve on 1:161, but listing
only eleven on 2:426.

63. *WTL*, 1:333–35.

64. For example, after the conquest some of the native freemen, who regarded
themselves as nobles, informed Edward I's government that Llywelyn ap Gruffydd had
tried to reduce them to the status of *rustici* and *ignobiles* by exacting building and
carrying services from them. Llinos Beverley Smith, "*Gravamina*," pp. 169, 174–75;
Davies, *Conquest*, pp. 118–22.

the prince's host, had broken down. During the thirteenth century many of the bondmen of Gwynedd appear to have become liable to military service under the same conditions as freemen.[65]

The number of bondmen in Gwynedd and the proportion of the total population that they comprised are difficult to estimate. In northwest Wales as a whole, G. R. J. Jones has calculated that there were 660 villages and hamlets. Of these, 267 were bond (40.5 percent), 220 free (33.3 percent) and 173 (26.2 percent) inhabited by both freemen and bondmen.[66] In what was to become the lordship of Denbigh, however, only 14.8 percent of the settlements were entirely bond. Another 25.9 percent were mixed bond and free. The rest, 59.3 percent, were wholly free.[67] In Anglesey, where the number of bond settlements slightly outnumbered free (36 percent bond, 31 percent free, 33 percent mixed), the population of bond vills tended to be much smaller than that of free settlements.[68] On the whole, although a not insignificant proportion of the population was unfree, bondmen seem to have been only a minority in Gwynedd.[69] Although there were some exceptions, the majority of bondmen were subject to the lordship of only the princes or the greater ecclesiastics. The conclusion that seems to emerge from this data is that, although the distinction between free and unfree was an important one in Gwynedd, the country did not know a serf system like that found in much of western Europe, where a numerous nobility was supported by a complex of estates worked in large part by the coerced labor of legally unfree tenants.

During the thirteenth century the princes of Gwynedd were endeavoring to create an administrative infrastructure for their lordship. Those areas of thirteenth-century Gwynedd that were under their control were divided into territorial units known as *cymydau* or commotes. How these were governed before the English conquest is not very clear. The two chief local administrative figures seem to have

65. Stephenson, *Governance*, pp. 90, 93.
66. Glanville R. J. Jones, "Distribution," pp. 22–23.
67. Owen, "Lordship," p. 12.
68. Pierce, "Medieval Settlement," p. 274.
69. R. R. Davies, *Lordship*, pp. 354–55. For a very different interpretation, see Jones's argument in "Distribution," p. 20, "that early Welsh society, far from comprising a majority of freemen, was made up of a majority of bondmen who supported a thin aristocratic crust of lords and notables (*uchelwyr*), and a minority of freemen who owed this status to their performance of official duties."

been the *rhaglaw* and the *rhingyll*. These officials collected the dues and services owed to the prince and executed his orders.[70]

The organization of the prince's immediate household is less obscure. The Welsh legal treatises portray a court that does not seem far removed from the world of Beowulf. The household's officials are said to number twenty-four, although the treatises vary as to their identity. The officials included the judge of the court, the bard, the doctor, the door-keeper, the candle bearer, the chief groom, the brewer, and the baker.[71] One would have expected to find a household similar in composition to this surrounding any great lord of the early middle ages.

The treatises, however, portray arrangements that were probably archaic by the end of the thirteenth century. Unfortunately, the scanty records from preconquest Gwynedd make it difficult to unravel the internal workings of the prince's household. However, it seems that specialization of function had not progressed too far among the prince's servants. Individual courtiers were charged with specific tasks on an ad hoc basis. Of the men who surrounded the prince, the most important seems to have been the *distain* or seneschal. This official was employed on a wide variety of tasks according to the needs of the moment and the skills of the man who happened to fill the post. In contrast to the situation in many other thirteenth-century principalities, the princes may not have had a specialized chancery, although they had a servant with the title of chancellor.[72] Financial arrangements also seem to have been rudimentary. The auditing of accounts apparently was conducted by men appointed by the prince on an ad hoc basis.[73] The princes were able to sustain a small-scale military

70. In many ways the duties of these officials seem to have been interchangeable. Vinogradoff and Morgan, eds., *Survey*, pp. lxxiv–lxxv, lxxix–lxxxiii. A species of sergeants of the peace, known as *ceisiaid*, may also have existed. However, the evidence for the existence of these officials is ambiguous, and opinion on whether or not they existed outside the eastern parts of Gwynedd is divided. See Stephenson, *Governance*, pp. 46–50.

71. *WTL*, 1:33–34.

72. Stephenson, *Governance*, pp. 11–24, 26–30. Stephenson observes that the evidence is such that one can neither prove nor disprove the existence of a chancery. For a different view, see Pierce, "Age," pp. 32–33.

73. On the princes' financial arrangements, I follow Stephenson, *Governance*, pp. 20–24, who criticizes the views of Jones Pierce, expressed in "Age," p. 33, that the princes possessed a specialized financial department of state headed by a treasurer.

organization, constructing a string of fortresses during the thirteenth century.[74]

My description of the political organization of Gwynedd has been very schematic. The chief point, however, should be clear. At the end of the thirteenth century this Welsh principality was, compared with some other contemporary polities, relatively backward. Although the princes of Aberffro had made determined efforts to build up a more effective administrative infrastructure within their domains, they seem to have been able to arrive at a degree of sophistication not much more advanced than that known by the greater territorial princes of western Europe a century or a century and a half earlier. Certainly their household government, with its unspecialized functionaries, does not compare favorably with the developed and quasi-bureaucratized royal administration that had come into existence in thirteenth-century England. Local administration also seems to have been relatively rudimentary. The chronic political turbulence of thirteenth-century Gwynedd, marked by periods of princely domination alternating with periods of civil war and English encroachment, made it difficult for the princes to consolidate their position.[75] In light of all this evidence, one is probably justified in saying that the authority exercised over the inhabitants of Gwynedd by the princes of Aberffro was relatively limited. Freemen were justiciable in the prince's court and owed him military service and a variety of economic dues. Yet on the whole the power of the princes rested rather lightly on the freemen of Gwynedd. The princes exercised more influence over their bondmen, but even in this case their rights extended to little more than the exaction of various dues. The small size of the princes' government and their exiguous material resources limited the rewards they could bestow on their servants and followers. As a result they were able to create a clientage network that bound to them on a quasi-permanent basis only a small number of important families.[76] The principality that fell into the hands of the English in the early 1280s was, in Welsh terms, a major achievement. But one should not exaggerate the degree of its success. Organized, coherent, coercive political authority wielded by trained administrators was not a very

74. See Glanville R. J. Jones, "Defenses," pp. 35–37. Compared to English castles, Welsh castles were inferior in design and construction; Davies, *Conquest*, p. 255.
75. Davies, *Conquest*, p. 265.
76. Stephenson, *Governance*, pp. 125–26.

important factor in the social life of Gwynedd in the days of its independence.[77]

These then are the components I have chosen for my model. On one side there are the French and English monarchies, which had emerged from similar social structures and whose institutional development was following parallel paths, with the Capetians lagging behind their English counterparts. On the other side there are Languedoc—with its often wealthy secular aristocracy, its powerful ecclesiastical lords, its diversified agriculture, its thriving and increasingly independent towns, and its peasantry, which was less thoroughly dominated by its masters than elsewhere in France—and Gwynedd—with its Celtic-speaking inhabitants, its less pronounced hierarchy of wealth and power, its poorer agrarian economy, its relatively undeveloped commercial sector, and its native princes struggling to fashion a coherent, territorial principality. My model may not satisfy purists, but in these matters purity is not possible.[78] Despite the flaws inevitable in the design of any comparative research strategy, I hope that the reader will decide it is capable of producing some observations that are, to be sure, not unassailable, but nevertheless interesting.[79]

77. This picture of the political development of Gwynedd may appear to be at variance with that given in Davies, *Conquest*, pp. 252–66. The divergence in our views may, however, be more apparent than real. Davies is quite right in reacting against older views that tended to depict Welsh society as chronically turbulent and politically undeveloped. His effort to situate the history of Gwynedd in the context of the European-wide trend toward the consolidation of political authority during the twelfth and thirteenth centuries is to be applauded. But, although the rulers of Gwynedd had made some impressive advances, it is clear that they had not been as successful as some of their contemporaries in creating a consolidated and durable territorial principality. Finally, the political history of preconquest Gwynedd, given the fragmentary nature of the sources, is a difficult subject, and intelligent historians can read the evidence in any of several different ways.

78. Tilly, in *Big Structures*, p. 80, argues that planning a comparative study does not "require a search for the perfect pair of structures or processes: exquisitely matched on every variable except the purported cause and the supposed effect." Our search is for useful knowledge, not perfection.

79. The reader may wonder why I have not chosen certain other seemingly obvious cases, such as the Norman conquest of England, the establishment of a Norman principality in southern Italy and Sicily, or the founding of the crusading states in Palestine and Lebanon. Studying these cases would be rewarding, but they are not really comparable to the phenomena considered in this book. In Languedoc and Gwynedd political incorporation took place when the new rulers from outside had fashioned for themselves embryonic state mechanisms. The earlier, eleventh-century conquests took place when such mechanisms were in their infancy. They involved not

One important observation is immediately apparent. Of the four polities we have considered, the one where political authority was least concentrated and institutionalized was Gwynedd. Yet it was to fall under the control of the most advanced and organized political entity in northwestern Europe. The differences between the political systems of Languedoc and the areas of northern France under Capetian leadership were not as marked.[80] Languedocian institutions must have looked fairly familiar to the men from the north who journeyed to the Midi to govern this new addition to the royal domain. Englishmen in Wales, however, felt themselves among an alien people, little removed from the state of savagery. The task of political integration was therefore a greater challenge for the people of England and Wales than it was for those of Languedoc and northern France.

Organization of the Inquiry

In examining how Languedoc and Gwynedd were incorporated into larger political organizations, I have organized the material into topical chapters, each divided into three sections: Gwynedd, Languedoc, and a conclusion. My reasons for this are twofold. First, despite much excellent scholarship on Gwynedd and Languedoc in the thirteenth and fourteenth centuries, there are few synthetic over-

---

so much the extension of the sovereignty of one political organization over new territory, but a physical transplantation of groups of aristocratic adventurers, often only loosely organized and led, from one region to another. By the time of the absorption of Gwynedd and Languedoc into larger polities, the institutions of the new state mechanisms of western Europe, while still in many ways embryonic, played an increasingly important role in the organization of political life.

80. I believe this to be true despite the fact that in recent years some historians of medieval Languedoc have become progressively more certain that its social arrangements differed in important ways from the "feudal" arrangements of northern Europe. This is a position, however, that other historians of medieval Mediterranean societies have challenged. The position that claims that Languedoc should not be regarded as a feudal society and that emphasizes its distinctiveness with regard to northern France is summarized by Ourliac in "Réalité," pp. 331–34. (See also Ourliac's "Féodalité méridionale," pp. 7–11.) The counterargument is presented by Bonnassie in "Du Rhône à la Galice," pp. 17–44. Even though the position of scholars like Ourliac may currently command the most respect, it is clear that, when we look at northern France, England, Gwynedd, and Languedoc together, Languedoc was more like Capetian France than Gwynedd was like England.

views of either region in this period.[81] I have therefore found myself compelled to fashion my own partial syntheses. Also, although specialists may be familiar with the outlines of either Welsh or Languedocian history, it would be a rare person who knew much about both regions. Readers will therefore find the detail in the Welsh and Languedocian sections helpful to their understanding. Second, one of my goals in this book is to draw attention to the dialectical interplay of the structures of our two encapsulated social formations with the political institutions of the outside organizations that were seeking to control them. Such an organization of the material enables me to present this interaction in a coherent fashion.

The chapters themselves divide into three groups. The first, which includes chapters 2 and 3, discusses the administrative and legal impact of outside rule on Gwynedd and Languedoc. The second section, embracing chapters 4 and 5, addresses the economic effects of the process of political encapsulation. The third section, chapters 6 through 8, examines how the political behavior of Welshmen and Languedocians was affected by the new regimes. The last chapter offers some general reflections on the implications of this exercise.

The Imposition of Outside Rule

It is not my purpose to recount in detail how Languedoc and Gwynedd came under outside rule. These are oft-told tales.[82] I will make only a few general observations. First, Wales was much more accessible from the centers of English power than was Languedoc from the core area of the Capetian monarchy. The mountains of Wales were immediately adjacent to the densely populated English lowlands. From England ready access to the country was available by land,

---

81. Roderick, ed., *Wales*; Wolff, ed., *Histoire du Languedoc*, and Le Roy Ladurie, *Histoire de Languedoc*, treat this period. But their discussions are only parts of works that address themselves to longer time periods. Their remarks, although often valuable, therefore tend to be schematic. The history of Wales is now well served by Davies's *Conquest*.

82. See, for Wales, Davies, *Conquest*, pp. 308–54; Lloyd, *History*, 2:716–64; John E. Morris, *Welsh Wars*; for Languedoc, *HL*, 6:275–751; Belperron, *Croisade*; Madaule, *Albigensian Crusade*; Oldenbourg, *Bûcher*; Strayer, *Albigensian Crusades*; Lea, *Inquisition*, 1:129–308; Wakefield, *Heresy*; and Griffe, *Débuts*, *Languedoc cathare de 1190 à 1210*, and *Languedoc cathare au temps de la croisade*.

along the coastal plains or up the river valleys that cut deeply into the mountains. Access by water was also easy, as English fleets repeatedly demonstrated. Languedoc, however, was much more remote from the Capetian core area around Paris and Orléans. Only a tedious journey of many days, usually made via the Saône and Rhône valleys and across the Rouergue, brought a traveler from the Ile de France to the country.

Second, the involvement of the members of our societies in one another's affairs had differed sharply. The English and the Welsh long had been deeply involved in one another's history. Indeed, since the late eleventh century much of mid- and South Wales had fallen under the control of the Anglo-Norman lords of the Welsh March. The English therefore had had a long experience of Welsh affairs before the end of the thirteenth century. Many had acquired a sophisticated insight into the nature of their neighbors' institutions.[83] The French monarchy, however, had had little to do with Languedoc since the break-up of the Carolingian empire. In the middle of the twelfth century the Capetians began to show a renewed interest in the affairs of the south. But when the wars that were to end Languedocian autonomy began in 1209, the French monarchy and the various southern lordships had behind them only a relatively brief history of important political contacts.

Gwynedd and Languedoc also had very different experiences of conquest. In the south of France the assertion of Capetian leadership was a protracted affair, one which began in 1209 and cannot be said to have ended until 1271, if then. Indeed, the Capetian monarchy had very little to do with the early stages of the conquest. The assault on Languedoc began as a crusade launched in response to Pope Innocent III's call to extirpate the Cathar heresy from the region. In the early years of these Albigensian crusades the task of conquest was shouldered by a miscellaneous assembly of aristocratic freebooters, most, but not all, from the north of France. These men elected as their leader Simon de Montfort. Although Simon and his followers enjoyed much initial success, they never managed to break the power of the counts of

---

83. See the interesting remarks of Gerald of Wales, himself of mixed Welsh and Anglo-Norman ancestry, on how the English might best conquer the Welsh and how, conversely, the Welsh might best resist the English, in *Opera*, 6:218–27. There had also been considerable cultural contact and influence between the Welsh and the English. See Davies, *Conquest*, pp. 104–6.

Toulouse. Indeed, following the death of Simon in 1218, Count Raimond VII managed to regain much of the ground his father had lost in the early days of the war.

Not until the 1220s did royal involvement become an important factor in the struggle for control of the region. In 1226 King Louis VIII, having bought out the claims of Simon's heir, led an army into the Midi. Although the king died on his way home from this campaign, his lieutenants carried on the war. In 1229 Count Raimond VII was persuaded to come to terms. The provisions of the Treaty of Paris incorporated eastern Languedoc directly into the royal domain. The county of Toulouse was left to Raimond, but his daughter and heiress Jeanne was married to the brother of King Louis IX, Alfonse de Poitiers, who thus inherited Toulouse on Raimond's death in 1249. The early years of the French regime in the south were troubled. Armed resistance by Cathar heretics, operating from strongholds in the Pyrenees, proved troubling. Not until the reduction of the castles of Montségur in 1244 and Quéribus in 1255 was this threat removed. The French also had to cope with the disaffection of the local nobles, many of whom revolted in 1240 and again in 1242. Not until 1271, following the death of Alfonse and his wife without heirs, was the county of Toulouse incorporated into the royal domain.

The destruction of the independence of Gwynedd was a conquest of a different sort. It was the work not of aristocratic freebooters but of the united English kingdom, led by one of its most forceful monarchs, Edward I. Moreover, it was not the result of a process protracted over many decades but of two sharp blows delivered in the 1270s and 1280s. The late 1260s had seen the power of the prince of Gwynedd at its height. Thanks to the political problems that had divided the English kingdom in the 1250s and 1260s, Prince Llywelyn ap Gruffydd was able to enhance his position. He eliminated his domestic rivals for power in Gwynedd and pushed the English out of the often contested country between the Conwy and the Dee rivers known as the Perfeddwlad. He also conducted a series of successful campaigns in mid- and South Wales. The Treaty of Montgomery in 1267 recognized his new importance. The English acquiesced in his conquests in South Wales, acknowledged that virtually all the other native princes were his vassals and recognized his claim to the title of Prince of Wales.

Llywelyn, however, soon fell from this pinnacle. Among his problems were the disloyalty of his own near kin, especially his brother

Dafydd, the disaffection of his new Welsh vassals, and increasingly strained relations with the king of England. All of this led to war in 1276. By the summer of 1277, Llywelyn was brought to yield to the English. Under the Treaty of Conwy the prince gave up the Perfeddwlad, renounced the homages of all but five of his erstwhile Welsh vassals and agreed to pay the English king tribute for the island of Anglesey. Dafydd, who had fought for the English, was given a lordship in the Perfeddwlad.

Dafydd was always a turbulent and untrustworthy character. Angered by the way crown officials treated him, he rose against the English in the spring of 1282. Prince Llywelyn threw in his lot with his brother and the rebellion soon spread to all of Wales. Unfortunately for the Welsh cause, Llywelyn was killed in December 1282. Dafydd remained at large for a few months more, but he was eventually betrayed to the English. Tried and condemned as a traitor, he was executed in October 1283. With the defeat and death of Llywelyn and Dafydd, the independence of Gwynedd was at an end.

In a way these two very different conquests are emblematic of the fates that would befall Gwynedd and Languedoc under outside rule. The speedy and thorough Edwardian conquest of Gwynedd was the opening phase in a major crisis in the lives of the people of Gwynedd. English rule was to bring profound changes that would affect almost every inhabitant of old Gwynedd. In Languedoc, however, the slow, piecemeal assertion of French rule was not to have such far-reaching, almost revolutionary consequences. The process of Languedoc's incorporation into the French polity was to result in much less change and upheaval.

2 State Apparatuses and Structures of Domination

Once masters of their new territories, the English and the French had to decide how to rule them. This was no easy question with a ready answer. From a theoretical point of view, one can postulate a wide range of solutions to the problem of how to govern a newly acquired possession. A minimalist solution would be merely to establish a loose hegemony over the local community. The activities of the outside rulers would be limited to little more than persuading the traditional ruling elites to acknowledge some form of superior lordship, coupled with the periodic levying of tribute. A maximalist solution would involve the total recasting of local political structures. Traditional mechanisms and techniques of rule would be abolished and replaced by ones modeled directly on those of the new masters. The governors who wielded these novel mechanisms of power would be either members of the outside ruling organization or local people who had been thoroughly educated in and assimilated to the outsiders' norms. Between these two poles one can imagine a whole spectrum of procedures involving the greater or lesser assimilation of local political institutions to those of the outside organization that had engulfed it. With this spectrum of possible solutions in mind, we can turn to an examination of the administrative arrangements made for the governance of Gwynedd and Languedoc.

Gwynedd

One can plausibly argue that the story of how England sought to govern Gwynedd should begin well before the final destruction of Llywelyn ap Gruffydd's principality in the 1280s. In many ways previous English dealings with the princes of Gwynedd can be interpreted as an effort to establish a species of indirect rule over the country. For much of the thirteenth century, English kings sought to influence events in Wales by binding various princes as their vassals and playing off one Welsh ruler against another. The rulers of Gwynedd, Llywelyn ab Iorwerth (1187–1240), Dafydd ap Llywelyn (1240–46), and Llywelyn ap Gruffydd all did homage to English kings, and Llywelyn ab Iorwerth married an illegitimate daughter of King John. By the terms of the Treaty of Montgomery in 1267, Henry III, in return for Llywelyn ap Gruffydd's homage and a pledge of an annual tribute payment of 25,000 marks, recognized him as prince of Wales and granted him the homages of all but one other Welsh prince.[1]

Even after his first victory over Llywelyn in 1277, Edward I did not contemplate destroying the principality of Gwynedd. Llywelyn was shorn of the homages of all but five of his Welsh vassals and required to pay a tribute of 1,000 marks a year for possession of the island of Anglesey.[2] Although Llywelyn's position had been significantly eroded, he still held, in the words of J. E. Lloyd, "a position which many an English earl might envy."[3] It was only following the rebellion against English hegemony in 1282 and 1283 that Edward resolved on the destruction of Gwynedd's autonomy.

The Institutional Framework of English Rule

One can speculate that if the princes of Gwynedd had been able to thoroughly dominate their fellow Welsh rulers and create a relatively well-integrated territorial state, they might have been able to fashion a workable relationship with England. True, they would have had at best a subordinate position in that relationship, but they would have been able to maintain their autonomy. But their achievements,

1. *Littere*, no. 1.
2. Ibid., no. 211.
3. Lloyd, *History*, 2:760.

while enough to arouse the anxieties of the English, were not enough to effectively tame their Welsh neighbors. Their ambitions antagonized their fellow Welsh rulers and some of their own subjects. The discontent thus aroused produced a turbulence in Welsh politics that both necessitated and facilitated English intervention. On the morrow of his victory in 1283, King Edward must have felt that the only way he could achieve an acceptable political situation in Gwynedd was to rule the country directly.

Edward and his assistants thus set about overhauling the country's government. Their labor was facilitated both by the relative weakness of native political institutions and by the speed and thoroughness of the victory in 1282 and 1283. The deaths of Llywelyn ap Gruffydd and his brother Dafydd meant the elimination of the only effective native concentration of authority. No other Welsh secular ruler had rivaled them in either power or sophistication of government. The local ecclesiastical lords—the bishops of Saint Asaph and Bangor and the few monastic corporations in Gwynedd—did not present a serious obstacle to the English. Edward and his helpers were thus free of the necessity to conciliate an important group of local potentates as they set about devising a scheme of government for Gwynedd.

Two separate policies were implemented. The western sections of Gwynedd, Gwynedd Uwch Conwy (Gwynedd beyond the Conwy), were ruled directly by the crown as the Principality of North Wales. Eastern Gwynedd, Gwynedd Is Conwy, and parts of the old principality of Powys, were carved up into new Marcher lordships, among them Denbigh, Dyffryn Clwyd, and Bromfield and Yale. These last areas will not be a major concern in this chapter. I will note parenthetically that the Marcher lords seem to have been more willing than royal agents to adopt and adapt native institutions. They followed the custom of the older Marcher lordships by dividing their seigneuries into Englishries and Welshries, the former governed largely according to English norms and rules, the latter according to Welsh traditions.

In the Principality of North Wales, however, Edward adopted a more draconian approach to the problem of governing the Welsh. On 21 March 1284 at Rhuddlan, he issued in the Statute of Wales a complete scheme for the governance of Gwynedd Uwch Conwy.[4] What the statute envisaged, and what the English accomplished over

4. Ivor Bowen, ed., *Statutes*, pp. 2–27.

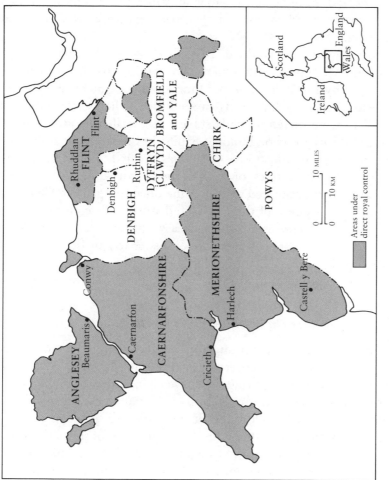

North Wales after the English conquest

the next few years, was the near total importation of an English-style government. The royal holdings in Gwynedd Uwch Conwy were incorporated into a single administrative unit presided over by the justice of North Wales. To handle the principality's financial affairs, an exchequer, closely modeled on that at Westminster and supervised by its own chamberlain, as well as a local chancery, were set up at Caernarfon.[5]

The principality was subdivided into three counties: Anglesey, Caernarfon, and Merioneth, each with its own sheriff. The Welsh commote was treated by the English as the functional equivalent of the shire subdivision generally known as the hundred. The rhaglawiaid and rhingylliaid were therefore made subject to the sheriffs and charged with the tasks imposed on hundred bailiffs in England.[6] In addition a variety of other administrative posts was created. County coroners were selected to keep track of pleas of the crown while foresters and woodwards were appointed to collect the dues charged the Welsh for access to the resources of the woods and wastes. To collect the payment known as *amobr*, due whenever a virgin was deflowered, officials known as amobragers were appointed. Early in the fourteenth century the office of escheator of North Wales was created to superintend the exploitation of lands that fell into the king's hands.[7]

Welsh Involvement in the New Administration

This English-style governing apparatus constituted a more thorough and effective set of governing institutions than the Welsh had previously known. In requiring the active cooperation of the Welsh in their operation, these new institutions also made novel demands on the time of the Welsh. Before the English conquest it seems that the relationship of the population with the government of the native princes had been largely passive. The people of Gwynedd had been called on periodically to disgorge some food renders, perform military service or various labor services, appear in courts presided over by the prince's judges, and on occasion find a few coins to swell his treasure hoard. The English, however, required a much more active involve-

5. Waters, *Edwardian Settlement*, pp. 15, 162–63.
6. Ibid., pp. 112–13.
7. From 1323 this office was usually held by the same man who served as chamberlain of North Wales; ibid., pp. 59–61.

ment of their subjects in the day-to-day functioning of the government.

The aspect of the new administration that made the most demands on Welshmen was the judicial system. County courts met approximately once a month, commote courts once every three weeks. Every freeholder in Gwynedd was liable to suit of court, that is, the duty to appear at the sessions of a particular tribunal in whose jurisdiction he held land. In the early days of English rule all free tenants were compelled to do suit to the courts of all the counties and hundreds in which they held land. Those bondmen who possessed some free land, a not uncommon occurrence, were also required to attend. Those who failed to appear were amerced.

The obligation of suit of court posed a difficult problem for the crown's Welsh tenants. In Gwynedd at the end of the thirteenth century, it was not uncommon for men to hold land scattered through several hamlets, often in different commotes and even in different counties. The result was a burdensome multiplication of suits of court.[8] Some Welshmen refused to do suit; as a result their land was confiscated.[9] In 1305 Welshmen complained to the prince of Wales— King Edward's son and the future Edward II, who had been granted the principality by his father—about the burdens of doing suit to his courts. Edward's response was two-fold. First, suit was henceforth held to be due to county courts only from those who possessed four bovates of land. Those with less freehold land were excused but still had to do suit to commote courts. Second, the problem of individuals who held land in several jurisdictions was dealt with by making the obligation of suit incumbent on only one piece of land. Thus, even if a tenant had holdings in several jurisdictions, he would have to attend only one county or commote court.[10]

Probably the most important judicial events of the year were the sheriff's tourns. Twice a year the sheriffs of North Wales held these special sessions of the commote courts. Every tenant, whether free or bond, was required to attend. It seems, however, that, as in England,

8. For example, in 1305 the abbot and convent of Cymer, located in Merioneth, complained that they were being distrained to do suit to the Caernarfonshire county court since they happened to own a fish weir and a few plots of land in the vill of Neigwl in that county; *RC*, p. 218.
9. Waters, *Edwardian Settlement*, pp. 100–101.
10. *RC*, p. 214.

bond tenants were not obliged to appear in person, each bond community instead sending a delegation of five men. At the tourn the sheriff empaneled a jury, which reported on such things as breaches of the king's peace or encroachment on his rights.[11]

Other features of the new legal system also required the active participation of the Welsh; among these was the hue and cry. In England whenever anyone discovered a felony, he was obliged to raise the hue. The inhabitants of the four neighboring villages were required to pursue the suspected criminal. As the Welsh pointed out to Prince Edward in 1305, the fact that their vills sprawled over large areas of land often made answering the hue and cry a major hardship.[12]

The activities of the newly created coroners also made demands on the time of the Welsh.[13] For the Welsh undoubtedly the most novel and exacting aspect of his duties was the inquest. Whenever someone was murdered or died accidentally or under suspicious circumstances, the coroner made an investigation. To his inquest he summoned the entire male population above the age of twelve of the locality where the body had been discovered, as well as the adult males from the four neighboring villages.[14]

The addiction of the English to the making of surveys also involved the Welsh in the operations of the royal government. Between March of 1284 and January of 1286, John de Havering, the justice of North Wales, and Richard Abingdon began compiling an extent of the crown's new dominions.[15] This was the first in a series of surveys that the English were to carry out in the next several years.[16] The periodic assessment of North Wales for taxation also involved the valuation of the property of the local inhabitants. Welshmen were deeply involved in the making of these surveys and tax lists. For example, when the

11. Waters, *Edwardian Settlement*, pp. 114–23.

12. *RC*, pp. 212–13. For examples of amercements levied on those failing to answer the hue, see G. Peredur Jones, ed., "Anglesey Court Rolls," pp. 34–38, and SC2/215/13, ms. 7d, 9d.

13. The 1284 Statute of Rhuddlan had envisaged a coroner in each commote. In practice, however, as in England there were only two coroners to a county.

14. Waters, *Edwardian Settlement*, pp. 139–41; James Conway Davies, "Felony," pp. 170–72.

15. Pierce, "Growth," p. 107.

16. See Edward A. Lewis, "Decay," p. 74.

great survey of Anglesey and Caernarfonshire was compiled in 1352, panels of Welsh jurors from each commote were sworn in to assist the surveyors in their work. The inhabitants of hamlets and villages were also summoned on pain of amercement to appear before the surveyors.

The Mobilization of Welsh Resources

The governing institutions introduced by the English thus made a larger demand on the time of the people of Gwynedd than had their native institutions. These new institutions also enabled the English to mobilize local resources on a much larger scale than previously. This facet of English rule is illustrated by a glance at the novel arrangements for raising military service introduced after the conquest.

Relatively little is known about the military practices of the Welsh before the destruction of Gwynedd's independence. According to Gerald of Wales, in the twelfth century, Welsh chieftains were attended by bands of young men, which could be put to various military and paramilitary uses. According to the legal treatises all freemen were required to do military service for the prince. Bondmen were also liable to military service, every unfree settlement being required to provide a man, a horse, and an axe to help fortify the prince's camp. The Welsh princes, however, were not free to draw on the resources of their subjects in an unrestrained manner. The service of freemen was limited. Although they had to answer the prince's call whenever he conducted a campaign in his own lordship, they were obliged to take part in an offensive campaign outside his dominions only once a year. That the prince was not free to do as he liked concerning the internal organization of his host is indicated by the note in some of the legal treatises to the effect that the men of Arfon had the right to claim the vanguard in the army of Gwynedd.[17]

In place of these old arrangements the English imposed a new and more demanding system of military service. The growing tactical importance of infantry had led the English to devise a system of forced conscription. All males between the ages of 15 and 60 were required to equip themselves with weapons the nature of which depended on

17. *WTL*, 1:336–41; *Ancient Laws*, pp. 37, 50; Emanuel, ed., *Latin Texts*, p. 204.

their wealth. When the crown wished to raise a force of foot soldiers, it appointed commissioners of array to survey a county's resources and select those most fit for service.[18]

This system was applied almost immediately to Wales. Welshmen pressed into military service were often organized according to English prescriptions into groups of twenty under a vintenar; five of these groups were placed under the command of a centenar. On many campaigns Welsh levies were led into battle by Englishmen. Welsh contingents were also on occasion supplied by their foreign leaders with chaplains, physicians, interpreters, and, from the mid-fourteenth century onwards, uniforms.[19]

The process by which Welsh troops were mobilized was no longer, as it had been in the days of independence, the organic outgrowth of native institutions. Instead Welshmen were recruited in accordance with a foreign scheme, organized according to foreign conceptions of tactics, and often commanded by foreigners. Above all, the Welsh no longer fought to further their own purposes but to serve the ambitions of their English masters.

The Regulation of Trade

Commissions of array, although frequent, had only an episodic impact on the Welsh. Other English administrative arrangements affected the Welsh in a more continuous fashion. To guarantee their mastery of Gwynedd, the English built a series of fortresses, jewels of the art of medieval military architecture. Associated with these strongholds were plantation boroughs peopled by small colonies of Englishmen. In addition, a few other places received the legal privileges associated with borough status. By the mid-fourteenth century there were nine boroughs in the principality. Although the population of most of these settlements remained small, they and the castles which some of them served had a profound impact on the life of Gwynedd.

The boroughs served as the poles around which the English government strove to reorient local trade. Although commodity exchange had not been highly developed in Gwynedd in the thirteenth century, the country had not been without commercial activity. Welsh peasants, like their counterparts throughout medieval Europe, were not

18. Prestwich, *War*, pp. 99–101.
19. Hewitt, *Organisation*, pp. 39–40, and Prince, "Strength," p. 355.

totally self-sufficient. They had to obtain certain specialized items, such as salt and various pieces of ironmongery, from outside sources. English rule also entailed a major increase in the amount of tribute that the Welsh had to render, tribute that usually had to be paid in cash. To obtain the increasing number of coins they were required to hand over to their new rulers, the people of Gwynedd were compelled to resort to trade on at least a petty scale.

Although the last native princes had claimed the right to establish markets, and seem to have done so in some places, the small-scale trade of independent Gwynedd appears to have been largely free of regulation. The English, however, proclaimed stringent rules designed to create a trade monopoly for the new boroughs. Sometime in 1304 or 1305 Edward I ordered that all goods offered for sale in an area within five leagues of the chartered boroughs of North and West Wales had to be traded within the town walls.[20] Initially attendance by the Welsh at the towns' weekly markets may have been compulsory.[21] This market legislation was anything but a dead letter. The English courts made a determined effort to enforce the provisions of the ordinances regulating trade.[22]

It is clear that the English adopted a maximalist approach to the problems of governing Gwynedd. There were, however, limitations to

20. Although the original text of this ordinance has not survived, confirmations of its provisions in the reign of Edward II make most of it reasonably clear. There were certain exceptions to the regulations. Some individuals, like the bishop of Bangor and a few others, had the right to hold their own markets and fairs. (For some examples, see *CChR, 1327–41*, pp. 187, 307, 461.) Certain items, like bread and ale, could be bought in gross and later resold at retail within the market district by the local burgesses. "Minute articles" such as flesh and fish, cut cheeses, eggs, and birds could also be freely traded by the Welsh outside the town markets; *CPR, 1307–13*, p. 578; *RC*, pp. 132, 212; *CCR, 1313–18*, p. 370; *Cal. Anc. Pets.*, p. 195.

21. At least in 1305 the men of North Wales petitioned for the suspension of the ordinance, which required that every household send one individual to "increase the people at the market." *RC*, p. 212; Edward A. Lewis, *Mediaeval Boroughs*, pp. 174–78.

22. For examples from early in the reign of Edward III of amercements imposed on Welshmen who attempted to trade outside the recognized markets, see SC2/227/34, ms. 1, 2, 2d, 3, 3d, 4d. See also Jones and Owen, eds., *Caernarvon Court Rolls*, pp. 113, 164–65, 177. The English also forbade the brewing of ale for sale by Welshmen living within the market districts. (For amercements levied on those guilty of illegal brewing, see ibid., p. 53.) Outside of the boroughs' market districts, the assize of ale (also a novel importation into Wales) regulating the quality and price of beer was in effect; Edward A. Lewis, "Development," p. 135; *RC*, p. 132.

this policy. On the one hand, North Wales was not directly incorporated into the English kingdom. Throughout the middle ages it remained constitutionally separate.[23] In the new lordships of northeastern Wales the traditional Marcher policy of preserving a Welshry institutionally and judicially separate from the Englishry was pursued. Only in the principality was the full panoply of English governing institutions deployed. Their impact there, however, was profound.

Languedoc

In the Principality of North Wales the English imposed one of the most advanced and thorough of medieval administrative machines on a society that had possessed relatively undeveloped techniques of rule. What transpired in Languedoc after the French conquest was very different. When the French monarchy gained control of Languedoc in the early thirteenth century, it deployed its usual array of governing institutions. These were in some ways more advanced than anything that had been previously possessed by local lords, and they continued to evolve during the thirteenth century. However, the imposition of royal rule did not mean the end of local concentrations of political authority. Many of these survived the coming of Capetian rule. The administrations of many local lordships and town corporations also grew in effectiveness and sophistication. Under royal domination, techniques of rule thus experienced major development. But progress in the art of exercising power benefited local lords almost as much as it benefited the crown.

The Institutional Framework of French Rule

In the royal administration established in Languedoc the chief figures were the seneschals, who were analogous to the baillis of the north. Seneschals were eventually located at Toulouse, Agen, Carcassonne, Beaucaire, and in the Rouergue. The seneschal was a virtual viceroy, combining in his hands military, administrative, legal, and fiscal duties. Beneath the seneschal in the administrative hierarchy

23. Edwards, *Principality*, p. 13.

came the viguiers. Presiding over territorial subdivisions of the *séné-chaussées*, they were primarily the seneschals' executive agents. In addition each sénéchaussée had a number of subaltern officials, among them *sous-viguiers* and bayles. Bayles fulfilled roughly the same functions as northern prévôts, being primarily concerned with collecting various royal revenues. There were also castellans charged with the keeping of royal fortresses.[24]

The development of specialized royal financial agents was a protracted process. During the tenure of Louis IX's brother, Alfonse de Poitiers, as count of Toulouse, use was made of a number of officials who were specially charged with financial affairs. Individuals known as *clercs enquêteurs* collected the *fouage* and the extraordinary subsidies that Alfonse levied. There was also a figure known as the *clerc du connétable*, who was a kind of general receiver for the lordship's revenues. The desire to ensure that the local bayles passed on to the count the dues they collected led to a variety of experiments. Alfonse for a time employed a *superbaiulus* to control the bayles, an expedient that does not seem to have been very successful. Eventually in Toulouse each *jugerie* (the sénéchaussée of Toulouse was divided, not into *vigueries* like the other sénéchaussées, but into jugeries) received a financial officer called a procurator. In the royal sénéchaussée of Carcassonne, each viguerie was equipped with a similar official, this one with the title of *clavier*. Finally, the sénéchaussées gradually acquired a flock of petty officials—sergeants, messengers, beadles, jailers, foresters, *banniers* (a species of rural police), and notaries. The supervision and discipline of these local officials was ensured by resort to a common technique of medieval administration, the dispatch of special envoys equipped with extraordinary powers, the *enquêteurs-réformateurs*.[25]

The administrative framework established by the Capetians was often unstable. This was due to the fact that the extent of royal authority in the region was itself uncertain. In addition to the surviving local lordships, the French kings at times had to contend with other princes who had claims to suzerainty or sovereignty over part of the country.

24. Auguste Molinier, "Etude sur l'administration de Louis IX," pp. 490–93, 496–99; Strayer, "Viscounts," pp. 216–19.

25. Lot and Fawtier, *Histoire*, 1:94; Strayer, *Reign*, p. 136; Molinier, "Etude sur l'administration de Louis IX," pp. 504, 508; Michel, *Administration*, pp. 90–93; Friedlander, "Sergents," pp. 235–51; *HL*, 6:793–94.

For example, for many years the kings of Aragon maintained a claim to lordship over several areas in Languedoc.[26] Even more vexing were the claims of the dukes of Gascony, who were also the kings of England, to the overlordship of the areas that lay on the border of their duchy and Languedoc. For example, the suzerainty of the county of Bigorre was the object of much competition in the thirteenth century, competition that finally turned in favor of the Capetians. On the other hand, the Agenais, although ruled for much of the century by the French, was ultimately ceded to the English king-dukes.[27] Finally, even in areas whose suzerainty was not contested, the process by which royal authority expanded was often slow, a matter of the piecemeal acquisition of estates and jurisdictional rights. All of these factors combined to create an administrative geography that was often anything but clearly defined.

Consequently the territorial framework of royal administration was slow to take definitive form. Although the sénéchaussée of Beaucaire was early divided into vigueries, that of Carcassonne was not. In this sénéchaussée royal castellans often exercised civil jurisdiction analogous to that of a viguier over the districts surrounding their fortresses. It was not until the late 1240s and early 1250s that most of the sénéchaussée of Carcassonne was divided into fixed vigueries.[28]

The boundaries between and even the existence of administrative districts were constantly in question. Between 1257 and 1271, when Alfonse de Poitiers was count of Toulouse, seven new bailies were created in the Agenais and four in Quercy. In the Toulousain itself three new bailies were created and three abolished.[29] Towns and villages were often transferred from one jurisdiction to another.[30] As a result royal servants often experienced considerable embarrassment in

26. By the terms of the treaty of Corbeil in 1258 the king of Aragon renounced his rights over a number of places in Languedoc. (Sivéry, *Saint Louis*, pp. 602–3.) In 1272, however, in the aftermath of a war between King Philip III and the count of Foix, a number of castles in the southern half of Foix were occupied by Aragonese troops. Not until 1277, when the count did homage to the French king for his entire county, were they persuaded to evacuate these strongholds; *HL*, 9:12–21.

27. See Lodge, *Gascony*; Gavrilovitch, *Etude*, especially pp. 68–75, 82–83; and Trabut-Cussac, *Administration*, pp. xxiv–xxv, 59–65, 72–77.

28. Friedlander, "Administration," pp. 25, 51, 58–62, 135–36.

29. Dossat, ed., *Saisimentum*, pp. 40–41.

30. *Regs.*, vol. 2, no. 3070; and Friedlander, "Administration," pp. 205–7.

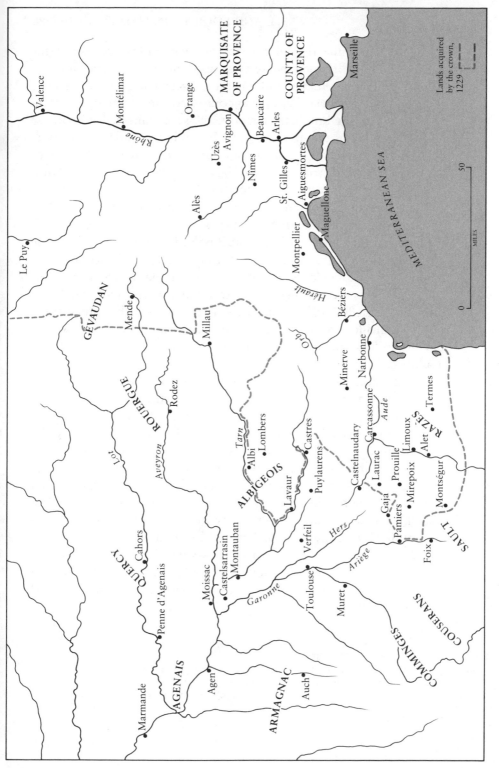

Languedoc in the thirteenth century

trying to determine the boundaries of their bailiwicks. When the agents of Philip III took possession of Toulouse after the death of Alfonse de Poitiers, they found much disagreement over the extent of some bailies. Moreover they even encountered considerable uncertainty as to where the boundary between the sénéchaussées of Toulouse and Quercy lay in the area around Montauban. Similarly, a dispute between the seneschals of Carcassonne and Beaucaire over the boundary between their districts required the appointment in 1294 of a royal commissioner to investigate the matter.[31]

The Capetian lack of interest in carrying out a thorough reordering of southern governing mechanisms is perhaps most clearly revealed by the fact that they failed to create during the first century of their rule any institutions that might have integrated their newly acquired dominions into a coherent whole. Because of complaints about the difficulties and expenses involved in prosecuting appeals before the Parlement of Paris, Philip III for a time experimented with sending some of his councillors to Toulouse to hold sessions there. This, however, did not prove satisfactory; after 1293 no more parlements sat in Toulouse.[32]

On occasion the French did convene assemblies within their sénéchaussées. In 1254 Louis IX promised that restrictions would not be placed on grain exports from the region without urgent necessity or prior consultation. On four occasions in the thirteenth century the French called general assemblies for particular sénéchaussées to discuss such prohibitions. These infrequent general meetings always remained narrowly concerned with the immediate issue that had caused their convocation. The rather mediocre attendance at some of these assemblies seems to indicate that they did not exercise any great attraction for the people of Languedoc.[33] Even among the ranks of the French administrators there seems to have been little regional cooperation.[34] Only in the fourteenth century did the demands of war with the English lead French royal agents to begin to fashion a unified administration for the province.[35]

31. Dossat, ed., *Saisimentum*, pp. 36–39; Ménard, *Nîmes*, 1:346.
32. Boutaric, *France*, pp. 216–17; *HL*, 10: *Notes*, 6 (n. 1).
33. Dognon, *Institutions*, p. 221; Bisson, *Assemblies*, pp. 214–15, 220.
34. Strayer, "Viscounts," pp. 219–20.
35. Dognon, *Institutions*, pp. 205–17, 329–34, 378bis–93.

The Survival of Local Concentrations of Political Authority

Although the French kings were recognized as suzerains throughout the region, large areas remained outside the immediate grasp of the royal administration. The peace associations that had been active in the late twelfth and early thirteenth centuries may have gradually faded away as the crown and the greater lords took on more of the business of enforcing public peace;[36] but many of the pre-existing political organizations that the Capetians found in Languedoc continued to live on, embedded within the royal sénéchaussées.

Among these were the numerous urban corporations. In the north of France the Capetians had long cultivated amicable relations with important urban communities. In Languedoc the kings displayed circumspection in dealing with the local urban polities. This is not to say that Languedocian towns found the coming of the French a painless experience. In the early thirteenth century many cities suffered cruelly as a result of the Albigensian crusades. Despite the travails that some cities experienced, the immediate period of the wars saw an expansion of urban liberties and influence. As various factions competed for their support, town consulates took advantage of the situation to acquire new privileges.[37] Toulouse, for example, made much political progress during this period. Its loyalty to Raimond VI and Raimond VII rendered the privileges that it had acquired from previous counts almost untouchable. The town's resistance to the crusaders also persuaded many of the local lords in the Toulousain to make concessions to its citizens.[38] Even Simon de Montfort found it worth his while to cultivate the goodwill of some Languedocian towns, as, for example, he attempted to do in 1216 when he granted the people of Nîmes various rights.[39]

The advent of royal control at first saw a reduction of some towns' privileges. For example, the consulate of Clermont-Lodève was suppressed. At Beaucaire the consulate was also abolished, while that of

---

36. Bisson, "Organized Peace," pp. 235–36; Bisson, *Assemblies*, pp. 118–21, 233.
37. Michel, *Administration*, pp. 223–25, 227–29.
38. Molinier, "Etude sur l'administration de Louis IX," p. 561.
39. Michel, *Administration*, p. 223.

Nîmes was much reduced.[40] At Toulouse the town consuls found themselves drawn into protracted controversies with their new master, Count Alfonse de Poitiers.[41] Yet, despite the trimming of the powers and autonomy of some towns, the French did not launch an all-out attack on them. Indeed, from the middle of the thirteenth century, Louis IX began restoring lost privileges to those towns that had had their wings clipped in the early days of royal rule.[42] At Toulouse, after the absorption of the city into the royal domain, the townsmen found the king's agents more accommodating than Count Alfonse.[43]

Capetian rule was thus not inherently inimical to the preservation of traditional centers of political authority. Indeed some members of the local ruling elites found that French hegemony was not incompatible with progress for themselves. Under the umbrella of Capetian over-lordship, some were able to consolidate and expand their own author-ity. Prominent among these were the prelates of the Languedocian church. The bishops were in many ways the great victors of the Al-bigensian crusades. Before the crusades, for example, the authority of the bishops of Toulouse had been limited. Bishop Fulk, however, suc-cessfully exploited the turmoil of the war, enhancing, among other things, his judicial authority. He also significantly improved the mate-rial situation of his see, prying tithes and church property out of the hands of the local aristocracy.[44] The bishop of Lodève also benefited from the crusades. The wars ended the pretensions of the counts of Toulouse to lordship over the diocese and enabled the bishop to weak-en the local aristocratic houses and impose tolls throughout the bisho-pric.[45]

The bishops of Albi were especially successful in consolidating their authority under French domination.[46] In the late twelfth century they had had to share power in the city with the Trencavel viscounts of Carcassonne. In the last decades of the century Bishop Guilhem Peire (1185–1227) began to improve his position. Supported by the towns-

40. Ibid., pp. 244–46.

41. Molinier, "Etude sur l'administration de Louis IX," pp. 561–66.

42. Michel, *Administration*, p. 265.

43. Molinier, "Etude sur l'administration de Louis IX," pp. 561–66; Auguste Mo-linier, "Commune," pp. 147–62; and Wolff, *Histoire de Toulouse*, pp. 139–43.

44. Mundy, *Liberty*, pp. 164–65, 390 (n. 14).

45. Ernest Martin, *Lodève*, 1:46, 64.

46. The following paragraphs are heavily indebted to Auguste Molinier, "Dé-mêlés," pp. 284–95, and Biget, "Procès," pp. 273–341.

men, he secured an agreement that recognized his claim to share with the viscounts rights of high justice in most of the town.[47] Moreover, the Albigensian crusades conveniently removed the Trencavels from the scene. Bishop Guilhem, through an adroit policy of changing alliances as the needs of the moment dictated, managed to bring Albi through the wars relatively unscathed.

In the late 1220s the major political problem for the bishops of Albi became the growth of royal power. From 1229 onward the bishops devoted much of their energy to trying to restrict royal authority. An inquest in 1229 found that Bishop Durand de Beaucaire (1228–54) had all rights of high justice in Albi and a share with the king in the profits of low justice.[48] This decision did not end friction between Albi and the royal administration. Royal agents came to feel that the bishop was defrauding the king of many of his rights.[49] Disputes over the king's rights often produced violence. Royal agents, like the bayle who was ejected from the city in 1235, were assaulted or arrested by the Albigeois.[50] Townsmen summoned to answer to the seneschal of Carcassonne for their misdeeds refused to heed their citations.[51] On two occasions, in 1252 and 1260, seneschals made armed incursions into the diocese. Finally, in 1264 Bishop Bernard de Combret (1254–71) and the royal government managed to work out a mutually acceptable compromise; this governed crown-episcopal relations until the end of the *Ancien Régime.*[52]

Ecclesiastical lords were not the only local potentates who expanded their authority in the aftermath of the French conquest. Many lay lords found that the imposition of Capetian overlordship was no bar to the consolidation of their own authority. Although Count Raimond VII of Toulouse made significant concessions to the French in 1229, he used the next twenty years to cement his control of what the Treaty of Paris had left him. By reviving his judicial authority in the city of Toulouse and curtailing the Toulousains' exemptions from tolls, Raimond managed to trim the feathers of the city's powerful

47. Compayré, *Etudes*, pp. 141–43.
48. *HL*, 8: cols. 919–20.
49. See, for example, *HL*, 8: col. 2401.
50. *HL*, 8: col. 1305.
51. See the complaints of the seneschal of Carcassonne about the behavior of the Albigeois in *HL*, 8: cols. 1301–10, 2399–2404.
52. See Compayré, *Etudes*, pp. 150–57.

bourgeoisie. In the early 1240s Raimond even succeeded in arrogating to himself the right to select Toulouse's consuls.[53]

Raimond also enjoyed success in consolidating his authority elsewhere in his lordships. He increased the size of his domain, wresting large tracts of land out of the hands of other lords. For example, when Bernard-Odon de Niort, lord of Montréal and Laurac, was condemned for heresy in 1237, Raimond was able to confiscate his extensive possessions in the Lauragais.[54] The count also increased his authority by founding approximately forty *bastides*.[55] A useful gauge of Raimond's activity is provided by the documents preserved in Paris among the *Layettes du Trésor des Chartes*. This collection contains ninety-four acts in which the count acquired various rights and privileges between October 1230 and May 1249. Forty-nine instruments record the acquisition of lands or rights in a minimum of forty-seven different localities. Four acts record exchanges between the count and other landholders. Three deal with transactions in which individuals converted their allodial holdings into fiefs held of Raimond. Another thirty-five acts record the acknowledgment by forty-three named individuals of the fact that they were the count's personal dependents.[56] Ultimately, of course, all Raimond's efforts served to enrich the Capetians. But the fact that his lands came into the possession of the crown should not blind us to the very real success that he enjoyed in laying the groundwork for a strong territorial principality.

Raimond VII was not alone in finding the imposition of French dominion no insurmountable barrier to the development of his own power. Although the lands and properties of some of the leading houses of the Midi, among them those of Toulouse and Carcassonne, found their ways into royal hands, many of the other regional dynasties survived the Albigensian wars intact. Some of these were very active in expanding their authority and improving their lordships'

53. Mundy, *Liberty*, p. 136; Wolff, *Histoire de Toulouse*, pp. 125, 138.
54. Ramière de Fortanier, *Chartes*, pp. 17–18.
55. Saint-Blanquat, "Comment," p. 280.
56. *Layettes*, vol. 2, nos. 2077, 2145, 2171, 2288, 2359, 2440, 2460, 2462, 2469, 2472, 2482–84, 2487, 2561, 2582, 2710, 2713, 2717, 2740, 2742, 2758, 2765, 2787, 2839, 2882, 2888, 2894, 2953, 2956, 3072, 3079, 3176, 3205, 3216–17, 3225, 3229, 3242, 3342, 3345, 3347, 3350, 3351, 3357–59, 3372–73, 3378–79, 3381, 3400, 3467–68, 3507, 3514, 3516, 3531, 3540, 3549–51, 3573[2]; vol. 3, nos. 3574–75, 3589, 3597, 3626, 3629, 3631–32, 3653–56, 3659–60, 3676, 3680, 3685–86, 3704, 3729, 3731, 3734–36, 3742–44, 3747–51, 3759, 3764–65.

administrations. This was especially true of the Pyrenean principalities, which long enjoyed a large degree of autonomy. By the end of the thirteenth century the counts of Comminges, who had previously had only primitive and makeshift tools for the governance of their lordship, were copying the administrative mechanisms that Count Alfonse de Poitiers was using in Toulouse.[57]

Among the most successful of these princely administrators and politicians were the counts of Foix. The counts gradually built up an elaborate administrative structure, complete with seneschals, bayles, procurators, and castellans. It appears that the effectiveness of this administration improved greatly in the late thirteenth and early fourteenth centuries. By 1320 it had become competent enough to carry out an enumeration of all the hearths in the county as well as all the services and dues owed the count.[58] The counts also experimented with the calling of general assemblies of the inhabitants of their lordship.[59]

Finally, even the peasantry was able to consolidate its political position under the umbrella of royal overlordship. It was during the period of the Albigensian crusades and their aftermath that the institution of the consulate began to spread widely throughout the villages of the region. For example, in the area of the county of Toulouse known as the Lauragais, no rural consulates seem to have existed before the beginning of the thirteenth century. After Count Raimond VII of Toulouse acquired the region in 1237, consulates began to appear, although their number remained limited during the count's reign. But once Alfonse de Poitiers inherited the county, consulates became more numerous, diffusing to even the tiniest villages. When King Philip III took possession of the Lauragais in 1271, his agents recorded consulates in ninety-six local communities.[60] In the area around the city of Béziers, consulates developed more slowly, only some four to ten having appeared by 1250; but in the next few decades close to fifty more appeared in the records. The authority of consuls varied fairly widely, being largely confined to supervision of local commercial and agricultural life, the collection of tailles, and the management of the

57. Higounet, *Comté*, p. 231.
58. Dufau de Maluquer, "Pays de Foix," pp. 3–5.
59. For example, in 1333 a body called the *Tres Status Comitatus* met at Pamiers; *HL*, 9:464 (n. 1).
60. Ramière de Fortanier, *Chartes*, pp. 40–46.

community's property in the Béziers region—but including important judicial powers in the Lauragais.[61] No matter the extent of their powers, however, it is clear that the imposition of royal rule did not constitute an effective bar to the spread of these institutions of self-governance among the castra of Languedoc.

The Mobilization of Resources

The continued vigor of local political groupings often posed problems for royal administrators. The potential for resistance preserved by these indigenous political entities considerably complicated royal agents' efforts to mobilize local resources. This is illustrated by a glance at Capetian efforts to draw on the military resources of Languedoc. The crown managed to fasten a liability to military service on its new vassals in the south and on the towns of the royal domain. But the exact nature and extent of this service remained often ill-defined and contested. Virtually every summons for military aid initiated a round of protracted negotiations with those called on to furnish it.[62] Many of the Languedocian nobles who fought in French armies made it clear that they were not obliged to do such service but performed it of their own free will.[63] The monarchy also exerted only limited control over the organization and leadership of the forces it raised. In many ways the Languedocian troops that followed the French kings to war remained the organic outgrowth of local social and political arrangements—raised, organized, and led to battle by Languedocians using Languedocian methods. Although Languedocians may not always have been able to impose on the monarchy limits to their military service, they certainly succeeded in imposing the forms for that service.[64]

The relative lack of coercive authority wielded by the French in Languedoc (compared with the English in Gwynedd) is revealed by the embarrassing, if not indeed perilous, situations in which the agents of royal authority often found themselves. For example, when

61. Bourin-Derruau, *Villages*, 2:147–50, 154–59.

62. Contamine, *Guerre*, pp. 53–55.

63. See, for example, the declarations by various Languedocian nobles who took part in the 1272 campaign against the count of Foix in *RHF*, 23:781–82.

64. See, for example, the forces mobilized by the count of Foix in 1339; *HL*, 10: *Preuves*, cols. 849–53.

Hugues d'Arcis, seneschal of Carcassonne from 1243 to 1246, paid a formal visit to Albi, he found the city appareled as if for war, with chains stretched across the gates and streets. Hugues found the inconvenience he experienced negotiating these obstacles humiliating. Even more outrageous was the fact that when he departed the city, some of the Albigeois urinated on him from the walls.[65]

Not only could high royal officials in Languedoc be humiliated, they could also be intimidated into pursuing courses of doubtful wisdom. In 1303 the royal enquêteur Jean de Picquigny, confronted with the demands of the political elite of the *bourg* of Carcassonne and a riotous mob, was forced to remove a number of convicted heretics from the prisons of the local inquisitors.[66] Even the king himself could be subjected to pressure. When Philip IV came to the Midi at Christmas of 1303, he was met at Toulouse by organized demonstrators demanding justice for those citizens of Albi who had, so it was claimed, been unjustly imprisoned for heresy. In Carcassonne he was treated by the leader of the town militia to thinly veiled threats of rebellion unless he redressed the grievances against the inquisitors.[67] The contrast with the situation in Gwynedd could not be greater. No Welshmen ever openly threatened an English king with rebellion or successfully coerced a great royal emissary into subordinating his desires to their own. The French may have been the suzerains of Languedoc, but they were not masters there in the same sense as were the English in Gwynedd.

Conclusion

There were a number of important similarities in the ways the French and English sought to rule their new territories. First, neither the French nor the English royal governments felt compelled to create governing institutions specifically adapted to the social and political institutions of their new subjects. Both governments simply deployed in their new territories mechanisms of government that they already utilized in their core areas. In Languedoc and the Principality of North

65. *HL*, 8: cols. 1305–6.
66. BN, Ms. Lat. 4270, fols. 155v–56r, 271v.
67. BN, Ms. Lat. 4270, fols. 214r, 226r–26v.

Wales, the outside rulers installed political institutions that were in most respects mere replications of those they knew at home. In the new Marcher lordships created in northeast Wales, the English continued a system of government already worked out by other Marcher lords in regions previously conquered from the Welsh.

Second, neither royal government sought to make its new territory completely adopt the norms of the outside rulers. With the exception of the effort to stamp out the Cathar heresy in Languedoc, neither royal government sought to impose the culture of its core area on its new subjects. Welshmen and Languedocians continued to speak their native languages and to live according to the social customs of their ancestors. In these two cases at least, it is clear that medieval state-building did not also involve nation-building.

Finally, neither group of rulers from the outside seems to have consciously pursued a policy of political demobilization in its new territory. Little effort was made to deconstruct native political institutions or to dissolve the pre-existing bonds that united Welshmen or Languedocians to one another. To be sure, the process of conquest in both regions did result in a measure of "demobilization." The house of Gwynedd, possessor of the most important concentration of political authority in independent Wales, perished during the conquest. In Languedoc a number of local aristocratic houses failed to survive the Albigensian crusades. But once the wars ended, neither set of outside rulers embarked on a policy designed to eliminate or reduce the political capacity of local organizations.

The ultimate impact of these basically similar policies on Gwynedd and Languedoc was, however, very different. English rule in the part of Gwynedd that became the Principality of North Wales resulted in what can be considered a political revolution. With the deaths of Llywelyn ap Gruffydd and his brother Dafydd, the power structure of the principality of Gwynedd was decapitated. No other lords, whether secular or lay, had been as successful as they in concentrating political authority. Thus, although the English after 1283 did not deliberately seek to reduce the political authority of the local elites, almost no significant concentrations of political power remained in native hands. Before 1283 Gwynedd had possessed relatively undeveloped political institutions and had taken only the first steps on the path toward the concentration of coercive authority. After 1283 it rapidly acquired one of the most developed sets of monarchical governing institutions known in western Europe.

Nothing this dramatic occurred in Languedoc. Although the French kings gained significant holdings and deployed a local administration throughout the region, native power holders and native institutions of governance continued in existence. Indeed, in many lordships and urban corporations techniques of rule progressed under the umbrella of Capetian overlordship.

The root cause of this striking difference in the consequences of outside rule is the different constellation of political forces that prevailed in Languedoc and Gwynedd when they came under outside rule. In Gwynedd no social class had in the days before the conquest achieved for itself a clearly dominant role. As a result the native state apparatus was ill-developed. This social formation—devoid of a clearly dominant group and with governing institutions that were still relatively new and, compared to those of neighboring England, relatively undeveloped—was unable to resist English aggression. Moreover, the lack of developed native organs of government permitted—indeed, perhaps required—that the administrative tools set in place by the new regime be English in nature.

In Languedoc the agents of the crown confronted a more developed and complicated political system. In the late twelfth and early thirteenth centuries a number of local lords, both secular and ecclesiastical, were in the process of building up their authority and trying to create territorial principalities. The immediate entourages of these princes may not have displayed as much specialization of function and professionalization as that of the Capetian kings; but their local administrations—with their seneschals, bayles, and local judges—display some similarity to arrangements known north of the Loire. Many of the local towns were also engaged in winning important degrees of self-government and, in some cases, were trying to extend their authority over the neighboring countryside. Although many Languedocian lords and town governments were sorely tried by the Albigensian crusades, their authority was too deeply rooted to be eradicated. As a result many native centers of authority survived the imposition of French rule and competed on a not-too-unequal footing with the royal government for control of the resources available within Languedoc.

More than a mere difference in the extent of royal authority was involved in this issue. At stake were the relations that were to exist between the "state," in the sense of the government of kings, and the rest of society. In general, in the kingdoms of medieval Europe, powers of command and coercion and the right to the legitimate employment of force were not monopolized by a single set of central political institutions. The kings of England and France were the heads of their political societies, but they were not sovereigns in the sense that their successors were to become in the days of absolutism. Monarchs confronted not a uniform mass of citizens, each one endowed with a formally equal set of rights and duties vis-à-vis the state, but a highly unequal array of subjects. The members of the dominant class, the landed aristocracy, were not merely economically dominant, but also politically dominant in a direct and unmediated fashion, with many possessing, as an integral part of their patrimonies, various political powers.

This typically medieval pattern persisted in Languedoc under Capetian rule. The kings from the north were the recognized overlords of the region, but they had to share political power with the local magnates as well as with the local town corporations. The Capetians constituted merely one group of power holders among others.

The political system of those parts of Gwynedd incorporated into the Principality of North Wales was very different. Not only did the introduction into the principality of English institutions of governance constitute a major departure in the political history of the country, it also resulted in the creation of a political system that was perhaps as different from that found in England as it was from that of independent Gwynedd. England, despite the centralization of political authority that had taken place there, was still marked by the wide diffusion of powers of command and coercion among the nobility. The English aristocrats may not have possessed as grand a set of political powers as did some of their counterparts on the continent, but they nevertheless had secure title to a respectable amount of political authority.

In postconquest Gwynedd the situation was very different. The web of royal authority that lay over the people of the principality was an almost seamless whole. Here, more so than almost anywhere else in the regions subject to the English king, there was little confusion between political authority and private rights in property. "State" authority assumed an unusually unified and unitary character. Very few native Welshmen emerged from the conquest possessing any parcels of sovereign power; what powers they succeeded in retaining or acquiring were not very extensive. Neither was a new, English aristocracy imported into the principality. To be sure, a small number of towns received a degree of political autonomy. But in contrast to the situation in Languedoc, these urban entities were mostly alien importations. And, by catering to the consumption needs of the great fortresses built by Edward I, they functioned as one of the chief supports of the new regime. The concentration of authority in the hands of a single directing agency and its servants was in Gwynedd pushed to a point possibly without parallel elsewhere in western Europe. The conquest may thus have produced one of the closest approximations to a unified state system known in medieval Europe.

The relationship between government and society in Gwynedd and Languedoc was thus very different. In Languedoc political authority remained widely diffused; in the Principality of North Wales it was concentrated in the hands of alien rulers. This meant that the English and French royal governments were to experience much different success in their efforts to mobilize the resources of their new subjects. Chapters 4 and 5 of this book will be taken up with a detailed discussion of some of these efforts to tap the economic resources of their new territories. Here I will restrict myself to a few general observations. In Languedoc a host of quasi-autonomous political structures interposed themselves between the agents of the crown and local resources, both human and material. In Gwynedd such intermediary political organizations were largely absent. Conditions in this subject Celtic society thus made feasible a much greater and more effective intervention by the royal government in local affairs. The state apparatus thus came to occupy a more pivotal role in the affairs of Gwynedd than in Languedoc. Indeed it probably played a more central role in this tiny country on the fringes of Europe than it did in either England or northern France.

Ultimately, Welshmen and Languedocians came to have a very different experience of the nature of authority. For the people of Gwynedd, the end of independence meant a radical alteration of the meaning of political power. Authority ceased to be an organic outgrowth of native social and economic institutions. As a result, the people of Gwynedd experienced a profound alienation from almost all sources of power and authority. Not only were they systematically kept away from the levers of power in the new administration, but the very mechanisms through which authority was wielded were foreign, the products not of Welsh but of English history. In Gwynedd the postconquest period thus saw the opening of a gulf between civil society and its state mechanism. Political power increasingly came to reside with a directing group that was not part of Welsh society.

In Languedoc, however, political authority after the French assertion of hegemony did not present itself in such a foreign, alienated, and alienating guise. The French may have established their supremacy over the region, but they had not ruled all of its indigenous political traditions invalid. Many of these persisted. Under French domination important advances were made in the skill and thoroughness with which power was wielded. But Languedocians were as likely to benefit from these innovations as were Frenchmen. Enough power was left in local hands for the people of Languedoc to be able with a measure of success to impose their will on their new masters. The gulf between local society and its state mechanism was much smaller than it was in Gwynedd. Unlike many Welshmen, Languedocians were not made to feel like exiles in their own land.

3   Authority and Law

When one social formation is subjected to the political domination of another, some adjustment of their respective legal systems is necessary. It is with this subject that we will be concerned in this chapter. Not every aspect, however, of the legal structures that came into existence in Gwynedd and Languedoc under outside rule will receive equal emphasis. We will be primarily concerned with the use of legal mechanisms as techniques of rule. In a sense we are still dealing with the subject matter of the previous chapter, that is, with the structures of domination that took shape in Gwynedd and Languedoc after the end of their independence.

A separate chapter on the use of legal mechanisms as techniques of rule is warranted by the unusually important role that legal matters played in medieval political life. Concepts of law and justice were central to the ideological self-conception and self-justification of the ruling elites of Europe in the central middle ages. By the thirteenth century several generations of legal thinkers, scholars, and practitioners had fashioned a large corpus of formal and often highly intricate scholarship on the various systems of law in effect in western Europe, much of it designed to exalt the authority of the ruling elites by providing a transcendental justification for their right to dispense justice. On the concrete level of pragmatic political practice, law also played a strategic role in the governance of medieval polities. To be a ruler in medieval Europe was to be primarily a collector of tribute and a doer of justice. Rulers, of course, concerned themselves with other matters, but they often did not have effective enough institutional means to make a real impact in those spheres. It was therefore in the form of courts, judges, juries, and lawyers that political authority most commonly manifested itself in the daily life of the people of western Europe. The impact of the English conquest of Gwynedd and the French conquest of Languedoc on the indigenous legal systems is therefore essential for the understanding of the fate of our two regions under outside rule.

Gwynedd

The Legal System of Independent Gwynedd

The legal system of independent Gwynedd displays many of the characteristics one would expect to find in a social formation with a limited concentration of political authority and a relatively undeveloped state apparatus. Legal mechanisms were in many ways beyond the control of the directors of Welsh political organizations. Although the princes of Gwynedd attempted to make themselves the masters and directors of their lordship's legal system, they had not completely achieved this goal before the English conquest. In preconquest days the settlement of disputes was in many important respects left up to procedures and institutions that did not owe their authority to princely validation.[1] The Welsh legal process seems to have put more emphasis

1. As with so many aspects of life in independent Wales, the study of the legal system is bedeviled by a shortage of documents. Only the merest scraps of evidence reveal the functioning of a Welsh court in the days of independence. Most generalizations about the legal system have therefore been based on the Welsh legal texts, sources that are difficult to use and often misleading. Although it is claimed in these texts that they were compiled at an assembly presided over by King Hywel Dda in the tenth century, they are patently not legal codes proclaimed by authoritative political institutions. Instead they are lawyers' treatises dealing with various points of substantive and procedural law. Similarly, although the treatises may contain traces of ancient laws and procedures reaching perhaps as far back as the days of Hywel Dda, the oldest surviving manuscript of one of these tractates dates only from the late twelfth century. In fact, most of the extant manuscripts were composed after the destruction of Gwynedd's independence. (See Emanuel, ed., *Latin Texts*, pp. 1, 97–104, 172–75, 269–72, 294–99, 408–18; Wiliam, *Llyfr Iorwerth*, pp. xix–xx; and Timothy Lewis, "Bibliography," pp. 159–72.) To what extent the material in these manuscripts, including that in the twelfth- and thirteenth-century texts, accurately represents contemporary Welsh legal practice is open to question. It is possible that much of the substantive law and procedure discussed in the texts from independent Wales was already archaic when the treatises were composed.

on arbitration, negotiation, and compromise between litigants than on the authoritative decrees of judges and courts. In many ways, therefore, legal business in independent Wales was transacted without much reference to the desires and wishes of the local princes.

Independent Wales possessed courts and legal professionals. But in many cases courts and judges were not integrated into a system completely organized and controlled by the local political authorities. Frequently the selection, training, and discipline of judges were matters beyond the purview of the princes. Outside of Gwynedd, judges appointed by one of the local rulers functioned side by side with men who owed their judicial office to something other than princely favor. The legal treatises associated with South Wales indicate that every landowner, by virtue of his lordship over land, was ipso facto a judge. Although "official" judges appointed by a Welsh king could be removed from office for false judgments, these judges by privilege of land could not.[2] In addition to these men who presided over the meetings of courts, there was also a group of professionally trained legal experts, the *ynaid* (sing. *ynad*), whose advice was sought on technical issues and who were required to identify the matter to be put to proof. There are indications that the right to the office of ynad was hereditary in certain families.[3]

It is thus clear that the princes of independent Wales did not completely control the judiciary. It even appears that in certain circumstances cases could be tried without the formal presence of legal experts.[4] Even when princes appointed judges, it is clear that the authors of the legal treatises felt that they were not free to appoint whomever they wished. The prologue to the section of the *Llyfr Iorwerth* known as the Proof-Book states that Hywel Dda and the wise men who supposedly helped him compile the laws in the tenth century called down a curse on "the lord who should confer, and upon the person who should undertake judicial authority, without knowing the three columns of the law; and the worth of wild and tame animals, and whatever pertains to them."[5] The *Llyfr Blegywryd*, usually associated with South Wales, specifies that any man appointed by the king as a

2. *WTL*, 2:204; Richards, *Laws*, pp. 43, 96; Emanuel, ed., *Latin Texts*, pp. 66, 349.
3. See *Cal. Var.*, p. 208. See also p. 195 and James Conway Davies, ed., *Welsh Assize Roll*, p. 70.
4. See Davies, ed., *Welsh Assize Roll*, p. 318.
5. *Ancient Laws*, p. 105. See also Emanuel, ed., *Latin Texts*, p. 199.

judge who does not know the law must go through a year's training before he can take up his office.[6]

Another indication of the relative freedom of the legal system from the control of local power holders is the fact that Welsh law gave much importance to extracurial proceedings, or at least to proceedings that did not require the presence of a judge. In South Wales, according to the Black Book of Saint David's, if a dispute arose in any of the five villages of Ystrad Tywi, it was to be settled by the landowners of the other four villages.[7] Even in Gwynedd, whose rulers did much to make the judicial system an instrument of their will, some matters escaped the jurisdiction of their courts. According to the *Llyfr Iorwerth* it was among the rights of the freemen of the *cantref* of Arfon to settle boundary disputes among the cantref's *maenolau* without the presence of a judge.[8]

The importance of extracurial proceedings is perhaps most dramatically illustrated by the way in which crime, especially homicide, was treated. A killing was primarily an offense, not against public order, but against the kindred of the victim; it gave rise to a blood-feud. A feud, however, was not an occasion for indiscriminate retaliatory killing. Instead it was a threat used to stimulate negotiations for a money compensation, known as *galanas*, paid by the kindred of the killer to the kindred of the victim.[9]

The blood-feud is not the only evidence of the large role that Welsh legal mechanisms gave to negotiations between disputants. The surviving records make it clear that the Welsh were fond of arbitration.[10] For example, when in the early 1260s a series of boundary disputes pitted the bishop and chapter of Bangor against Prince Llywelyn ap Gruffydd of Gwynedd, the parties agreed to submit their differences to settlement by a board of arbitrators.[11] The replies collected in 1278 by English justices inquiring into methods of holding pleas of land in Wales and the Marches make it clear that the Welsh envisaged litigation as a process by which the judges should bring the contending

---

6. Richards, *Laws*, pp. 34–35; Emanuel, ed., *Latin Texts*, pp. 325–26.
7. *WTL*, 2:204–5.
8. *WTL*, 2:263; *Ancient Laws*, p. 51. A *maenol* was a subdivision of a commote.
9. See Pierce, "Laws of Wales," pp. 296–98.
10. Richards, *Laws*, p. 114.
11. *Littere*, no. 192.

parties to a settlement.[12] Since the element of negotiation was so prominent in Welsh legal process, it is not surprising to find that the initiation of a suit often involved the exchange of hostages between the parties.[13] The modes of proof employed in Welsh legal proceedings were also not easily subject to the direction or influence of political authorities. Whereas in English courts most issues were submitted to the verdict of juries, the Welsh still made extensive use of oath-helpers, both in civil and criminal matters.[14]

The Growth of Princely Control

Welsh legal mechanisms, as they emerge from the legal treatises and the scanty records of judicial proceedings, thus appear to have been relatively free of control by local political directors. Yet it is also clear that in the thirteenth century Welsh law and legal mechanisms were evolving rapidly in a different direction, one that was turning them into more effective tools for the wielding of princely authority. This was especially true in Gwynedd. There the princes attempted to create a legal system that was not a mere amalgam of various quasi-autonomous dispute settlement mechanisms but was instead an instrument with which they could control the social life of the country. To this end they reduced the autonomy of local courts and introduced various changes in procedural and substantive law.

In the thirteenth century the princes experienced much success in making all judges and courts in Gwynedd agents of their will. Under the dynasty of Llywelyn ab Iorwerth, there were no judges by privilege of land. All judges were officials, appointed by the prince. In the commote courts it was these individuals who presided.[15]

The court of the prince's household also seems to have become more important in the country's legal and political life during the thirteenth century. Among the figures in attendance on the last princes was an officer called the justice of Wales.[16] Jones Pierce has seen in this

---

12. The records of litigation, at least from the border areas of Wales, illustrate the frequent recourse to arbitration. For examples, see Davies, ed., *Welsh Assize Roll*, pp. 188, 246–48, 262–63, 312. See also *Cal. Inq. Misc.*, vol. 1, no. 1109.

13. Davies, ed., *Welsh Assize Roll*, pp. 224, 253, 264–65.

14. *WTL*, 2:303–9; Emanuel, ed., *Latin Texts*, p. 87; Richards, *Laws*, p. 85.

15. Lloyd, "Law," p. 112.

16. *Littere*, no. 32.

figure the chief judicial officer of Gwynedd. He has further claimed that in this period there developed a right of appeal from the local commote courts to the prince's household court. Moreover, as the princes either compelled or enticed the neighboring rulers into becoming their vassals, they began to claim the right to adjudicate cases relating to their vassals' lordships.[17]

The growing political power of the princes of Gwynedd allowed them to make some changes in substantive law. Many of these seem to have been intended to give the prince a more authoritative voice in the settlement of disputes. Increasingly, crime came to be regarded as an offence not only against the kindred of the victim but also against the prince. One-third of the compensation payable by the kindred of a slayer was held to be due to the prince. It also appears that certain especially heinous killings came to entail extra penalties imposed by the prince, among them execution and "harrying spoliation" of the slayer's property.[18]

Princely control of judicial mechanisms was also enhanced by changes in procedural law. Modes of proof more amenable to the control of judges began to be utilized. Borrowing from English procedure, the princes made greater use of jury trials. Evidence collected in 1281 by an English commission makes it clear that the use of the jury had become fairly common in certain areas of Gwynedd in the late thirteenth century. For example, one Welshman from Tegeingl in Gwynedd Is Conwy reported that the lord of a region where a dispute occurred was free to choose whether the parties should settle the matter according to *cyfraith*, that is, by Welsh law, or by jury. He also stated that in the early thirteenth century Prince Llywelyn ab Iorwerth had been unwilling to allow the use of cyfraith and had insisted "that the truth of the matter should be enquired."[19] Trial by jury is, of course, more "rational" (at least in our terms) than the old methods that had depended on oath-helpers. But the increased use of juries also

17. Pierce, "Age," pp. 34–35.
18. *WTL*, 2:107–8, 125–26. See also Stephenson, *Governance*, pp. 87–88. In 1281 Ithel ap Philip told English commissioners investigating certain aspects of Welsh law that Prince Dafydd ap Llywelyn had in the 1240s completely abolished the law of galanas throughout Gwynedd, holding that "a crime ought to bind its authors and not others who had not offended"; *Cal. Var.*, p. 199.
19. See *Cal. Var.*, pp. 195–200, 202–3, 206, 208–9.

gave the princely agents who controlled the courts and selected the jurors more influence in shaping the outcome of a case.

The legal system of independent Wales thus presents a picture of great complexity. On the one hand, much legal business was in the hands of men and institutions whose existence did not depend on any central political authority. The law was also marked by numerous survivals of procedures and techniques that had become archaic elsewhere in western Europe—blood-feud, proof by compurgation, and the extensive use of arbitration. On the other hand, the development of princely power, especially in Gwynedd, was leading to significant changes. Courts were becoming less the expressions of local communities assembled to resolve differences among their members and more the creatures of princely authority.

The princes of Gwynedd were in the thirteenth century thus making progress in converting what had previously been largely autonomous legal mechanisms into tools with which they could more effectively enforce their will on their subjects. They had, however, not completely succeeded by the time of the conquest.

The Refashioning of Gwynedd's Court System

When Edward I crushed the last vestiges of Welsh independence, he took up the unfinished work of the native princes. In the border areas that were carved into lordships for some of the king's most important followers, the new masters were left free to make what legal arrangements they saw fit. In the royal Principality of North Wales, however, the monarchy pursued a more innovative policy. Probably the most profound change was the complete overhaul of the court system, a process which has been described in chapter 2. In place of the court of the prince's household and the courts of the commotes, the conquerors introduced the full panoply of royal courts known in England. In creating these the English completed the process begun under the last native Welsh princes, that is, the transformation of the local court system from a mechanism used by local communities to resolve internal disputes into a tool of authoritative rule and coercion wielded by a dominant elite.

That the English sought to overhaul the Welsh court system is not surprising. In many ways the courts formed the linchpin of royal authority in thirteenth-century England. They were the arenas in which the king's agents most frequently came into contact with his subjects. They were also the places where royal judges settled the most politically significant cases concerning landholding and other rights. Moreover, the courts played a strategic role in the administrative and political integration of the kingdom. The county court in particular was the chief institution through which the king communicated with local elites. In it were read out royal proclamations, newly enacted statutes, and announcements of important royal grants. The court's suitors elected such officials as coroners, verderers, members of parliament, and, at times, sheriffs. The county court also played various auxiliary roles in the assessment and levying of taxes.[20] The fines, fees, and amercements generated by the courts also formed a respectable portion of royal revenue. Given the great importance of the court system in the machinery of royal government, it is clear why the crown lost no time in introducing it into the principality. As in England the courts in Gwynedd Uwch Conwy became the most frequent and common manifestations of the king's power.

The royal effort to remake the court system of Gwynedd was helped by the fact that the English kings acquired a monopoly over the principality's legal business that was even more complete than what they enjoyed in England itself. Although by the end of the thirteenth century the English legal system was one of the most centralized in western Europe, there was still a large number of lords with recognized rights to various forms of jurisdiction. Royal legal theory regarded these rights as franchises, all of which were held to derive ultimately from a grant from the crown. Although few lords outside the Marches were equipped with anything to match the judicial privileges of the greater French aristocrats, there were many members of the English ruling elite who held title to franchises of one kind or another.[21]

Legal privileges of this sort were, however, a rare commodity in Gwynedd. *Quo warranto* proceedings in the principality in 1348 reveal only a paltry number: three individuals put forward claims to what can be classified as extensive rights. Both the bishop of Bangor and the dowager Queen Isabella claimed return of writs on their

20. William Alfred Morris, *County Court*, pp. 107, 132–42; Stubbs, *Constitutional History*, 2:215–26; Jewell, *English Local Administration*, pp. 45–46, 84; Palmer, *County Courts*, pp. 293–94.
21. See Hilton, *Medieval Society*, pp. 230–36.

lands. The bishop also claimed the right to try his tenants concerning all pleas, save those of the crown. Walter de Mauny, the sheriff of Merioneth, claimed all fines and amercements levied on his men and tenants within the county. Aside from these individuals, few others claimed any franchises. The abbots and convents of Aberconwy and Beddgelert and the prior of the Hospitallers all claimed various minor rights such as private gallows and the amercements of their men. Only eleven lay Welshmen, almost all from the commote of Edeirnion in Merioneth, claimed any franchises, none of them very extensive.[22]

The Refashioning of Welsh Law

In addition to remodeling the court system, the English made some significant changes in Welsh substantive law. The English found Welsh criminal law morally repugnant. To them it appeared barbarous, savage, and contrary to the dictates of reason and revelation. This attitude is clearly manifested in the letters that John Peckham, archbishop of Canterbury (1279–92), exchanged with Llywelyn ap Gruffydd. In a missive that he sent to the prince in October 1279, Peckham observed that many provisions of the law of Hywel Dda were said to be contrary to the dictates of the Decalogue. In August 1280 he stated that much Welsh law was contrary to reason. Among its defects was the fact that homicide and other crimes were not punished by condemnation of the offender or by weight of reason, but instead were resolved by compelling the parties involved to negotiate a settlement. In the archbishop's opinion, such procedures were contrary to the strictures of both the Old and the New Testaments. Finally, in a letter written to Llywelyn in 1282, Peckham observed that Hywel Dda had been inspired by the devil when he codified Welsh law.[23]

More than moral indignation, however, was involved in the substitution of English for Welsh criminal law. A near monopoly of criminal justice was an integral facet of royal government in England. Only insignificant aspects of criminal justice were in seigneurial hands. The infliction of punishment for felonies was therefore deeply bound up with the prestige and self-conception of the monarchy. And the steady stream of fines, amercements, and confiscations generated by the op-

22. *RC*, pp. 133–205.
23. Peckham, *Registrum*, 1:77, 136; 2:475–76.

erations of the criminal justice system was a welcome addition to the royal exchequer's revenues.

The English therefore set about remaking Welsh criminal law. The Statute of Rhuddlan prescribed the almost complete application of English criminal law in the Principality of North Wales. Felonies were defined in Gwynedd as they were in England. The English system of jury trials presided over by royal justices was imposed on the country. In place of the elaborate tariffs of money compensation known in Welsh law came the English system of punishment, liberal in its application of execution, mutilation, confiscation of property, and disherison. In place of negotiations between the kinsmen of the killer and of his victim came the whole administrative panoply of English criminal justice—coroners, presenting juries, sheriffs' tourns, gaol deliveries, appeals, outlawry, and abjuration of the realm.[24]

These innovations may have resulted in the final abolition of any responsibility on the part of a criminal's kindred for his actions. But in place of the old collective responsibility of the kinship group the English imposed new collective responsibilities that lay on the inhabitants of a given administrative unit as a whole.[25] Welsh villagers were now required to answer the hue and cry and assist at coroners' inquests. In 1285 the criminal provisions of the Statute of Winchester were also made applicable to the principality. A commote's inhabitants were henceforth required to make good the damages suffered by victims of robberies within its boundaries. Also, if any malefactors loitered in the countryside, the people of the commote were required to apprehend them or else forfeit all their goods at the will of the king.[26]

Noncriminal aspects of Welsh law experienced less dramatic change. In litigation concerning movable property, the Statute of Rhuddlan allowed the Welsh to continue using their traditional modes of trial and proof. In actions involving immovable property, the statute specified that "the truth may be tried by good and lawful men of the neighbourhood chosen by consent of parties."[27] To bring civil law more into line

24. James Conway Davies, "Felony," pp. 145–96, and Waters, *Edwardian Settlement*, pp. 134–44.
25. Davies, "Felony," p. 180; Waters, *Edwardian Settlement*, p. 136.
26. *RC*, p. 131; Davies, "Felony," p. 180.
27. If the plaintiff could prove his case through the testimony of unimpeachable witnesses, he was to recover the object in demand; the defendant was to be amerced. If the plaintiff could not establish his point in this fashion, the defendant could be put to purgation and be required to produce as many oath-helpers as the gravity of the matter required; Ivor Bowen, ed., *Statutes*, p. 26.

with English norms, Edward excluded bastards from inheriting land, permitted widows to hold as dower one-third of their deceased husbands' land, and allowed women to inherit land in the default of male heirs.[28] The statute also introduced into Gwynedd the English system of initiating litigation through writs obtained from the royal chancery.

The Survival of Welsh Law

Despite the important changes implemented by the new regime, Welsh law was not completely displaced by English. The evidence for the survival of aspects of Welsh law is strongest in the Marcher lordships. There traditional Welsh criminal law, virtually abolished in the principality, continued to live on. Galanas payments can be found in Dyffryn Clwyd, Clun, and Denbigh. In Dyffryn Clwyd the prosecution of thieves by means of oath-helpers continued through the late middle ages. Other aspects of Welsh law also survived. Although the Statute of Rhuddlan had abolished the right of bastards to inherit in the principality, the men of Cydweli in 1356 gained the right to demise property to their illegitimate sons.[29]

In the Principality of North Wales it is harder to trace the survival of Welsh law. Nevertheless, despite the creation of an English-style court system, the abolition of most Welsh criminal law, and some changes in civil law, it is clear that the basic system of rules concerning tenure of land was largely unaffected by the English conquest. The bulk of land in Gwynedd continued to be held in accordance with traditional rules. Even in criminal matters, guilty individuals were occasionally allowed to redeem themselves by means of cash payments.[30]

Despite these survivals it is clear that the role of law and legal procedure changed significantly as a result of English rule. In independent Wales the legal system had enjoyed a relatively large measure of autonomy with respect to the embryonic native state apparatuses. Many issues under litigation were settled not by the definitive sentences of authoritative judges who owed their position to the will of the local princes, but by arbitration and negotiation between the parties involved. Even when a dispute was decided by a princely court, this was often done using modes of proof, such as compurgation, that

28. R. R. Davies, *Conquest*, pp. 368–69.
29. R. R. Davies, "Survival," pp. 346–47; R. R. Davies, "Twilight," pp. 154, 158.
30. Davies, "Survival," p. 353.

were not readily susceptible to manipulation by those who presided over the court's deliberations. During the thirteenth century the princes of Gwynedd endeavored with some success to capture native legal mechanisms and make them instruments for the expression and enforcement of their will. The English regime completed this process. The king was, at least in the principality, the undisputed master of the legal system. The courts were his property and the judges his appointees. The mode of proof employed with increasing frequency, trial by jury, was authoritarian and coercive. These changes in legal procedure, coupled with the administrative reforms discussed in the previous chapter, gave the new English rulers of the Principality of North Wales far more effective tools for intervention in the country's affairs than its native rulers had ever possessed.

Languedoc

The Legal System of Independent Languedoc

The evolution of Languedoc's legal system following the disintegration of the Carolingian empire was similar to what took place elsewhere in Gaul. During the tenth century the principle of the personality of the laws gradually died out. In place of Salic, Gothic, and Roman law (the last known through the Breviary of Alaric), there grew up a series of local customs that applied to all the residents of a particular lordship. The court system set up by the Frankish kings from the north also eroded. With the weakening of the authority, first of the king-emperors from the north and then of the local counts and viscounts, some of the petty lords who became the effective masters of much of Languedoc usurped the jurisdiction of the old Frankish courts presided over by counts and viguiers.[31]

The end result of this evolution was a complex sharing of rights of justice among the ruling classes. In a single locality many different seigneurs often had a claim to some form of jurisdiction.[32] In some places rights of justice became the subject of *pariage* agreements. In

---

31. Auguste Molinier, "Etude sur l'administration féodale," pp. 202–3, 208. See also Archibald R. Lewis, *Development*, pp. 313–14.

32. For an example, treating the division of the rights of justice in Albi, see Molinier, "Etude sur l'administration féodale," p. 209; *HL*, 8: cols. 909–16.

these a common bayle would be named to administer justice in the name of all the lords claiming jurisdictional rights. Another factor that contributed to the complex mosaic of legal rights in Languedoc was the growth of urban autonomy, which allowed many towns to gain a significant degree of legal jurisdiction.

Languedoc was thus divided into competing and overlapping jurisdictions. Few of the region's legal mechanisms seem to have been very authoritarian in nature or possessed of developed means of coercion. Among the nobles, especially, legal business for the most part seems to have been settled through various forms of negotiation and arbitration rather than through the definitive verdicts of courts equipped with sufficient coercive authority to enforce their decisions on recalcitrant litigants.[33]

At the beginning of the thirteenth century, however, legal procedure within certain Languedocian polities was taking on a more authoritarian and coercive guise. In Toulouse the town consuls were at work solidifying their judicial prerogatives. They waged a successful struggle against the efforts of the local seigneurial courts to act as mediatory tribunals. By the middle years of the thirteenth century, it seems that privately constituted panels of arbitrators had disappeared from the city. No longer were judge arbitrators simply chosen by the litigants in a case; they now received their authority from the consuls. Legal procedures applied by the consuls themselves became steadily more coercive. At the end of the twelfth century and the beginning of the thirteenth, litigants who submitted their cases to arbitration were required to abide by the decision reached by the assessors. In cases of appeal the decision of the consuls was made binding on the courts from which the appeals had emanated.[34] By mid-century the consuls

33. Dognon, *Institutions*, p. 52. For example, in 1201 a dispute between Raimond Roger of Foix and Raimond VI of Toulouse over whether the counts of Foix owed homage to the counts of Toulouse for the castle of Saverdun was submitted to arbitration; Castillon, *Histoire*, 1:239–40. In at least one area in the Pyrenees, criminal affairs were still often settled through the payment of wergelds; Berthe, *Comté*, pp. 71–72. Finally, in the late twelfth century it also seems that much of the litigation involving the inhabitants of Toulouse was settled by arbitration; Mundy, *Liberty*, pp. 140–41; Wolff, "Noblesse," pp. 223–24. There is a discussion of the extensive use made of negotiation and arbitration in tenth-century Languedoc in Lewis, *Development*, pp. 217–19. Further remarks on arbitration in the eleventh century can be found in Magnou-Nortier, *Société*, pp. 277–81.

34. Mundy, *Liberty*, pp. 144–47.

had supplemented the old accusatory procedures of the criminal law with new and more authoritarian inquisitorial procedures.[35]

The Growth of Coercive Judicial Mechanisms under Capetian Hegemony

After the assertion of royal suzerainty, local power holders continued to acquire greater control over local judicial mechanisms. In Albi, for example, Bernard de Castanet, bishop from 1275, devoted much effort to trying to make local judicial institutions more effective instruments of seigneurial control and less expressions of the sentiments of the community. On the one hand, he tried to assert greater control over the diocesan notaries.[36] On the other hand, he endeavored to restrict the right of those townsmen, known as prud'hommes, who formed part of his criminal court to decide questions of guilt and innocence and to determine penalties.[37] At roughly the same time, Amauri II, viscount of Narbonne, was engaged in a similar endeavor to restrict the participation of Narbonese prud'hommes in the business of his courts. The viscount was also trying to expand his jurisdiction in the city by claiming that his court could intervene ex officio in certain so-called *cas vicomtaux* (such as assaults on agents of the court, homicide, adultery, and counterfeiting) regardless of the claims of other local courts and without consultation with the prud'hommes of the suspect's place of residence.[38]

35. Mundy, *Liberty*, pp. 163, 320 (n. 41). As for the rules of substantive law applied by the multiplicity of tribunals that had grown up in Languedoc, it is difficult to generalize. In Roussillon, which eventually was to be incorporated into the Spanish political orbit, Visigothic law continued to be applied in the local courts. Elsewhere in Languedoc classical Roman law was coming to have a greater influence on local legal customs. Molinier, "Etude sur l'administration féodale," p. 210. (The spread of Roman law in Languedoc is described by Gouron, "Diffusion," pp. 54–67. On the tendency of modern legal historians to exaggerate the importance of classical Roman law in the region, see Rogozinski, *Power*, pp. 84–87.) Despite the spread of Roman law, the substantive rules enforced by the courts continued to vary from one place to another.

36. Doat, vol. 107, fols. 274r–75v; and Biget, "Procès," p. 317. See also the complaints of the people of Cordes about Castanet's efforts to regulate local notaries in AM Cordes, FF49.

37. ASV, Collectorie 404, fols. 19r, 31v. See also AM Albi, FF7; Gilles, "*Doctores*," p. 319; and Compayré, *Etudes*, p. 159.

38. Régné, *Amauri II*, pp. 102–5, 304–5.

The Struggle over Jurisdiction

Into this pre-existing and constantly developing complex of judicial systems, the French monarchy inserted its own network of courts and judges. The most important royal courts were those of the seneschals. Each viguerie or jugerie also had a royal judge. Litigants dissatisfied with the verdicts of these local courts could appeal to the Parlement of Paris (or, when Alfonse de Poitiers was count of Toulouse, to his court.)[39] These changes made by the French were important. For the first time, Languedoc became part of a unified, supraregional legal system.

However, the implantation of a royal legal system did not alter the fact that many aspects of local legal life were beyond the control of the king's government. Although royal agents were often zealous in pushing their master's claims to hear and settle disputes and collect the revenues thus generated, native lords and town consulates were often just as dedicated in their resistance to such efforts. Even within royal lordships the king's servants met with determined defiance. In the city of Toulouse the town consuls and their new French masters spent long years wrangling over jurisdiction. In 1255 Count Alfonse's council complained that the consuls were unjustly claiming jurisdiction in all matters concerning inhabitants of Toulouse, including acts committed outside the city. The council further remonstrated with the consuls for ignoring the jurisdiction of the count's viguier and instructing advocates who were inhabitants of the town that they were not to plead in his court or to give their services to any outsider litigating against a citizen. Finally, the council accused the consuls of excluding the viguier from the sessions of their criminal court and forbidding appeals from the city courts to those of the count. Differences over the extent of the consuls' jurisdiction continued to bedevil relations throughout Alfonse's reign. These disputes were not settled until 1283, when King Philip III established a common court for Toulouse, composed of the consuls but presided over by his viguier.[40]

If the French encountered challenges to their legal authority within the royal domain itself, it is hardly surprising that they found local

39. Molinier, "Etude sur l'administration de Louis IX," pp. 522–23, 526–28.
40. Ibid., pp. 562–65; *HL*, 8: cols. 1370–74, 1551–60; Auguste Molinier, "Commune," pp. 153, 160–61; Auguste Molinier, ed., *Correspondance*, vol. 2, no. 2058.

lords, whether ecclesiastic or lay, equally troublesome. Among the more intractable foes of the extension of royal jurisdiction were the Languedocian prelates. Relations between royal agents and the bishops were often little more than a series of wrangles over jurisdiction. For example, around 1255 Guillaume, bishop of Lodève, complained that the seneschals of Carcassonne had been trying criminal affairs that rightfully belonged to his courts.[41] In 1265 the bishop of Béziers was at loggerheads with the crown over his right to appoint notaries and hear cases from certain villages.[42] In 1267 the bishop of Toulouse complained that Alfonse de Poitiers's seneschal had destroyed his lawful gallows in the village of Castelmarou.[43] Around 1275 this bishop was protesting yet again, this time over the fact that the royal viguier of Toulouse was trying clerics on criminal charges.[44] In 1322 Augier, the almoner of Ferrals, appealed to the Parlement of Paris against the impounding of his property by royal servants. Augier had been accused of leading an armed assault on the village of Villerouge-Termenès in the sénéchaussée of Carcassonne, during which several hundred goats and sheep belonging to Arnal Dorban, one of the village's lords, were driven off. In his defense Augier claimed that he had been acting well within his rights as the agent of the abbey of La Grasse, which had high and low justice in the neighboring village of Thézan. According to Augier he had been carrying out a legitimate distraint at Villerouge. Although his men had indeed been armed, he claimed that the custom of the sénéchaussée of Carcassonne allowed anyone who had such jurisdiction, as did his masters, to bear arms with impunity on his own land.[45]

In these struggles over legal jurisdiction, royal servants often found themselves overmatched. Around 1300, royal agents complained to the king that the Languedocian bishops were making widespread use of the threat of excommunication to force litigants to bring cases involving temporal matters into church courts. The church courts were also compelling lay arbitrators to deliver opinions foisted on

41. *Layettes*, vol. 3, no. 4208.
42. Boutaric, ed., *Actes*, vol. 1, no. 995A.
43. Molinier, ed., *Correspondance*, vol. 1, no. 362.
44. Campbell, "Clerical Immunities," p. 414; *HL*, 10: *Preuves*, cols. 133–36.
45. Boutaric, ed., *Actes*, vol. 2, no. 6688. For other examples of disputes over jurisdiction, see *Regs.*, vol. 1, nos. 1310 and 1962; and *HL*, 10: *Preuves*, cols. 536–37.

them by church authorities. Finally, ecclesiastical judges were forcing royal officials to execute their decisions.[46]

The secular aristocracy, both great and small, was as jealous of its legal prerogatives as the church hierarchy. The surviving records bristle with disputes between royal agents and local seigneurs over matters of jurisdiction.[47] The greater the power and influence of the local noble, the more frequent and intractable were the disputes. Among the most important northerners planted in Languedoc by Simon de Montfort were the Lévis, marshals of France and lords of Mirepoix. The seizure in the late 1260s of certain prohibited coins by the marshal's agents involved the Lévis in a dispute with the seneschal of Carcassonne. Matters reached such a pass that the king's ministers arrested several of Mirepoix's servants. In 1270, however, the Parlement ruled that the marshal's actions had been lawful. In 1321 another Lévis was at odds with the king's government. Early in January animosity between the people of Caudeval and Corbières intensified into a pitched battle between the two villages. The royal castellan of Montréal claimed the resulting case for his court. However, the procurator of Mirepoix asserted his master's right to try the matter, thereby precipitating a long round of litigation from which Mirepoix eventually emerged victorious.[48]

The counts of Foix, masters of lordships scattered across Languedoc, were a constant source of trouble for royal servants bent on increasing the king's jurisdiction. In 1265 the crown was at law with the count over the question of who had rights of high justice at Pennautier in the sénéchaussée of Carcassonne. Within the county of Foix itself, the counts enjoyed great success in restricting royal authority. In late 1305 or early 1306 one Bonetus de Fortis committed a murder in Pamiers. He was arrested by comital agents, and a criminal action began against him. The seneschal of Carcassonne, however, alleging that Bonetus was a royal valet, removed him from the count's prison. However, after much controversy and negotiation, the accused was returned to Foix's jurisdiction. In 1306, following a riot at Pamiers, the count and the royal government found themselves in yet another

46. Boutaric, ed., "Notices," pp. 132–33.
47. For examples, see Boutaric, ed., *Actes*, vol. 1, nos. 232, 438, 1313; vol. 2, nos. 6450, 6452; and *Regs.*, vol. 2, no. 3448; vol. 3/1, no. 3020.
48. Boutaric, ed., *Actes*, vol. 1, nos. 1479–80; vol. 2, no. 6570.

jurisdictional dispute. The lieutenant of the *juge mage* of Carcassonne came to the city and cited several townsmen to appear at Carcassonne. The count's procurator protested, asserting that jurisdiction over the affair belonged in the first instance to the town consuls, and on appeal, to the count. The juge mage's lieutenant replied that the illegal bearing of arms was a *cas royal* and therefore pertained to the king. This produced an appeal by the count to the Parlement of Paris. In 1309 the count was again pestering the royal government, this time asserting his right to execute all those condemned for heresy in his domains and to confiscate their property. Litigation over this matter dragged on through 1326.[49]

The Persistence of Indigenous Legal Forms under Outside Rule

The factors discussed above—the survival of local power centers, their resistance to the expansion of royal jurisdiction, and the development by the directors of some of these encapsulated polities of more coercive and authoritarian legal mechanisms of their own—meant that the French found it difficult to make significant changes in local rules governing property holding. This is seen clearly in the complex of rules governing fief-holding. During the first stage of the Albigensian crusades, when the French monarchy was as yet uninvolved in the conquest, Simon de Montfort was confronted by the problem of how to secure a group of loyal, militarily competent followers to assist him in subjugating the region. In an effort to solve this problem, Montfort embarked on a policy of confiscating land from the native aristocrats and parceling it out among his followers. These lands were distributed as fiefs held in return for military service. The local rules governing fief-holding were, however, not as satisfactory to a would-be military despot as they might be, the legal obligations of Languedocian vassals to their lords being lighter than in the north. Simon therefore decided that his vassals would be required to hold their fiefs on more exacting and burdensome terms. In the statute he issued in 1212 at Pamiers he declared that all the fiefs he had given to his followers would be held in accordance with the customs of the Ile de France.[50] The resurgence

49. Boutaric, ed., *Actes*, vol. 1, no. 46A; Doat, vol. 93, fols. 79r–86r; *HL*, 9:284 (n. 1), 354 (n. 1); 10: *Preuves*, cols. 453–57, 484–89, 659; Lea, *Inquisition*, 1:538.
50. Timbal, *Conflit*, p. 26; Boutaric, *Saint Louis*, pp. 494–95.

of the house of Toulouse in the later phases of the crusades, however, meant that fiefs held in accordance with the customs of the Ile de France were restricted primarily to the area around Carcassonne.

Eventually some descendants of the newly planted lords from the north decided that they preferred the local customs governing fief-holding. The custom of the Ile de France, while not requiring the equal division of a fief among all male heirs, mandated that each surviving son receive a portion of his father's patrimony. Given the right chain of circumstances, this rule could lead to a serious reduction in the size of a lordship. In Languedoc, however, the spread of notions derived from Roman law resulted by the late thirteenth century in the recognition of a wide degree of testamentary freedom on the part of those who held their fiefs by local custom. This freedom made it possible to protect the integrity of an estate by willing much of it to a single heir. By the fourteenth century such great lords as those of Mirepoix and of Capendu wanted the French king to allow them to hold their fiefs in accordance with local custom. The result was a gradual supplanting of the imported rules of fief-holding by the prescriptions of local custom.[51]

Even royal efforts to change certain aspects of Languedocian procedural law could meet with the opposition of those who felt their interests threatened. In 1291 Philip IV tried to expand his gracious jurisdiction in the sénéchaussée of Carcassonne by creating royal seals that were to be used to give official authentification to contracts. His action offended the local notaries, who felt that it was both unnecessary and a threat to their livelihood. Their opposition forced Philip to acknowledge that notarial acts, even those without a royal seal, were legally valid.[52]

The relatively light impact of the royal legal system on the region's social life is also revealed by the continued prominence of arbitration as a method of settling disputes. For example, in 1255 a dispute between the consuls of Pamiers and Sicard de Montaut over the tolls the latter claimed to collect at Auterive on the Ariège river was sub-

51. Timbal, *Conflit*, pp. 144–48; *HL*, 10: *Preuves*, cols. 723–24. In criminal matters the French also made little in the way of alterations to local customs. In 1312, for example, the *donzel* Etienne de Montpezat was accused of murder. The king's government instructed the two commissioners assigned to determine the case that, although the royal court utilized its own style in making inquests, it was accustomed to take into consideration local custom. The commissioners were therefore to follow local usages in investigating the charges against Etienne; *Regs.*, vol. 1, no. 1689.

52. Gouron and Hilaire, "Sceaux," pp. 48–49.

mitted to the judgment of Aymeri Palherii, the judge of Toulouse, chosen by both sides as an "arbiter, arbitrator or friendly peacemaker."[53] When in the early fourteenth century the Franciscan friar, Bernard Délicieux, found himself at odds with the consuls of the bourg of Carcassonne concerning money they owed him, he called on the seneschal and viguier of Carcassonne to mediate the dispute.[54] As a final example, in 1308 the Parlement of Paris registered the arbitration by the seneschal of Toulouse of a dispute between Guillaume de Nogaret, one of King Philip IV's most important advisers, and the people of his seigneurie of Lunel.[55]

To sum up, the thirteenth century saw the growth of more coercive and authoritarian judicial mechanisms in Languedoc. As was the case elsewhere in medieval Europe, legal procedures were being transformed into techniques of rule wielded by the dominant classes. In Languedoc, however, this process did not benefit only monarchical authority. Certainly, the French created a new system of courts in Languedoc and made it possible for litigants to appeal from local courts, whether royal or seigneurial, to Paris. But the strength of the local ruling elite meant that it was impossible for the French to supplant all of the old traditional lords who had rights of justice. Seigneurial justice therefore persisted under French rule. So also did the jurisdiction of many of the urban communes. This continued fractioning of rights of jurisdiction meant that even the new forms of procedure devised in the thirteenth century remained only partially useful as means by which political directors, whether French or Languedocian, could intervene in the affairs of local society.

Conclusion

The legal developments in Gwynedd and Languedoc examined in this chapter were typical of a general European phenomenon: the progressive transformation of legal systems from community-based dispute settlement mechanisms into tools of coercion and discipline wielded by western Europe's dominant classes. Despite their overall similarity, however, there were some important differences in how

53. *HL*, 8: cols. 1367–70.
54. BN, Ms. Lat. 4270, fols. 32r, 57r–57v, 134r, 280v.
55. Boutaric, ed., *Actes*, vol. 2, no. 3479.

Welsh and Languedocian legal arrangements evolved under outside rule. Gwynedd experienced a more far-reaching series of changes. Its native courts were replaced by an English system of courts and judges. Traditional modes of proof, which had already been under attack, were largely replaced by English procedures. Welsh criminal law, whose rules and procedures offended English sensibilities, was also substantially reworked. The changes wrought in the legal system of Languedoc by the French conquest were not as extreme. To be sure, the French set up a new royal court system. For the first time all of Languedoc belonged to a single, supraregional legal system. But the French kings did not enjoy as complete a legal monopoly in Languedoc as did the English kings in Gwynedd. Local lords and urban corporations maintained important elements of jurisdiction. These local lords were jealous of their privileges and were prepared to defend them, often successfully, against royal pretensions. Royal courts and judges had to fit themselves into the interstices of a local, on-going system.

In neither Gwynedd nor Languedoc did the French or the English royal governments try to work major changes in civil law. Aside from a few modifications, traditional land law was left largely unchanged. The reason for this conservatism is easy to understand. The French and English kings sought to exploit their new dominions largely by extracting tribute from the inhabitants. They were not concerned with changing local production processes so as to make them yield either more traditional goods or entirely new products. It was therefore not necessary for them to alter the legal superstructure of rules concerning the possession and transmission of land.

In this and the previous chapter, we have surveyed the governing institutions created in Gwynedd and Languedoc in the aftermath of their incorporation into larger polities. The changes that took place in Gwynedd were more dramatic and far-reaching than those in Languedoc. In Gwynedd native social organizations were largely stripped of effective political power. Authority was concentrated to an unusual degree in the hands of the directors of the formal state apparatus. In Languedoc, however, authority remained widely diffused throughout society. The agents of the French crown did not enjoy as great a monopoly of power as did their English counterparts in Gwynedd. In the next two chapters we will examine how the directors of the English and northern French political organizations sought to use the governing institutions they had fashioned to intervene in the economic affairs of their new territories, the success they enjoyed in mobilizing the resources of their subjects, and the impact of their policies on the Welsh and Languedocian economies.

4 The Land Settlements

Economics and politics are tightly linked. An economy is not merely an amalgamation of techniques of production and distribution. It is also a political system, in which public power is used to preserve the property relationships that lie at the heart of a society's methods of production and distribution of wealth. Politics or economics should therefore not be considered in isolation. A change in economic structure has real and profound consequences for political life. Conversely, changes in the structures of authority have tangible economic effects.

This was especially true in medieval Europe. On the one hand, medieval Europe did not know the distinction, essential to capitalist societies, between the state (all of whose inhabitants are formally equal citizens) and civil society (in which differences of birth, education, occupation, and property ownership—things to which the state is formally indifferent but which make up the real life of a society— are allowed to act, free of direct political intervention).[1] In medieval Europe the distinctions of civil society were directly represented in the structures of its political institutions. On the other hand, surplus was siphoned out of the medieval peasant and artisan economies into the hands of the dominant elites, not primarily through economic means,

1. On the distinction between state and civil society, see Marx, "Jewish Question," pp. 33–34.

but through politically based levies and charges. The crucial role of the political sphere in the economy thus stands clearly and unambiguously revealed in medieval Europe. The functioning of regional economies cannot be understood without an analysis of the politically based forms of intervention in those economies. Therefore, in this chapter and the next, we will examine how the incorporation of Gwynedd and Languedoc into larger political entities affected them economically.

In the thirteenth century the economies of Languedoc and Gwynedd presented strong contrasts. Languedoc was a fairly advanced and prosperous region. To be sure, compared with the agricultural systems to be found on the alluvial plains of northern France, Languedocian agriculture appears somewhat unproductive. Agrarian practices, especially in eastern Languedoc, were those typical of the Mediterranean world, well adapted to a dry climate but of relatively low productivity. Instead of the three-field system of crop rotation found in many places in the north of France, in much of the Midi two-field systems were employed. In place of the heavy-wheeled plow of the north, Languedocian tillers used a lighter, wheelless instrument. This meant that more labor had to be employed in tilling a given amount of land. Like northern peasants, those of the south engaged in animal husbandry as well as in the raising of crops. Indeed, in the mountainous areas of Languedoc such as the Pyrenees, the Montagne Noire, and the Cévennes, animal husbandry probably played a more important role in peasant life than it did north of the Loire.[2]

Despite a level of productivity lower than that of some other areas of Europe, Languedocian agriculture in the thirteenth century was relatively diversified and rewarding. Large tracts of fertile soil (e.g., the terrefort of the Toulousain) were well suited to the growing of cereals. Viticulture and arboriculture were also well developed; grapes, figs, olives, almonds, cherries, and chestnuts were all grown.[3]

One of the more thoroughly Romanized regions of France, Languedoc had had a long history of urban development. Numerous towns dotted the region. By the middle of the twelfth century an active current of commercial exchanges had developed. The sizable urban

2. Le Roy Ladurie, *Paysans*, 1:76–83, 88–89.
3. Wolff, *Commerces*, p. 4; Wolff, ed., *Histoire du Languedoc*, pp. 148–49; Magnou-Nortier, *Société*, pp. 209–10.

populations provided an internal market for the agricultural produce of the countryside.[4] Some towns had become hosts to important annual fairs. From around 1100 Italian merchants were in regular contact with the region.[5]

Although the merchants of Languedoc may not have been as enterprising or as wealthy as those of Italy or Flanders, they maintained important commercial ties with the outside world. By 1215 traders from Montpellier had found their way to the fairs of Champagne in northern France. Wine, especially from the Lomagne and the vineyards around Gaillac on the Tarn, was exported to England via Bordeaux.[6] At the end of the thirteenth century merchants from the city of Toulouse were to be found conducting their affairs in a number of English towns.[7] There was also a relatively important mining industry in the region.[8] The most flourishing nonagricultural sector of the economy was cloth manufacturing. From the end of the twelfth century Montpellier was already known for the quality of its dye work. During the thirteenth century Languedocian cloth merchants established a network of trade relationships with much of northwestern and Mediterranean Europe.[9]

Gwynedd's economy was very different.[10] Compared with that of neighboring England, with its great grain-producing regions and its small but numerous towns, the economy of northern Wales was both backward and unproductive. In Gwynedd the cultivation of cereals was less developed, animal husbandry more important, commercial activity small-scale, and urbanization little developed. The climate, topography, and geology of Wales all militated against grain production on a significant scale. High relief and high rainfall, cool temperatures, bleak, wind-swept mountain slopes, and poorly drained, acidic soils made good arable land rare.[11]

---

4. Wolff, *Commerces*, pp. 169–230, discusses Toulouse as a consumption center during the thirteenth and fourteenth centuries.

5. Wolff, ed., *Histoire du Languedoc*, pp. 153; Combes, "Foires," pp. 233–36.

6. Wolff, *Commerces*, p. 15; Allègre, "Vie," p. 335.

7. Wolff, *Commerces*, pp. 120–21. See also Auguste Molinier, ed., *Correspondance*, vol. 1, no. 882.

8. Chevalier, *Vie*, p. 549; and Wolff, ed., *Histoire du Languedoc*, p. 150.

9. Wolff, "Draperie," pp. 442–44; Reyerson, "Rôle," pp. 20, 25–26; Wolff, ed., *Histoire du Languedoc*, p. 150; Wolff, *Commerces*, p. 11; Allègre, "Vie," p. 335.

10. For fuller references, see Given, "Economic Consequences," pp. 13–15.

11. E. G. Bowen, ed., *Wales*, p. 272, and David Thomas, ed., *Wales*, p. 122.

In much of medieval Europe wheat was the prize crop, the bread made from it being a highly esteemed item in the diet. Wheat production in Gwynedd, however, was of only secondary importance. The 1292–93 lay subsidy returns for the portion of the Llŷn peninsula included in the Cafflogion commote of Caernarfonshire indicate that the output of oats, a hardier grain more suited to poorer soils and conditions, was five and one-half times that of wheat. Compared to that of England, animal husbandry played a more important role in the Welsh economy. In the twelfth century, Gerald of Wales noted the importance of pastoralism to the Welsh. He remarked that they ate little bread but much meat, as well as milk, cheese, and butter. The Cafflogion lay subsidy reveals that animals accounted for about two-thirds of the commote's assessed wealth.[12]

The utilization of space for agricultural production in Gwynedd presented a complicated picture. Lowland arable and highland pastures were linked by a system of transhumance. During the summer, while some members of a family worked small plots of arable, others drove cattle to the upland pastures, known as *hafodydd*. There the family cows, ewes, and goats were grazed and their milk processed into cheese and butter.[13]

The large pastoral component of the Welsh rural economy made it very different from that of lowland England. The English found this economy—with its different emphases and different methods and rhythms of production—puzzling, if not indeed offensive. John Peckham, archbishop of Canterbury and a product of a society that emphasized the growing of grains, found the less labor-intensive pastoralism of the Welsh incomprehensible. To him the people of Gwynedd seemed a hopelessly idle race, sunk in sloth and sin, that should be forced to live in towns and undertake useful labor.[14]

The economy of Gwynedd was also very little commercialized. As far as is known, Wales in the thirteenth century had no native coinage. Although trade undoubtedly existed throughout the period, it is certain that it played a relatively minor role in the economic life of Gwynedd. Some of the small settlements along the coast were centers of trade. Tenures that the English were able to recognize as akin to

12. Colin Thomas, "Thirteenth-Century Farm Economies," pp. 8–9, 12; Gerald of Wales, *Opera*, 6:179–80.

13. Pierce, "Aber," p. 42; Sylvester, *Rural Landscape*, p. 222; Elwyn Davies, "*Hendre*," pp. 49–50. See also Hughes et al., "Review," p. 376.

14. Peckham, *Registrum*, 3:776–78, 991–92.

their own burgage tenure existed in a few places.[15] Local markets existed before the 1280s.[16] But, with the possible exception of Llanfaes in Anglesey, these embryonic towns were little more than local market centers. Trade on a size and scale similar to that of England or Languedoc was unknown.

Gwynedd and Languedoc thus represent two poles of the economic arrangements to be found in Europe in the central middle ages. Languedoc possessed an economy of the type that has drawn most of the attention of historians. Although it was perhaps less developed and prosperous than that of some regions, it presents a familiar picture with its large production of cereals, its active commercial life and its small cities with their cloth-working artisans. Gwynedd provides an example of the economies to be found in some of the fringe areas of western Europe, with a much less productive agriculture, an emphasis on pastoralism, a tiny current of commercial exchanges, and an almost complete absence of urban life.

I will begin my discussion of the economic consequences of outside rule by examining what happened to land tenure and patterns of landholding. We are dealing with a very important aspect of medieval economic and social organization. The economy of medieval Europe was based on agriculture. Within that economy the single most important factor of production was the land, for on its exploitation rested the entire social edifice. Knowledge of who owned land, how much, and under what conditions is crucial to an understanding of economic behavior in the middle ages.

Gwynedd

Landholding in Gwynedd after the English conquest was marked by both dramatic change and remarkable stability.[17] Overlordship of virtually all the land of Gwynedd passed directly into the

15. Pierce, "Ancient Meirionydd," p. 19, and Pierce, "Caernarvonshire Manorial Borough," pp. 143, 146.

16. As at Llan-faes in Anglesey; *Cal. Anc. Pets.*, pp. 82–83; Lewis, *Mediaeval Boroughs*, pp. 9–11. Pierce, in "Growth," pp. 121–23, makes much of "the flourishing condition of markets and fairs." His picture, however, seems to be overly optimistic, as is indicated by the fact that his estimate of Llywelyn ap Gruffydd's total revenue from tolls on commercial transactions in Gwynedd amounts to only about £17 a year (70 percent of which came from Llan-faes).

17. For fuller references, see Given, "Economic Consequences," pp. 15–24.

hands of Englishmen. The wealthiest landholders, for the most part members of the old royal families of Gwynedd and Powys, disappeared in the wake of the conquest. The last prince of the house of Aberffro, Llywelyn ap Gruffydd, was killed in the war, and his property in Gwynedd Uwch Conwy was seized by the crown. The other great landholders in northern Wales had been members of the royal house of Powys. The northern half of this ancient kingdom passed into the hands of English aristocrats. Gruffydd ap Gwenwynwyn, lord of the southern half of Powys and a firm ally of the English, kept his lordship. But by 1309 marriage alliances and accidents of birth had brought most of his lands into the hands of an Englishman, John Charlton, the husband of Gruffydd's granddaughter.[18]

So after 1283 all land in Gwynedd came under the overlordship of one English master or another. But the actual physical occupation of the land seems to have changed relatively little as a result of the conquest. For the most part Welshmen continued in occupation of the land of their ancestors. Although the wealthiest stratum of native lords disappeared shortly after the conquest, this was not true of the less-well-endowed owners of land. Many of the wealthier members of native society supported the English in the wars of the 1270s and 1280s. The English government recognized that these men had baronial status, and left them in control of their estates. At the bottom of the social hierarchy, the peasants of Gwynedd, both bond and free, were undisturbed in the possession of most of their property.

Landholding in Gwynedd Is Conwy

In discussing the impact of the conquest on patterns of landholding in Gwynedd, it is necessary to make a distinction between the areas that were incorporated into the Principality of North Wales and the regions that were turned into new Marcher lordships. Gwynedd Uwch Conwy, the core area of Llywelyn ap Gruffydd's lordship, was largely absorbed into the principality. Gwynedd Is Conwy and other parts of northeast Wales experienced a different fate. Much of this region had been bitterly contested by the English Marcher lords and the Welsh since the eleventh century. For extended periods, parts of it had been under English rule. English influence was accordingly

18. Morgan, "Barony," p. 12.

strong, and ethnically English peasants were settled on the region's fringes. Much of this area was divided by Edward I among the great English aristocrats. The northern half of Powys was carved into the lordships of Chirk and Bromfield and Yale. The areas known as Rhos and Rhufoniog were given to the earl of Lincoln to form the lordship of Denbigh. Dyffryn Clwyd went to a member of the Grey family and became the core of the lordship of Ruthin.

Our best information about events in these new lordships comes from Denbigh. A terrier produced in 1334 by the lordship's administration shows that much land had changed hands since the 1280s. In part this was the direct consequence of the military operations of the conquest. The wars of the 1270s and 1280s, together with a rebellion in the 1290s, produced a sizable crop of disinherited rebels. Since the land actually belonged to the gwelyau of which the rebels were members, the English confiscated from the kinship groups those fractions of their land that they felt corresponded to the deceased rebels' share in the clan lands. Large amounts of land were involved in these operations. There were 104 settlements in the lordship; in thirty-seven of these (35.6 percent) the deaths of rebellious Welshmen had led to the confiscation of land.[19]

Other mechanisms also brought land into the lord's hand. If a tenant died without collateral descendants related to him within the third degree of consanguinity, his land escheated. Those who were unable to perform the services due for their land also saw their tenancies seized. The exact mechanism by which the escheats listed in the 1334 survey took place is often not clear. What is indisputable, however, is that a great deal of land had escheated in one fashion or another. Altogether escheats were recorded in ninety-six of the 104 settlements in the lordship, or 92.3 percent of the total. Direct seigneurial control of land was also acquired by a program of exchanges, which often brought entire villages directly into the hands of the lord.[20]

The acquisition of sizable tracts of land allowed the English to work some changes in Denbigh's ethnic and social composition. The new rulers made a determined effort to establish an English colony. Through

19. These figures are derived from Vinogradoff and Morgan, eds., *Survey.*
20. Vinogradoff and Morgan, eds., *Survey*, pp. 17, 27–28, 41, 278; David Huw Owen, "Englishry," pp. 62–63, 68.

one mechanism or another, all of the original Welsh inhabitants of the vill adjoining the head of the honour at Denbigh were removed, and an English-style borough was created in the castle's shadow.[21] Other Englishmen were settled nearby. In the town of Lleweni, for example, only one Welshman was allowed to retain land. The rest of the village was divided among about 120 English colonists.[22] All told, in the commote of Rhufoniog Is Aled, there were 223 Englishmen holding a total of 6,561 acres, approximately a quarter of the commote's land. Ceinmeirch commote also experienced a sizable wave of immigration. Here 158 Englishmen, who were not also tenants in Is Aled, held 3,126 of the commote's approximately 11,000 acres. Elsewhere in the lordship English settlement was much less dense. Altogether 412 Englishmen held 10,979 of the lordship's approximate total of 97,500 acres.[23]

In addition to settling Englishmen in the lordship, the administration introduced English forms of land tenure. The alien immigrants of course held their land by tenures common in England. In places, the 1334 survey also reveals Welshmen holding their land under forms of tenure that can be regarded as recently introduced.[24] The majority of the native inhabitants of the lordship, however, seem to have continued to hold their land according to traditional rules of Welsh land tenure.

Although the conquest of this part of Wales saw some important changes—the establishment of a small colony of Englishmen, the spread of some forms of English land tenure—the extent of these changes should not be exaggerated. The English settlement was both small and confined primarily to the eastern parts of the lordship. Denbigh remained overwhelmingly Welsh in population and social structure.

In the other new Marcher lordships, the conquest does not seem to have had as large an impact. In Bromfield and Yale, English rule made little difference to the traditional distribution of property. An extent made in 1315 indicates that escheats and exchanges had not occurred on anything near the scale of what had taken place in Denbigh. English settlers were few in number and seem to have been confined

21. David Huw Owen, "Denbigh," pp. 172–74, and "Englishry," p. 69.
22. R. R. Davies, Lordship, pp. 346–47.
23. Ellis, "English Element," pp. 189–90, 192–98.
24. Vinogradoff and Morgan, eds., Survey, pp. cx–cxiii, 284–85.

mostly to the towns of Holt and Wrexham.[25] English settlement in Dyffryn Clwyd was also small. Most Englishmen seem to have lived in the borough of Ruthin; even so the majority of the town's population was probably Welsh.[26] In Chirkland the 1292 lay subsidy roll shows only a tiny number of Englishmen resident in the lordship.[27]

The distribution of land and the structure of the population in northeast Wales thus seem to have changed relatively little as a result of the English conquest. Although Englishmen migrated into the area, they did so in small numbers, except in parts of the lordship of Denbigh. Even this tiny current of immigration was confined to the first twenty years of the postconquest period.[28] English-style tenures spread in these new Marcher lordships, but most land continued to be held by Welshmen under the old native forms of tenure.

Landholding in the Principality of North Wales

In the Principality of North Wales the royal government applied a different policy to the question of land. No great lordships were carved out of the three new shires of Caernarfon, Anglesey, and Merioneth. The only lord of note remained the king of England or, on occasion, his heir, the prince of Wales. The creation of a strong military presence in the principality did, however, involve the introduction of small colonies of Englishmen. The cornerstone of English domination in Gwynedd was the string of castles erected by Edward I. To cater to the consumption needs of these fortresses, the royal administration established a number of boroughs and enticed English settlers to take up residence in them. The boroughs of Caernarfon and Conwy received foundation charters in 1284. In the following years boroughs were established at Cricieth, Harlech, and Bere. In 1295 the borough of Beaumaris was founded.[29]

The creation of these towns required some rearrangement of the social landscape. The government took care, however, to minimize the

---

25. Ellis, ed., *Bromfield and Yale*, p. 4; Davies, *Lordship*, p. 345.
26. Jack, "Ruthin," pp. 249–50.
27. Davies, *Lordship*, p. 304.
28. Ibid., p. 342.
29. Ultimately four more settlements were given borough status: Newborough in 1303, Bala in 1324, and Nefyn and Pwllheli in 1335; Lewis, *Mediaeval Boroughs*, pp. 33–35.

impact of the new boroughs and castles on local patterns of landholding. For the most part, towns were carved out of lands that before the conquest had been part of Llywelyn ap Gruffydd's maerdrefi. In some cases this core was supplemented with other lands, usually escheats or other bond tenancies. The lands of free gwelyau were seldom expropriated to endow the English immigrants.[30]

In only a few cases did the erection of the castles and their dependent boroughs result in significant exchanges of land and resettlement of Welshmen. At Conwy the king's government had to strike a bargain with the Cistercian monastery of Aberconwy. When Edward I decided to use the abbey's site at the mouth of the Conwy river for one of his castles, the monks moved inland to Maenan in Nantconwy commote. This relocation meant that some of Nantconwy's inhabitants had to be dispossessed. Some were resettled in the nearby commote of Creuddyn; others were sent further afield to Anglesey. The creation of Beaumaris in the 1290s also involved the relocation of Welshmen. The people of Llan-faes, on whose site Beaumaris was built, were removed to the old maerdref of Rhosyr. There the government obligingly established for them their own town, known as Newborough.[31]

All told, the demographic and tenurial impact of borough creation seems to have been small. Conwy, Caernarfon, and Beaumaris were the most important of the castle-towns. The acreage taken for these settlements was not, however, very large. Only about five thousand acres were incorporated into the nine boroughs in the principality.[32] Moreover, subsequent efforts by the townsmen to expand their holdings were not very successful.[33] It would not be until the early decades of the fifteenth century that members of English burgess families would begin to build up fairly large estates in the Welsh hinterland.[34]

The number of Englishmen who took up residence in the new boroughs was small. The minor castellated boroughs of Cricieth and Harlech came quickly to number a substantial Welsh element among their inhabitants. In the early fourteenth century the chief centers of

30. Ibid., pp. 43–44.
31. Ibid., pp. 44–45, 49–53; Hays, *Aberconway*, pp. 71–74; Edward A. Lewis, "Decay," pp. 41–42.
32. Lewis, *Mediaeval Boroughs*, pp. 45, 47, 50, and "Decay," p. 39.
33. For an example, see Lewis, *Mediaeval Boroughs*, pp. 45–46.
34. Pierce, "Landlords," pp. 373–74. See also Carr, *Medieval Anglesey*, pp. 217–21.

ethnically English burgesses were Caernarfon, Conwy, and Beau-maris.[35] The population of these three most thoroughly English bor-oughs was not very large. Beaumaris seems to have been the biggest with 132¼ burgage tenements in 1305. By 1351 the number had reached 154¼. Conwy was the second largest with 121¾ burgages in 1309, a number which by 1312 had risen to 124. Caernarfon was the smallest. In 1298 it had a mere 59 burgages; until the middle of the fourteenth century the largest number of burgage tenures recorded was only 63.[36] The conclusion to be drawn from this evidence is that the English policy of castle building and town plantation, although a major facet of their plan for the administration of Gwynedd, did not have an important impact on patterns of landholding. Not much land was taken for the new towns and the number of Englishmen who settled in them remained small.

Outside the towns little effort was made to change the preconquest distribution of landed property. There was almost no systematic re-grouping of lands as occurred in parts of Denbigh. Although many of the inhabitants of the three counties of the principality fought against the English in the 1270s, the 1280s, and the 1290s, the English did not expropriate the lands of deceased rebels on a large scale.[37]

Some land was nevertheless confiscated as the result of rebellion. Since sheriffs were required to account for the management of land escheated to the crown, the records of the exchequer of Caernarfon allow us to estimate the extent of these confiscations. Table 1 lists the lands that these accounts indicate were taken from the estates of deceased rebels.[38] This list is undoubtedly incomplete. But the overall impression remains that very little land was confiscated from rebels in the three counties that made up the principality of North Wales.

Other forms of escheat also brought property into the hands of the

35. In the mid-fourteenth century, however, Beaumaris experienced considerable native immigration. During the Black Prince's reign it was stated that the greater number of its burgesses were Welsh; Lewis, *Mediaeval Boroughs*, pp. 258–60.

36. Ibid., p. 66. Williams-Jones, in "Caernarvon," p. 83, estimates that Caernar-fon's population in 1300 was 300 to 400.

37. Edward I deliberately pursued a policy of clemency towards those who had resisted him. During the conquest his government proclaimed that all who came to the king's peace would be allowed to enjoy their lands; *RC*, p. 137; Lewis, *Mediaeval Boroughs*, pp. 178–79.

38. Table 1 printed here corrects errors and omissions in Given, "Economic Conse-quences," p. 23.

Table 1
Lands confiscated from Welsh rebels in the Principality of North Wales

Name of rebel	Commote	Amount of land
Merioneth County		
Adda ap Dafydd	Tal-y-bont	16 acres
Peredur ap Llywelyn	Tal-y-bont	16 acres
Llywelyn ap Cadwgan	Ystumanner	4 acres
Rhirid ab Einion	Penllyn	9 acres, 2 carucates
"Aurifaber"	Penllyn	6 bovates
Gronw ap Heilin	Ardudwy	6 bovates
Caernarfon County		
Adda ab Iorwerth	Arllechwedd Isaf	3 bovates
Iorwerth ap Hywel	Arllechwedd Uchaf	1 bovate, 1/16 gafael
Tegwaredd Fychan	Arllechwedd Uchaf	1/2 bovate
Dokyn Crach	Nantconwy	1 bovate
Madog ab Iorwerth	Nantconwy	?
Einion ap Hywel	Nantconwy	?
Ednyfed ab Einion	Nantconwy	?
Owain ap Madog	Nantconwy	?
Cynwrig Foel	Dinllaen	12 acres
Anglesey County		
Ieuan ap Philip ap Daniel	Aberffro (cantred)	?
Einion ap Gruffydd	Aberffro	1/2 acre
Hywel Duy ap Gronw	Aberffro	1 carucate
Cynwrig ap Tegwaredd	Menai	60 acres
Iorwerth ap Madog	Menai	1/2 acre
Trahaearn ap Bleddyn	Talybolion	5 bovates
Llywelyn ap Madog	Talybolion	?
Gronw Byng	Twrcelyn	4 acres

Note: Other escheats are reported in Dindaethwy commote, Anglesey, but no particulars are given (SC6/1227/3, m. 1).

The meaning of Welsh land measures is a difficult subject. The Welsh acre was smaller than the English. The *Llyfr Iorwerth* indicates that it equaled only 1,440 square yards. The *Llyfr Blegywyrd* indicates an acre equal to only 512 square yards. Bovates seem to have varied in size from two to five acres, but were probably around four acres in Gwynedd. Carucates, at least in 1332, were sixty acres in extent. (Glanville R. J. Jones, "Post Roman Wales," pp. 327–28; *Cal. Inq. Misc.*, vol. 2, no. 1275; T. Jones Pierce, "Note," p. 203 (n. 36); Carr, *Medieval Anglesey*, p. 172.)

Sources: SC6/1170/5, ms. 4, 5, 8; SC6/1170/6, m. 13; SC6/1227/4, m. 1; SC6/1227/8, ms. 1, 3; SC6/1227/9, m. 2; SC6/1227/11, m. 1; SC6/1227/13, m. 2; SC6/1230/2, ms. 1d, 2; RC p. 33.

crown. Almost invariably these lands were relet, as tenancies at will and at increased rents, to the neighbors or relatives of their former possessors.[39] Very little of the land that found its way into the crown's custody was used to endow Englishmen. The one major grant to an English person went to Edward I's wife, who in 1284 received the manor of Rhosyr, the commote of Menai, a carucate of land in Llanfaes (all in Anglesey), and a few villages in Caernarfonshire.[40] Gifts to other Englishmen were usually small and were given only for limited time periods.[41]

The survey of 1352 shows that the number of Englishmen who held land in the rural districts of Anglesey and Caernarfonshire was small. Aside from the queen, nine English tenants were listed. None of their possessions seems to have been very extensive. Thomas de Mussynden was the best endowed, with the manor of Cemais and sixteen hafodydd in Caernarfonshire.[42] It is clear that in the Principality of North Wales, the English government made no effort to create a new landholding class or to effect significant transformations in the landholding patterns prevailing among the indigenous Welsh.

Two main conclusions emerge from the preceding pages. First, the conquest vested ultimate ownership of virtually all land in the hands of Englishmen. All landholders in Gwynedd were now tenants, whether of the crown or of the new Marcher lords. A privileged few were required to do knight service for their holdings. Most were compelled to pay cash rent.

Second, despite this important change, the conquest did not produce major alterations in the actual possession of the land or the uses to which it was put. Some Englishmen took up tenancies in Gwynedd, primarily in the new Marcher lordships in the northeast and in the boroughs established in the principality, but their numbers were not large. Among the Welsh the imposition of English rule did not result in a major reorganization of the hierarchy of wealth. True, the greatest native landholders, the members of the royal families of Gwynedd and Powys, disappeared. But since their possessions were used to enrich

39. For examples, see SC6/1170/5, ms. 4, 5; and *RC*, pp. 8, 16.
40. These grants were made with the stipulation that they were never to be separated from the crown of England; *Cal. Var.*, pp. 291–92.
41. For examples, see *Cal. Anc. Pets.*, pp. 26–27; *BPR*, 3:123–24; and *CCR*, 1323–27, p. 19.
42. Mussynden's holdings are detailed in *RC*, pp. 18–19, 35. The holdings of the other English tenants are listed on pp. 3, 11, 18, 32–34, 55, 68, 70.

Englishmen, either Marcher lords or the English king, their elimination did not result in a major redistribution of land among other native proprietors. No social group in Gwynedd was able to exploit the postconquest situation in such a way as to significantly improve its wealth.[43] In the very long run, some squires would eventually be able to build up respectable estate complexes. But this was primarily a phenomenon of the late fourteenth and early fifteenth centuries and probably owed more to the opportunities presented by the demographic changes that followed the Black Death than to conditions created by the imposition of English rule.[44]

English policy toward land in Gwynedd seems to have been dictated by goals more military and political than economic. Land was taken from Welshmen and given to Englishmen not with the primary aim of making that land either more productive or productive of different kinds of goods. Rather, the purpose of most land transfers was to guarantee the continued military dominance of what was perceived to be a turbulent and rebellious people. As the English chronicler Rishanger noted, Conwy castle was erected to contain the attacks of the Welsh, and Beaumaris was designed to repress their insolence.[45] Similarly, the English colony in Denbigh was intended to surround the lordship's administrative headquarters with tenants whose loyalty could be regarded as certain. The English conquest of Gwynedd thus did not result in a massive transfer of land, the dispossession of large numbers of Welshmen, the importation of an alien landed ruling elite, or the concentration of land in the hands of a newly wealthy group of native proprietors.

Languedoc

What transpired in Languedoc with regard to landholding after the French conquest shows some similarities with events in Gwynedd. The Capetian kings managed to establish their claim to overlordship over much of the land of Languedoc. Many seigneuries passed directly into the royal domain. Virtually all the lords of the Midi eventually became the vassals of the French kings. Certain lordships, which pre-

43. See the material on the Anglesey gentry in Carr, *Medieval Anglesey*, pp. 196–217.
44. On the construction of one estate complex, see Carr, "Making," especially pp. 150–57.
45. Rishanger, *Chronica*, pp. 105, 148.

viously had been regarded by their masters as allods, that is, as free of any superior lordship, were either recognized to be, or were formally transformed into, fiefs held ultimately of the French crown.[46]

Yet, as in Gwynedd, the French conquest ultimately had a relatively minor impact on actual patterns of landholding. The policies pursued by the French were, however, not as consistent as those adopted by the English. This difference stems from the fact that the acquisition of Languedoc was completed in two stages. In the first, the conquest was the work of freebooters led by Simon de Montfort, who from 1209 onwards answered Pope Innocent III's appeal for a crusade against the Cathar heretics and their sympathizers. The second and more methodical stage began in the 1220s when the French monarchy took over the struggle from the failing hands of Amaury de Montfort. The first stage saw a determined effort to expropriate many of the indigenous nobles and replace them with men imported from the north. The French monarchy, however, put an end to this policy and in many cases either restored or compensated those Languedocian nobles who had been deprived of their lands.

The Crusading Policy of Confiscation

The policy of confiscation and expropriation applied by Simon de Montfort and his followers in the early stages of the Albigensian crusades was most thoroughly carried out in the area around Carcassonne. When this town surrendered to the crusaders in 1209, its lord, Viscount Raimond Roger Trencavel, became their prisoner, an experience he did not long survive. His son was disinherited and forced to seek refuge in Spain. Thereafter Carcassonne became Montfort's base of operations in his struggle with the counts of Toulouse and their allies. In the course of these wars many local lords were driven from their estates, which were given to Simon's supporters.[47]

46. Dognon, *Institutions*, pp. 29–32; Sivéry, *Saint Louis*, p. 209.
47. Auguste Molinier, "Etude sur l'administration de Louis IX," pp. 542–43. See the material assembled in Auguste Molinier, ed., *Catalogue*. The lack of any study of what Friedlander has called the crusading nobility is surprising. Friedlander's researches have made it clear that this group played an important role in the governance of the royal sénéchaussée of Carcassonne; "Administration," pp. 58, 65–66, 195–96, 357, 378–80, 261–62. Timbal in his *Conflit* has compiled a list of fiefs held in accordance with the customs of Paris. But as yet we lack a systematic study of this important topic.

Ultimately there emerged from the crusades some major fiefs in the hands of families originally from the north of France. Gui de Lévis, one of Montfort's most trusted companions, acquired the lordship of Mirepoix. Simon's nephew was rewarded by King Louis IX with the southern half of the diocese of Albi.[48] The Languedocian nobles of the regions under Montfort's domination were not, however, completely rooted out. Some important houses, like those of Lautrec and Narbonne, never lost their lands. In the later years of the crusades, when Count Raimond VII reduced the area controlled by the Montforts, many of the lesser lords who had been expelled from their estates managed to recover them.

The Royal Policy of Magnanimity

When the monarchy began to take a direct interest in the conquest of the south, it adopted a more cautious and conciliatory policy toward the Languedocian aristocracy. During Louis VIII's campaign in 1226, many nobles of the Carcassonne region were quick to make their peace with the king. They were thus assured of the untroubled possession of their estates. Moreover, the 1229 Treaty of Paris that ended the wars declared null all confiscations that had taken place in the lands left under the lordship of Raimond VII of Toulouse.[49]

A series of rebellions in the early 1240s forced the French to return for a time to a policy of confiscation. In 1240 Raimond Trencavel, heir to the lordship of Carcassonne, crossed the Pyrenees at the head of a group of exiles and tried to reclaim his inheritance. His effort aroused much support. For over a month Trencavel besieged the *cité* of Carcassonne, the center of royal power in the province. The rebellion, however, collapsed; those who had supported Raimond lost their lands. This group included more than just the nobles of the Carcassès. Many of the people of Carcassonne's bourg had joined the rising and were forced to flee. The bourg itself was razed.[50] In 1242 Raimond VII of Toulouse staged his own uprising. This proved no more successful than Trencavel's rebellion and resulted in another round of confiscations.

Yet the government of Louis IX was willing to behave magnani-

48. Molinier, "Etude sur l'administration de Louis IX," p. 544.
49. Ibid., pp. 543–44; *HL*, 8: col. 889; Timbal, *Conflit*, p. 33.
50. *HL*, 6:720–21.

mously toward those who repented of their deeds. Rebels who submitted to the crown often got their lands back. Even Raimond Trencavel was persuaded to make his peace with the king; in 1247 Louis IX gave him fairly large estates in the sénéchaussée of Beaucaire. In that same year the exiled Carcassonnais were pardoned and allowed to rebuild the bourg.[51] The people of Béziers also benefited from royal clemency. After a terrible sack of the town in 1209, the crusaders had seized much land owned by their victims. In the early 1240s, however, Saint Louis allowed the heirs of those who had perished in 1209 to reclaim their inheritances.[52]

The career of Olivier de Termes illustrates nicely the vicissitudes of fortune that nobles from eastern Languedoc could experience. The son of Raimond, lord of the castle of Termes, he was born around 1197. In 1210 Raimond, besieged by Simon de Montfort, was forced to surrender himself into captivity. Olivier became an outlaw. Like many other outlaws, or *faidits*, he entered the service of Count Raimond VII of Toulouse. In 1240 he joined Trencavel's rebellion. Not until 1247 did he make his peace with the king. Thereafter, he proved a firm supporter of Louis IX, accompanying the king on his first crusade. In reward for his services, he was given the castle of Aguilar and all of the Terminès with the exception of Termes itself. In the 1250s he played an important role in the capture of the Cathar stronghold of Quéribus. By mid-century he had thus managed to regain much of his father's land.[53] Among other seigneurs who benefited from Louis IX's generosity was Olivier's brother-in-law, Guilhem de Minerve. In 1254 Louis granted him rents equal to 50l.t. After his death, Louis gave his widow a further annual income of 60l.t. Such examples of royal restitution to former opponents could be easily multiplied.[54] The available evidence clearly indicates that the royal government never contemplated a wholesale expropriation of the ruling elite of eastern Languedoc. Indeed the government took steps to conciliate and preserve it.

51. *HL*, 6:783–86, 790–91.
52. *RHF*, 24:361 (no. 5). See also p. 331 (no. 51).
53. Eventually, however, he sold off most of his possessions and left Languedoc for Palestine where he died in 1275; Madaule, *Albigensian Crusade*, pp. 124–28; Guiraud, *Histoire*, 2:232–33.
54. For other examples of Languedocian nobles who recovered forfeited lands and rights, see Guiraud, *Histoire*, 2:234–35; *HL*, 6:849–50; Michel, *Administration*, pp. 415–16; and *RHF*, 24:250*.

Elsewhere in Languedoc the local nobility was not subjected to as severe a trial. The lesser nobles of the county of Toulouse survived the Albigensian crusades. Large numbers can be identified in the decades after the end of the wars. Between 1259 and 1261 approximately 244 *milites* or *domicelli* (or people who were said to be close relatives of men so termed) did homage to Alfonse de Poitiers. When Philip III's agents took possession of the county of Toulouse in 1271, approximately 565 nobles, knights, and barons did homage.[55]

Although the wars of the early thirteenth century undoubtedly made times difficult for the indigenous nobles, most seem to have weathered the storm. French royal policy thus did not envisage the systematic dispossession of the local ruling elite. Even those northerners established in the region seem to have rather quickly assimilated themselves into the ranks of the local nobility; they thus ceased to be aliens in any meaningful sense. The Lévis family, lords of Mirepoix, are a good example of this phenomenon. They formed especially close ties with the ruling family of the county of Foix, into which they married. In 1316 Jean de Lévis was one of those named to the provisional regency council set up to administer Foix following the death of Count Gaston I.[56] Some descendants of the crusaders from the north even became devotees of the very Cathar heresy that their ancestors had fought against.[57]

The Inquisitors and the Expropriation of Land

Before we leave the subject of landholding, we must consider the work of an institution that, although not royal in nature, owed much of its effectiveness to the changed conditions in Languedoc that arose from the imposition of Capetian hegemony: the inquisition. Established in the 1230s to root out Cathar heretics and their sympathizers, the inquisition had an impact on the possession of land. Among the penalties that it could impose on convicted heretics were the confisca-

55. The figures for the Albigeois are derived from Cabié, ed., *Droits*; those for the county as a whole from Dossat, ed., *Saisimentum*. Exact figures of those who did homage cannot be given since many men had the same name and several individuals evidently did homage more than once.

56. Castillon, *Histoire*, 1:369, 390.

57. For an example, see Friedlander, "Administration," pp. 65, 378–79.

tion of their property and the disinheritance of their kin. The extent of these confiscations can be judged only with difficulty today. The inquisition itself did not profit from the property it ordered seized. Forfeitures went instead to benefit the treasury of one of the local lordships, whether secular or ecclesiastic. One of the most important recipients of such confiscations was the royal government.

Confiscated property was often very extensive. At times entire lordships were seized. In the 1220s the viscount of Fenouillèdes, convicted of heresy, lost his lordship; in 1237 the large holdings of the Niort family in the Lauragais were confiscated.[58] Surviving royal financial accounts from Languedoc give a rough indication of the extent to which the crown benefited from these confiscations. In his account for 1293 and 1294, the royal official charged with the management of heretics' forfeited property in the sénéchaussée of Toulouse reported revenue from this source of 1,255l. 11s. 11d.t. Since total receipts from the sénéchaussée in that year amounted to 32,992l. 17s. 6d.t., the property of condemned heretics thus produced a respectable 3.8 percent of the entire royal income from Toulouse. Similarly, in 1299 the accounts of this same sénéchaussée reveal that the 1,808l. 0s. 3d.t. derived from the property of the condemned constituted 4.3 percent of total royal receipts. Information on royal income in the sénéchaussée of Carcassonne is unfortunately very fragmentary. However, we possess part of an account for this district for the year 1302–3. Total receipts amounted to 28,250l. 5s. 9d.t., of which 9.6 percent (2,711l. 8s. 3d.t.) came from the exploitation of property taken from heretics.[59]

Discovering who forfeited property is easier than learning who ultimately acquired it. Although many confiscations went to the crown, the king's government realized that other individuals might have a legitimate interest in them.[60] This was especially true of lords whose tenants had been condemned. In 1260 Louis IX issued an ordinance that allowed the seneschal of Carcassonne to sell the lands and other

58. *HL*, 7:86–87; Ramière de Fortanier, *Chartes*, pp. 17–18.
59. Fawtier and Maillard, eds., *Comptes*, vol. 1, nos. 9570, 11647, 12748–49 and pp. 473, 567.
60. See the provisions made by Louis IX in 1259 for the wives and creditors of those condemned as well as for certain categories of repentant heretics; *HL*, 8: cols. 1440–41.

properties confiscated from certain heretics to the lords of whom those lands and rights were held in fee.[61] Indeed, the crown seems to have leased or sold much of the confiscated property that it acquired. Although without detailed local research one cannot generalize with much confidence, it seems that land transfers attendant on confiscations for heresy, extensive as they may have been, did not result in any important restructuring of patterns of landholding in Languedoc. For the most part, confiscated land was probably acquired by individuals who already owned property in the neighborhood.[62]

Not infrequently the families of condemned heretics succeeded in recovering their kinsmen's property. In the sénéchaussée of Toulouse, Raimond Baldrici of Avignonet and his brothers were allowed to re-possess the property that their father had forfeited when he was imprisoned for heresy. Similarly, in Le Mas-Saintes-Puelles Pierre Barravi (or Barrani) and his brothers were allowed to redeem their father's property. In the same village another pair of Barravis, Arnaud and Bernard, the heirs of Pons Barravi, secured their inheritance with a payment to the royal government.[63]

It was even possible for condemned heretics themselves to recover their property. Alfonse de Poitiers allowed a number of former heretics, once they had been released from prison, to do so.[64] A notable example was Guillaume Garric of Carcassonne. In the 1290s Garric, a lawyer, was one of the ring-leaders of Carcassonne's resistance to the inquisitors. His behavior earned him excommunication, arrest, and condemnation as a heretic. When he was released from prison in

61. Boutaric, ed., *Actes*, vol. 1, nos. 429, 457; Beugnot, ed., *Olim*, 1:470. In March of 1303 Philip the Fair announced that he would not keep possession for more than a year and a day of any property he acquired in the *mouvance* of another lord; Dossat, *Crises*, p. 286, citing Laurière et al., eds., *Ordonnances*, 1:358.

62. See Dossat, *Crises*, pp. 303–4. At times the benefactors of such transactions were great landholders, like the abbot of Alet who in 1311 was allowed to acquire the rents and tolls that had belonged to some of his vassals condemned for heresy; *Regs.*, vol. 1, no. 1310. In other cases quite modest individuals leased confiscated property from the crown. The account of Reginald de Dugny for the sénéchaussée of Toulouse reveals several such individuals. See, for example, Fawtier and Maillard, eds., *Comptes*, vol. 1, nos. 9629, 9653–54.

63. Fawtier and Maillard, eds., *Comptes*, vol. 1, nos. 8998, 9000–9001, 10871–72. For the recovery in 1279 by members of the Roaix family of Toulouse of property confiscated in the 1230s and 1240s, see Mundy, *Repression*; Wolff, *Commerces*, pp. 30–31.

64. Dossat, *Crises*, pp. 314–15.

1312, King Philip IV granted him whatever rights the crown had acquired in the property seized from him.[65]

The success with which the families of condemned heretics managed to recover their property was so marked that it aroused the ire of the church authorities. In 1253 the archbishop of Narbonne and his suffragans called on Alfonse de Poitiers to put an end to the scandalous practice of allowing the heirs of condemned heretics to redeem their relatives' property.[66] It seems that the existing evidence leads one almost inevitably to agree with Philippe Wolff's opinion that the inquisition's prosecution of heretics did not effect any major social changes in Languedoc.[67]

In conclusion, one can say that the assertion of royal domination produced some minor changes in the patterns of landholding in Languedoc. Especially in the early days of the crusades, some members of the local nobility were dispossessed and replaced by Frenchmen. This process largely came to a halt, however, once the monarchy took charge of the conquest of Languedoc. Indeed, the Capetian kings returned to many Languedocian faidits some of the property that they had lost in the early days of the wars. The penal operations of the inquisition resulted in a transfer of landed property which, while it cannot be accurately measured, seems at times to have been substantial. The bulk of this property, however, was dispersed among other Languedocian landholders. It did not go to enrich a new class of landlords, whether native Languedocians or foreign French.

Conclusion

Comparison of the effects of outside rule on patterns of landholding in our two regions has revealed one significant difference: In Gwynedd, to a much greater extent than in Languedoc, outsiders gained direct overlordship of land and tenants. In Languedoc the French kings acquired extensive lands and a number of northern French families were installed in the region. But large numbers of

65. In 1321, however, Garric again fell afoul of the inquisitors and was condemned a second time for heresy; Douais, "Guillaume Garric," pp. 7–10; *Regs.*, vol. 1, no. 1517; *HL*, 10: *Preuves*, cols. 526–27.

66. *Layettes*, vol. 3, no. 4054.

67. Wolff, ed., *Histoire du Languedoc*, pp. 208–9. This opinion seems to be shared, with reservations, by Dossat, *Crises*, pp. 319–20.

indigenous aristocrats remained rooted in the countryside. Although the French kings were the ultimate overlords of the region, their lordship over much of the land was indirect. Immediate property rights over land and tenants remained to a large degree in the hands of the local nobles.

In Gwynedd, however, the major secular, native landholders were either expropriated during the conquest or died out in the succeeding decades. The lands that had been subject to the houses of Gwynedd and Powys came into the possession of Englishmen. In eastern Gwynedd the beneficiaries of this process were the new Marcher lords, recruited from among the leading aristocrats of England; in the principality the crown became the immediate lord of much of the population. To be sure, the English did not gain a complete monopoly of lordship over land in Gwynedd. Local ecclesiastical corporations and a small group of Welsh "barons" remained masters of land and tenants. But this element of continuity does not alter the fact that direct overlordship over the bulk of the land in Gwynedd had now passed into foreign hands.

English rule, by encouraging migration to Gwynedd from England, also helped create a multi-ethnic society. Although only small numbers of Englishmen settled in Gwynedd, the foreign enclaves they established were of great importance. Attached to the fortresses of Gwynedd, they played a pivotal role in ensuring the military domination of the country. The settlers developed many contacts with the native Welsh, but they were not assimilated into local society. Throughout the middle ages the English burgesses maintained an acute sense of their differences from the natives.

In Languedoc there was nothing akin to this English program of planned colonization. Some northern French barons settled in Languedoc, but their number was not large. They also seem to have been quickly absorbed into the regional nobility. Subsequently, if people from northern France settled in Languedoc, they did so as individuals pursuing their own private destinies, not as part of a deliberate policy of colonization.[68]

If we look at how different social classes in Gwynedd and Languedoc were affected by changes in landholding, it appears that in

68. On immigration into Languedoc, see Higounet, "Mouvements," pp. 1–24. See also in Wolff, Commerces, maps Ia–Ic (pp. 677–80), which show the origins of apprentices in Toulouse.

both regions it was members of the dominant classes who were primarily affected. Members of these groups had to surrender claims over land to outsiders. Outside rule had much less important consequences for the distribution of land among other strata of the local populations. To be sure, in both Gwynedd and Languedoc much property changed hands. But this mobilization of land, although it enriched some and impoverished others, did not result in a fundamental transformation of the native patterns of land distribution. The petty agricultural producers who were in effective control of the bulk of the land in both areas remained in possession of their property after the assertion of outside rule. Some (indeed, in the case of Gwynedd, most) now held their lands of new masters who were outsiders; but the rules by which they held their lands, whether of new masters or old, remained largely what they had been in the days of independence. Nor, as far as we can see, did the transfers of land attendant on the assertion of outside rule produce radical realignments of wealth in either society. Finally, patterns of land use do not seem to have changed.

Even when outsiders acquired extensive holdings, they do not appear to have been interested in trying to reorganize the internal structure of their holdings. The Frenchmen who established themselves in Languedoc adapted readily to local norms and behaved like traditional Languedocian seigneurs. Even in the new Marcher lordships of northeast Wales, where extensive transformations in landholding patterns took place, English administrators left the majority of Welsh tenants in place and allowed them to continue to organize the process of agrarian production according to traditional techniques.

The reason for this continuity in landholding and land use is clear. Medieval aristocrats were only tangentially involved in direct economic production. For the most part lords were content to let peasants and others manage the production process. Only after these petty producers had created an economic surplus did their masters attempt to appropriate some of it through politically based charges. Committed to a strategy of extraeconomic exploitation of their estates, the new rulers from outside had little incentive to change local processes of economic production, and hence little incentive to alter the distribution of property that underpinned the peasant economy. It is to the ways in which the English and French sought to extract surplus value from their new territories that we will turn our attention in the next chapter.

5 The Struggle for Surplus Value

The incorporation of Gwynedd and Languedoc into the English and French polities was a process in which political coordination preceded economic penetration. Although there had been economic contacts between our two sets of social formations before their political amalgamation, the economies of Languedoc and Gwynedd had not been subordinated to those of northern France or England. Neither the French nor the English had dominated their future subjects' systems of production and exchange. Although there were differences in levels of productivity and wealth between our two pairs of social formations (very significant in the case of Gwynedd and England, less so in that of Languedoc and northern France), neither Gwynedd nor Languedoc had in the days of its independence been an economic colony of its future master.

After the English and French monarchies acquired possession of Gwynedd and Languedoc, they sought to siphon off some of the economic surplus of their new territories. The techniques they employed to this end were primarily political rather than economic. Neither the English nor the French sought to exploit the economies of their new territories from the inside, by introjecting themselves directly into local processes of economic production. Instead the exploitation of the Welsh and Languedocian economies was conducted from the outside, through politically based levies on the surpluses of the local communities.

In this chapter I will discuss the methods the French and English employed to extract surplus from their new subjects in Gwynedd and Languedoc. Although the fragmentary nature of the surviving evidence makes the task difficult, I will also try to assess the success they enjoyed in mobilizing local resources. Finally, I will offer some very tentative speculations about the possible impact of these English and French fiscal demands on the economies of Gwynedd and Languedoc.

Gwynedd

To the task of extracting wealth from its Welsh subjects, the English monarchy was able to bring to bear one of the most elaborate and skilled financial administrations in northern Europe. The crown quickly put the techniques perfected by this administration to work in the Principality of North Wales. Edward I's plan for the principality included the creation of an exchequer at Caernarfon. Supervised by this office, royal officials lost no time in battening onto the country's financial resources.

English Demands for Tribute

Their most striking achievement was the overhaul of the principality's rent structure.[1] Under the Welsh princes the people of Gwynedd had provided their rulers with a variety of food renders, labor services, and compulsory hospitality.[2] By the end of the thirteenth century such renders in kind were, as far as the English government was concerned, archaic. This reality had also become apparent to the last native princes of Gwynedd. In their efforts to solidify their domination of the other princely houses in Wales and to fend off the English, the princes of Gwynedd had found themselves in need of much hard cash. They had therefore begun the process of converting renders in kind into money dues.[3] The English completed this process at one blow, commuting virtually all renders in kind into cash payments.

Data compiled by T. Jones Pierce, although it is incomplete, omit-

1. For fuller references, see Given, "Economic Consequences," pp. 24–43.
2. *WTL*, 1:275–352.
3. See Stephenson, *Governance*, pp. 55–56.

ting the demesne vills that had belonged to the Welsh princes, provide us with a useful gauge of the extent of the English achievement.[4] In Jones Pierce's sample, the cash rent due from the free tenants of the principality increased 78.5 percent, from £210 10s. 11d. to £375 17s. 8½d. A greater change, however, took place in the assessments of the bondmen. Before the conquest they had paid only £37 12s. 5½d. The English increased this total to £272 6s. 0 ¾d. All told, the English more than doubled the amount of money paid by the inhabitants of Gwynedd (see table 2), whether bond or free, from around £248 to around £648.

These greatly increased cash dues constituted one of the most striking consequences of the English conquest. Rent was, however, not the only means of surplus extraction that the English employed. Among the more lucrative of seigneurial dues in the areas of classic manorialism in medieval Europe were those known as banalités. These involved the right to compel individuals to grind their grain at the lord's mill, press their grapes at his wine press, bake their bread in his oven, and so forth, and to charge for these services.

Among the most lucrative of these banalités were compulsory milling charges. Before the conquest such dues seem to have been little developed. The prince's bondmen were required to grind their grain at his mills. Most freemen, however, had their own mills. Those who did not ground at the lord's mills, some at fixed rates, others for free.[5]

The English lost little time in trying to generalize compulsory milling. Suit to the king's mills was enforced by the conquerors' new court system.[6] Among the petitions addressed to English sovereigns by the people of Gwynedd, many contain complaints about novel requirements to grind grain at royal mills. Sometime between 1300 and 1302 the "commonalty of the more noble of all Anglesey" protested that they were being compelled to make suit to royal mills.[7] A petition of 1305 asked that the prince of Wales not compel his subjects to grind their grain at his mills.[8] In northeast Wales the masters of the new

4. Pierce, "Growth," p. 118.
5. R. R. Davies, *Lordship*, p. 127; *WTL*, 1:330–31; Ellis, ed., *Bromfield and Yale*, p. 33; Stephenson, *Governance*, p. 61.
6. See, for example, SC2/227/27, m. 2; SC2/227/34, ms. 1, 3d.
7. *Cal. Anc. Pets.*, p. 452.
8. *RC*, p. 212. For other petitions on this subject, see *Cal. Anc. Pets.*, pp. 108, 503. See also petitions relating to the efforts of crown agents to block the construction or operation of private mills on pp. 241–42, 449–50.

Marcher lordships pursued similar policies. In the lordship of Chirk, for example, the free tenants complained that they had always had their own mills until Roger de Mortimer began demanding rent for them.[9] In Bromfield and Yale compulsory milling dues were systematically introduced in the late thirteenth and early fourteenth centuries.[10]

The English also collected market tolls on a large scale. Before the conquest, the Welsh seem to have paid such dues only at local fairs. The English generalization of market tolls produced no small measure of discontent. In 1305 the people of the principality petitioned for permission to pay only those tolls they had known in the days of the native princes, a request to which Edward of Caernarfon, then prince of Wales, turned a deaf ear.[11]

The creation of an English-style court system in the principality also resulted in new financial exactions. Royal justice was anything but cheap. The writs that initiated certain forms of litigation had to be purchased from the local chancery. The chattels of those convicted of, or outlawed for, felonies were confiscated. Those objects, known as deodands, which caused accidental deaths were also appropriated by the crown. The king's government, however, did not have to rely exclusively on these casual incidents. Over the centuries the crown had perfected means of using its legal system to extract money from even its law-abiding subjects. In its normal operations, the English justice system required the active cooperation and involvement of many of the crown's subjects; those who failed in any of their manifold obligations were liberally amerced.

For example, the work of the coroners produced a steady stream of revenue for the crown. Coroners held inquests into violent or suspicious deaths, calling on all adult males from the four neighboring villages to help. Those who failed to attend were amerced. Coroners also secured the profits of sea wrecks for the crown, a royal prerogative that in Gwynedd could pose some peculiar problems. In 1315–16 the abbot of Bardsey informed the king that on the Llŷn peninsula it was not uncommon for cattle to kill themselves by drowning or by falling over cliffs facing the sea. The abbot complained that crown

---

9. *Cal. Inq. Misc.*, vol. 2, no. 1203.
10. Ellis, ed., *Bromfield and Yale*, pp. 32–33. See also Davies, *Lordship*, pp. 127–29.
11. *RC*, p. 213; Edward A. Lewis, *Mediaeval Boroughs*, pp. 176–77.

Table 2
The increase of money dues in the Principality of North Wales after the English conquest

Commote	Pre-1284 dues			Post-1284 increase			Post-1284 dues		
	£.	s.	d.	£.	s.	d.	£.	s.	d.
Anglesey									
Dindaethwy	14	0	5	15	17	5	29	17	10
Aberffro	37	9	0-3/4	26	8	7	63	17	7-3/4
Talybolion	20	4	3-1/2	17	10	10-1/4	37	15	1-3/4
Twrcelyn	20	16	8	20	16	3-1/2	41	12	11-1/2
Menai	17	1	11-1/4	18	18	7	36	0	6-1/4
Total	109	12	4-1/2	99	11	8-3/4	209	4	1-1/4
	(100%)			(90.8%)			(190.8%)		
Caernarfon									
Creuddyn	3	0	0	4	2	0-1/2	7	2	0-1/2
Arllechwedd Isaf	7	5	7-1/2	3	10	10-1/2	10	16	6
Arllechwedd Uchaf	12	19	10	1	18	10	14	18	8
Is Gwyrfai	6	11	8-1/2	15	1	4	21	13	0-1/2
Uwch Gwyrfai	11	16	2-1/2	25	12	2	37	8	4-1/2
Dinllaen	18	0	0-1/2	33	0	7	51	0	7-1/2
Cymydmaen	14	6	4	22	9	11	36	16	3

Cafflogion	13	14	9	17	9	2	31	3	11
Nantconwy	8	7	9	16	0	7-1/2	24	8	4-1/2
Total	96	2 (100%)	3	139	5 (144.9%)	6-1/2	235	7 (244.9%)	9-1/2
Merioneth									
Ystumanner	15	8	0	17	5	11-3/4	32	13	11-3/4
Tal-y-bont	15	16	0	22	2	5-3/4	37	18	5-3/4
Eifionydd	4	14	11	47	7	0	52	1	11
Ardudwy	5	6	8	50	2	6	55	9	2
Penllyn	1	4	0	24	4	4	25	8	4
Total	42	9 (100%)	7	161	2 (379.3%)	3-1/2	203	11 (479.3%)	10-1/2
Grand Total	248	4 (100%)	2-1/2	399	19 (161.1%)	6-3/4	648	3 (261.1%)	9-1/4

Note: These figures do not include the rents from the demesne vills of the native princes.
Source: Pierce, "Growth," p. 118.

servants were treating his tenants' cattle that died in such accidents as "sea-wreck" and confiscating the carcasses.[12]

One could continue at great length detailing the ways in which the English crown used its legal system to extract money from its subjects' purses. Maitland and Pollock were of the opinion that in thirteenth-century England amercements were handed out in such volume for such a multitude of petty transgressions that the typical subject could expect to be amerced on average at least once a year.[13] The situation must have been little different in Gwynedd.

The income derived by the crown from Gwynedd was, although variable from one year to the next, often substantial. The accounts rendered by the chamberlain of the exchequer of Caernarfon for the fiscal year 1305–6 illustrate the sums that could be raised in the principality. The single largest item of income was composed of "rents of assize." The total collected each year from the three counties of the principality amounted to £1309 4s. 8d. The operations of the justice system brought in £611 5s. 11³/4d., a sum equal to 47 percent of the rent.[14]

The growing success enjoyed by the English crown in extracting surplus from its possessions can be seen in table 3. This lists the annual receipts accounted for by chamberlains of North Wales at the English Exchequer during the years 1284 to 1300 and 1304 to 1307.[15] The middle column shows the sums received by the chamberlain. To make the long-term trends stand out more clearly, these figures have been converted to a common index, with the fiscal year 1286–87 as base 100. (This is the first year that the chamberlain's account covered the normal twelve-month accounting period of the Exchequer, which began in late September. The first account recorded covered the period from March 1284 through December 1285, the second the period from February through September 1286.) As one can see, receipts at the exchequer of Caernarfon were basically stable from 1286 through 1289. In the early 1290s they began to rise, reaching index figures in the 120s. This increasing fiscal pressure may help

---

12. *Cal. Anc. Pets.*, pp. 140–42.
13. Maitland and Pollock, *English Law*, 2:513.
14. Figures from Griffiths, "Early Accounts," pp. 111–17.
15. In constructing the table, I have counted only receipts generated within the Principality of North Wales. I have omitted transfer payments made to the chamberlain from sources outside the principality.

Table 3
Royal revenue from the Principality of North Wales, 1284–1307

Year	Revenue			Index number
	£.	s.	d.	1286–87 = 100
1284–1285[a]	922	7	11-1/2	94
1286[b]	573	9	7	59
1286–87	976	16	9-1/2	100
1287–88	869	8	0	89
1288–89	849	13	9	87
1289–90	1231	12	7	126
1290–91	706	14	11	72
1291–92[c]	1187	11	9-3/4	122
1292–93[c]	1187	11	9-3/4	122
1293–94	423	15	4	43
1294–95	606	0	15-1/2	62
1295–96	1133	5	3-1/2	116
1296–97[d]	1048	7	8-1/4	107
1297–98[d]	1165	16	5-1/2	119
1298–99[d]	1319	17	9-1/4	135
1299–1300[d]	1691	1	5-3/4	173
1304–5	1688	3	0	173
1305–6	2400	3	3-3/4	246
1306–7	2673	5	9-1/4	274

[a] Covers period from March 1284 through December 1285.
[b] Covers period from February through September 1286.
[c] Average of the total receipts of the two years 1291–93.
[d] Includes revenues from the lands of the late Queen Eleanor.
Source: John Griffiths, "Early Accounts"; Edward A. Lewis, "Account Roll of the Chamberlain."

to explain the outbreak of the major uprising of 1294–95. This rebellion produced a marked fall in revenue, receipts declining to index figures of only 43 in 1293–94 and 62 in 1294–95. With the end of the rebellion there began a steady climb in revenue. In 1299–1300 receipts reached the index figure of 173. Revenue continued to rise in the last years of Edward's reign. In 1306–7 receipts reached the index figure of 274. In a period of twenty years, thanks to steady and determined application, the English administration had managed to increase its take from its territories in Gwynedd almost threefold.[16]

16. These figures should be adjusted to take account of such things as price movements and monetary debasement. English silver coinage was debased in the fourteenth century, the number of troy grains of silver in a pound falling from 5,332 in 1272 to

Ground rent, profits of justice, and other seigneurial dues thus brought in substantial sums to the royal treasury. However, the English need for cash was insatiable. Taxation was therefore also employed. By the late 1200s the English crown had had much experience with taxation and had developed a body of techniques for its assessment and collection. The most lucrative royal levy was a tax on movable property, known as the lay subsidy. Such a tax required parliamentary approval. With the exception of lepers and clergymen, everyone subject to the crown was obliged to pay. Until 1334 assessors evaluated the movable goods of subjects—such as animals, grain, and other crops—for each levy. Those not found too poor to pay had to part with a sum that corresponded to a fraction, agreed by king and parliament, of the total assessed value of their chattels.

The English lost little time in imposing lay subsidies on Gwynedd. In 1291 Edward I demanded a tax at the rate of a fifteenth. More taxes followed in 1300 and 1318. Despite the early application of lay subsidies to North Wales, the principality in the middle ages was not normally subject to such parliamentary levies.[17] This did not mean that the Welsh escaped scot-free from the clutches of the tax collectors. Instead, in place of the lay subsidies, the crown resorted to

---

4,320 in 1351, a decline of 19 percent. But significant debasement did not begin until the 1340s, after the period with which we are concerned here. (Craig, *Mint*, p. 74.) Moreover, although the coins paid by the Welsh to the English treasury may have had less intrinsic value by the middle of the fourteenth century than they had at the end of the thirteenth, their decline in value does not offset the greatly increased number that the Welsh had to disgorge. Adjusting Welsh renders for the effects of inflation is a more challenging problem. Price statistics from Gwynedd are hard to come by. English statistics indicate a tendency for prices to move upward in the late thirteenth and early fourteenth centuries, although the year-to-year fluctuations are very great. Whether a trend can be validly distinguished amid the "noise" present in these statistics is therefore a difficult question. (See Farmer, "Grain Price Movements," pp. 212, 214, and Rogers, *History*, 1:225–32.) If Wales did experience significant inflation, this phenomenon would have tended to reduce the impact of the conversion of all rents into cash dues. In fact, in the long run inflation might have meant that the Welsh peasants benefited by being able to pay their rents in cash rather than in kind. Given our woefully inadequate data, this is an argument that can be neither proved nor disproved. In the short run it is clear that the sudden increase in cash dues probably posed a problem for the peasants of Gwynedd. At least we shall see below that many Welshmen were prepared to complain about the rents they had to pay.

17. Williams-Jones, ed., *Merioneth Lay Subsidy*, pp. vii–viii; and Willard, *Parliamentary Taxes*, pp. 26–29.

various nonparliamentary levies. For example, from 1346 at the latest Flintshire was subjected every seven years to a "mise" of 1,000m. On at least one occasion, in 1437, this levy was extended to Anglesey.[18]

Taxation had, it seems, not been completely unknown in Gwynedd before the English conquest. In 1273 Llywelyn ap Gruffydd had demanded a "tribute" from his subjects. In late 1275 he had also imposed a tax of 3d. on every head of cattle in his lands. (This was such a novelty that Anian, bishop of Saint Asaph, noted that it provoked astonishment and fear among the people of his diocese.)[19] But in its frequency and its weight, English taxation marked an innovation in the social life of Gwynedd.

Little information concerning the amount of money raised in postconquest Wales by means of the nonparliamentary subsidies has survived. However, records of some of the taxes on movables have survived, among them those from the counties of Merioneth and Flint for the subsidy of 1292–93. For this tax these two counties together paid about £1,030. It is possible that the Principality of North Wales as a whole disgorged around £2,300. The subsidy of 1300 was not as heavy as that of 1292–93, North Wales parting with only £1,333 6s. 8d. In 1318 the amount demanded was smaller still, the three counties of the principality paying £929 12s. 9½d.[20]

The impact of this tax burden is difficult to assess. Williams-Jones, the editor of the 1292–93 Merioneth lay subsidy roll, has argued that the crown's Welsh territories were taxed more heavily than its English.[21] For the 1292–93 lay subsidy, the inhabitants of Merioneth were obliged to hand over a total of £566 11s. 10d. When compared with the amounts paid by the larger and more populous counties of England, this sum appears rather impressive. In 1290 all of England was assessed at less than £120,000. Of the English counties, both Cornwall and Rutland were called on to contribute less than Merioneth. The areas incorporated into the new Marcher lordships also

18. Williams-Jones, ed., *Merioneth Lay Subsidy*, p. ix. For other examples of nonparliamentary levies, see *BPR*, 1:67–68, 86.

19. Stephenson, *Governance*, pp. 69–70; *CCR*, 1272–79, p. 57; *Cal. Anc. Corr.*, pp. 105, 179; Williams-Jones, ed., *Merioneth Lay Subsidy*, p. xx.

20. Williams-Jones, ed., *Merioneth Lay Subsidy*, pp. xxiv–xxv; Natalie Fryde, ed., *Welsh Entries*, p. xix.

21. Williams-Jones, ed., *Merioneth Lay Subsidy*, p. xxvi.

had to bear a heavy burden of taxation, although these funds went to enrich their immediate lords and not the king's government. For example, in Dyffryn Clwyd seven extraordinary grants were made to the lord between 1338 and 1371.[22]

What proportion of its total revenues did the crown derive from its dominions in Gwynedd? Making an estimate is very difficult. J. H. Ramsay tried to calculate the revenues of the English kings. His figures are not very reliable, but a consideration of them is perhaps not completely without value for our purposes. Ramsay concluded that in the last two years of his reign Edward I's revenues amounted to £112,739 15s. 4¾d.[23] The income from the Principality of North Wales (see table 3) for this period amounted to £5,084 11s. 2d., or about 5 percent of the total. Crown financial servants occasionally prepared estimates of royal revenue. Although the accuracy of these is open to question, they nevertheless provide an indication of what some royal servants believed the king's revenues were likely to be. In 1284 total royal income was estimated at £26,828 3s. 9¼d.[24] In 1324 the king's net income was thought to be £60,549.[25] Finally, in the reign of Edward III royal revenue was estimated at 70,397 marks 5s. 5d. for the year 1362–63.[26] In 1433 the crown estimated its total annual revenue from England and Wales at £58,794. Of this sum £2,238, or 3.8 percent, came from the Principality of Wales. The income from the principality was equal to 24.1 percent of the £9,290 of revenue expected from the farms of all the shires and towns in England (Chester and the duchies of Lancaster and Cornwall not included).[27] On the whole it seems that income from Gwynedd made a not insignificant contribution to the general revenues of the English kings. Indeed, given its small population and its unproductive econo-

22. Davies, *Lordship*, pp. 184–87.
23. Ramsay, *History*, 2:89.
24. Mills, "Exchequer Agenda," p. 234.
25. Natalie Fryde, *Tyranny*, pp. 97–98. See also Harriss, *King, Parliament, and Public Finance*, pp. 523–24.
26. Tout and Broome, "National Balance Sheet," p. 412. This figure differs from the 53,444 marks 10s. 5d. that Tout and Broome rather misleadingly identify as the crown's total revenue (p. 407). Their figure represents not gross revenue, but net revenue after the deduction of various expenses.
27. See Ralph A. Griffiths, *Henry VI*, p. 108.

my, Gwynedd may have been called on to shoulder an unusually heavy burden of royal finance.

The Mobilization of Military Manpower

To the crown's strictly financial demands should be added its requisitions of military manpower. By the end of the thirteenth century, English armies were no longer predominantly collections of vassals performing knight service. To be sure, the crown's vassals continued to be summoned to the host. But increasingly military forces were raised through other mechanisms. Tactical developments had given a more important role to foot soldiers after a long period of almost complete dominance of the battlefield by the heavily armored, mounted knight. In large part the infantry required by late thirteenth- and early fourteenth-century armies was raised through a process of conscription. By the 1270s the normal mechanism of enlisting infantry for a campaign was to set up commissions of array, charged with the responsibility for raising troops in a specified area, most frequently a county.

Using this device the English quickly pressed Welsh troops into service against the Scots. In 1297 Welshmen fought at Stirling, where some 350 perished.[28] For the Bannockburn campaign of 1314, the crown envisaged enlisting 21,540 infantry, of whom 4,740 (22 percent) were to come from Wales, 2,000 (9.3 percent) from North Wales alone.[29] In 1322 Edward II led another 23,000 men into Scotland. Wales provided about 6,500 infantry, some 3,700 coming from North Wales.[30] In the reign of Edward III more Welshmen saw service in Scotland.[31]

Welsh troops, though not in such large numbers, were shipped across the channel to participate in the French wars. In 1297, 5,297 Welsh foot, led by 45 mounted constables and a captain, were sent to

---

28. Carr, "Welshmen," p. 23. Thereafter infantry from Wales regularly journeyed north to fight the Scots. See ibid., p. 23; John E. Morris, *Welsh Wars*, p. 287; CCR, 1302–7, pp. 446–47, 505; *Cal. Anc. Pets.*, pp. 119–20; CPR, 1307–13, p. 82; and CCR, 1313–18, pp. 367, 562–63.
29. John E. Morris, *Bannockburn*, p. 40.
30. Fryde, *Tyranny*, p. 128, and "Welsh Troops," pp. 82–83.
31. Prince, "Strength," pp. 354–60.

Flanders. Slightly over 1,900 of these men came from the Principality of North Wales and northeastern Wales.[32] Throughout the Hundred Years' War, Welshmen regularly fought on the continent.[33]

Just as the Welsh may have had to bear a proportionately heavier share of taxation than the English, so it appears that they made a disproportionately large contribution to royal armies. Whereas Welshmen were recruited for almost every major campaign, many English counties were called on for only relatively minor levies.[34] Welsh contingents often constituted a large proportion of royal armies. For example, of the 12,500 infantry raised for the 1298 Falkirk campaign, 10,500 or 84 percent of the total, were Welsh. The contingent from the three shires of Caernarfon, Anglesey, and Merioneth, together with that from the Perfeddwlad, amounted to 3,200 men, or 26 percent of the total.[35] If one accepts 300,000 as an estimate of the size of the population of Wales in the late thirteenth century[36] and also assumes that the population was divided roughly evenly between males and females, this would mean that about one out of every fourteen Welsh males took part in this campaign.[37] Similarly, during the 1322 Scottish expedition, Welsh troops accounted for 30 percent (6,490) of the total infantry muster of 21,700. The contingent from North Wales alone amounted to at least 3,711, or 17 percent of the total.[38] Although we cannot tell exactly what proportion of the native population served in the wars of the fourteenth century, it is clear that Gwynedd was called on to make a relatively large contribution to the military efforts of the late medieval English kingdom.

32. Norman Bache Lewis, "English Forces," pp. 311, 317.

33. See Prince, "Strength," pp. 361, 363, 368; Carr, "Welshmen," p. 24; Hewitt, *Black Prince's Expedition*, p. 21.

34. Maddicott, *English Peasantry*, p. 37.

35. John E. Morris, *Welsh Wars*, p. 287.

36. Williams-Jones, ed., *Merioneth Lay Subsidy*, p. lix. If one accepts Williams-Jones's estimate, this means that the Welsh population was about one-twentieth the size of the population of England, which many historians put at around 6 million in the early fourteenth century.

37. If one accepts the figure of 150,000 proposed by Edward A. Lewis ("Contribution," p. 95) as a minimum estimate of the population of Wales, then approximately one out of every 7 Welshmen was recruited for this campaign.

38. Fryde, *Tyranny*, p. 128, and "Welsh Troops," p. 83.

English Investment in Gwynedd

If the English took much out of the local economy, they seem to have put little back into it. True, they spent a great deal on building fortifications. But they made very little in the way of capital investments designed to increase economic productivity. For example, although the new English administration set up two new manors in the lordship of Denbigh, these were allowed to fall into decay within a few decades, along with the old demesne estates of the last native princes.[39]

The English showed no greater desire to invest in nonagricultural production. The chief industry of medieval Europe was cloth manufacturing. Among the major technological developments in the production process during the middle ages was the spread of fulling mills. The new rulers of Gwynedd, however, were reluctant to make the heavy expenditures necessary to build such mills. Of the seventy-two fulling mills known in Wales before 1349, only one was located in the Principality of North Wales. The Marcher lords did rather better. At least twelve fulling mills are recorded in Flint and Denbigh before 1349.[40] On the whole, however, it appears that the English did little to make the economy of Gwynedd more productive.

The Welsh Reaction

The demands of their English masters seem to have confronted the people of Gwynedd with serious difficulties. Not only did the English require them to part with a larger portion of their surplus, they also demanded that it be paid in cash. The necessity of finding large sums of money put the peasants of Gwynedd in a difficult dilemma. In Gwynedd at the end of the thirteenth century and the beginning of the fourteenth, there was no certainty that either a buyer or a commodity to sell could be found.

The first problem that a would-be purveyor of agricultural surplus encountered was an extremely small internal market. Although North Wales knew distinctions of social status, there was no great concentra-

39. David Huw Owen, "Lordship," pp. 211–14; Vinogradoff and Morgan, eds., *Survey*, pp. cvi–cix.

40. Jack, "Cloth Industry," p. 449. See also his "Fulling Mills," pp. 70–130.

tion of wealth in old Gwynedd. Internal trade was therefore probably mostly small-scale, concerned with petty items of local consumption.

The castles constructed by the English and the boroughs they founded presented a potential market. The garrisons and burgesses required corn, meat, and materials for building and heating; some Welshmen probably profited from this demand. Edward I's campaign of castle construction stimulated the local stone quarries.[41] But once the initial spurt of building was over, the demand generated by the boroughs and castles must have been small. The towns never enjoyed very large populations, nor were the castle garrisons especially numerous.[42] The burgesses also had their own plots of arable land outside the town walls. Since these were often among the most fruitful lands in Gwynedd, the townsmen must to a large extent have been self-sufficient in cereals.

From the surviving records it seems that the current of commodity exchange flowing through the plantation boroughs was not very large. Royal revenue from the tolls of markets and fairs was small in the first half of the fourteenth century.[43] In the reign of Edward II, the burgesses of Conwy wrote to the king about the sad state of their trade. According to their lament, no merchants (with the exception of some Irishmen from Dublin and Drogheda, other North Welsh burgesses, and a few individuals from English towns near the Welsh border) visited them.[44] It is clear that the boroughs in the Principality of North Wales were but tiny markets at best for the country's surplus agricultural produce.

The peasants of Gwynedd were also confronted by the fact that very little of what they produced interested the outside world. One of the most important agricultural goods produced for market in medieval Britain was wool. Since the economy of Gwynedd had an important pastoral component, one might have expected the Welsh to be able to export substantial quantities of wool. However, it appears that northwest Wales was not a significant producer in the middle ages.[45] Welsh sheep seem to have been small, and, with the exception of those of the

41. Edward A. Lewis, "Development," pp. 140–42.
42. Lewis, *Mediaeval Boroughs*, pp. 25–26.
43. Ibid., pp. 300–304.
44. *Cal. Anc. Pets.*, pp. 311–12.
45. The rest of this paragraph draws on Lewis, "Development," pp. 152–58. See also Munro, "Wool-Price Schedules," especially pp. 157–59.

Radnor region (outside the Principality of North Wales), to have produced wool of the poorest type. In 1341 the wools of Wales were described as "coarse and of little value, so that for their poorness they are not numbered among wools of any sort of the realm of England."[46] Foreign merchants rarely visited the country in search of the clip of its flocks. Of the sixteen towns established as wool staples in 1327, only two were in Wales, at Carmarthen and Cardiff in West and South Wales respectively.[47] By 1353 only Carmarthen was recognized as a staple town. Although some cloth was manufactured in Wales, most of it was intended for local consumption.

Gwynedd did export some timber, millstones, honey, wax, butter, cheese, and hides.[48] In Flintshire the conquest saw an increase in iron and lead mining, but much of the work, and therefore of the profit, was in the hands of imported German and English miners.[49]

On the whole Gwynedd's external trade was very small. Furthermore, most of it was handled by outsiders, there being very few native Welsh merchants.[50] Most of the little profit therefore went to fill non-Welsh purses. In the light of all this evidence, one can readily sympathize with the complaint voiced by Iorwerth Foel in the 1320s that "the people of Wales have nothing to sell except their cattle for which they can do nothing."[51]

Medieval Welshmen thus had few products to sell and few markets in which to sell them. Some made an effort to merchandize their labor. Late fourteenth-century court rolls from Caernarfon show that Welshmen in search of employment were not uncommon in the borough.[52] But in selling their labor, the Welsh encountered many of the same problems as they did in selling the products of their agriculture. Within Gwynedd itself there was not much demand. Large amounts of coin

46. *CPR, 1341–43*, p. 272.
47. *CCR, 1327–30*, p. 116. Although northern Wales was not a significant wool exporter, the wools of the border districts of eastern and southern Wales had a good reputation. Cistercian monasteries in these regions produced much wool for sale. See R. R. Davies, *Conquest*, pp. 156–57, 169–70, and Donkin, *Cistercians*, pp. 79–84.
48. Lewis, "Development," pp. 140, 148, "Contribution," p. 95; *BPR*, 1:155; Jones and Owen, eds., *Caernarvon Court Rolls*, p. 97; Carr, *Medieval Anglesey*, pp. 108–10.
49. Rees, *Industry*, 1:41.
50. Lewis, "Contribution," p. 99.
51. *Cal. Anc. Pets.*, pp. 115–16.
52. Jones and Owen, eds., *Caernarvon Court Rolls*, pp. 30, 42, 48, 66, 69, 76.

were lavished by Edward I on wages for the construction of his castles, but it seems that for the most part the laborers employed in his building campaign were English.[53] Moreover, once the fortresses were built, the government had only a limited need for labor.[54]

The English also tried to ensure that Welsh laborers received anything but a fair day's pay for their work. Some of the labor needed on royal building projects was extorted from the Welsh without any compensation. For example, in 1305 the people of North Wales complained to Edward of Caernarfon that they were being compelled to do unreasonably heavy carting services for work on the king's castles, manors, and mills.[55] More importantly, the English instituted rules setting maximum wages. Edward I seems to have made an ordinance on this subject early in the fourteenth century. Although the text of this has not survived, D. L. Evans has argued that it was probably similar to an ordinance issued in 1299 for Ireland which decreed that wages were to be no higher than they had been in the previous year. Similar regulations were enforced in the Marcher lordships.[56]

With wage levels blocked at home, Welshmen often looked for work in England. The preamble to the Statute of Labourers of 1351 refers to Welshmen seeking employment in the kingdom during harvest time.[57] The same year eleven men from Dyffryn Clwyd were amerced in the lordship's court for going to England in search of work. Amercements for similar offenses were imposed on sixteen men in 1367 and on twenty-two in 1384. In places in the Marches the movement of labor was organized by professional recruiting agents.[58] Finally, at the beginning of Glyndŵr's rebellion in the early fifteenth century, English observers noted that considerable numbers of Welsh laborers were leaving England to return home to join the uprising.[59]

All in all, it seems that the people of Gwynedd must have experienced much difficulty acquiring the cash needed to pay the increased dues demanded by the English. When in 1318 some of the men of

53. Edwards, "Edward I's Castle-Building," p. 17.

54. In 1304–5 the crown spent £632 19s. 4¼d. on work at Caernarfon castle, but the bulk of the wages paid seems to have gone to English laborers; Edward A. Lewis, "Account Roll," pp. 268–69.

55. RC, p. 213.

56. D. L. Evans, "Some Notes," pp. 81–82; Davies, Lordship, p. 233.

57. Great Britain, Record Commission, Rotuli Parliamentorum, 2:234.

58. Davies, Lordship, pp. 398, 233 (n. 10).

59. Lloyd, Owen Glendower, p. 35.

South Wales sent a petition to Edward II, they observed that they were never accustomed to having money in their possession; their counterparts in North Wales could undoubtedly have echoed this complaint.[60]

Some other English measures after the conquest also may have had negative consequences for the economy of Gwynedd. It has been pointed out in the previous chapter that the coming of English rule resulted in little change in the patterns of landholding. Despite this fact, it is possible that some of the changes may have produced complications for local agrarian practices. Among these was the assertion of a more rigorous lordship over the pasture resources of the country. This process is well documented in the Marcher lordships of northeastern Wales. In Denbigh seigneurial woods and parks were created throughout the lordship.[61] For access to the pasture and woodland resources over which it had asserted dominion, the administration often charged substantial fees.[62] In Dyffryn Clwyd the seigneurial administrators claimed that all trees, even those growing on a tenant's own land, belonged to the lord.[63] In Bromfield and Yale in the first decade of the fourteenth century, Welshmen complained that they were not allowed to make use of anything in the woods, from which they derived the greater part of their sustenance, without the permission of the lord's foresters.[64]

Within the Principality of North Wales, the assertion of royal control over woods and wastes seems to have occasioned similar problems. In the reign of Edward I, the bishop of Bangor protested that his tenants were being deprived of their traditional rights to common of pasture. In 1315–16 the abbot of Bardsey voiced a similar complaint.[65] The 1352 extent of Caernarfonshire shows that those few Englishmen who obtained land from the king displayed a definite interest in the upland summer pastures. Thomas de Mussynden was holding sixteen hafodydd, Robert de Chirbury eleven, and Robert Pollard one.[66] In Merioneth in 1316 John Colier, a burgess of

60. *Cal. Anc. Corr.*, p. 179.
61. Vinogradoff and Morgan, eds., *Survey*, pp. 25, 275; Owen, "Lordship," pp. 224–25.
62. See, for example, Vinogradoff and Morgan, eds., *Survey*, pp. xlii–xliii.
63. Davies, *Lordship*, p. 123.
64. *Cal. Anc. Pets.*, pp. 74–75.
65. Ibid., pp. 464–65, 142.
66. *RC*, pp. 11, 18–19, 35.

Harlech, held a number of hafodydd from the king in return for provisioning Harlech castle.[67] Thus, some of the inhabitants of Gwynedd found themselves either excluded from their old pasture lands or forced to pay for the privilege of using them. It is possible that this factor may have helped to dislocate the system of agricultural production.

Signs of Economic Dislocation

All this evidence suggests that the English regime posed an economic problem for the inhabitants of Gwynedd. The portion of their surplus with which they had to part was increased. They also had to pay these increased renders largely in the form of cash, which, as we have seen, was no easy matter. To meet these new demands, the Welsh may well have been forced to reduce their own level of consumption or to forgo replacing tools, seed, and animals. Both of these strategies, if employed, might eventually result in declining agricultural yields. Many Welshmen tried to sell their labor to their new masters. During the fourteenth and fifteenth centuries, there was a steady outflow of Welshmen into England seeking service in the royal armies or employment as laborers. Although this may have served to inject a few coins into the cash-starved economy of Gwynedd, the rewards of this migration were probably not great. To an extent it was self-defeating, for it served to remove labor from the domestic economy, which, in the absence of any significant advances in agricultural technology, probably reduced productive capacity. Finally, the alacrity with which the English fastened onto the pasture and forest resources of their new possessions may have served to dislocate the native economy, dependent as it was on the linking of small lowland plots of arable with upland pastures.

This is admittedly a speculative argument. The agrarian economy throughout Britain was entering a difficult period in the early fourteenth century. The standard explanations for the rural economy's difficulties tend to stress biological and climatological factors—the supposed development of a Malthusian check on the economy's productive ability, deteriorating weather, cattle plagues, the appearance of famines, and so forth. But, as J. R. Maddicott has argued, in trying

67. *Cal. Anc. Pets.*, pp. 516–17; Great Britain, PRO, *Calendar of the Fine Rolls, 1307–19*, p. 271.

to understand the economic difficulties of the early fourteenth century, we should not focus our attention on these factors to the exclusion of all others. Maddicott has argued that in England the greatly increased crown levies of the early fourteenth century served to compound the difficulties in which peasants already found themselves.[68] One could argue that this fiscal pressure was even more dire in its consequences in Gwynedd, a relatively poor country and one that had not been nearly as rigorously exploited before 1283 as it was afterward.

Whether one chooses to accept this argument or not, it is impossible to miss the signs of economic distress in Gwynedd that appear in many of the surviving financial records. In 1291–92 the sheriff of Anglesey reported that because of a number of factors, including the poverty of the tenants, £34 2s. 6½d. of the usual dues from the county could not be collected. In the same year the sheriffs of Caernarfonshire and Merioneth reported shortfalls of £15 15s. 10d. and £13 12s. 7½d.[69] In the late 1290s the Exchequer at Westminster was aware that revenues from the manor of Rhosyr in Anglesey had for several years been well below normal because of the tenants' poverty.[70] In 1304–5 the sheriff of Caernarfonshire claimed an allowance on his account of £67 15s. 0 ½d. for uncollectible dues. This figure amounted to 14 percent of the county's standard annual payment of £483 14s. 1¾d.[71] In 1309–10 the escheator of North Wales reported that in Glyndyfrdwy some of the mills for which he was responsible were in such a bad state of repair that he could get only 4s. a year for one (originally worth 60s.) and 18d. for another (previously valued at 25s.).[72]

Other records also depict a gloomy situation. Sometime early in the fourteenth century, eight men of Cafflogion commote in Caernarfonshire, in a petition delivered to Edward II, informed the king that because of their poverty and impotence they had left their lands, unable to pay their rents, reliefs, and other dues. In 1324 the villeins of the commote of Eifionydd in the same county complained that they were so vexed and impoverished by the demands of the men who were

68. Maddicott, *English Peasantry*, pp. 3–5, 74–75.
69. John Griffiths, "Two Early Ministers' Accounts," pp. 53–54, 58, 60.
70. Fryde, ed., *Welsh Entries*, no. 144.
71. Waters, "Account," pp. 151–53.
72. Waters, "Documents," p. 366.

farming the king's mills and fish-weirs that they experienced great difficulty in holding their land. As a final example, in 1330–31, the king's bondmen complained that the royal purveyors had so impoverished them that they could barely live.[73]

The economic consequences of the coming of English rule thus seem to have been dire. The ever needy royal administration compelled the Welsh of the principality to give up a larger amount of the surplus they produced. The country was systematically bled of manpower to feed the growing needs of the adventuristic military policies of the alien kings. All these demands fell on an economy that was not only decidedly unproductive, but was one that produced little of anything wanted by the outside world. The peasants of Gwynedd therefore found it difficult to acquire the growing masses of coin that their new masters required. The quest for money led to the growth of a current of migratory laborers, whose search for work in England probably brought little cash into the country but subtracted from it the benefits of their labor. These factors combined to make at least the first few generations of English rule a period of economic difficulty for the impecunious peasants of Gwynedd.

Languedoc

If the imposition of outside rule in Gwynedd produced a profound alteration in the way in which surplus value was appropriated, it had no such impact in Languedoc. Despite the differences between the north and the south of France, the social structures of Languedoc and northern France were more alike than were those of Gwynedd and England. Both regions of what is today France possessed nobilities, although that in the north was probably more powerful and richer than its Languedocian counterpart. In both regions peasants were grouped into seigneuries and paid dues, which, although differing in detail, were not altogether dissimilar. In both areas the political elite collected a wide variety of legal dues, tolls, banalités, and so forth. When the French monarchy gained control of Languedoc, it found already in existence a familiar system of extractive techniques.

73. *Cal. Anc. Pets.*, pp. 112, 123, 283–84.

Royal Tribute Collection in Languedoc

On the whole, the monarchy probably gained financially from the acquisition of Languedoc. Ultimately it acquired direct possession of some of the richest lands. From the Montfort family it received the region around Carcassonne; from the Raimondines it acquired the county of Toulouse. These areas—with their fertile fields, vineyards, and numerous cloth-working and commercial towns located astride major trade routes—were among the wealthiest in the south.

Unfortunately, the scattered survival of French financial records makes it difficult to assess just how much revenue these areas brought in. It seems, however, that by any estimate substantial sums were derived from royal possessions in Languedoc. A century ago Edgard Boutaric analyzed the accounts of Alfonse de Poitiers for the county of Toulouse. In 1258 the fixed revenues of the sénéchaussée of Toulouse amounted to 4,725l.t. Deducted from this sum were 1,634l. 8s.t of regular expenses, leaving a net income of 3,090l. 12s.t.[74] For this same sénéchaussée there survive two accounts compiled in the reign of Philip IV, by which time the Toulousain had come into the crown's possession. In the earliest, from 1293–94, the king's receivers accounted for revenues of 32,992l. 17s. 6d.t. and expenses of 15,424l. 4s. 11d.t. In the later account Simon Louard reported, for the period from 15 May 1298 to 24 June 1299, receipts of 42,535l. 6s. 3d.t. and expenses of 23,444l. 4s. 3d.t.[75] This one southern sénéchaussée at least was paying for itself nicely at the end of the thirteenth century.

The total contribution of Languedoc to royal finances is, however, difficult to estimate. Joseph Strayer, using figures assembled by Borrelli de Serres, has estimated that in the 1290s the sénéchaussées of Carcassonne, Beaucaire, and Toulouse produced about 84,000 *livres parisis* a year at a time when total royal revenue was about 450,000l.p.[76] The share of royal revenue coming from Languedoc was clearly substantial. However, it appears that Normandy, a smaller region also acquired by the Capetians in the thirteenth century, made

---

74. This sum represents only "fixed" revenues, and does not include income obtained from variable sources, such as fees for licenses of alienation, fines, confiscations, and so forth; Boutaric, *Saint Louis*, pp. 275–76.

75. Fawtier and Maillard, eds., *Comptes*, 1:473, 494, 567, 590.

76. Strayer, "Normandy and Languedoc," pp. 46–47, using data from Borrelli de Serres, *Recherches*, 2: appendix A, table 8.

an equally large contribution. Baldwin has estimated that Philip Augustus's acquisition of Normandy and other areas in northern France added about 80,000 livres parisis to his income.[77]

Although the Capetian kings profited from the incorporation of Languedoc into their realm, their assertion of hegemony does not seem to have resulted in as significant an increase in the fiscal exploitation of local society as occurred in Gwynedd. Rule by a dynasty from beyond the Loire may have meant that the old elites found a new mouth present at the traditional feeding trough of peasant production, but it does not seem to have had as dramatic an impact on the way in which surplus was extracted from the local economy as English rule had in Gwynedd. Royal agents were, of course, as avid as anyone else for more revenue in the thirteenth century, and over the years they increased crown revenue in the south. For example, in 1257 the Agenais, then under the lordship of Alfonse de Poitiers, yielded 1,870l.t. In 1259 this area provided the count with 2,246l.t. By 1271, when the Agenais had become part of the royal domain, revenue had risen to 3,351l.t.[78]

This growth in revenue was not, however, the result of anything as dramatic as the sudden increase in cash rent effected by the English in Gwynedd. Instead, increases in royal income were for the most part the result of slow, piecemeal acquisition of a ground rent here, of tolls or perquisites of justice there. The laborious nature of this process is illustrated by the literally hundreds of purchases of small parcels of land and various rights made in the king's name in 1275 by the seneschal of Toulouse, Eustache de Beaumarchais.[79]

One of the ways in which the crown expanded both its power and its revenue base was through the creation with local seigneurs of joint lordships, known as pariages. Languedoc was fertile ground for such arrangements. Many abbeys and bishoprics were happy to enter into these arrangements with the king as a way of protecting themselves from the designs of their neighbors. In 1307 and 1308, for example,

77. Baldwin, *Government*, pp. 247–48. Sivéry (in *Saint Louis*, pp. 294–95) argues that a comparison of royal accounts from 1202–3 and 1286–87 indicates that royal acquisition of territories south of the Loire resulted in only relatively small increases in crown revenue. In his opinion, lands acquired by the kings north of the Loire contributed far more to the thirteenth-century increase in the size of their revenues.

78. Dossat, "Divisions," p. 311.

79. Dossat, "Restauration," pp. 289–316.

Philip IV arranged five important pariages, with the abbot of Candeil for Labessière, the bishop of Pamiers for all his possessions, apart from the episcopal city itself, with the bishops of Cahors and Le Puy for their episcopal cities, and with the bishop of Mende for his entire diocese. Pariage agreements with the secular nobility were also common. Since many nobles in Languedoc observed the practice of partible inheritance, family lordships were often split up amongst a host of petty and needy heirs. The king's government was thus able to purchase for relatively modest sums pariage rights in a seigneurie, which often paved the way for the total absorption of the lordship into the royal domain.[80]

Royal authority and revenue were also expanded by the creation of planned settlements known as bastides. Alfonse de Poitiers was especially fond of this sort of activity. During his lifetime several bastides were created in the valley of the Dropt and around the towns of Villemur and Buzet. By founding such settlements in pariage with local lords, Alfonse managed to extend his authority into the county of Comminges, where at least nine such settlements are known to have been made during his reign.[81] The creation of royal bastides continued in the early fourteenth century.[82] The revenues derived from these foundations could be substantial. In 1256 Count Alfonse founded Montflanquin. From it in 1268 he collected 140l.t. By 1271 its income had risen to 203l.t. The revenues from Villeneuve, founded in 1264, revealed a similar upward trend, being 150l.t. in 1268 and 193l.t. in 1271.[83]

A variety of other measures was employed by the crown to improve its revenue. Royal estates were often consolidated through exchanges, such as the one in 1306 by which Bernard, viscount of Lautrec in the Albigeois, exchanged his holdings in the sénéchaussée of Carcassonne for the castle and town of Caraman and its dependencies in the sénéchaussée of Toulouse.[84] To increase its revenue, the crown also bought up the right to collect tolls. Between 1273 and 1275, for example, the ministers of King Philip III acquired such rights from several impor-

---

80. Dognon, *Institutions*, p. 23. For references to some other pariage agreements, see *Regs.*, vol. 1, no. 1146; vol. 2, nos. 2900, 3303, 3305, 3276, 3479.
81. Latour, "Dramatiques," pp. 36–37.
82. See for example, *Regs.*, vol. 2, nos. 2088, 2092.
83. Dossat, "Divisions," pp. 309, 311.
84. *Regs.*, vol. 1, no. 265.

tant families in the city of Toulouse.[85] To ensure that the king got the lion's share of the revenue derived from the coinage of money, restrictions were placed on the circulation of coins issued by seigneurial mints.[86]

Obstacles to the Mobilization of Languedocian Resources

One should be careful of forming too optimistic a picture of the case with which royal revenue was increased. The survival of indigenous political structures made it possible for Languedocians to offer effective resistance to royal demands for tribute. The royal government frequently had to part with some of its sources of revenue. The enquêteurs whom Louis IX sent to Languedoc to investigate complaints often surrendered various dues and exactions. In 1254, for example, enquêteurs lightened royal financial demands on the people of Sommières. Similarly, a year later enquêteurs ruled that the king's ministers had illegally usurped the legal jurisdiction of the lords and consuls of Montaren.[87] Even the notoriously grasping regime of Alfonse de Poitiers could be persuaded to surrender some of its sources of revenue. When the county of Toulouse was taken into the hands of King Philip III in 1271 following Alfonse's death, the villagers of Ondes and Castelnau-d'Estrétefonds reported that they had secured from the count certain reductions in their dues.[88] To finance his participation in Louis IX's last crusade, Alfonse was also forced to sell off numerous pieces of land, the partial recovery of which cost his royal successors at least 4,412l. 17s. 4d.t.[89]

Royal efforts to tax commercial exchanges were often successfully resisted. In the early thirteenth century, for example, the burgesses of Toulouse had managed to win exemption from numerous tolls and sales taxes. When in the 1270s the royal viguier tried to claim that only goods intended for the Toulousains' immediate consumption were exempt from these imposts, the townsmen persuaded the king to relax his demands.[90]

85. Mundy, *Liberty*, p. 45 and n. 10.
86. Bisson, "Coinages," pp. 407–18; Castaing-Sicard, *Monnaies*, pp. 75–81.
87. Michel, *Administration*, pp. 410–14.
88. Dossat, ed., *Saisimentum*, pp. 128–29, 138–39.
89. Dossat, "Restauration," p. 263.
90. Wolff, *Commerces*, pp. 465–66.

Pariage agreements were often fraught with expensive difficulties. This can be seen clearly in the history of one of the most vexing of these arrangements, the pariage of Pamiers. At the beginning of the Albigensian crusades, the counts of Foix and the abbots of Saint-Antonin had exercised codominion in Pamiers. In 1209 the abbot took advantage of the arrival of the crusaders to deprive the count of his share in the town's lordship, giving it to the Montforts. In 1225 the abbot was compelled to recognize once again the rights of Count Roger Bernard II. But when in the following year Louis VIII campaigned in Languedoc, Saint-Antonin installed him in the place of the count, a situation, however, which did not survive Louis's death. In 1269, after violent confrontations with Count Roger Bernard III, Abbot Bernard Saisset arranged a pariage with Louis IX for a period of ten years. But the count of Foix did not abandon his claims. After a stormy period in which the county was invaded by a royal army and the count himself lodged in a French prison, Roger Bernard won himself into the king's good graces. As a result, in 1285 the French agreed to restore his rights in Pamiers.

Despite Saisset's efforts the royal garrison that had been installed in Pamiers left the city in 1295. The result was war between the abbot and the count. In 1300 the count and Saisset, who had become the first bishop of the new diocese of Pamiers, agreed to the terms of an arbitration delivered by Gui de Lévis, the lord of Mirepoix. With the accession in 1302 of a new count, Gaston I, however, disputes between the house of Foix and the bishop resumed. Once again Saisset turned to the king. Pretending that the pariage with the count concerned only the city of Pamiers itself, Bernard offered to establish a new pariage with the crown for all his see's other rights and privileges. In 1308 Philip IV agreed to this scheme, which prompted Gaston to protest. As late as 1344 one of his successors, Gaston III, was still trying to vindicate his dynasty's rights in Pamiers. Nevertheless the agreement of 1308 remained final. Henceforth Pamiers was ruled in a double pariage, between the count and the bishop on one side and the bishop and the king on the other.[91]

Royal efforts to tax Languedoc also reveal the difficulties that the king's agents experienced in separating southerners from their wealth. Royal taxation became especially heavy at the end of the thirteenth century because of Philip IV's wars with the Flemings and the English.

91. J.-M. Vidal, "Bernard Saisset," vol. 5, pp. 426–38, 565–90; vol. 6, 50–58.

Languedoc had to bear its share of this burden. The sums collected in the Languedocian sénéchaussées were often considerable. The people of Carcassonne promised to pay a total of 71,548l.t. during 1297 and 1298.[92] In 1304 this same sénéchaussée contributed 59,465l.t. in taxes, while the sénéchaussée of Beaucaire was compelled to disgorge 15,831l.t.[93] The tax of 1305 brought in from Carcassonne about 13,464l.t.[94]

In the collection of these revenues, royal agents were often willing to resort to chicanery and outright brutality. For example, in October 1297 Raimond Durand, a notary, and other royal agents descended on Laurac in the sénéchaussée of Toulouse. Durand assembled the leading men of the village and informed them that he had come to raise a variety of dues, the most important of which were taxes for the Flemish war. When the villagers proved recalcitrant, Durand's reply was twofold. He told them that they had eight days to find the money; anyone who did not pay would be arrested. While Durand delivered this ultimatum, sergeants, armed with lists of those liable to pay the quête levied on the unfree, scoured Laurac. They evicted the inhabitants of the houses on their lists, locked the doors, and confiscated the keys. When the sergeants delivered the impounded keys to Durand, the village notables caved in and agreed to go to Toulouse to negotiate the amount of their payment with Durand's superiors. Before leaving Laurac, Durand and his assistant demanded a payment of 50s. to defray their expenses, forced every notable to give them between 4d. and 6d., and required those villagers whose keys had been confiscated to pay 5d. to recover them.

When the notables arrived in Toulouse, they were confronted with a demand for the extraordinary sum of 50,000s. Eventually they were allowed to offer 3,000s., still an impressive figure. The royal ministers, anticipating reluctance on the part of the other villagers to go along with this agreement, once again sent Durand to Laurac. He secured compliance with the levy by arresting every household head in the village. After a long day spent under armed guard, the villagers agreed to pay whatever was required of them.[95]

The brutality that royal servants like Durand displayed was, how-

92. Strayer, "Consent," p. 51.
93. Mignon, *Inventaire*, no. 2058; Strayer, "Consent," p. 74.
94. Mignon, *Inventaire*, no. 2059.
95. Favier, *Philippe le Bel*, pp. 86–89.

ever, more than anything else a confession of weakness. The royal government experienced much difficulty in collecting taxes. Almost every demand for taxation was the occasion for protests and protracted negotiations. For example, when a property tax of one-fiftieth was levied in 1296, the parts of the town of Montpellier that belonged to the king of Majorca protested at being called on to contribute. The crown's demand for a subsidy in 1297 aroused much discontent. The town of Narbonne and the counts of Armagnac, Astarac, and Rodez—among others—protested. The people of Albi, after much negotiation, managed to get the crown to compromise on how the tax would be levied. Instead of paying 8s. per hearth, the Albigeois were to pay, for each year that the war in Flanders lasted, a lump sum equal to the proceeds that would have been raised by a tax at the rate of 6s. a hearth. In return they were to be spared all other demands for loans, gifts, aids, and additional taxes. In Béziers the government could collect nothing at all until a dispute between the local nobles and commoners over the former's tax liability was settled. In 1303 opposition forced the abandonment of efforts to collect fines for exemption from military service in the diocese of Toulouse.[96]

Resistance to the crown's request in 1304 for subsidies for the Flemish war was also widespread. Grants were hedged about with many conditions. Nobles insisted on the right to pay their taxes in installments, to cease paying if peace were made, and to make their own estimates of their income. Debts owed by the king to Languedocian nobles for previous military service were to be settled out of the proceeds of the tax. The towns of the sénéchaussée of Carcassonne agreed to contribute only if they were allowed to determine the number of hearths liable to taxation and were exempted from all other royal demands for a year. The towns of the sénéchaussée of Beaucaire gained the right to deduct from the tax debts owed to them by the king.[97]

The county of Foix often presented particularly thorny problems of tax collection. In the reign of Philip IV almost every effort to raise taxes there was met either with protests or outright defiance. In 1292 an attempt by the crown to tallage the Jews of Foix produced a remonstrance from Count Roger Bernard III.[98] Efforts to impose

96. Strayer, "Consent," pp. 49, 51, 53, 55, 63.
97. Ibid., pp. 67–69; *HL*, 10: *Preuves*, cols. 432–35.
98. *HL*, 9:164; Castillon, *Histoire*, 1:362.

hearth taxes in 1294 and 1297 produced further protests from the count that his subjects were exempt from such exactions.[99]

An attempt in 1300 to levy a tax on personal property produced tumult throughout the county. Pierre de Bogis, a royal viguier, was charged with the task of collecting the subsidy. Together with several assistants, he made his way to the town of Foix. There he found the gates shut and chains stretched across the bridge spanning the Ariège river. Confronted by these warlike preparations, Pierre read his letters of commission to the assembled mob, an oration to which the crowd turned a deaf ear. Bogis, having accomplished nothing at Foix, made his way down the Ariège to Varilhes where he managed to raise some cash. With seven mules loaded with coin he set off for Carcassonne. His journey was interrupted by the bayle of Foix and a group of his henchmen who relieved Bogis of his mules and his money. Pierre appealed to the count's castellan at Varilhes for aid, but was ignored.

When the viguier arrived in Carcassonne, he had the rebellious Fuxéens cited to appear before royal justices to answer for their contempt of royal authority. Two sergeants were dispatched to deliver the summons. Their experiences were no more pleasant than those of Bogis. At Foix they were confronted in their turn by a closed town and a threatening mob. At Tarascon they also found the town gates barred against them. And in the village of La Barguillère they were set upon and nearly killed by an enraged crowd. The counts of Foix, Roger Bernard III and his son Gaston I, refused all royal requests to turn over for trial those responsible for these acts. Faced by this steadfast contumacy, the king's courts in 1305 sentenced the people of Foix, Tarascon, and four other localities to heavy fines. In 1308, however, these were drastically reduced. Thereafter the French apparently decided that raising direct taxes in the county was more trouble than it was worth and gave up the effort.[100]

Among the more determined opponents of royal taxation were the local prelates. The privileges claimed by the church included exemption for its personnel from certain types of subsidy. For this reason, among others, numbers of Languedocians sought out the protections and immunities that went with clerical status. Bishops were very liberal in bestowing these benefits, obligingly conferring holy orders on

99. Castillon, *Histoire*, 1:362–63; Strayer, "Consent," p. 53.
100. Llobet, *Foix*, pp. 54–56; Doat, vol. 96, fols. 40r–56v.

large numbers of men who were clerics in name only.[101] When it came to protecting these nominal clerics from the tax collectors, the church was often willing to use the full arsenal of its spiritual powers. According to complaints made by the seneschal of Carcassonne sometime in the mid–1250s, when the men of the town of Siran tried to get a woman who held land of the king to contribute to a royal taille, the archbishop of Narbonne excommunicated them because the woman's husband was a cleric.[102] In 1283 the consuls of Béziers protested to the king that the town was full of clerics who did not live as churchmen should, being either married or engaged in various "mechanical" arts, but who nevertheless refused to let themselves be assessed for the contributions made to the king.[103] Similar complaints were voiced in Albi, Toulouse, Narbonne, and Montpellier.[104]

The collection of taxes in Languedoc thus posed real problems for the king's administrators. Each levy aroused opposition, which was often not only violent but effective. Every time a new tax was proclaimed, the royal collectors found themselves forced to engage in protracted negotiations with the natives. It is true that levies in Languedoc could bring in large sums of money, but the cost to the French government in time, labor, and good-will used up in the business of collection may have been very high.

The Mobilization of Military Manpower

The Capetian monarchy, like most of its contemporaries, found recruiting military manpower an often difficult proposition. Every mobilization effort was greeted with foot-dragging, cries of poverty, and claims of exemption. The situation in Languedoc was no different from elsewhere in France. The Capetians often found that raising local troops was as difficult as tapping Languedocian purses. To be certain, Languedocians frequently took part in royal campaigns. Since the French were often at war with the English kings, who were also dukes of Gascony, Languedocians were called on to do service there. For example, in 1329, for a projected campaign in Gascony, the king's

101. Boutaric, ed., "Notices," p. 133.
102. *HL*, 8: col. 1420.
103. Langlois, "Rouleaux," p. 199. See also p. 206 (n. 1) for similar complaints from the sénéchaussée of Carcassonne.
104. Compayré, *Etudes*, p. 273; *HL*, 9:133–34.

ministers anticipated raising 1,000 men-at-arms and 16,000 foot in Languedoc. Similarly, in 1330 they planned on calling out 2,000 men-at-arms and 16,000 foot.[105] Despite their service in royal armies, Languedocians do not seem to have been required to make disproportionately heavy manpower contributions. For the most part the kings raised troops primarily in areas close to the theaters of campaign. Northerners served in the north, Languedocians in the south.

As in the case of taxation, the French found that their southern subjects presented many difficulties concerning military service. The local aristocracy expected to be well paid for its campaigning. The homages done by local nobles to the king often included the proviso that they were required to do military service only at the crown's expense.[106] The great aristocrats who served the king expected to be recompensed on a lavish scale.[107]

The monarchy's attempts to raise troops in Languedoc were often met with claims to exemption. In the 1250s, for example, the archbishop of Narbonne argued that he, his bishops, his abbots, and all their subjects were not required to provide troops for the king's armies.[108] Around 1255 the bishop of Lodève denounced as illegal the efforts by the king's seneschal to summon his men for military service.[109] In the 1330s the men of Lunel protested that the conditions of their tenures did not require them to do military service.[110] Calls on the manpower resources of the region's towns and cities produced the same protracted negotiations and litigation as did demands for taxation.[111]

Royal Stimulation of the Economy

The French monarchy thus experienced considerable difficulty in mobilizing the resources of its Languedocian subjects. One could

105. Contamine, *Guerre*, p. 66. Southerners did go north to campaign in Flanders, but for the most part the armies that fought there were recruited in the north; Lot, *Art militaire*, 1:264–65, 270.

106. See, for example, the homage offered in the 1250s by the *domicellus* Raymond de Meyrueis in Michel, *Administration*, p. 419.

107. For example, the military services of Roger Bernard III of Foix were rewarded by the crown with the restoration of some of the rights he claimed in the disputed pariage of Pamiers; *HL*, 9:111.

108. *HL*, 8: col. 1423.

109. *Layettes*, vol. 3, no. 4208.

110. Contamine, *Guerre*, pp. 53–54.

111. For an example from the city of Albi, see Doat, vol. 108, fols. 37r–39v, and *HL*, 8: cols. 1506–9.

therefore infer that the potentially deleterious effects of an overly effective royal fiscality were minimized. Beyond this conclusion it is very difficult to gauge the impact on the region's economy of its incorporation into the royal political system. In some ways French rule may have served to promote the Languedocian economy. The crown appears to have made a number of productive investments in the region. As noted above, one of the ways in which the French expanded their authority was through the creation of bastides. All told, the crown or Alfonse de Poitiers patronized the creation of at least eighty-seven of these settlements in Languedoc during the thirteenth and early fourteenth centuries.[112] By fostering the growth of these plantations, the French not only enriched themselves, they also contributed to the expansion of local production.

Given the developed state of Languedocian trade and manufacturing, the French often plowed much of what they took from Languedoc back into the local economy. Thanks to the survival of the accounts of one royal servant, Master Arnaud Mestre, we are well informed about some royal purchases in Languedoc in the 1290s. In connection with the planning in 1295 of an invasion of England, Master Arnaud was instructed to acquire weapons and armor in Toulouse and its environs. To fill his order, Arnaud was forced to call on the resources of merchants and artisans scattered all across the region from the county of Comminges to the Mediterranean coast. Eventually he spent 3,192l. 16s. 9d.t. on purchasing, packaging, and transporting various war materials. Most of the money found its way into the hands of Languedocian merchants, artisans, and mule skinners.[113] To be sure, this is only one example. But it is clear that the economy of Languedoc produced many things that the royal government found worth its interest, and for which it had to pay good money. It is therefore not unreasonable to deduce that much of the surplus extracted from the Midi in the form of ground-rent, taxation, seigneurial dues, and so forth was plowed back into the local economy.

In addition to spending money in Languedoc, the royal government took other steps that may have fostered local economic development. The gradual ousting of coins struck by local seigneurs by the issue of royal mints may have eased commercial transactions. Most coins pro-

112. This figure is based on the material contained in Curie Seimbres, *Essai.* See also Higounet, "Pour l'histoire," pp. 387–94.

113. Mestre's account is published in Fawtier and Maillard, eds., *Comptes,* vol. 2, nos. 25020–309, and is analyzed by Wolff in "Achats," pp. 395–402.

duced by the native mints were of small value. With the steady inflation of prices in the thirteenth century, their usefulness was decreas-
ing. Their replacement by the more valuable royal coins may thus have
helped increase the velocity of exchanges.[114]

The king's government also took steps to protect the economic
interests of Languedocian merchants and artisans. At the end of the
thirteenth century and the beginning of the fourteenth, the region's
cloth merchants began to fear competition from Roussillon and
Catalonia. Their complaints resulted in the issue of royal ordinances
in 1277, 1305, and 1318 restricting the export of raw wool and
undyed cloth from Languedoc. Although these restrictions were ultimately lifted in 1333, they coincided, in the opinion of Guy
Romestan, with a period of great prosperity for the Languedocian
cloth industry.[115]

Economic Progress under Royal Hegemony

On the whole, it does not seem that French rule was a bar to
progress, at least for those engaged in the commercial and manufacturing sectors of the local economy. Evidence that these sectors were
expanding under French domination in the thirteenth and early fourteenth centuries is abundant. The contacts of Languedocian merchants with the outside world steadily expanded. The most active
period of trade between England and the city of Toulouse fell between
1255 and 1270. At the same time, trade with the northern half of the
French kingdom grew. The activities of merchants from Montpellier at
the fairs of Champagne were so extensive that the city's consuls felt it
advisable to elect a captain of merchants who would have jurisdiction
over Montpellier traders visiting the fairs.[116]

Within Languedoc itself there were unmistakable signs of economic
expansion. The royal patronage of the planned settlements known as
bastides has already been mentioned. The kings were not alone in
encouraging such colonizing activities. Between 1222 and 1340 about
400 to 500 bastides were established in the area stretching from Aquitaine to the Rhône valley. Manufacturing and mining also grew. By
1240 small-scale coal mining was under way in the Cévennes.[117] The

114. Castaing-Sicard, *Monnaies*, pp. 79–81.
115. Romestan, "Gabelle," p. 219; Wolff, "Draperie," pp. 444–46.
116. Wolff, *Histoire de Toulouse*, pp. 123–24; Combes, "Montpellier," p. 382.
117. Le Roy Ladurie, *Paysans*, 1:140, citing Bardon, *Exploitation*, pp. 3–4.

last half of the thirteenth century also saw the beginnings of local silk production.[118]

Most striking, however, was the steady development of the local cloth industry. Montpellier, which by the end of the twelfth century had already become well known for the quality of its dye work, continued to expand its markets. By the end of the thirteenth century, its merchants were importing cloth from England and Arras. They were also exporting finished cloth to Italy, Constantinople, Armenia, and Palestine.[119] At least seventy-six other towns in the region supported a cloth-working industry of some kind.[120] If in Gwynedd outside rule had been attended by economic difficulty, in Languedoc it meant business as usual.

Conclusion

The approach of the English and French to the mobilization of the resources of Gwynedd and Languedoc reveals one major similarity: the importance of politically based forms of surplus extraction. Before their absorption into the political systems headed by the French and English monarchies, the economies of Gwynedd and Languedoc had not been effectively subordinated to those of England or northern France. The assertion of outside rule made little difference to this situation. The incorporation of Gwynedd and Languedoc into larger political organizations was not the prelude to an increased penetration of their local economies by those of their outside masters. Neither the French nor the English sought to work any significant structural changes in the Welsh or Languedocian economies. Relations of production were not altered so as to make Languedoc or Gwynedd produce new forms of economic surplus. Both the French and the English were content to let their subjects continue organizing the tasks of production largely as they had always done. The English did try to redirect trade through the new plantation boroughs, but this was done not to stimulate new types of economic behavior but to facilitate the taxation of Welsh trade and to ensure that it benefited the imported English burgesses. The English and the French sought to exploit the resources of their new territories not by directly subsuming

118. Le Roy Ladurie, *Paysans*, 1:216–17.
119. Sayous and Combes, "Commerçants," p. 370; Wolff, "Draperie," pp. 442–44.
120. Wolff, "Draperie," pp. 456–58.

their economies under those of their core regions but by extracting tribute through extraeconomic, politically based charges. In a world where the market played only a secondary role in the economy and where most exchanges took place outside of it, this was probably inevitable.

If our two sets of outside rulers had similar policies concerning resource extraction, the consequences of these policies for Gwynedd and Languedoc were very different. English rule in Gwynedd meant an intensification of resource extraction. The rulers of independent Gwynedd had certainly devoted much effort to mobilizing their lordship's resources, but their success had been relatively limited. After 1283 the English brought to bear on their Welsh subjects far more effective means of surplus extraction than the native rulers had ever wielded. All rents were immediately converted to cash, banalités such as compulsory milling dues were generalized, a court system that was an effective means of generating cash income was imposed on the Principality of North Wales, and taxation was imposed on a scale unimaginable in the days of independence. The assertion of lordship over woods, wastes, and upland pastures by the crown and the new Marcher lords made access to these crucial means of production more expensive. In the principality, ordinances designed to give the new English boroughs a stranglehold over the country's commercial exchanges were decreed. In the late thirteenth and early fourteenth centuries the people of Gwynedd probably faced a system of surplus extraction that was more vigorous and demanding than anything they had previously known.

The assertion of Capetian lordship in Languedoc seems to have had no such dramatic consequences. Before the coming of the French, the rulers of Languedoc had already fashioned a relatively developed set of techniques for extracting surplus from the hands of direct producers. The bulk of the peasantry was composed of dependant tenants paying rent for their land. Many lords had also established their exclusive ownership of the region's forests and wastes, crucial to the peasants as a source of fuel, building materials for dwellings and tools, and pasture for their animals.[121] The members of the dominant classes had also secured control of such means of production as forges, ovens, mills, and wine presses, whose compulsory use they forced on their tenants.[122] The coming of the royal administration meant little

121. On the viscount of Narbonne's forest rights, see Régné, *Amauri II*, p. 348.
122. Auguste Molinier, "Etude sur l'administration féodale," pp. 186–88.

change in this situation. The monarchy merely acquired various seig-neurial rights already possessed by some local lords. The kings, as possessors of what passed for supreme authority in the French king-dom, also tried to mobilize resources through taxation and calls for military service. But on the whole it seems that the imposition of royal authority did not have as profound an impact on the forms of surplus extraction as did English rule in Gwynedd.

The evidence we have examined in this chapter tends to lead to the conclusion that the English crown extracted more surplus from Gwynedd than did the French monarchy from Languedoc. This is, unfortunately, a conclusion that cannot be demonstrated with any certainty. Our figures concerning revenue and the population base are so vague as to preclude any firm conclusions. But some statistical speculation is not completely without utility. For comparative pur-poses, we will examine the revenue collected by the English crown in the Principality of North Wales in 1306–7 with that collected by the Capetian monarchy in 1293–94 in the sénéchaussée of Toulouse-Albigeois.[123] English revenue from the Principality was £2,673 (rounded to the nearest pound). French revenue from Toulouse in 1293–94 was (rounded to the nearest livre) 32,993l.t.[124] According to the tables in Spufford's *Handbook of Medieval Exchange*, the En-glish pound sterling in 1292 equaled 82s. 6d. of money of Tours.[125] Converting *livres tournois* to pounds sterling using this rate of ex-change, we find that royal revenues from Toulouse in 1293–94 equal-ed 7,998 pounds sterling.

Using this figure we can try to calculate the average amount of revenue paid per village or parish in our two areas. The Principality of North Wales seems to have contained around 500 villages and ham-lets.[126] Dividing £2,673 by this figure, we get a figure of £5.3 as the average return to the crown. The sénéchaussée of Toulouse is reported

123. The year 1293–94 was chosen because it fell just before the French monarchy began to devalue its currency. The rapid changes in the value of French coins over the next several years makes the task of comparing English and French revenue difficult. See Borrelli de Serres, *Recherches*, 2:510–11.

124. Fawtier and Maillard, eds., *Comptes*, 1:473.

125. Spufford, *Handbook*, p. 209.

126. The county of Anglesey had 209 villages (Davies, *Conquest*, p. 130), Caernar-fon 142 villages (*RC*, pp. 1–43, 92–97), and Merioneth 125 villages (Williams-Jones, ed., *Merioneth Lay Subsidy*). These figures added together give a total of 476 villages. To account for omissions, 24 villages have been added to this total.

to have contained 1619 parishes in the fourteenth century.[127] Dividing £7,998 by this figure gives us an average return from each parish of £4.9. Since Welsh settlements tended to be small,[128] this measure would seem to indicate that English royal fiscal pressure on the people of Gwynedd Uwch Conwy was heavier than that of the French monarchy on the sénéchaussée of Toulouse.

If we try to calculate French and English fiscal demands per capita, we enter very unstable terrain. Nevertheless the exercise has some merit. If we accept Williams-Jones's belief that in the early 1290s the population of the county of Merioneth was between 12,500 and 13,500 and that each of the other two counties in the Principality probably had larger populations,[129] we can estimate that the total population of the principality was about 60,000.[130] Using this figure, we can calculate that the crown was collecting £44.6 in revenue per 1000 inhabitants in the principality in 1306–7.[131] A 1328 survey recorded 153,590 hearths in the sénéchaussée of Toulouse-Albigeois. If we multiply this figure by 4, we can estimate the total population of the sénéchaussée at 614,360.[132] Calculating on this basis we find that the Capetians were collecting £13 from every 1,000 inhabitants. These calculations are, of course, speculative. But combined with the rest of the evidence that has been assembled in this chapter, they suggest that the weight of English royal fiscal demands in the Principality of North Wales was probably heavier than that of Capetian fiscal demands in Languedoc.

Assessing the impact of French and English fiscal demands on their new subjects is also an uncertain business. However, the evidence assembled in this chapter suggests that outside rule may have had a more deleterious effect on the economy of Gwynedd than on that of

127. Lot, "Etat," p. 308.
128. Williams-Jones (*Merioneth Lay Subsidy*, p. lxvii) was of the opinion that Welsh villages probably numbered only around 100 inhabitants.
129. Williams-Jones, ed., *Merioneth Lay Subsidy*, pp. xli–xlii.
130. In 1801 the population of the three counties of Anglesey, Caernarfonshire, and Merioneth was about 106,000. See Mitchell, *Abstract*, p. 20.
131. If we performed this same calculation on the basis of the 1801 population, the figure would be £25.2 per 1,000 inhabitants.
132. The number of hearths comes from Lot, "Etat," p. 308. The multiplier is one less than the five suggested by Lot as appropriate (p. 297). Since I am trying to demonstrate that English fiscal pressure on Wales was greater than French royal pressure on Languedoc, it seemed that I should try to *minimize* the size of the population of the sénéchaussée of Toulouse-Albigeois.

Languedoc. The Welsh—forced to pay higher rents and dues; compelled to buy access to the upland pastures and forests of the region; and mulcted by the courts, tax collectors, and military arrayers—saw the resources of their country stripped to supply the needs of their foreign masters. For the peasant producers of Gwynedd, English rule ushered in a period of economic dislocation and decline. The early fourteenth century was, of course, a period when a general decline began to manifest itself in the European economy as a whole. But this general trend may have been exacerbated in Gwynedd by the new demands made on its surplus. In Languedoc, French rule seems to have had no such negative impact. The demands made by the French on the Languedocian economy, which in the thirteenth century was still in an expansionary phase, do not appear to have been too difficult to cope with. Moreover, the French, unlike the English, showed themselves solicitous of the wishes of native producers. As we have seen, the royal government was willing to shape its export policy to meet the demands of its Languedocian subjects. As a result the economy of Languedoc seems not merely to have come through the crisis of the Albigensian crusades and their aftermath relatively intact but to have thrived and expanded.

In Gwynedd outside rule meant that surplus collection was largely concentrated in the hands of Englishmen, whether agents of the crown or of the Marcher lords, while in Languedoc the surplus appropriated from direct producers was more widely distributed. In the Principality of North Wales the governing apparatus of the crown captured the lion's share of what surplus was available. With few exceptions, the crown was the immediate landlord of almost every Welshman in the principality. Since political authority was concentrated in the hands of crown servants to a degree almost without parallel in western Europe, the majority of the cash appropriated through directly political means also passed into the hands of crown agents. The same situation obtained in the Marcher lordships of the northeast, where the Marcher lords occupied the same structural position as the crown held in the principality. Surplus appropriation in Gwynedd after 1283 was thus largely the monopoly of Englishmen.

The situation in Languedoc was quite different. Although the crown was an important landlord, it did not dominate landholding in the same way the English did in Gwynedd. Moreover, political power in Languedoc was not as concentrated as it was in Gwynedd, but was shared by the crown with members of the locally dominant classes. These local authorities possessed their own politically based methods of extracting surplus from the economy. The appropriation of the local economy's surplus production was thus shared between the French crown and the dominant classes within Languedoc. Unlike the situation in Gwynedd, surplus extraction in Languedoc did not become a near monopoly of the directors of the outside, encapsulating political organization.

6 Old Rulers and New Masters

In this and the next two chapters I explore how the integration of Gwynedd and Languedoc into larger polities affected the political practices of certain classes within these societies. Before the loss of their independence, both Gwynedd and Languedoc had had their own native ruling classes. With the incorporation of these areas into larger polities, these elites faced the problem of fitting into the structures of larger organizations. In dealing with this challenge the elites of Gwynedd and Languedoc experienced different fates. Although one cannot say that the Languedocian ruling classes were thoroughly integrated into the Capetian polity, they were able to play a considerable role in the affairs of the kingdom. The new outside authorities treated them with circumspection and consideration. The ruling elites of Gwynedd experienced different treatment. Not only were they not allowed to participate as equals in the affairs of the English kingdom, but they were allowed to play only a marginal role in governing their own country.

Gwynedd

For the leading elements of the dominant classes of Gwynedd, the English conquest was a catastrophe. During the conquest in 1282 and 1283, the ruling house of Gwynedd was almost completely eradicated. Both Prince Llywelyn ap Gruffydd and his brother Dafydd perished; their children were carted off into captivity in England. On the morrow of the conquest, the only major Welsh lord left in northern Wales was Gruffydd ap Gwenwynwyn of Powys, who had supported Edward against Llywelyn. Within a few decades, however, Gruffydd's dynasty had been extinguished. By 1309 marriage alliances and the accidents of birth and death had brought most of his lordship into the hands of an Englishman, John Charlton, husband of Gruffydd's granddaughter.[1] The top layer of the ecclesiastical ruling elite was also affected by the conquest. Before 1283 most bishops of the two sees in North Wales, Bangor and Saint Asaph, had been ethnically Welsh. Under English rule, however, access to high church office became increasingly difficult for Welshmen.[2] From the late 1320s on, Bangor was regularly in the possession of an English bishop. Saint Asaph remained open to Welshmen for a few decades longer, but from the late 1370s on, this see was also normally held by Englishmen. The advent of English rule thus meant that top leadership positions within Gwynedd were largely closed to Welshmen. In the fourteenth century members of the upper strata of Welsh society would have to focus their ambitions on less lofty goals.

The Welsh Ruling Elite under English Domination

The English recognized that some of their Welsh subjects were of baronial status. These men were regarded as holding their land by a special tenure, *tir pennaeth*, or "Welsh barony." In northern Wales these men included the descendants of Llywelyn ab Iorwerth's seneschal Ednyfed Fychan,[3] some members of the former ruling house of Powys,[4] and descendants of Owain Brogyntyn, one branch of which

1. In 1283 the only other major Welsh lord had been Rhys ap Maredudd of Dryslwyn in South Wales. Like Gruffydd ap Gwenwynwyn, he had supported Edward I against Llywelyn ap Gruffydd. In 1287, however, Rhys rebelled against the English. His rebellion quickly foundered, and he was executed for treason. On Gruffydd and Rhys, see Carr, "Aristocracy," p. 109, and Morgan, "Barony," p. 12.
2. This point is discussed in greater detail in chapter 8.
3. On this family's holdings and privileges, see Glyn Roberts, "Wyrion Eden," pp. 182–84; RC, pp. 150, 167–68; and Carr, Medieval Anglesey, p. 72.
4. These men were masters of the barony of Glyndyfrdwy. In 1328 Gruffydd ap Madog succeeded in entailing this estate. Glyndyfrdwy thus descended intact to Gruffydd's grandson, Owain Glyndŵr, and made this eventual rebel one of the most powerful and wealthy of early fifteenth-century Welshmen; R. R. Davies, "Race Relations," p. 55.

enjoyed a privileged status in the Merioneth commote of Edeirnion, the other occupying a similar position in the commote of Dinmael in the lordship of Denbigh.[5]

This "baronial" group did not cut a very impressive figure under the new regime. Their number was few and their lands not very extensive. With the exception of the barons of Edeirnion, they possessed little in the way of franchises. Compared with the prosperous and powerful English aristocracy, these tenants by Welsh barony were petty lordlings indeed. Beneath them in the hierarchy of wealth and status came the group that the Welsh referred to as the uchelwyr, who were neither numerous nor wealthy.

Under the new regime the members of this "gentry" stratum found it difficult to progress either economically or politically. The English kept in place those aspects of native law that hindered the accumulation of land. For example, traditional custom made alienation *inter vivos* extremely difficult. Despite repeated petitions from Welshmen that they be allowed the same powers of alienation as Englishmen, the crown never agreed to a permanent alteration of this rule. Similarly, the English refused to change the fundamental rule governing inheritance of land, which called for the equal division of an estate *per stirpes* among all male heirs.[6]

I do not want to give the impression that material progress was impossible for the members of this stratum of Welsh society. Despite the fact that the English rulers did not foster the accumulation of land by the Welsh gentry, some in the late fourteenth and early fifteenth centuries succeeded in amassing respectable estates.[7] This, however, was a protracted process. And no one, no matter how successful, managed to create anything that rivaled the estate complexes of the more comfortable elements of the English aristocracy.

The Welsh Gentry and the English Political System

The members of the relatively impecunious Welsh squirearchy were not the most impressive candidates for admission to full part-

5. Carr, "Barons," p. 189, and "Some Edeyrnion and Dinmael Documents," p. 246; *RC*, pp. 150–51, 157, 169, 183; Carr, "Medieval Dinmael," pp. 9–12.

6. In 1316 Edward II allowed free alienation for a period of three years, but this concession was not renewed; Ivor Bowen, ed., *Statutes*, pp. 25, 29; Carr, *Medieval Anglesey*, p. 177. See also *RC*, p. 214.

7. See R. R. Davies, *Conquest*, pp. 415–17, 428–29, and Carr, "Making," pp. 150–57.

nership with their English counterparts in the governance and exploitation of the English polity. Throughout the fourteenth century, Welshmen participated in the political life of the English kingdom in only a marginal fashion. For example, Welsh attendance at Parliament, an institution that grew in importance during the century, was minimal.[8] Between 1284 and 1399, members of the Welsh laity attended only two, both in the reign of Edward II.[9] The political world of the English kingdom was, for all practical purposes, closed to ethnic Welshmen. Although there were Welshmen in the king's household,[10] almost no Welshmen ever held high office in England, whether in the royal household, in the great central bureaucratic offices, or in local administration. Within the English polity, Welshmen had only two roles, as *condottieri* and, less frequently, as counterweights to baronial opponents of the king.

This fact is illustrated by the career of Gruffydd Llwyd. A descendant of Llywelyn ab Iorwerth's seneschal, Ednyfed Fychan, Gruffydd served in the households not only of Edward I but of his wife and his eldest son. He was heavily involved in royal military efforts, raising troops in Wales and campaigning in Flanders and Scotland. When Roger Mortimer and Queen Isabella landed in England in 1326 to overthrow Edward II, Gruffydd was one of the men commanded by the king to assemble the military forces of North Wales to resist them.[11]

In the mid-fourteenth century other Welshmen continued Gruffydd's tradition of military service. Sir Hywel ap Gruffydd, the famous Sir Hywel of the Axe, fought at Poitiers. Indeed it was generally believed by later generations of Welshmen that he personally had captured the French king there.[12] In the last half of the fourteenth century

8. Some Welsh abbots were on occasion summoned to Parliament. But the abbot of the principal monastery in Gwynedd, Aberconwy, was never called to parliament after the conquest; Hays, *Aberconway*, p. 80.

9. W. R. Williams, *Parliamentary History*, p. 1; CCR, *1318–23*, p. 539; CCR, *1323–27*, p. 626.

10. In 1294 and 1295 nine Welshmen were drawing wages as *scutiferi* in Edward I's household; E. B. Fryde, ed., *Book of Prests*, pp. 25–27, 30–31, 47, 51, 164.

11. *Dictionary of Welsh Biography*, p. 319; Edwards, "Gruffydd Llwyd," pp. 589–600; CCR, *1302–7*, p. 505; CPR, *1307–13*, p. 82; CPR, *1324–27*, p. 325; Natalie Fryde, *Tyranny*, p. 128.

12. Wynne, *History*, p. 38. See also the poem of Iolo Goch, active in the second half of the fourteenth century, in Gwyn Williams, *Welsh Poems*, pp. 62–63.

Gregory Sais of Flintshire spent much of his life in English armies in France.[13]

For the most part, the Welsh role in English politics was restricted to such military service. But for a brief period in the reign of Edward II, the Welsh elites were allowed to play an important part in the affairs of the kingdom. This was due to the fact that the king alienated a large segment of the English nobility and found himself forced to depend to an unusual degree on Welsh support. Welsh hostility to some of the great English aristocrats involved in the governance of Wales and the March made them in turn willing to support the king. Among the chief enemies of the king in the 1320s were members of the Mortimer family, Roger Mortimer of Wigmore and Roger Mortimer of Chirk. Not only were these men Marcher lords, they were heavily involved in the governance of royal Wales, Mortimer of Chirk having been appointed in 1317 justice of all Wales for life.[14] His rule and the influence of his nephew, Mortimer of Wigmore, were unpopular with the Welsh.[15]

Hostility to the Mortimers caused many prominent Welshmen to rally to the king in the civil war of 1321 and 1322. Welsh support continued to be important to the king in the last years of his reign. Gruffydd Llwyd was one of those alerted in 1323 after Mortimer of Wigmore's escape from the Tower of London. When Mortimer and his paramour, Queen Isabella, returned to England to raise a rebellion late in 1326, it was to Glamorgan in South Wales that the king fled, there to be captured on 16 November 1326. Even after Edward had been captured by his enemies, many of his Welsh supporters remained loyal. Gruffydd Llwyd, summoned to the parliament at which the king was deposed, refused to attend.[16] In the summer of 1327 a number of Welshmen hatched a plot to rescue Edward from captivity.[17]

The Welsh role in the political life of the English kingdom may not have been insignificant during the unhappy reign of Edward II, but it was short-lived. With the accession of Edward III, the loyalties of the

13. Carr, "Welsh Knight," pp. 40–51, and "Welshmen," p. 30.
14. Waters, *Edwardian Settlement*, p. 47.
15. See *Cal. Anc. Pets.*, p. 30.
16. J. Beverley Smith, "Edward II," pp. 159–61, 166–67.
17. This plot may have been the goad that spurred the new regime to murder its embarrassing prisoner; Tout, "Captivity," p. 165. For other examples of Welshmen who remained loyal to Edward II, see Ralph A. Griffiths, *Principality*, p. 100, and Carr, *Medieval Anglesey*, pp. 247–48.

Welsh political elite no longer figured significantly in the calculations of English politicians. That men like Sir Gruffydd Llwyd had been able to take part in shaping the political destinies of England had been an aberration, a product of the crisis of authority during Edward II's reign. With the restoration of normal political life, the Welsh ceased to play a part in English affairs, other than as fodder for the royal military efforts in Scotland and France.

The Welsh Gentry and the Governance of Gwynedd

For much of the fourteenth century the political horizon of the Welsh was therefore rather narrowly limited to their own country. But to what extent were they allowed to participate in the governance of their native land and to share in the benefits that service to the crown could bring? There exist materials out of which a *Wallia Regia* could be constructed. Ralph Griffiths has already produced a large list of men who held office in South Wales in the later middle ages. Unfortunately no similar list of royal officials in Gwynedd has yet been published. Nevertheless the material assembled by Griffiths is very suggestive. Between the late 1270s and the middle of the fourteenth century, some 815 appointments were made to crown office in South Wales.[18] Of these, 531 (65.2 percent) went to individuals whose names indicate that they were ethnically Welsh.

The situation in Gwynedd seems to have been similar. It is beyond the scope of this work to produce an exhaustive list of Welshmen who held crown office in the north. Nevertheless, there is readily accessible certain material that gives an indication of the extent of Welsh participation in royal government. In his account for the year 1303–4, the sheriff of Caernarfon listed 16 Welsh rhingylliaid and rhaglawiaid, 9 Welsh woodwards and 6 Welsh farmers of amobr fines.[19] In 1343 an inquiry carried out by agents of Edward the Black Prince revealed that in the Principality of North Wales there were one sheriff, one coroner, two woodwards, two rhingylliaid and three rhaglawiaid who were Welsh.[20]

18. This figure includes individuals who served as deputies or lieutenants of the actual office holders. Since some men held more than one office, the actual number of individuals who held crown appointment during this period was less than 815.

19. Waters, "Account," pp. 147–49.

20. "Roll of Fealty," pp. cliii, clvi, clxviii–clxix.

Given the significant differences between medieval Welsh and English culture, it is not surprising that the Welsh came to have a strong hold on the lower levels of the royal administration. Of the 598 appointments made before 1350 in South Wales to offices other than those of justice, chamberlain, sheriff, or constable of a major castle, 498, or 83.3 percent, went to men who seem to have been ethnically Welsh. In the Principality of North Wales the surviving records reveal no shortage of Welsh officials on the local level.[21]

The Welsh may have had a strong grip on the lower levels of the royal administration in Gwynedd, but higher office was for a long time largely closed to them. The two most important offices in the principality were those of justice and chamberlain of the exchequer of Caernarfon. None of the thirty-three men appointed to one of these offices between 1284 and 1343 was Welsh. Similarly, of the fourteen men who served as controller of the chamberlain of North Wales, none was Welsh.[22] It was unusual for Welshmen to command any of the great fortresses built by Edward I. Only two natives did so before 1382.[23] Welshmen were more successful in securing appointment to the office of sheriff. Of the thirty-five men who served as sheriff of either Anglesey, Caernarfonshire, or Merioneth between the conquest and 1343, eight (22.9 percent) were ethnically Welsh.[24] In the fourteenth century as a whole, only nine Welshmen held office as sheriff of Anglesey.[25] Of the twenty-five sheriffs of Caernarfonshire between 1286 and 1399, six were Welsh. In Merioneth three of the twelve sheriffs between 1283 and 1400 were Welsh.[26] In the new Marcher lordships in Gwynedd Is Conwy, there seems to have been a similar desire to keep Welshmen away from the most important administrative posts. In the lordship of Denbigh, for example, between 1297 and

21. For some examples, see *CCR, 1313–18*, pp. 109, 152; *CCR, 1323–27*, pp. 24, 205; *CPR, 1317–21*, pp. 502, 525; *Cal. Anc. Pets.*, pp. 64, 132, 440–41; and *BPR*, 1:67–68, 155. In some gentry families service to the crown became something of a tradition. For examples, see Carr, "Medieval Gloddaith," pp. 12–21, "Aristocracy," p. 117, and "Barons," pp. 290–91.

22. Waters, *Edwardian Settlement*, pp. 168–70.

23. One of these held office for only five days. See Edward A. Lewis, *Mediaeval Boroughs*, p. 149 (n. 4); Griffiths, *Principality*, p. 112; Tout, *Chapters*, 6:60, 63.

24. See Waters, *Edwardian Settlement*, pp. 171–73.

25. Carr, *Medieval Anglesey*, p. 77.

26. Great Britain, PRO, *List of Sheriffs*, pp. 236, 248, 260.

1424 no Welshman served as steward or receiver; between 1344 and 1424 none was named constable of Denbigh castle.[27]

If Welshmen were largely excluded from high office, this did not mean that they had exclusive control over the minor posts open to them. Englishmen, or at least ethnically English burgesses from the fortified plantation boroughs, managed to secure control of many lesser crown offices. In his account for the fiscal year 1303–4, the sheriff of Caernarfonshire listed twenty-one rhaglawiaid and rhi-ngylliaid in his bailiwick, five of whom were English. Furthermore, one of the ten woodwards the sheriff named was English, as was one of the seven farmers of the county's amobr fines.[28] Similarly, of the fourteen men who were holding the office of woodward in 1343, twelve were English. In that same year nine of the eleven recorded rhi-ngylliaid were English, as were ten of the thirteen rhaglawiaid.[29]

The role that the natives of Gwynedd played in the new royal administration of their country thus appears to have been limited.[30] In part the failure of the Welsh elites to secure access to the commanding heights of the royal administration can be attributed to the fact that few Welshmen at the time of the conquest possessed the technical skills necessary to occupy positions of trust in the new administration. Native governing institutions were less developed than their English counterparts. Service in the relatively elaborate accounting, writing, and judicial departments of the English government required a higher degree of training and intellectual discipline than many members of the Welsh elite could command on the morrow of the conquest. This, of course, was a factor that weighed less heavily with the passage of time. The Welsh were eager to acquire new skills, as can be seen by the alacrity with which they strove to enter the royal household or to attend the English universities.

More important in the long run than the relative lack of skills necessary for royal service was the fact that the English did not trust the Welsh. The crown often tried to prevent Welshmen from securing

27. David Huw Owen, "Lordship," pp. 293–94.
28. Waters, "Account," pp. 147–49.
29. Figures derived from "Roll of Fealty." See also the material on officeholding by Englishmen in Carr, *Medieval Anglesey*, pp. 78–79, 82–83.
30. In the fifteenth century, after the failure of the Glyndŵr rebellion, Welshmen were even more rigorously debarred from office. See Carr, *Medieval Anglesey*, pp. 78–79, 84.

positions of power and influence. It appears that in the aftermath of a rebellion that took place in 1294 and 1295, Edward I issued an ordinance barring Welshmen from royal office.[31] This decree was not consistently enforced, but the spirit of mistrust that it embodied lived on among the English. For example, in 1309 Edward II's councillors wrote to the justice of Wales to express their concern about the number of Welshmen who were acquiring royal office. They instructed him that henceforth sheriffs, bailiffs, and other officers "be not Welshmen if he can find Englishmen there sufficient to execute those offices."[32]

In later decades the crown became rather more uneasy about the holding of important posts by Welshmen. In December 1330 Gruffydd, son of William de la Pole and a member of the baronial family of Powys, was appointed sheriff of Merioneth, only to be removed from office within a few weeks. On 20 February 1331 the justice of North Wales was ordered to seize the shrievalty of Merioneth into the king's hands, if it was being held by anyone other than an Englishman, and to entrust it to Richard de Holand.[33] In the late 1340s Roland Deneys, keeper of the southern fortress of Cardigan and steward of Cardiganshire, appointed Adda ap Llywelyn Fychan as his lieutenant. In 1348 the Black Prince, observing that Adda's appointment was "in contravention of the ordinance made by Edward I, on his conquest of Wales that no Welshman should have the keeping of a castle or other office of charge in those parts," ordered Deneys to remove him.[34] Similarly, when in 1347 the Black Prince granted the burgesses of Newborough the right to elect a mayor, he stipulated that they must select an Englishman, despite the fact that the majority of the town's inhabitants were Welsh.[35] The middle of the fourteenth century also saw action taken against Welsh burgesses in the castle towns of North Wales. In 1337 three burgages held by Welshmen in Cricieth were seized into the king's hand. About 1345 the liberties of Beaumaris, most of whose burgesses were Welsh, were suspended on the grounds that they were intended for Englishmen.[36]

31. No copy of this ordinance has survived. However, there are frequent references to it in later years, for example in *BPR*, 1:159–60. See also Ralph A. Griffiths, *Principality*, pp. xviii–xix.

32. *CCR, 1307–13*, pp. 88–89.

33. Great Britain, PRO, *Calendar of the Fine Rolls, 1327–37*, p. 236.

34. *BPR*, 1:159–60.

35. *BPR*, 1:155.

36. Carr, *Medieval Anglesey*, pp. 248–49.

The Rewards of Royal Service

Although the Welsh were largely excluded from occupying the highest offices in the principality, many nevertheless spent long years in the service of king or prince. The question naturally arises as to what they gained from this service. The answer seems to be something, but not too much.

It is clear that the big prizes in Gwynedd were reserved for individuals who were not Welsh. In the fourteenth century the man who was most munificently rewarded by the crown with offices and revenues in North Wales was Sir Walter de Mauny, who probably never set foot in the country. A native of Brabant in the Low Countries, Walter made a successful career in England. In 1332 he received a life grant of the shrievalty of Merioneth, an office he held until his death in 1372. In 1341 he was permitted to retain for his own use most of the county revenues.[37] This was certainly the largest grant made to an individual who was not a member of the royal family. But other members of the royal entourage did well in Gwynedd. In 1353, for example, the Black Prince gave to Sir John of Saint Peter lands in Anglesey worth £111 19s. 0½d. a year, to be held by him for life.[38]

For the Welsh the cornucopia of royal patronage produced less striking rewards. This is not to say that they were so trivial as to be not worth pursuing. The Hendwr branch of the barons of Edeirnion found their service rewarded in the 1330s with a charter allowing Gruffydd ap Madog and his heirs to hold a weekly market and an annual fair at Llandrillo.[39] Some Welshmen received annual fees levied on the exchequer at Caernarfon.[40]

The profits of office were themselves nothing to be scorned. Most of the lesser posts in the royal administration in Gwynedd, those which were most likely to find their way into Welsh hands, were let at fixed farms; that is, the office holder contracted to pay a fixed sum every

---

37. D. L. Evans, "Walter de Mauny," pp. 194–97.
38. *BPR*, 3:123–24.
39. *CChR, 1327–41*, pp. 307, 328.
40. For examples see *CPR, 1317–21*, pp. 342, 344; *CCR, 1327–30*, pp. 76, 193, 281, 455; Natalie Fryde, ed., *Welsh Entries*, no. 656; *CCR, 1318–23*, p. 76. Royal offices could also be let to favorites at advantageous farms. For an example, see *CCR, 1323–27*, p. 205. Royal lands were also entrusted to deserving Welshmen for low rents or no rents at all. For some examples, see *Cal. Anc. Corr.*, p. 209; *Cal. Anc. Pets.*, p. 62; *Cal. Var.*, p. 288; *CPR, 1313–17*, p. 355; *CPR, 1317–21*, p. 499.

year. In return he was allowed to keep whatever excess he managed to collect. It is next to impossible to gauge what level of reward an office holder in Gwynedd could expect to derive from his public responsibilities, but at times there must have been a handy profit to be made. An inquiry made in 1343 reveals that royal offices were often worth a good deal more than the farms paid for them.[41]

The rewards of office were not necessarily all financial or all strictly legal. A royal post gave its incumbent the opportunity to manipulate crown authority for his own ends. This could take the fairly benign form of securing leases on advantageous terms or ensuring that the petitions of friends and relatives obtained a favorable hearing. Possession of royal office could, however, allow one to pursue a rewarding career of peculation. Cynwrig Sais, from 1336 to 1339 rhaglaw of Tegeingl in the county of Flint, flagrantly abused his position, making false indictments, harassing the bishop of Saint Asaph, demanding exorbitant fees, levying wrongful reliefs, and extracting enormous corn dues from the people of Tegeingl.[42]

Cynwrig was not the only royal servant to vex the people of Tegeingl. In 1358 the commote's liege men complained to the Black Prince concerning the high-handed behavior of his agents. According to the petition, the king's escheator had seized lands and rents without any legal process. The local rhaglaw had extorted double reliefs from those individuals unfortunate enough to have lost the tallies they had received when they originally made fine to inherit their ancestors' estates. Together with the sheriff, he had imposed illegally heavy amercements on those convicted of petty trespasses. The two officials had also formed a "confederacy of false presenters, swearers and accusers," which they used to procure indictments of individuals who were then afflicted with "great fines and ransoms" as punishment for their imaginary felonies and trespasses. The sheriff, Rhys ap Roppert, and his predecessor, Ithel ap Cynwrig, were also accused of packing juries with their kinsmen, allies, and special friends. According to the petitioners, the sheriff, when carrying out his tourns, "browbeats his inquests, makes threats, false suggestions and other insinuating speeches in front of the jurors, and causes them in one point or another to leave the truth and present what is false on account of the

---

41. "Roll of Fealty," pp. clxix–clxx.
42. D. L. Evans, ed., *Flintshire Ministers' Accounts*, pp. xxii–xxviii.

fear they have of him and the confederacy mentioned above." The petitioners also accused the commote rhingylliaid of various malversations. In August they were said to demand that the men of Tegeingl reap and carry their corn. During the winter and Lenten plowing seasons they extorted gifts of seed corn. And in the summer they requisitioned lambs and wool.[43]

An ambitious and pushing uchelwr undoubtedly found the extra coins he obtained through farming the office of rhaglaw, rhingyll, or woodward a pleasant addition to his budget. The influence, whether for good or ill, that could be obtained by holding crown office was also nothing to be despised. The profits of royal office in Gwynedd should not, however, be exaggerated. Income derived from royal service may have been a valuable supplement to the fortunes of the Welsh political elite, but it was not a road to riches. Service to the crown allowed some lucky Welshmen to siphon off part of the surplus extracted from the local economy by the English administration. It rarely enabled them to acquire extensive lands or authority over tenants, the real source of economic well-being and political influence in medieval Europe. The descendants of Ednyfed Fychan—despite the fact that one of them, Gruffydd Llwyd, was among Edward II's strongest supporters in Gwynedd—did not do very well out of royal service. By the end of the fourteenth century their power and influence had declined drastically.[44] The grants of land that Welshmen received from the crown were almost always temporary. Although some Welshmen held royal manors, the government preferred to give such leases to Englishmen. For example, in 1343 only three of the eighteen men who were recorded as farmers of royal manors and mills were Welsh, and the estates in their custody do not appear to have been very profitable. By far the wealthiest royal manors were in the hands of Englishmen.[45]

The material rewards of office holding in the principality therefore seem to have been rather modest as far as the Welsh were concerned.

43. BPR, 3:318–22.

44. Roberts, "Wyrion Eden," p. 197. This is not to say that the acquisition of land was impossible for Welshmen in the fourteenth century. Escheat records from early fifteenth-century Anglesey show that some of those who forfeited property to the crown because of their participation in the Glyndŵr rebellion had amassed estates of some seventy to eighty acres. (Carr, Medieval Anglesey, p. 175.) These accumulations are not to be despised, but they still would have put their holders into only the lower ranks of the English gentry.

45. "Roll of Fealty," pp. clxvii–clxviii, clxx.

Indeed, for some, royal office could prove a disaster. Even Sir Gruffydd Llwyd, one of the more prominent of King Edward II's servants, spent several periods as a captive in the king's prisons.[46] He was not the only Welsh royal servant to languish in a royal jail. Cynwrig ap Gruffydd, sheriff of Anglesey in the 1330s, died during a captivity that was probably the result of unpaid arrears owed to the king's treasury.[47]

Welsh office holders often found themselves vexed about the size of the farms they owed to the Caernarfon exchequer.[48] Some, indeed, were overwhelmed by their debts to the treasury. Late in the reign of Edward II, Ieuan ap Trahaearn, rhingyll of Nantconwy commote in Caernarfonshire, was £21 10s. behind in his payments. Thanks to a cattle murrain and other misfortunes, he claimed that he could not pay his debt without selling some of his lands and tenements.[49] Iorwerth Foel, rhingyll of Eifionydd commote in Caernarfonshire, experienced similar difficulties. In the early 1320s he informed Edward II that he was £32 in arrears on his account. He asked that he might be allowed to discharge this debt by means of annual payments of 40s. "Otherwise," as he put it, "he will be destroyed for ever."[50]

The material we have examined points to the following conclusion: the coming of English overlordship in Gwynedd resulted in a process of marginalization for the local political elites.[51] During the wars of conquest the native political hierarchy was decapitated. Some members of the Welsh political elite who survived the conquest were acknowledged by the new English regime to be of baronial status. But, compared to the barons of England, their wealth and influence was unimpressive. Throughout the first generations of royal rule, members of this group found access to positions of authority and responsibility within the English kingdom denied them. Within Gwynedd itself the Welsh elite occupied a secondary position in royal government. The highest ranks of royal officialdom were, until the end of the fourteenth century, largely closed to them. The Welsh enjoyed more success in entering the lower levels of the administration. But even for these posts

46. J. G. Edwards, "Gruffydd Llwyd," pp. 596–97.
47. Fryde, ed., *Welsh Entries*, no. 996.
48. For examples, see Fryde, ed., *Welsh Entries*, no. 144; *RC*, p. 219; *CCR, 1313–18*, p. 544; *Cal. Anc. Pets.*, pp. 454–55.
49. *Cal. Anc. Pets.*, p. 110. See also pp. 58–59 for another rhingyll who in the 1320s was unable to pay his dues to the crown.
50. *Cal. Anc. Pets.*, pp. 115–16.
51. A point that is made by Carr in "Aristocracy," p. 128.

they had to compete with Englishmen. Royal service had its rewards, whether in money or influence, for those who secured crown office. These rewards, however, seem to have been rather modest on the whole. The native officeholder who in the first century of English rule in Gwynedd managed to translate royal service into a significant enlargement of his landed patrimony was a rare individual. Before 1277 the members of the Welsh political elite, as unprepossessing as they may seem compared with those of other regions of contemporary Europe, were the masters of their country. After 1284 they were at best the junior partners of the English in the governance and exploitation of their native land.

Languedoc

In considering the fate of the leading classes of Languedoc under the French regime, it must be remembered that these groups differed significantly from their Welsh counterparts. In Gwynedd the native political elite did not cut a very impressive figure. Little concentration of wealth or authority had taken place before the English conquest. In Languedoc, however, the French monarchy had to deal with groups that were well endowed with wealth and authority. Within the area organized into the sénéchaussées of Toulouse, Carcassonne, and Beaucaire, the most powerful of the local aristocratic houses were eliminated as a result of the Albigensian crusades. But a numerous middling and lesser nobility survived. On the fringes of the sénéchaussées, there remained entrenched a number of powerful dynasties. In addition to this secular aristocracy, Languedoc also contained important town corporations and ecclesiastical lordships, many of which emerged from the early thirteenth-century wars with their authority enhanced.

The Languedocian Aristocracy
and the French Kingdom

Given these facts, it is not surprising that the native elites of Languedoc played a much different role in the polity of the French kingdom than did the people of Gwynedd in the English kingdom. For example, the great aristocratic houses of the south were very active in the politics not only of their own region but of the kingdom as a whole. During the Albigensian crusades the counts of Foix had been among the most determined enemies of the crusaders and the French kings. Although their loyalty remained problematic throughout much of the thirteenth and fourteenth centuries, they quickly became major figures on the French political scene. Roger Bernard III took part in Philip III's campaign against Aragon in 1285. Under Philip IV he was active in the Gascon wars and was named governor of the dioceses of Auch, Aire, Dax, and Bayonne, which had been seized from the English. Gaston I took part in campaigns against the Flemings in 1304 and 1315. Gaston II continued the tradition of military service. In 1324 he served against the English in Gascony. In 1328 he was at the battle of Cassel in Flanders. In the late 1330s he again served in Gascony. In 1338 he went north to Amiens to help ward off a threatened English invasion of the kingdom. With the title of captain-general, he returned to Gascony. In 1339 and 1340 he was back in the north, where he defended Tournai against the English. His son, Gaston Fébus, twice held the title of lieutenant-general in Languedoc.[52]

The counts of Armagnac, whose principal estates lay to the west of Toulouse on the borders of Gascony, also served regularly in royal armies. In 1352 Jean I of Armagnac was named lieutenant-general of Languedoc. He also campaigned in Normandy. When the treaty of Brétigny transferred his allegiance to the English, he participated in the Black Prince's 1367 Nájera campaign. But in 1369 he took part in the revolt against English overlordship. Jean II also led an active military career in service to the French kings, campaigning in Gascony, Burgundy, and the Rouergue. Count Bernard VII (1391–1418), named constable of France after the battle of Agincourt in 1415, was until his assassination the effective ruler of the kingdom. The lords of the Pyrenean county of Comminges were also active in French armies. In 1319 Count Bernard VIII was named royal captain on the frontiers of Flanders.[53] Pierre-Raimond I (1339–42) fought for the king in Gascony, Flanders, and Hainault. Pierre-Raimond II supported the French until the treaty of Brétigny transferred his allegiance to the English. He served in the Black Prince's Castilian campaign in 1367. In 1369, like the count of Armagnac, he revolted against the English

---

52. *Dictionnaire*, 14:190–94; Castillon, *Histoire*, 1:363–64; Tucoo-Chala, *Gaston Fébus*, p. 59; *HL*, 9:503.
53. *Regs.*, vol. 2, no. 2673.

and took an active role in French military operations during the next few years.

Some of the more prominent Languedocian aristocrats maintained important ties with rulers outside the French kingdom. This was especially true of the counts of Foix, with their interests in Gascony (where in 1290 they inherited the viscounty of Béarn) and Spain. Roger Bernard in the 1270s and 1280s fought the count of Ampurias, the bishop of Urgel, and the king of Aragon over his rights in lordships south of the Pyrenees. Gaston II went to Spain to aid the king of Castile in his war against the Moslems of Morocco. Indeed, he died in Seville in 1343 of an illness he had contracted during the siege of Algeciras. In 1358 Gaston III helped the Teutonic Order wage war against the grand-duke of Lithuania.[54]

Members of less exalted local families also played a significant role in French politics, among them representatives of the house of L'Isle-Jourdain. Jourdain IV, who inherited the lordship in 1240, took part in Charles of Anjou's effort to seize the kingdom of Sicily, became one of Charles's councillors, and participated in the 1285 invasion of Aragon.[55] Other members of the family served in royal armies and held office as seneschal of Beaucaire and Gascony and captain of the Flemish frontier.[56] The viscounts of Narbonne also regularly served in royal armies.[57]

Despite their active participation in French affairs, the greater nobles of the Midi were not merely clients of the king. They served because to do so was to their advantage. Some were more than capable, during the turbulence of the Hundred Years' War, of pursuing their own interests at the expense of the king. This was especially true of Gaston Fébus of Foix. He took advantage of the war to try to build up a territorial state stretching through the Pyrenees from Béarn to Foix. On a less exalted level, Gui de Comminges obstinately defied the royal government. From the early 1320s his claims to his mother's inheritance in the Albigeois brought him into conflict with the house of L'Isle-Jourdain and the countess of Vendôme. For nearly thirty

---

54. Tucoo-Chala, *Gaston Fébus: Un grand prince*, pp. 29–30.

55. Dossat, ed., *Saisimentum*, p. 87 (n. 3); Régné, *Amauri II*, p. 52.

56. *Regs.*, vol. 2, no. 2673; *RHF*, 24:222*.

57. Aymeri V took part in the 1285 Aragon expedition. Amauri II participated in Charles of Anjou's wars in Italy. In 1369 Aymeri IX received the title of admiral of France; *Dictionnaire*, 1:991–93; Régné, *Amauri II*, pp. 52–85.

years, despite repeated royal prohibitions, Gui, the "little king of the Albigeois," intermittently waged war against his neighbors.[58]

Faced with such a powerful, locally dominant class, it is not surprising that the monarchy was careful to conciliate and placate it. The service and allegiance of the great southern aristocrats, whether shaky or firm, were rewarded with ample gifts. The counts of Foix received liberal rewards for their services, or at least for their benevolent neutrality. When Roger Bernard did homage to Louis IX in 1229, he was granted rents worth 1,000l.t. a year.[59] Because of his usefulness to the crown, Roger Bernard III was allowed to keep the viscounty of Béarn, which he had acquired in 1290, despite the competing claims of the count of Armagnac. In 1298 he was also granted the right to collect the tolls of Béziers.[60] Gaston I was sufficiently highly regarded by the crown to be allowed to marry Jeanne d'Artois, a member of the royal family. More concretely, in 1303 Gaston was confirmed in his possession of Béarn and given Saint-Gaudens and the Nébouzan. In 1338 Gaston II received, in return for his services against the English, the viscounty of Lautrec.[61] Undoubtedly the most powerful of the counts of Foix was Gaston III Fébus, who also married into the French royal family, wedding Agnes de Navarre, daughter of Philippe d'Evreux, king of Navarre and descendant of Philip III. In 1390 Charles VI had to buy this dangerous magnate's benevolence with 100,000 francs and the county of Bigorre.[62]

Other aristocratic houses also received their share of rewards. When the count of Armagnac revolted against the English in 1369, he was given the counties of Bigorre and Gaure. The lords of L'Isle-Jourdain in 1306 were allowed to appropriate for their own use some of the property the king had seized from the Jews. In the 1340s Bertrand de L'Isle-Jourdain received from Philip VI various properties located in the Agenais.[63] In 1341 the king elevated the lordship to the status of a county.

The kings found it wise to regularly consult the opinions of their Languedocian subjects. Whereas English kings only summoned repre-

---

58. *HL*, 9:568 (n. 2).
59. *Layettes*, vol. 2, no. 2019.
60. Castillon, *Histoire*, 1:369.
61. *Regs.*, vol. 3/1, no. 2292.
62. Tucoo-Chala, *Gaston Fébus*, pp. 333–34.
63. *Regs.*, vol. 3/1, nos. 2487, 2490–91; *HL*, 10: *Preuves*, cols. 913–14, 916–17.

sentatives of the Welsh laity to two parliaments in the fourteenth century, French kings frequently called the politically important groups of Languedoc to take part in royal assemblies. Within the sénéchaussées of Languedoc, conclaves were periodically held to discuss such matters as the prohibition of grain exports from the region.[64] Languedocians were also called to general assemblies of the entire kingdom.[65] Between 1305 and 1345, representatives from the southern sénéchaussées were called to eight assemblies in the north of France and to another six meetings in Languedoc itself.[66]

Languedocians and the Government of the French Kingdom

The French monarchy was willing not only to consult Languedocians, it was also prepared to recruit them into the ranks of its administrative agents. A definitive answer to the question of how many men from Languedoc were royal servants and what offices they held would require an exhaustive study of the personnel of royal government, a task that transcends the scope of this essay. Enough evidence, however, can readily be assembled to show that, although there was no massive influx of Languedocians into the higher levels of royal administration, southerners were not uncommon among the ranks of the king's servants.

Languedocians pursuing careers in the king's central government in Paris were never very numerous. During the middle decades of the thirteenth century, Louis IX preferred to draw his closest councillors from among the ranks of those men born in the old royal domain centered on Paris and Orléans.[67] His successors were more open to employing men from other regions of the kingdom, although they continued to show a preference for men from the old royal domain. Of the 145 individuals whom J. R. Strayer has identified as having served Philip IV in high-ranking positions, the majority were from the old

---

64. *HL*, 10: *Preuves*, cols. 587–89.
65. For example, among those summoned in 1302 by Philip the Fair to the great meeting at Paris at which his agents tried to inflame public opinion against Pope Boniface VIII were the count of Comminges, the viscount of Narbonne, the lord of L'Isle-Jourdain, and representatives of various towns; *HL*, 9:229–31.
66. Dognon, *Institutions*, pp. 202–3.
67. Quentin Griffiths, "New Men," p. 246.

domain; only nine (6.2 percent) were natives of Languedoc.[68] It is clear that Languedocians did not dominate the central organs of royal government. But, in contrast to the experience of Welshmen, there were at least some who were close to the king. Indeed, among the most powerful and influential of Philip IV's advisers was a native of the Toulousain, Guillaume de Nogaret. This Languedocian played a key role in some of the great affairs of the reign, directing the assault on Boniface VIII at Anagni and helping bring about the destruction of the Templars.[69]

Southerners served not only in the great offices of state, but in other posts in the royal administration of northern France. Guillaume de la Barrière, in addition to the positions he held in Languedoc, was also governor of the bailliage of Vermandois.[70] Peire-Raimond de Rabastens, although much of his career was spent in the south, where he was seneschal of Bigorre, also held posts further north. In the 1320s he was bailli of Amiens and in the 1330s seneschal of Poitou.[71] Peire de Roquenégade served as a royal procurator in negotiations with the Flemings in 1317.[72] Men from Languedoc were also entrusted with military commands outside Languedoc. In 1317 Guilhem de Carsan was castellan of La Royère (Creuse) and Raimond de Tourouzelle was in charge of Cassel in Flanders.[73] Jean de Burlas, son of a seneschal of Carcassonne and master of the king's arbalesters, died fighting the Flemings at Courtrai in 1302.[74]

Languedocians and the Royal Government of Languedoc

Not surprisingly, men from Languedoc were more strongly represented in the local government of Languedoc than in the kingdom's central government. Unfortunately no one has yet compiled a list of royal servants in Languedoc comparable to that produced by Ralph

---

68. Among the 112 men who held less important royal posts in Paris, only six (5.4 percent) came from Languedoc and the Auvergne; Strayer, *Reign*, pp. 42–43.

69. On Nogaret, see Favier, *Philippe*, pp. 29–35; Pegues, *Lawyers*, pp. 99–101; Holtzmann, *Wilhelm von Nogaret*; and Louis Thomas, "Vie," pp. 161–207.

70. Cazelles, *Société*, pp. 267–68.

71. *Regs.*, vol. 2, no. 3469; vol. 3/1, nos. 1152, 1439.

72. In 1318 he was a member of the Parlement of Paris; *RHF*, 24:195*.

73. *Regs.*, vol. 2, nos. 385, 355.

74. Friedlander, "Administration," p. 295. See also p. 146.

Griffiths for the southern half of the Principality of Wales.[75] The materials out of which such a list could be constructed, however, are not hard to come by. Letters issued by the royal chancery during the reign of Philip IV contain the names of 164 men who were royal officials in Languedoc.[76] Of this number the geographic origin of ninety-five can be identified with reasonable certainty. Forty-six (48.4 percent) were natives of Languedoc. Financial accounts also allow us to see who held crown office. The 1293–94 account for the sénéchaussée of Toulouse names 188 royal employees. Of these, the origins of ninety-five can be identified. Fifty-nine (62.1 percent) were Languedocians. Similarly, the 1298–99 account for this same sénéchaussée mentions 203 officials.[77] Of the ninety-six whose origins can be identified, fifty-six (58.3 percent) originated in Languedoc.

Many of the lesser nobles of the region sought to advance their careers by a period of royal service. For example, the first native Languedocian to become a seneschal was Guilhem de Pia, placed in charge of the sénéchaussée of Carcassonne in 1248.[78] Rostaing Payrier, the co-seigneur of Bagnoles, was in the early fourteenth century juge mage and lieutenant of the seneschal of Carcassonne.[79] Orri de l'Anglade from the Toulousain was in the reign of Philip IV castellan of the fortress of Le Fousseret.[80] Pons d'Aumelas, a royal knight and doctor of laws, had a long career in royal service in the early fourteenth century: juge mage of the sénéchaussées of the Rouergue and Toulouse, réformateur in that of Carcassonne, and member of the Parlement of Paris. He was entrusted with such important affairs as the investigation of the dispute between the countess of Vendôme and the family of the count of Comminges concerning property in the Albigeois.[81] Similarly, Bertrand de Roquenégade was a valued servant of the crown. He served as seneschal of Saintonge from 1312 to 1316,

75. A beginning, however, has been made: See Strayer, *Gens*, together with the addenda and corrigenda of Maillard, "A Propos," pp. 325–58; Rogozinski, *Power*, pp. 146–61, 171; and Friedlander, "Administration," pp. 264–483.

76. This figure does not include royal notaries.

77. Fawtier and Maillard, eds., *Comptes*, 1:432–95, 524–92.

78. Friedlander, "Administration," pp. 15–17.

79. *Regs.*, vol. 2, nos. 1445, 2043.

80. Dossat, ed., *Saisimentum*, p. 98 (n. 1).

81. Boutaric, ed., *Actes*, vol. 2, no. 4565; *HL*, 9:409 (n. 1); *Regs.*, vol. 2, no. 2139; vol. 3/1, no. 2357; Strayer, *Gens*, pp. 149–50; Langlois, "Pons d'Aumelas," pp. 259–62.

was often employed on judicial matters and was consulted on such affairs as Philip V's plans for a crusade.[82]

There was in the thirteenth century, however, a tendency for the higher levels of the royal administration in Languedoc to be reserved for men recruited among the nobility of northern France. Of the thirty-two men who served as seneschals of either Beaucaire, Carcassonne, or Toulouse during the reign of Philip the Fair, only six (18.8 percent) may have been natives of Languedoc.[83] Southerners were, however, better represented among the ranks of viguiers. Of the approximately sixty men known to have held this post during the reign of Philip IV, twenty-two were from Languedoc; only ten were northerners.[84]

Other offices in the region were heavily staffed with natives. In the receivers' account for the sénéchaussée of Toulouse for 1293–94, seven of the ten judges whose place of origin can be determined came from Languedoc. Half of the twelve judges and notaries whose origins can be determined mentioned in the 1298–99 account for this sénéchaussée were Languedocians.[85] Not surprisingly the lower levels of the royal administration were heavily infiltrated by southerners. Of the eighteen bayles listed in the account of the sénéchaussée of Toulouse for 1293–94 whose origins can be determined, sixteen were from Languedoc. In the 1298–99 account, eight of the twenty-four bayles named can be safely regarded as Languedocians; none of the remaining sixteen can be identified as a native of northern France.[86] Men from the Midi were also found in significant numbers among the ranks of royal castellans. In 1293–94 nine of the twenty-five castellans recorded in the sénéchaussée of Toulouse can be identified as south-

82. *Regs.*, vol. 2, no. 2653; Boutaric, ed., *Actes*, vol. 2, nos. 4702, 5015, 5330, 5473, 5506, 5533, 5590, 5819; *RHF*, 24:195*.

83. These figures are derived from Strayer, *Gens*, pp. 49–53, 99–101, 166–67. From 1266 to 1320 only three of the seneschals of Carcassonne were southerners; Friedlander, "Administration," p. 138. In the fourteenth and fifteenth centuries 28 percent of the seneschals of Beaucaire, Carcassonne, Toulouse, and the Rouergue were Languedocians; Chague, "Contribution," pp. 361–62.

84. Strayer, "Viscounts," p. 220.

85. Of the thirty-seven judges in the sénéchaussée of Carcassonne between 1266 and 1320 whose origins can be identified, only one was a northerner; Friedlander, "Administration," pp. 184–85.

86. Friedlander has argued that most bayles in the sénéchaussée of Carcassonne were local burgesses; "Administration," pp. 102–3, 204.

erners; of the rest, eight can unambiguously be assigned an origin outside the region. Similarly, in the 1298–99 account ten of the twenty-seven castellans listed can be assigned an origin in the Midi; only seven can definitely be regarded as not native to the south.

The Rewards of Royal Service

The preceding evidence suggests that offices of importance in royal government were relatively more open to Languedocians than to Welshmen. Royal service may also have been more rewarding for Languedocians. Whereas the English crown was sparing with its patronage of Welshmen, the French kings were more generous to their southern subjects. An exact count of the monarchy's gifts to its Languedocian servants and favorites is, unfortunately, impossible. Such grants, however, seem to have been fairly common. In 1318 one of the reasons advanced by royal enquêteurs for canceling a pariage agreement with the viscount of Narbonne concerning the castrum of Laure was the fact that the king and his predecessors had already granted away so many localities in the viguerie of the Minervois that there was no longer any place left where the viguier or the judge could hold their assizes.[87]

The letters preserved by the French chancery give some indication of the scope of royal generosity. By my count, which is based on a survey of the printed guides to the registers and which is probably incomplete, a minimum of seventy-seven royal grants to Languedocians in return for their services were recorded between 1285 and 1347. These varied dramatically in importance. Some of the more impressive grants made to the greater local aristocrats have been touched on above. Other royal gifts could be fairly minor, such as the right granted in 1321 to Etienne Lombart of Moissac to collect dead wood in the forest of Gandalou.[88] Although the crown was reluctant to grant estates outright as fiefs, a number of its more important favorites did receive such gifts.[89] Much more common, however, seem to have been gifts of rents and pensions, which constituted 27.3 percent of the grants recorded by the royal chancery between 1285 and 1347.[90]

87. *Regs.*, vol. 2, no. 1927.
88. *Regs.*, vol. 2, no. 3509.
89. For examples, see *Regs.*, vol. 2, nos. 1658, 2842–43; vol. 3/1, no. 29.
90. For examples, see *Regs.*, vol. 1, nos. 1136–37; vol. 2, no. 1347.

As one might expect, the rewards of royal service were not limited to fees and gifts. The ability to manipulate royal authority to serve one's own ends was undoubtedly one of the more attractive aspects of service to the crown. Indeed, given the differing levels of institutional development attained by the French and English monarchies, French royal oversight of its local officials was perhaps less thorough than English. Accordingly, royal servants in Languedoc may have enjoyed greater latitude in making their posts serve their own needs than did their counterparts in Gwynedd. For example, during the anti-inquisitorial agitation that disturbed Languedoc shortly after 1300, one of the more inveterate enemies of the inquisitors and their ally, the bishop of Albi, was Guilhem de Pezens of Montgiscard, the royal viguier at Albi.[91] When some of the townspeople of Albi refused to contribute to the taxes levied by the consuls to support their campaign against the bishop and the inquisitors, Guilhem used his authority to force them to pay up.[92]

Guilhem's deputy, Peire Nicholay, also used his authority to thwart the work of the inquisitors. When, in the summer of 1303, the royal enquêteur Jean de Picquigny removed a number of Albigeois who had been found guilty of heresy from the inquisitors' prison in Carcassonne, he was excommunicated. In the town of Castres the duty of publishing the anathema fell on Peire de Recoles, a stipendiary priest. For his pains, he was arrested by Nicholay. Nicholay ordered him to revoke the sentence of excommunication. Should he refuse, he was told, he would be removed to Albi and lodged in such a place that he would gladly comply. When the archpriest of Albi finally came to retrieve Recoles, Nicholay refused to release him until he had had a document drawn up prohibiting the priest from leaving the viguerie of Albi.[93]

Such intimate glimpses of royal officials wielding their authority to help their friends are unfortunately all too rare. We are much better informed about those men who exploited their positions in a criminal manner and consequently ran afoul of the king's government. For example, in the late 1260s Raimond Martin was using his position as bayle of Pezens to acquire property fraudulently. In 1317 Arnal La Roque, clavier of the king at Montréal, was accused of embezzle-

91. Bernard Gui, *De fundatione*, pp. 203–4.
92. BN, Ms. Lat. 4270, fol. 266r.
93. Hauréau, *Bernard Délicieux*, pp. 176–87.

ment.[94] In 1319 Hugues du Sourniès, a former royal treasurer at Carcassonne, offered the king's enquêteurs 2,000l.t to be pardoned for bribery and counterfeiting.[95] In 1322 François Luliani, a royal notary of Béziers, was prosecuted for accepting bribes and sexual favors in return for hampering criminal investigations.[96] In 1327 royal réformateurs investigated charges of forgery, arbitrary arrest, and theft against Peire Bonassie, former lieutenant of the viguier of Carcassonne and farmer of the royal notariate. Peire's kinship with the sénéchaussée's procurator had enabled him to so terrorize the region that the local notaries dared not even record the complaints of his victims.[97]

Nonroyal Sources of Patronage

Thus access to royal office was relatively easy for Languedocians, and the profits of such office could be substantial. The attractions of royal service for the men of the Midi should not, however, be exaggerated. The king and his government were not the only sources of patronage and reward in Languedoc. For the ambitious Languedocian there were paths to success other than royal service. If the king was looking for clients among the Languedocian political elite, so were the great native aristocratic houses. Some of these built up impressive retinues. For example, in the fourteenth century Gaston III Fébus of Foix-Béarn constructed an extensive network of clients through the granting of fief-rents.[98] Even trusted royal servants could be absorbed into these alternate clientage networks. For example, Pons d'Aumelas, when he was juge mage of the sénéchaussée of Toulouse in 1309–10, was said by the procurator of the count of Foix to be the familiar of the count of Armagnac.[99]

Many of the Languedocian lordships had their own administrative infrastructures in which an ambitious man could make a career. For example, throughout the thirteenth and fourteenth centuries, the counts of Foix developed a progressively more elaborate administra-

94. Boutaric, ed., *Actes*, vol. 1, no. 1577, vol. 2, no. 5003.
95. *Regs.*, vol. 2, no. 3066.
96. Boutaric, ed., *Actes*, vol. 2, no. 6901.
97. *HL*, 9:446 (n. 6); *Regs.*, vol. 3/1, no. 56.
98. Tucoo-Chala, *Gaston Fébus*, pp. 289–94.
99. *HL*, 9:320 (n. 1); Langlois, "Pons d'Aumelas," p. 261.

tion. Many of the counts' servitors originated in their own lordships; but individuals from elsewhere were also recruited. In the mid-thirteenth century Arnaud Morlana, a member of a prominent family of Carcassonnais, was the count's seneschal.[100] Other aristocratic houses—such as those of the counts of Comminges, the lords of L'Isle-Jourdain, the countess of Vendôme, and the lords of Castres—also had respectable numbers of men in their employ.[101]

Some Languedocians combined careers of service with both the king and one of the great local lords. For example, Jacques de Béraigne was for a brief period in the 1290s a criminal judge in the séné-chaussée of Toulouse, but for most of his career he labored for the lords of L'Isle-Jourdain.[102] In the late thirteenth and early fourteenth centuries, some Languedocians also sought employment with masters outside the French kingdom.[103] For example, many men served both the king of France and the king of Majorca, who held part of the city of Montpellier from the French crown.

Of the outsiders who exercised influence and patronage in Languedoc, undoubtedly the greatest was the pope. After the Albigensian crusades, papal influence in the Languedocian church grew dramatically. Increasingly, local prelates acquired their sees not through the normal procedures of canonical election by their cathedral chapters but by papal provision.[104] The establishment of the popes at Avignon intensified their interest in the region. All of the Avignonese popes were natives of Occitan-speaking regions, and they recruited large numbers of servants from their homeland. Of the 134 appointments made to the cardinalate during this period, twenty-six (19.4 percent) went to men whose origins lay in the south of France.[105] Similarly, of the 1,333 men employed at the papal curia whose diocese of origin can be determined, 113 (8.5 percent) came from the provinces of Narbonne and Toulouse. If ones adds to this figure those men who

---

100. Doat, vol. 28, fol. 129r.

101. For the administration of the county of Comminges, see Higounet, *Comté*, pp. 215, 224, 231; for the governor of the countess of Vendôme's lands, see Boutaric, ed., *Actes*, vol. 2, no. 6017. On the lords of Castres, see Friedlander, "Administration," pp. 143–44.

102. Strayer, *Gens*, pp. 175–76.

103. For examples, see Strayer, *Gens*, pp. 55, 59, 60–61, 83–84, 171–72.

104. Guillemain and Martin, "Elections," p. 110; Catherine Martin, "Episcopat," pp. 154–55.

105. Guillemain, *Cour*, p. 187, and carte 5.

originated in the dioceses of Albi and Cahors, the total rises to 248 (18.6 percent).[106]

Within Languedoc itself not a few of the men who attained episcopal rank owed much of their good fortune to papal patronage. Eight of the men who became bishops in the province of Narbonne between 1249 and 1317 had previously held posts in papal government.[107] Some Languedocian prelates combined royal and papal service. The most notable example was Gui Foucois. Son of a man who had been chancellor and judge for Count Raimond V of Toulouse, Gui received legal training at Paris and entered the service of Count Raimond VII. On the count's death Gui transferred his loyalty to the new French ruler, Alfonse de Poitiers, whom he served as councillor and enquêteur. In the 1250s he entered royal service. Late in that same decade he embarked on an ecclesiastical career, which culminated with his election as Pope Clement IV in 1265.[108]

The incorporation of their native land into a larger political entity thus did not pose as profound a problem for the Languedocian elites as it did for the Welsh. The dominant classes of Languedoc were treated with respect by the French monarchy. To insure the loyalty of the more powerful local aristocrats, the kings were liberal with appointments to high office and with gifts of lands and rents. The urban corporations and the great prelates of the south were treated with similar circumspection. Languedocians were regularly consulted in the assemblies held by the French kings.

Moreover, Languedocians readily found their way into the royal administration. Although the great offices of state headquartered in the Ile de France were not deluged with southerners on the make, access to high office in Paris was possible. It was not even out of the question for a man like Guillaume de Nogaret to become one of the king's most trusted and influential henchmen. Languedocians were well represented in the ranks of the administration of the southern sénéchaussées. There was a tendency for the highest positions, such as that of seneschal, to be reserved for men recruited among the northern French nobility. But these northerners often appointed southerners as

---

106. Figures from Guillemain, *Cour*, pp. 454–75.
107. Catherine Martin, "Episcopat," pp. 165–66.
108. Dossat, "Gui Foucois," pp. 23–57. For other examples of men who combined royal service with attainment of high office in the papal bureaucracy, see Gilles, "Clergé," pp. 397–400.

their lieutenants. And with the passage of time southerners began to gain appointment to even the highest offices in the local royal administration. Certainly the lower levels of government were open to men of Languedocian birth. Procurators, notaries and judges were overwhelmingly Languedocian; so too it seems were most bayles. Southerners were also well represented in the ranks of viguiers and castellans.

A career of royal service was, however, not the only path open to an ambitious and talented Languedocian. There were other avenues of advancement he could pursue. The powerful aristocratic houses and the great prelates of the region all had their own administrative infrastructures, which became more complex and effective with the passage of time. The rewards of service to such local potentates might not be potentially as great as those that could be won through serving the king, but they were not to be despised. The establishment of the papacy at Avignon made the popes some of the most influential patrons in the Midi. The incorporation of Languedoc into the French polity required the old regional elites to find new parts for themselves in the larger political world of which they had become members, but the logic of their situation did not compel them to play only a marginal role in that world.

Conclusion

Before their incorporation into larger political organizations, Gwynedd and Languedoc were social formations in which there were marked differences in the distribution of power and authority. These differences were less pronounced in Gwynedd. Although Gwynedd was by no means an egalitarian society, its ruling class was not nearly so dominant in local affairs as its Languedocian counterpart. The members of the preconquest ruling elite of Gwynedd did not cut a very impressive figure, at least compared to their English neighbors. A few princely families, the most striking being the ruling house of Gwynedd, had managed to build up a measure of wealth and political authority. Their position was not, however, very solidly rooted. Not only were they unable to preserve their independence from the English, but most of them disappeared during or shortly after the conquest. The English recognized a few families as being of baronial status. But in Gwynedd this was a tiny group. Moreover, many of its members steadily declined in wealth and influence with the passage of time. Since Gwynedd had had a relatively undeveloped commercial and urban life before the Edwardian conquest, the English government did not have to contend with a well-entrenched corps of self-conscious and quasi-autonomous urban corporations. Instead the crown set about creating a series of urban settlements whose largely English population was one of the pillars on which it rested its power in the region.

In Languedoc the situation was different. Languedoc possessed a dominant aristocracy, both lay and ecclesiastical. Although these Languedocian power holders could not prevent the imposition of royal overlordship, many of them survived the Albigensian crusades. Moreover, unlike Gwynedd, Languedoc was dotted with numerous towns, rich, populous, and jealous of their privileges.

The dominant classes of Languedoc and Gwynedd, given their different structures and their different command of their societies' resources, experienced different destinies under outside rule. In Gwynedd the advent of English rule led to a change in the structure of the native ruling elite as its top strata were eliminated. For lesser Welsh members of the ruling elite who survived, the English conquest produced a deflation of their importance. A few Welshmen found a niche in the royal household. But it seems that virtually no one of ethnic Welsh background occupied a position of importance or influence in the kingdom of England. Welsh ambitious outside their native land were limited to service in the king's armies in Scotland and France. Within Gwynedd itself Welshmen were often systematically and consciously kept away from the levers of power.

In Languedoc, however, the indigenous ruling classes found that Capetian rule had few such negative consequences. Outside rule here did not radically alter the structure of the native ruling elite. Although some of the leading baronial dynasties lost control of their lands during the Albigensian crusades and their aftermath, most members of the local ruling elite survived the establishment of royal hegemony. The French kings proved solicitous of the feelings and interests of the members of the Languedocian ruling strata. The Capetians, and after them the Valois, were willing to recruit Languedocians for positions of importance and influence, both in the local and central royal administrations. The politically significant elements in the region were regularly consulted by the monarchy, whether in regional assembles or in the kingdomwide councils periodically summoned to discuss important matters of state.

In essence, in Languedoc the groups that had been dominant before the assertion of Capetian overlordship remained dominant afterwards; in Gwynedd the native ruling groups were either eliminated or pushed into a marginal position in the new political system. The relationship of these two ruling elites to the royal governments that claimed authority over them became very different. It has already been observed (in chapter 2) that postconquest Gwynedd saw an unprecedented concentration of political authority in the hands of the royal government. In the Principality of North Wales, state power presented itself as a nearly unified and unitary whole. As a result the royal government (and in the new Marcher lordships the seigneurial administrations of the English lords) occupied a strategic role in the life of the local political elites. Economic and political progress was possible only through service to the alien masters. Indeed, if a Welshman wanted to serve a master other than an Englishman, he often had to accept permanent exile from his homeland, as did a number of men who joined the armies of the French king. Despite the great importance of the state apparatus to the fortunes of the Welsh, they were barred from playing an influential role in it. The major political decisions affecting Gwynedd were made by Englishmen; and the profits, political and financial, that derived from its government flowed largely to the same alien masters.

In Languedoc the king's government played a much less important role in the life of the dominant classes. This was true despite the fact that the French royal government was much more open, at all levels, to ambitious Languedocians. Political power in Languedoc was not centralized and unified as it was in Gwynedd Uwch Conwy. Instead it was dispersed among a large number of local aristocrats, prelates, and town corporations. The royal government thus did not monopolize the political life of the region. In many important ways this still revolved around the local power centers and on occasion, as with the rise of papal influence, around power centers extrinsic to the kingdom.

In essence, outside rule had produced in Gwynedd and Languedoc two highly divergent political systems. In these new systems the native leading classes made their presence felt on the political scene in different ways. In Languedoc the dominant classes retained their traditional influence. Although heavily involved in the structures of the new state apparatus, their political lives were not completely monopolized by it. In Gwynedd, however, the local political elite was reduced to a supporting role in the new political system. Although the state apparatuses operated by the English came to monopolize the region's political life, the Welsh were condemned to at best a marginal role in those structures. Under outside rule the political elite of Languedoc, although it now had to operate in the context of a complex, kingdom-wide political system, remained the master of its own house. In Gwynedd, however, alien rule ultimately succeeded in making many members of the native political elite feel like exiles in their own land.[109]

109. In a fourteenth-century manuscript of the squire Hopcyn ap Thomas ab Einion of Ynystawe there is a note about the travails of "those who suffer pain and deprivation and exile in their native land." Brynley F. Roberts, "Lawysgrifau," p. 227; R. R. Davies, "Colonial Wales," p. 22; Davies, "Race Relations," pp. 46–47.

7 Internal Conflict and the New Order

At the time of their incorporation into larger political organizations, neither Languedoc nor Gwynedd was a unified polity. In neither region had anyone succeeded in welding the disparate local communities and power centers into a coherent, organized, and imperatively coordinated whole. Both areas were riven by deep conflicts that pitted local groups against one another. In this chapter we will examine what effect the assertion of outside authority had on these internal patterns of conflict. Once again we will observe an important difference in the impact of outside rule in Gwynedd and Languedoc. In Gwynedd, English rule put an end to the most fruitful sources of internal conflict, the state-building aspirations of the princes of Gwynedd. In Languedoc, however, outside rule did not end internal conflict. Indeed, in some cases the royal regime may have contributed to the intensification of conflict, giving local political actors opportunities to pursue their interests at the expense of their neighbors and on occasion providing some of the contending local parties with access to new resources with which to prosecute their quarrels.

Gwynedd

In the thirteenth century the politics of Wales had been largely determined by the efforts of the princes of Gwynedd to establish a strong territorial principality and, from this base, to dominate the rest of Wales. As we have already noted, however, Gwynedd was not very promising ground for the creation of such a political organization. The unproductive and largely noncommercial nature of the economy made it difficult for a would-be political leader to accumulate enough wealth to attract a large group of followers. Predation on one's neighbors, a traditional technique of acquiring surplus in medieval Europe, was also not a very rewarding option for a Welsh prince. His Welsh neighbors were equally poor, and the English, although rich, were too powerful and too dangerous to be raided with impunity.

The Welsh kinship system also worked against the construction of a territorial principality. At bottom Welsh society, at least among the freemen and among many bondmen as well, was organized around the patrilineal descent group. The power of the princes never quite managed to escape from the limitations set by this kinship system. Older historians argued that the notion that princely authority was qualitatively different from that inherent in any family group was not very developed. The prince's authority was often treated as though it were merely part of his family patrimony. As such it was subject to the same rules of inheritance that governed the transmission of any other form of property. When a prince died, it was often felt appropriate that his authority be shared among all his surviving sons.[1] Every time a prince died, his dominions were thus threatened with dismemberment. Doubt has recently been cast on this interpretation by J. B. Smith. Whether or not one wishes to accept his argument that Welsh legal theory and practice recognized that only one heir should succeed to a kingdom,[2] it is clear that disputed successions were a common feature of Welsh political life.

Problems of dynastic succession were complicated by the common Welsh practice of fosterage. A prince's male children were not reared by their father but were instead entrusted to the care of one of the local magnates. This custom served to cement ties between a prince and his followers. However, it also fomented rivalry among brothers. When their father died, the heirs—conscious of their hereditary rights, frequently strangers to one another, and able to call on the support of their foster parents—often strove to maximize their own

1. Jenkins, "Law," p. 26; *WTL*, 1:29; *Littere*, pp. xxxvi–xxxvii.
2. J. Beverley Smith, "Dynastic Succession," pp. 199–232.

share of the paternal inheritance. The result was chronic civil war, pitting heirs against one another and resulting, as Gerald of Wales put it, in "murder, arson and wholesale destruction."[3]

Political Consolidation by the Princes of Gwynedd

In the face of such difficulties, it is a tribute to the ambition, energy, and effectiveness of the thirteenth-century princes of Gwynedd that they were able to achieve as much as they did. In an effort to prevent the dismemberment of princely authority among their heirs, they tried to alter inheritance customs so as to guarantee that only one son would succeed to power. Llywelyn ab Iorwerth (1195–1240), who built up the fortunes of the dynasty in the early thirteenth century, had two sons. His eldest, Gruffydd, was illegitimate. His second, legitimate son was Dafydd. By Welsh law, which recognized the inheritance rights of illegitimate children if they were acknowledged by their father, Gruffydd had a very good claim to share power with his younger brother. Llywelyn, however, sought to ensure that only Dafydd should succeed him.[4]

In addition to trying to guarantee the succession of a single heir, the rulers of Gwynedd sought to put their dominance of the other Welsh princes on a more solid juridical foundation. Borrowing from English practice, they endeavored to make all the other Welsh princes their feudal vassals. From 1258 Llywelyn ap Gruffydd styled himself prince of Wales and began demanding homage from the other native rulers. In 1263 Llywelyn managed to bring his most important rival, Gruffydd ap Gwenwynwyn of Powys, to do homage and recognize that he held his lands in the southern half of this ancient kingdom as a vassal of Gwynedd. The Treaty of Montgomery between Llywelyn and the English in 1267 recognized that he was the direct feudal overlord of most of the petty princelings of Wales.[5] During the thirteenth century the princes of Gwynedd also sought to fashion a more effective administration with which to govern the areas under their domination. They created an embryonic central administration, built a string

3. Gerald of Wales, *Opera*, 6:225. See also 6:211–12. The translation is from Thorpe, *Journey*, p. 273.
4. Lloyd, *History*, 2:686–87.
5. *Littere*, pp. xlii–xliii, and nos. 1, 147, 204.

of castles and tried to bind certain families to them with the gift of landed estates held under special, privileged forms of tenure.[6]

Resistance to the Princes' Ambitions

This drive to create a coherent territorial principality in Gwynedd aroused much discontent. The Welsh princes who had been compelled to do homage to Llywelyn ap Gruffydd for their lands had no special reason to love his overlordship. There is considerable evidence that even at the height of his power in the late 1260s and early 1270s, Llywelyn was not sure of their loyalty. At least he found it wise to demand that they give him hostages. In 1261 Maredudd ap Rhys, who had done homage in 1258, had to offer Llywelyn twenty-four hostages. In 1274 the lord of Powys, Gruffydd ap Gwenwynwyn, was required to hand over his son Owain. Various lords from mid and South Wales had to give the prince similar sureties.[7]

These restless vassals proved willing to throw off their allegiance to Gwynedd when the opportunity presented itself. Indeed, it was Llywelyn's difficulties with his vassal Gruffydd ap Gwenwynwyn of Powys that helped bring about the first of his disastrous wars with Edward I. In 1274 Gruffydd, in collusion with Llywelyn's brother Dafydd, concocted a plan to assassinate the prince. The two conspirators intended that Dafydd should succeed his brother. Owain, Gruffydd's son, would marry Dafydd's daughter; Gruffydd would also receive various lands to add to his patrimony in Powys. When the details of the plot were discovered, Gruffydd fled into exile in England. There he found more potent allies in his effort to destroy the power of Prince Llywelyn.[8]

When war came with the English in 1276, the lords of southern Wales quickly went over to Edward I. Among those from South Wales who deserted the prince were some who had been employed in his administration. Ifor ap Gruffydd, who led a contingent from Elfael against Llywelyn, had probably once been the prince's bailiff for Elfael-Is-Mynydd. Rhys ap Gruffydd, who had been bailiff of Builth,

---

6. Pierce, "Age," pp. 33–34; Glanville R. J. Jones, "Defenses," pp. 29–43; Glyn Roberts, "Wyrion Eden," pp. 181–82.

7. *Littere*, pp. xliv–xlv.

8. Lloyd, *History*, 2:748–50; Stephenson, "Powys," pp. 46–49.

rallied to the English side and by 1278 was a member of the king's household.[9]

Even within Gwynedd the princes found that there was discontent with their rule. Dissension and strife were common within the ruling family itself. The princes of Aberffro never managed to solve the problem of orderly succession to power. Despite efforts to guarantee that only one brother inherited all of his father's authority, disputes among siblings plagued the princely house. The reign of Llywelyn ap Gruffydd, the last prince of Aberffro, was constantly bedeviled by troubles with his brothers. Owain, with whom Llywelyn had originally shared power after the death of their uncle Dafydd in 1246, went to war against Llywelyn in 1255. He was defeated and kept in prison until 1277. Another of Llywelyn's brothers, Dafydd, supported Owain in 1255. He shared Owain's defeat and, for a time, his incarceration. Released in 1256, he remained loyal to Llywelyn until 1263. In that year he threw in his lot with Henry III. By 1267, however, he had once again reconciled himself with Llywelyn. But in 1274 he plotted with Gruffydd ap Gwenwynwyn of Powys to murder his brother. When the conspiracy misfired, he fled to England. In the first of Edward I's wars, he fought for the English.

The financial exactions of the princes also stirred up much discontent in Gwynedd. The negotiation of treaties with the English, the creation of alliances with other Welsh rulers, the construction of castles, and the maintenance of an administration all cost a great deal. The princes' need for cash forced them to pursue aggressive, grasping, and avaricious policies. Traditional dues in kind and labor were increasingly converted into cash payments. Experiments were made with taxation, a novel procedure that produced much consternation.[10]

The churchmen of Gwynedd were especially outraged by some of the princes' financial expedients. For example, the abbot and canons of the Augustinian house of Haughmond (near Shrewsbury in England) had various rights in the township of Neigwl. Until the beginning of the thirteenth century they had been accustomed to giving the prince an occasional gift of 23s. 2½d. In the reign of Llywelyn ab

9. J. Beverley Smith, "Middle March," p. 87; James Conway Davies, ed., *Welsh Assize Roll*, pp. 120–21.

10. See Llinos Beverley Smith, "*Gravamina*," pp. 166–67.

Iorwerth, however, the prince's rhaglaw began demanding this sum every year, a practice which was continued under each subsequent prince. The monks of Basingwerk also felt the heavy hand of the prince. In the reigns of Llywelyn ab Iorwerth and his son Dafydd, they had been accustomed to entertaining the prince and 300 of his men once a year when the prince came to hunt in the commote of Penllyn. If the prince did not personally visit the commote, they owed nothing. Llywelyn ap Gruffydd, however, claimed that the monks were required to support not 300, but 500 men. Furthermore, they were obligated to do this every year, even if he did not personally set foot in Penllyn. In this case, their debt was to be discharged in cash.[11] Llywelyn ap Gruffydd's brother Dafydd was also busy in the last half of the thirteenth century tightening the financial screws on the local monasteries. In 1305 the abbot of Bardsey was still complaining about the injustices done decades earlier when Dafydd, at that time master of the Llŷn peninsula, had arbitrarily assessed on the abbot's tenants an extra *cylch* payment of 68s. 6d. a year.[12] Similarly, the monks of Cymer claimed that Dafydd had imposed on their tenants in Neigwl a payment of 39s. above their customary obligation.[13]

These unpopular demands made many in Gwynedd willing to see the English trim the powers of the princes. In 1277 several ecclesiastics supported Edward I against Llywelyn. Both north Welsh bishops, Anian of Saint Asaph and Anian of Bangor, were in the royal camp.[14] The Dominicans of Bangor and Rhuddlan also favored the king.[15] Support for Edward was not limited to the ranks of churchmen. Many laymen, like Cadwgan Goch of Anglesey and Dafydd ap Gruffydd of Hendwr, fought for the king.[16]

Even members of the privileged "official aristocracy," who had received lands on special terms from the prince, were willing to desert their master. Among the men who supported Edward I were descendants of Ednyfed Fychan, the seneschal of Llywelyn ab Iorwerth.[17] During the 1282–83 war, some of Prince Llywelyn's own household

---

11. *Cal. Inq. Misc.*, vol. 2, no. 667; vol. 1, no. 1357.
12. *RC*, p. 221. See also *CPR, 1313–17*, pp. 469–70.
13. *CPR, 1313–17*, pp. 394–95.
14. See *Cal. Anc. Corr.*, p. 112.
15. Glyn Roberts, "Dominican Friary," pp. 221–23.
16. *Cal. Var.*, p. 354; *Cal. Inq. Misc.*, vol. 2, no. 181.
17. Roderick, ed., *Wales*, 1:119; Glyn Roberts, "Wales and England," p. 381. See also Stephenson, *Governance*, pp. 104–5, 126–27.

may have tried to assassinate him.[18] Llywelyn's brother Dafydd, who tried to carry on resistance after the prince's death, was betrayed to the English by some of his countrymen.[19]

Internal Conflict under the English Regime

The ambitions of the princes of Gwynedd were thus a source of much conflict within their polity, conflict which helped facilitate the English conquest. To these disruptive ambitions of the house of Aberffro the English put a definitive end. The other Welsh princes were either eliminated or sank into vegetation and decay. Allowed to play only a marginal role in the English political system, the former rulers of Gwynedd lived out a mediocre existence. With their ambitions limited to relatively minor posts in the new administration or to service in royal armies, they no longer cut a very impressive figure in the politics of their own country. The rivalries of this group, closely circumscribed and controlled by the English, ceased to play a significant role in generating conflict in Welsh society. The English conquest thus put an end to one of the most fertile sources of strife in Gwynedd.

What other effects English rule had on patterns of internal conflict is hard to say. Some bondmen may have seen the end of the old order as an opportunity to improve their lot. Although most of the unfree in Gwynedd seem to have been under the direct lordship of the princes of Aberffro, others were subject to different lords. There is some evidence that these individuals took advantage of the coming of English rule to try to shake off their former obligations. For example, in 1305 Llywelyn Foelhron of Cornwy and the archdeacon of Anglesey complained that their bondmen had transferred themselves to the advowry of the king.[20] Sometime in the reign of Edward II, Adam ap Dafydd of Cilan in Caernarfonshire complained to the king that four of his bondmen had similarly withdrawn themselves from his control and placed themselves in the king's advowry.[21]

English rule may also have spurred some bondmen to try to improve their legal position. In preconquest Gwynedd there had been two types of bond community: one characterized by tir gwelyog tenure, in

18. Lloyd, "Death," p. 350.
19. Williams ab Ithel, ed., *Annales Cambriae*, p. 107.
20. Carr, *Medieval Anglesey*, p. 143.
21. *Cal. Anc. Pets.*, p. 164.

which the bondmen were organized in gwelyau similar to those of the native freemen; and another characterized by tir cyfrif tenure, in which the settlement's land was periodically redistributed among the tenants. After the conquest some bondmen in tir cyfrif villages tried to convert their holdings into tir gwelyog. In 1352 the bondmen of four villages and hamlets in Dinllaen commote in Caernarfonshire, all characterized by tir cyfrif, endeavored to convince the English extentors that they held their land in tir gwelyog.[22]

Tir cyfrif bond tenants were not alone in trying to take advantage of the making of the extents to conceal their former obligations. Many others did the same thing. Of course, if they succeeded, this meant that their neighbors were faced with the prospect of shouldering the evaders' share of the burden as well as their own. Not surprisingly the neighbors of these defaulters were willing to denounce them. For example, in the lordship of Dyffryn Clwyd, the entire community of the commote of Dogfeiling sued the brothers Gruffydd ap Tudur and Tudur Fychan. According to the community's attorneys, the brothers held land in Llangynhafal and were therefore bound to contribute to the cylch paid to the lord's foresters. Gruffydd and Tudur, claiming exemption from this cylch, had refused to pay their share.[23]

The propensity of the royal government to assess lump sum amercements on entire villages and commotes also produced a regular crop of disputes as people sought to evade contributions. For example, in 1346 the government imposed an amercement on the bondmen of the commotes of Malltraeth and Llifon in Anglesey. This touched off a series of suits in which each commote's bondmen claimed that they were not obliged to contribute to payments by the other commote.[24] Amercements and fines levied by the sheriffs at their biannual tourns also produced spates of litigation, in which Welshmen claimed that they had been unfairly forced by their neighbors to contribute to the funds raised to pay off these charges.[25]

The advent of English rule also exacerbated the tensions within the kinship group. There were several sources of potential conflict within the gwelyau. A permanent tension existed between the gwely as a whole and the smaller four-generation kindreds that were its constitu-

22. *RC*, pp. 34–35.
23. SC2/215/69, m. 9.
24. SC2/215/13, m. 2.
25. SC2/227/28, ms. 1, 3; SC2/227/27, m. 1.

ent parts. It was membership in these smaller groups that determined the possession and transmission of land by inheritance. Only male kin who shared a common great-grandfather could inherit land directly from one another. Similarly, it was this group that had to approve any alienation of land by one of its members. There was also tension between loyalty to the kinship group and loyalty to the neighborhood. The lands and members of kinship groups were scattered across often very extensive areas and intermixed with the lands and members of other gwelyau. The ties established with neighbors who belonged to a different kindred must often have conflicted with ties of loyalty to one's own gwely.[26]

There were thus many fissiparous factors at work within the gwelyau, which English rule seems to have encouraged. One factor that exacerbated conflict among kinsmen was the fact that English local government was firmly based on units defined primarily by territorial contiguity. For the English the basic building blocks of their administration were villages, commotes, and counties, on which various collective responsibilities were imposed. This facet of English rule heightened the potential for conflict between loyalty to kin and loyalty to neighbor. The internal coherence of the gwelyau was also threatened by the unprecedented mobilization of land that took place after the conquest. For one reason or another much land came into the crown's possession, to be relet to tenants at improved rents. To a large extent the lands involved in this process were freed from the old restrictions that Welsh family law had placed on their use and alienation. The weakening of the kinship groups' control over land helped contribute to their gradual disintegration.[27]

To sum up, English rule in Gwynedd promoted certain types of conflict between Welshmen. The divisive tendencies within the gwelyau were given greater freedom to operate. The fastening of collective responsibilities on villages and commotes created tensions within and between these entities. Elements of the native population tried to take advantage of the turmoil occasioned by the imposition of the new regime to escape from their traditional responsibilities. Yet among the most striking aspects of the English regime was the fact that it put an end to one of the most fertile sources of conflict between Welshmen,

26. R. R. Davies, *Lordship*, pp. 358–68, 370–71, 377.
27. On the disintegration of the gwely, see Edward A. Lewis, "Decay," pp. 1–50.

the political ambitions of the native princes. The efforts by the princes of Gwynedd to create a territorial principality out of the unpromising material offered by their native country had engendered much conflict, pitting them against the other Welsh princes, against the inhabitants of their lordship, and against the members of their own family and entourage. With the coming of the English regime, the state-building aspirations of the princes were made permanently irrelevant. Although domestic stress and strain were undoubtedly to be found in fourteenth-century Gwynedd, as in any social formation, the most important social, economic, and political divisions in Gwynedd under outside rule were, as we shall see in the next chapter, to pit Welshmen against Englishmen.

Languedoc

In Languedoc outside rule had a different impact on local patterns of conflict. The imposition of Capetian leadership failed to eliminate some of the most important sources of internal cleavage. More than that, in some respects the new regime served to exacerbate the conflicts that set Languedocian against Languedocian. Under French rule the consolidation of authority by local political organizations continued, a process that had begun before the coming of outside rule and that had engendered much conflict in independent Languedoc. The growing fiscal demands that came with French domination also intensified indigenous social conflict. Finally, the royal regime allowed certain groups to attempt to carve out for themselves new positions of power, a process that did much to envenom local political life.

The Consolidation of Local Political Authority

The conflicts engendered by the consolidation of seigneurial control and the ambiguous role of the royal government in this process can be illustrated by glancing at the internal history of some of the more important Languedocian towns. Narbonne, for example, was the scene of a series of complex struggles. This city, like many others in Languedoc, was divided into two parts, the old cité around the cathedral and the more commercially oriented bourg. Before the coming of the French, Narbonne had had three different lords: the viscounts, the archbishops, and the abbots of Saint Paul. Moreover, by the early thirteenth century consulates had emerged in both halves of the town. During the Albigensian crusades the townsmen and Viscount Aymeri III (1194–1238) cooperated closely, the citizens loyally following the viscount in his tortuous policies vis-à-vis the crusaders.[28]

The period after the end of the crusades, however, saw recurrent conflicts between the Narbonnese and their lords. Initially the archbishop was the more prominent enemy of the townsmen. From 1234 to 1237 Archbishop Pierre Amiel engaged in a bitter quarrel with the bourg, which originated in a dispute between the people of the bourg and the inquisitors. Amiel, supporting the inquisition, sought to make use of this affair to increase his authority. He tried to force the bourg's inhabitants to swear fealty to him; he may also have envisaged dissolving the consulate. Pierre also managed to quarrel with the people of the cité. When he died in 1245, he was at odds with the consuls of both the bourg and the cité, as well as with members of his cathedral chapter and the viscount.

From the middle of the thirteenth century, however, the townsmen found themselves more vexed by the viscount than by the archbishop. Royal involvement also became a more important factor in the struggle over the distribution of political authority. The consuls of the bourg and the cité began to claim that they were immediately subject to the king of France as duke of Narbonne. In 1280 the viguier of Béziers gave the consuls the king's safeguard and ordered the viscount not to molest them, an action that caused him to appeal to the royal courts.[29] Royal protection of the townsmen did not prevent Viscount Amauri II from vigorously prosecuting his struggle against them. Frustrated by the long disputes over the question of from whom the consuls held their authority—the king, the viscount, the archbishop, or no one—Amauri in 1307 arranged the excommunication of the consuls and named syndics to replace them. This action brought him into conflict with the crown, which proceeded to nominate the cité's consuls and to sequester the bourg's consulate.[30]

The role played by the king's government in the disputes that pitted townsmen against lords bent on aggrandizing their power is also illus-

28. Much of the following discussion is based on Emery, *Heresy*, pp. 25, 53–65, 79–82, 91, 98–101.
29. *HL*, 9:73.
30. Régné, *Amauri II*, pp. 168–72.

trated by events in the city of Albi.[31] In the early thirteenth century the bishops of Albi had taken advantage of the coming of the French to expand their authority. As part of this campaign, the bishops were at first careful to cultivate the people of the city of Albi, granting them many privileges. But once the bishops had worked out the rules that would govern their dealings with the king of France, their relations with the Albigeois deteriorated. This process seems to have begun in the late 1260s.

With the accession of Bishop Bernard de Castanet to the see in 1276, following a long vacancy during which the townsmen had usurped some privileges for themselves, life in the diocese became envenomed.[32] Castanet wasted little time in antagonizing the townspeople. He set about trying to exert greater control over judicial affairs in his lordship. He also tried to reduce the various rights that the townspeople had arrogated to themselves during the see's vacancy. Finally, he may have attempted to infringe on the right of the citizens to elect consuls.

The result of his actions was a reversal of the old patterns of alliance. Some of the townspeople decided that their interests would best be served by an understanding with the royal authorities. The concrete form in which this was expressed was a growing number of appeals from the bishop's courts to those of the king. In 1297 matters came to a head when the bishop arrested thirteen townsmen for cutting down trees and vines. Before the bishop's bayle would agree to release them, he demanded what seemed to the Albigeois to be excessive guarantees for their subsequent appearance in court. The detainees, claiming that the customs of the town had been violated, appealed to the king. The royal viguier took custody of the accused, allowed them to offer what they claimed to be the customary sureties, and released them. This action began a dispute between Castanet and the royal authorities that dragged on for years.[33] The difficulties that grew out of this controversy may have been among the reasons that led Castanet in 1299 and 1300 to arrest a number of leading townsmen as heretics. The condemnation of these men touched off an explosion that saw rioting in Albi, complaints to the king, the seizure of the

31. Much of the following discussion is based on Biget, "Procès," pp. 273–341.

32. During the vacancy the townspeople arrogated to themselves the right to possess an *hôtel de ville* and adopted an aggressive attitude toward diocesan administrators. On one occasion they invaded the episcopal palace and arrested the archdeacon of Albi; Doat, vol. 107, fol. 13r. See also Boutaric, ed., *Actes*, vol. 1, no. 1984.

33. Documents relating to this dispute can be found in Doat, vol. 103, fols. 57r–58v; vol. 108, fols. 61r–62r, 108r–9r; and AM Albi, FF7–12.

diocese's temporalities by royal agents, a papal investigation of Casta-net, and his eventual transfer to another see.

Certainly the conflicts that grew out of the consolidation of political authority during the thirteenth century would have disturbed the re-gion even if the French kings had never appeared on the scene. Royal agents, however, did little to stop these quarrels. Here the contrast with the English regime in Gwynedd is striking. There English author-ity ended such conflicts by ending indigenous political development. This did not happen in Languedoc. The French may have imposed some limits on the violence with which such conflicts could be pros-ecuted, but they did not halt them altogether. Furthermore, the ability of the parties involved in these struggles to call on royal aid may have served merely to prolong internal strife by preventing one side from winning a final victory over the other.

The French Regime as a Factor for the Exacerbation of Internal Social Conflict

The coming of the French regime seems to have exacerbated the tensions that set local social groups against one another. These ten-sions were, of course, not created by the French. Like the political issues that divided Languedocians, they were the result of the develop-ment of a complex social system. Nevertheless, royal policies, which affected certain groups in the region in a differential fashion, served to sharpen some of the indigenous sources of social strife.

For example, the royal regime helped promote the forces that were working to set the local nobility more sharply apart from the rest of society. In Languedoc, as in Italy, the members of the lesser nobles had often been deeply involved in the life of the towns. In many places they elected members of the town consulates.[34] After the crusades, how-ever, nobles began to withdraw from the life of the cities. At Nîmes they were ejected. In June 1226 this city submitted to the overlordship of Louis VIII. The king, to ensure his control of the town, expelled the nobles from their lodgings in the Roman Arena and installed a royal garrison. He also purged the town consulate of its noble members.[35]

34. Dognon, *Institutions*, p. 68 (n. 1). See also Michel, *Administration*, pp. 212–13; *HL*, 6:274–75.

35. *HL*, 6:605; Michel, *Administration*, p. 230. In 1270 they were readmitted to the consulate, but the days when they had played a decisive role in the history of the city were over; ibid., pp. 257–58; Dupont, "Evolution," pp. 295–96.

Most petty nobles, however, did not have to be pushed out of the cities; they withdrew voluntarily. For example, before the crusades nobles had often undertaken to help defray their town's public expenses.[36] From the middle of the thirteenth century, however, the burden of taxation grew steadily heavier. To increased local levies were added the demands of the royal treasury, which became especially needy because of Philip IV's wars. In the face of this growing fiscal pressure, nobles began reassessing their role in the towns. Because royal taxes were justified on the grounds of necessity for the king's wars, nobles, pointing to their personal liability for military service, claimed to be exempt. Disputes over the validity of these claims can be found all over Languedoc.[37] To escape the burden of taxation, some nobles physically abandoned the cities. Those who did not, often asserted that they formed a community legally distinct from that of the bourgeoisie.[38] Under French rule noble participation in the affairs of the southern towns thus declined. At Agde, for example, nobles seem to have been regularly represented on the town consulate before 1319. After that date almost none served as either consuls or councillors.[39]

Within the ranks of nonnoble townsmen, social tension became ever more acute under the French. The towns of Languedoc had participated in the general growth of a mercantile capitalist sector within the medieval economy. This development had brought great wealth to a few and grinding poverty to others.[40] With the growing disparity of wealth there came a steady increase in tension between rich and poor. For the most part the consulates that governed the cities became the creatures of a small handful of wealthy merchants. The practice of selecting consuls by cooptation, common in Languedoc, guaranteed that consular office remained in the hands of the same small number of families for generations. The consuls in turn usually appointed the town treasurers and councillors and often the men who supervised the guilds. This stranglehold on urban government permitted the wealthy to determine how the burden of taxation was distributed.

36. Dognon, *Institutions*, pp. 156–57.
37. For examples, see *RHF*, 24:332, 334 (nos. 51, 61); Auguste Molinier, ed., *Correspondance*, vol. 2, no. 1517; AM Albi, FF13; and Castaldo, *Agde*, pp. 204–7.
38. Dognon, *Institutions*, p. 160.
39. Castaldo, *Agde*, p. 210.
40. On the highly asymmetric distribution of wealth in Toulouse revealed by the surviving fragments of a 1335 tax register, see Wolff, *Estimes*, pp. 22, 79.

It was around this issue that many political disputes revolved in the thirteenth and fourteenth centuries. The rich not surprisingly preferred regressive forms of taxation, such as consumption and head taxes. The poor just as adamantly wanted taxation to be proportional to wealth, often coupling this demand with a call for revisions of the modes of selection of consuls and councillors. In the fourteenth century, conflict became ever more intense as the economy began to falter and as war and increasing royal financial demands exacerbated ill will between rich and poor.[41]

Royal agents inevitably found themselves involved in these affairs. At times they were criticized for claiming exemption from taxation for those immediately subject to the king's lordship.[42] More frequently, however, crown servants were called on to intervene in the squabbling over taxation within the cities. In 1268 the common people of Toulouse appealed to Alfonse de Poitiers, demanding that the consuls be required to levy all tailles *à sou et livre*, that is, proportionately to wealth.[43] In the mid-thirteenth century, controversies over the levying of tailles at Montauban led the royal government to suppress the consulate.[44] At Nîmes in the 1280s Rostaing de Pujault, the lieutenant of the seneschal of Beaucaire, was involved in trying to work out a settlement over the selection of consuls and the imposition of tailles.[45]

Chapter 2 noted that the prelates of the church benefited greatly from the assertion of French leadership. This consolidation of episcopal lordship helped generate strife in Languedoc. Probably the most universally detested aspect of the reinvigorated church was its tithe offensive. All across Languedoc, bishops in the thirteenth century were at work prying tithes out of the hands of their lay possessors. This process is best known for the diocese of Albi.[46] At the beginning of the Albigensian crusades a large number of parish churches and their

---

41. The 1330s in Languedoc were to see a series of uprisings of the poor at Toulouse, Cahors, Montpellier, Foix, Narbonne, and Millau; Wolff, "Luttes," pp. 81–83. The situation at Foix is discussed in Pélissier, "Lutte," pp. 96–103.

42. For an example from Saint-Geniès-le-Bas (Hérault) in 1247, see *RHF*, 24:346–47 (no. 125).

43. Wolff, *Histoire de Toulouse*, p. 140.

44. Wolff, "Réflexions sur l'histoire médiévale de Montauban," p. 341.

45. Ménard, *Nîmes*, 1:321. For royal intervention in the fiscal affairs of Alais in 1294 and 1295 and of Lodève in the early 1300s, see Bardon, *Alais*, pp. 15–25, and Ernest Martin, *Lodève*, 1:182–83.

46. For the following paragraph, see Biget, "Restitution," pp. 226–56.

tithes were in the hands of the diocese's petty nobility. Thanks to the crusades, the church was able to recover almost all of the tithes that had been in lay hands in the southern half of the diocese. In the middle decades of the thirteenth century the church authorities continued to gather in tithes. But it was not until the accession to the bishopric of Bernard de Castanet in 1276 that the campaign was pressed with true ruthlessness and effectiveness. So successful was Bernard in augmenting his income that the men who accused him of various misdeeds before a papal commission in 1307 estimated that his annual revenue was 20,000l.t., a figure at least ten times greater than that received by any of his predecessors.[47]

Not only did the Languedocian episcopate achieve greater control over tithes, it also began to claim that ever more categories of goods were subject to this levy. In the mid-1250s the seneschal of Carcassonne complained that the local bishops were trying to collect tithes on such previously exempt things as ovens, mills, roof-tiles, nuts, pears, and rabbit warrens and to claim first fruits from the grape and olive harvests.[48] The passage of time only saw growing ill-will over this issue. Around 1300, royal agents were still complaining about the church's effort to make ever more products subject to tithe.[49] In the early decades of the fourteenth century, the attempt to levy tithes on the increase of animals in the county of Foix produced protracted conflict between the bishop of Pamiers and the people of the mountainous region of the Sabarthès.[50]

The royal regime also served to exacerbate religious strife in the region. The Albigensian crusades, although directed against Catharism, did not destroy it; they merely drove the sect underground. To deal with this problem the church authorities in the second quarter of the thirteenth century created the inquisition. Charged with the extirpation of heresy, the inquisitors were given extensive powers by the papacy and the French monarchy. Eventually permanent inquisitorial

47. ASV, Collectorie 404, fol. 7r. In recovering tithes, Castanet adopted a very tough attitude toward their lay possessors. These men were declared *ipso facto* excommunicate; Doat, vol. 107, fols. 353r–57r. In certain cases Castanet was willing to threaten those who hindered his campaign of tithe recovery with the terrible threat of prosecution for heresy; see ASV, Collectorie 404, fol. 104.

48. *HL*, 8: col. 1422.

49. Boutaric, ed., "Notices," p. 134.

50. Llobet, *Foix*, pp. 28–31, 49–54.

tribunals staffed by Dominicans were established at Toulouse and Carcassonne. At times some of the more zealous bishops set up their own heresy-hunting machinery, as at Pamiers and Albi. Equipped with a fairly elaborate staff consisting of inquisitors and their assistants, notaries, scribes, sergeants, spies, and jailers, and able to call on secular officials for aid, the inquisition proceeded to track down and punish heretics and their sympathizers in Languedoc.[51]

Possessed of extraordinary powers and dedicated to destroying a heresy that had found widespread sympathy in Languedoc, the inquisitors stirred up trouble almost everywhere they undertook their investigations. In 1234 when Friar Ferrier tried to arrest a citizen of the bourg of Narbonne, his actions set off a riot and an uprising against the archbishop.[52] The inquisitor Guillaume Arnaud's effort in 1235 to begin proceedings against members of the leading consular families of Toulouse not only led to his own expulsion from the city but to the exile of all his fellow Dominicans as well. At Albi in 1234 Arnaud Catalan's attempts to exhume and burn the bones of a deceased heretic called into the streets a mob that almost lynched him.[53] In May 1242 a party of inquisitors was massacred at Avignonet by members of the Cathar garrison of Montségur.[54]

The inquisition evoked not only opposition to itself, it also created divisions among Languedocians. As the inquisitors drove on their investigations, their activities set neighbor against neighbor, friend against friend, and kinsman against kinsman. The evidence in Jacques Fournier's inquisitorial register is eloquent on this subject. Under the baleful regard of the inquisitors in Pamiers and Carcassonne, the most important social bonds in the county of Foix, those that united kinsmen, withered. For example, because of her husband's hostility to her heretical beliefs, Sibille den Baille, who ultimately died at the stake, drove him out of her house. Because of inquisitorial pressure kinsmen became unwilling to honor the traditional obligations of familial ties. When the earnest Cathar believer Pierre Maury returned to his native

51. See Given, "Inquisitors," pp. 336–59.

52. Emery, *Heresy*, p. 77.

53. Pelhisson, *Chronique*, pp. 32–38, 44–47. I have been unable to consult the Latin edition of Célestin Douais in his *Les Sources de l'histoire de l'inquisition au moyen âge* (Paris, 1881).

54. Dossat, "Massacre," pp. 343–50.

Montaillou after a sojourn in Catalonia, his uncle refused to welcome him into his home because of his fear of the inquisition.[55]

The Lack of a Consistent Royal Policy toward Social Conflict

None of these internal divisions was created by Capetian rule. But aspects of the new royal regime exacerbated their severity. Furthermore, the policies adopted by royal agents toward contending Languedocian interest groups did little to resolve these disputes. The king's agents appear to have almost never consistently supported a specific interest group against its opponents. Assistance was often given first to one contending party and then to its enemy. Moreover, one set of royal officials often favored one side in a controversy, another set the other. This is not a surprising conclusion. French governing institutions were not strong enough to allow the king's servants to impose any solution they wished on squabbling local factions. Also, as Jan Rogozinski has pointed out, royal government in Languedoc was largely staffed by local men. These individuals had complex sets of ties of mutual sympathy and interest with various factions in the south, ties that often kept the government from pursuing a consistent policy toward the controversies that agitated the region.[56]

Even a cursory examination of the role of the king's government in the numerous internal struggles in Languedoc reveals that royal servants behaved in a fashion that can at best be described as opportunistic. As we shall see in chapter 8, royal support of the inquisitors often wavered in the face of local opposition.[57] In the chronic disputes that pitted townsmen against their lords, the royal government seldom consistently supported one social group against another. For example, in the quarrels that agitated Moissac in the 1260s, the government of Alfonse de Poitiers favored now the monks, now the townspeople.[58]

55. Duvernoy, ed., *Registre*, 2:28, 174–75. The surviving inquisitorial records reveal that the tensions generated by heresy hunting in Foix often resulted in violence, as Cathar sympathizers resorted to assassination and mutilation to protect themselves. See ibid., 1:281; 2:222, 333, 427; 3:76, 276–77; Pales-Gobilliard, *Geoffroy d'Ablis*, pp. 150–55, 276–77; Charles Molinier, *Inquisition*, pp. 155–56; and Duvernoy, "Pierre Autier," p. 39.

56. Rogozinski, *Power*, p. 61.

57. See Friedlander, "Agents du roi," pp. 199–220.

58. Dossat, ed., *Saisimentum*, pp. 63–65.

In the protracted difficulties over how authority was to be shared at Le Puy among the bishop, the community, and the king, Philip IV's agents constantly shifted sides, showing favor to the bourgeoisie when it served their interests, abandoning them when negotiations with the bishop proved fruitful, only to return later to a renewed alliance with the townsmen.[59] At Agde in the 1330s and 1340s, royal agents showed little consistency during the long dispute over the liability of ecclesiastics to contribute to the tailles, favoring first the consuls, then the bishop and the cathedral chapter. Similarly, in the 1360s various royal servants supported both the bishop and the consuls in a controversy over which of the two parties had the right to appoint a captain for the city's troops.[60]

In the bitter disputes that pitted rich against poor and "ins" against "outs" over taxation and the election of communal officials, the king's government can be found supporting all factions. At Alais in 1294 royal agents were involved in arbitrating a dispute that had grown out of the *populaires'* discontent with the method used to elect the consuls and councillors. The arbitration award gave the popular party a greater voice in selecting councillors. Yet, when in the next year the consuls and some councillors unilaterally changed the method of election, the king's agents showed little interest in the protests of the outraged popular party.[61] When a dispute about the levying of tailles broke out in Montpellier in the 1320s, the government alternately favored the town consuls and the dissatisfied popular party. Similarly, in 1328 the protests of the popular party that the tax of that year was grossly unfair provoked the government to order the seneschal of Beaucaire to investigate. But before he could do so, the government changed its mind and ordered the collection of the tailles to proceed despite the "frivolous appeals" of the people.[62] At Roujan in 1319 two leaders of the town's popular party acquired letters from the seneschal of Carcassonne ordering the king's bayle to put an end to the unjust tailles levied by the consuls. Instead, the bayle, who was in league with the consuls, arrested the two and threatened them with death unless they surrendered the seneschal's letters.[63]

59. Delcambre, "Paréage," pp. 151–57, 323–25.
60. Castaldo, *Agde*, pp. 299–322, 363–66.
61. Bardon, *Alais*, pp. 18–28.
62. Rogozinski, *Power*, pp. 1–2, 6, 16–19.
63. Friedlander, "Administration," pp. 249–50.

The Lack of a Consistent Policy by Contending
Local Factions toward Royal Intervention

If the crown had no consistent policy toward the conflicting forces at work in its southern sénéchaussées, few of the local factions seem to have been consistent exponents of royal intervention. Depending on their short term interests, various groups alternately appealed to the king against their enemies or tried to keep royal intervention to a minimum. This phenomenon is illustrated by the behavior of the bourgeoisie of Albi. In the first half of the thirteenth century, the townspeople supported their bishop in his efforts to restrict royal authority. In the second half of the century, however, when relations with the bishops deteriorated, they worked to expand the king's power. Even then they were not committed royal partisans. When it served their purposes, they were willing to oppose the king's agents. For example, sometime slightly before 1291 the inhabitants of the town celebrated the feast of St. John the Baptist with a bonfire on a hill outside the town. The residents of Castelnau de Bonnafous, who claimed possession of the site, attacked the Albigeois. When the lieutenant of the seneschal of Carcassonne sent commissioners to investigate the matter, the people of Albi informed them that they had always had the right to light their bonfire at the place in question. Aside from that, they intended to answer concerning this affair only to their lord and judge, the bishop of Albi.[64]

The townsmen of Narbonne offered a similar display of inconsistency. When in 1301 Viscount Amauri II's court condemned a man to death without consulting the opinion of prud'hommes from the city, the consuls appealed to the king. Royal agents arrived to take custody of the condemned man, only to discover that the situation had changed. The viscount had had the culprit retried. He had again been convicted, but this time he had been sentenced to imprisonment. This maneuver had allayed the discontent of the townsmen. Therefore, when the royal agents forcibly removed the prisoner from the viscount's jail, they touched off a riot in which they almost lost their lives. Similarly, in the dispute over whether the king, the viscount or the archbishop was the immediate lord of the town consulates, the townsmen pursued an ambiguous course, with those of the cité

64. AM Albi, FF4–5. For a similar case in 1295, see AM Albi, FF6.

claiming to hold their authority from the king and those of the bourg claiming to hold of no one.[65]

French rule in Languedoc seems often to have exacerbated internal tensions. The imposition of French overlordship removed some of the constraints that had held various interest groups together in often uneasy alliance. By allowing local power holders to consolidate their authority, often with royal patronage, the French regime even encouraged internal dissension. Finally, the royal government adopted no systematic policy of favoring one faction over another. The king's administration, relatively weak and thinly spread, staffed mostly by local men who frequently had important personal ties with the rival factions bidding for royal assistance, pursued policies that were often inconsistent if not indeed contradictory. In Languedoc the advent of royal rule fostered not calm and tranquility, but chronic turmoil.

Conclusion

English and French domination had different effects on patterns of internal strife in Languedoc and Gwynedd. In Languedoc the advent of French rule helped ensure the continuation of significant internal strife. In Gwynedd, on the other hand, the English regime ended some of the most important internal causes of friction while contributing in only a minor fashion to the exacerbation of preexisting tensions. Two factors present themselves as possible explanations for this difference. The first is the differing predisposition of Languedocian and Welsh society to significant internal conflict. The second involves the contrasting nature and effectiveness of English and French rule in their new territories.

In considering the first factor, it is clear that Languedocian social arrangements offered a great potentiality for serious internal conflict. Languedoc was among the more advanced of the regional social formations of which medieval Europe was composed. By advanced I mean that specialization of political, economic, and social function had progressed relatively far. Languedoc's rural sector was marked by

65. Régné, *Amauri II*, pp. 102–5, 168–77.

an asymmetrical distribution of wealth and power among peasants and lords. Its substantial urban sector—with its merchant protocapitalists, urban landlords, and laboring artisans—was also characterized by strong asymmetries in the distribution of wealth and power. Each of the social strata that composed Languedocian society had its own particular interests to pursue at the expense of others. Yet, given the advance of economic specialization, each was locked into a necessary interdependence with the others. In such a context it is not surprising that there was a potentiality for chronic and significant internal strife.

Gwynedd presents a somewhat different picture. The social structure was characterized by less specialization of function or differentiation of social status. Although North Welsh society was not completely undifferentiated, it did not display the pronounced asymmetries found in Languedoc. The concentration of wealth was not as far advanced. Although independent Gwynedd knew freemen and bondmen, the rights and duties of the two groups were not very different from one another, except on the demesne estates of the local princes, which were few in number. This does not mean that Welsh society was devoid of conflict. Anyone familiar with Welsh history in the twelfth and thirteenth centuries is well aware that conflict was chronic. But it does mean that conflict was often small-scale, pitting relatively tiny groups against one another.

The nature of the governing apparatuses established by the French and the English also played a role in determining the intensity of local conflict in our two social formations. In Gwynedd the governing institutions of the English enjoyed a relatively large degree of autonomy vis-à-vis local society. This was not true of Capetian institutions in Languedoc. In Gwynedd the agents of royal power came to constitute a social category in their own right, over and apart from the rest of society. In Languedoc this did not happen to the same degree.

For a governing bureaucracy to operate as a social category in its own right, it must have a specific unity in the way in which it functions, and it must be relatively autonomous from the social classes present in its polity.[66] In Languedoc neither condition existed. In common with other feudal bureaucracies, the royal government in Languedoc lacked a specific unity in its method of functioning. First

66. Poulantzas, *Political Power*, pp. 341–50.

of all, it did not possess a monopoly of coercive authority. Important powers of sovereignty remained in local hands, whether of landed aristocrats, church prelates, or urban corporations. Royal agents had to fit themselves into the interstices of this preexistent system of power-sharing. The particular mix of rights and powers of command enjoyed by the royal government therefore varied from one place to another in its southern possessions. Secondly, the royal government did not deal with a polity composed of a level and uniform mass of citizens, all formally equal in rights and privileges. Instead it was confronted by a host of unequal actors, each endowed with a highly varied set of rights and privileges. These two factors made it impossible for crown servants to adopt a uniform method of procedure in dealing with the tasks of governing its Languedocian subjects.

The fragmentation of political power also reduced the relative autonomy of the state apparatus's staff vis-à-vis local social classes. First, the power and authority of the indigenous ruling class enabled its members to impose themselves, or their clients, on the royal government.[67] Second, the retention of significant authority by local power holders meant that the loyalty of the servants of the crown was often divided. Royal agents were not infrequently also servants or clients of one of the local potentates. Finally, the local recruitment of many royal administrators meant that these officials often had intimate ties with the contending factions whose disputes they were supposed to regulate.

For these reasons the royal bureaucracy in Languedoc was not able to function as a separate social category, with a specific set of group interests and coherent policies designed to serve those interests. As a result, its behavior was often inconsistent and opportunistic. The role of the royal government in provoking internal conflict in Languedoc was thus more negative than positive. By integrating Languedoc into a wider polity, the French kings removed the external threats that had kept various social groups often willing to ally with one another

---

67. For example, despite the fact that Gaston Fébus of Foix-Béarn pursued a policy that was often inimical to royal interests in the second half of the fourteenth century, he was nevertheless able to secure appointment as royal lieutenant-general in Languedoc. Cazelles, in *Société*, pp. 267–68, has noted that some of Philip of Valois's bureaucrats were protégés of prominent Languedocian noble houses. Cazelles has argued that these men functioned as a species of ambassador, continuing to advise and serve their former masters while simultaneously making a career in the king's government.

against outsiders. After the end of the crusades, the social and political groupings of Languedoc were left free to turn against one another. Furthermore, the intimate connection of the royal bureaucracy's staff with local social structures kept the government from developing a consistent policy toward the social conflicts that arose in the region. As a result, many a local disputant discovered that it was possible to enlist, at least for a time, the aid of the king's government in a particular controversy. The royal government thus often appeared not as an arbitrator of the conflicts generated within the local political system but as merely another potential ally to be enlisted in the ranks of one of the local, competing factions. In this way royal rule may have exacerbated some indigenous conflicts, by injecting into Languedoc new resources that could be captured by local politicians and used by them to prosecute their domestic quarrels with renewed vigor and greater resources.

In Gwynedd, on the other hand, local conditions enabled the English government to fashion itself into more of a separate social category, and to pursue a more coherent, self-contained policy. As I have already remarked, the Principality of North Wales after the conquest was, by medieval standards, a peculiarly homogeneous polity. The process of conquest stripped native institutions of almost all of what political authority they possessed. The royal government (and in the Marches the governments of the new English lords) was thus able to act on this relatively uniform political society in an equally uniform fashion, largely free of the necessity to fit itself around any rival concentrations of authority.

It therefore enjoyed what was, for a medieval state apparatus, a relatively large degree of autonomy with relation to local social classes. The members of the political elite of Gwynedd, reduced to a supporting role in the new polity, were usually incapable of imposing their wishes on the administration. Within that administration, moreover, positions of authority tended to be reserved for Englishmen, who often had few intimate bonds with the structures of native society. The result was that the English regime had a very different impact on local internal conflict than did the French government in Languedoc. By ending the ambitions of the Welsh princes, the English wrote *finis* to the most intense conflicts within Gwynedd. Their monopoly of power meant that they did not find it necessary to seek allies among various factions of contending Welshmen or to favor one group of quarreling natives over another. Even when certain groups in Gwynedd tried to enlist English support for their efforts to free themselves from some of the traditional constraints of Welsh social life, the English were reluctant to let themselves become involved. For example, attempts to get the English to agree to alter the traditional rules of landholding so as to facilitate the concentration of estates generally received an unsympathetic hearing. The English government thus remained largely apart from and indifferent to the sources of tension within native society. Moreover, its resources were not readily available to those who wished to promote local quarrels.

French and English rule therefore had different effects on local patterns of political strife. French domination in Languedoc served to exacerbate domestic tensions. The result was chronic turbulence in the south of France. This very climate of strife, however, helped to preserve the French hegemony. It prevented all the elements of Languedocian society from aligning against the French. It also allowed royal agents to intervene on the side of various disputants and thus win for themselves a measure of loyalty from at least some members of local society. By contrast English rule brought relative peace to Gwynedd. It eliminated the principal cause of political conflict in independent Gwynedd. It was also largely indifferent to internal conflict among the natives. The most important and explosive differences in Wales after the conquest were accordingly not those that separated Welshman from Welshman but those that pitted Welshman against Englishman.

8   Resistance and Rebellion

In this chapter we turn to the efforts made within Gwynedd and Languedoc to resist the rule of the new masters. Those forms of resistance intended merely to delimit or restrict the authority of the outsiders will not be a principal concern. Instead our attention will focus on attempts by Languedocians and Welshmen to eliminate altogether the domination of outsiders. In Languedoc, although the French regime was not universally popular and there were a number of conspiracies and rebellions directed against the kings from the north, there was never a large-scale movement that organized a broad-based political front against outside rule. In Gwynedd, despite almost a century of relative quiet, English rule produced widespread discontent, which ultimately in the early fifteenth century produced a major uprising, involving not only Gwynedd but virtually all of Wales. Here I seek to clarify the reasons for this difference.

Gwynedd

The chronicle of Welsh resistance to outside rule after 1283 presents a paradoxical picture. The first decades of the new regime saw a number of uprisings. But thereafter, for nearly a century, Gwynedd was largely quiet. To be sure, there were a number of Welsh exiles on the continent with dreams of expelling the English.[1] But within Wales itself, despite the chronic uneasiness of the English administrators and colonists about the malevolence of the natives, there was surprising calm. This quiescence, however, was not a sign of satisfaction with the new regime. In the opening years of the fifteenth century Welsh discontent produced a major upheaval. Under the leadership of a number of squires, the most prominent of whom was Owain Glyndŵr, much of Wales rose against the English in a rebellion that lasted, with varying degrees of success, from 1400 through 1413.

Welsh Resistance to English Rule before 1400

The first decade of English rule in Gwynedd was an uneasy one that was closed by a major rebellion. The event that triggered a rising in late September 1294 was the mustering of Welshmen for military service in Gascony. Initially the rebels met with much success. In Gwynedd, led by Madog ap Llywelyn, they seized the unfinished castle at Caernarfon, put the fortress and its town to the torch, and killed the sheriff of Anglesey. The revolt spread from North Wales into West and South Wales. The rebellion forced Edward I to cancel his Gascon plans and redirect his resources to a new conquest of Wales. By the summer of 1295 he had once again conquered the country.[2]

The middle of the fourteenth century, however, did see some restiveness.[3] In 1344 an anti-English riot took place at the fair of Saint Asaph. In 1345 Henry Shalford, burgess of Caernarfon and royal servant, was assassinated. John de Huntingdon, acting sheriff of Merioneth, was also, according to the burgesses of Caernarfon, "by the assent and compassing of the leading Welshmen of the county," killed as he was holding the county court. Although the murder of Shalford

1. See Contamine, *Guerre*, pp. 576–77, 592–93; Chotzen, "Yvain de Galles," pp. 231–40; Edward Owen, "Owain Lawgoch," pp. 6–105; Carr, "Rhys ap Roppert," pp. 163–67; and Carr, *Medieval Anglesey*, pp. 314–15.

2. This campaign is described in E. B. Fryde, ed., *Book of Prests*, pp. xxvi–xlvi; and John E. Morris, *Welsh Wars*, pp. 240–70.

3. In 1316 there was a short-lived revolt in Glamorgan, but this rising turned on local issues and remained confined to a small area in South Wales. See Ralph A. Griffiths, "Revolt of Llywelyn Bren," pp. 186–96; and J. Beverley Smith, "Rebellion," pp. 72–86.

touched off a wave of near panic among the English burgesses, it did little to disturb the stability of the regime.[4]

The reasons for Welsh quiescence in the fourteenth century are not difficult to understand. The native political elite had been either eliminated or neutralized during the wars of the 1270s, 1280s, and 1290s. For a number of years the patronage that the English directed toward the Welsh squirearchy was sufficient to keep it loyal. The prelates of the Welsh church might have formed a rallying point for resistance to the English. However, many Welsh churchmen had favored the English against the princes of Gwynedd. Throughout the fourteenth century the crown also kept firm control over appointments to higher church office. There were therefore no traditional centers of political authority that could serve as rallying points for those dissatisfied with the new regime. The string of fortresses constructed by Edward I also gave the foreigners unquestioned military superiority in the country.

The Persistence of Ethnic Hostility

The English may have successfully held the Welsh in obedience, but that did not mean that they did not mistrust the people of their new territories. To the English the Welsh were little better than savages. Already in the twelfth century, Gerald of Wales, himself partly Welsh but unable to speak the tongue of his Celtic ancestors, had waxed eloquent on the character faults of his countrymen. In his *Description of Wales* he remarked on the Welsh penchant for treachery and theft: "When they see a chance of doing harm, they immediately forget all treaties of peace and friendship."[5] These feelings of hostility were only intensified by the conflicts that marked Anglo-Welsh relations in the late thirteenth century. John Peckham, archbishop of Canterbury, denounced the Welsh as a perniciously idle people, whose leisure gave rise to savagery and criminality. In Peckham's opinion they were a bloodthirsty race, more cruel than even the Saracens.[6] The writ of summons to the parliament that condemned Dafydd ap Gruffydd to death in 1283 dwelt on the deceptions and

4. *Cal. Anc. Corr.*, pp. 231–32; D. L. Evans, "Some Notes," pp. 42–45.
5. Gerald of Wales, *Opera*, 6:207. The translation is from *Journey*, p. 257.
6. Peckham, *Registrum*, 2:436, 742; 3:776–77. See also R. R. Davies, "Buchedd," pp. 155–79.

plots that the Welsh, "with the stealth of foxes and with utter lack of respect for God and man," had hatched against the English.[7]

In the context of the wars of the thirteenth century, such opinions are not surprising. But the English remained mistrustful of their new subjects even after the destruction of Gwynedd's independence and long after the Welsh had ceased to pose a serious threat to the kingdom of England. Throughout the fourteenth century the English settlers in Gwynedd were convinced that the natives were hatching sedition. In its second decade a Scottish campaign in Ireland aroused fears of possible collaboration between Welshmen and Scots.[8]

In 1345 the murder of Henry Shalford provoked a series of near-hysterical letters from the burgesses of North Wales to the Black Prince. John de Pirye informed the prince's council that "all the great men of North Wales, clerks and others," had been party to the scheme to kill Shalford. The men of Denbigh claimed that "the Welsh have never since the conquest been so disposed as they are now to rise against their liege lord." The situation, according to the tremulous townsmen, had reached such a pass that "the Prince's English tenants in these parts hardly dare to go out of the towns of the franchises to plow and sow and trade; and his English bailiffs hardly dare to do their work for fear of being slain and plundered, so numerous are the evildoers and rebels who are outlaws in the woods." The inhabitants of Caernarfon reported that "the Welsh have become so proud and cruel and malicious towards the English in the said land, that they dare not go anywhere for fear of death." From Rhuddlan came the frantic announcement that "Englishmen residing in Wales in boroughs and in the geldable were never since the conquest in such perilous plight as they are now."[9]

Hand-in-hand with this mistrust of the Welsh went contempt. For an example, one need look no further than Owain Glyndŵr, leader of the great rebellion of the early 1400s. Owain was about as thoroughly steeped in English ways as a Welshman could be. His father-in-law

---

7. Stubbs, ed., *Select Charters*, p. 460, as translated in R. R. Davies, "Race Relations," p. 45.

8. J. Beverley Smith, "Gruffydd Llwyd," p. 473; and R. R. Davies, *Conquest*, pp. 387–88.

9. *Cal. Anc. Corr.*, pp. 230–33.

was a justice of King's Bench; Owain himself had probably been a student of English law at the Inns of Court in London; he had fought for the king in Scotland and had been a squire of the earl of Arundel. But he found that he got scant justice, or even civility, from Parliament when he submitted to it a petition concerning a dispute with the lord of Dyffryn Clwyd. When the House of Commons refused to give his complaint a hearing, the bishop of Saint Asaph warned the house of the discontent its behavior might cause. To this the members replied that they cared nothing for the "bare-footed buffoons" of Wales.[10] The depth of English contempt can be seen in the lordship of Dyffryn Clwyd, where it was argued in court that it was a punishable offense to call someone a Welshman when he was not.[11]

The Welsh, in their turn, seem to have felt little affection for the English. As Iolo Goch (fl. 1328–1405), poet and friend of Owain Glyndŵr, put it, "Where once there were Welshmen, now we have Englishmen and the Welsh suffer daily thereby."[12] But ethnic hostility alone does not explain the wide support for Owain Glyndŵr's rebellion in the early fifteenth century. The Welsh and the English detested one another after 1415 without an attempted revolution. The seeds of Glyndŵr's rebellion lay not so much in ethnic antipathy, no matter how deeply felt, but in policies of the royal government that systematically alienated all important segments of the social formation, not only of Gwynedd, but of all of Wales.

The Sources of Welsh Discontent with English Rule

In the late thirteenth century many in Gwynedd had not been hostile to the English conquest. Welshmen may not have had any great love for their English neighbors, but in general they had not much love to spare for any of their neighbors, English or Welsh. The political ambitions of the princes of Gwynedd had aroused much hostility and suspicion, not only among the other princely houses that feared the

---

10. Lloyd, *Owen Glendower*, pp. 20–22; Davies, *Conquest*, p. 448; Haydon, ed., *Eulogium historiarum*, 3:388.

11. R. R. Davies, *Lordship*, p. 317.

12. Welsh hostility to the English was only intensified by the failure of Glyndŵr's rebellion. See, for example, the poems of Lewis Glyn Cothi (one possibly by Tudur Penllyn) in Clancy, ed., *Medieval Welsh Lyrics*, pp. 166–68, 187–88.

supremacy of the Llywelyns, but also among many in Gwynedd itself who had to bear the burdens of their rulers' ambitions. Edward I thus had many Welsh allies during the wars of conquest.

But in the course of the fourteenth century, the English regime made the old divisions that had pitted Welshman against Welshman less important. The actions of the English administrators instead fused members of almost all important social groups into a single discontented mass that saw English overlordship as a mechanism of exploitation and a source of frustration to its ambitions.

One of the aspects of English rule that had the potentiality to offend nearly every inhabitant of Gwynedd Uwch Conwy was the new judicial system. The introduction into the Principality of North Wales of a foreign court system created novel and unpopular burdens. Some of these—suit of court, the hue and cry, and the activities of the coroners—have been discussed in chapter 2. Although it is clear that the Welsh found the administrative aspects of the new legal system a source of annoyance, it is harder to detect how they felt about the English mandated changes in substantive law. Although some of the alterations to local law made by the English may have met with Welsh approval, others did not. For example, when the lordship of Denbigh was in the hands of the Black Prince in 1361, a large number of its inhabitants complained that the local ministers, out of their desire for amercements, were not allowing disputants to settle their differences through the time-honored processes of negotiation.[13] There is also some evidence that the bloody punishments imposed by English criminal law offended Welsh sensibilities.[14]

The English rent offensive gave almost everyone in Gwynedd a common grievance. The making of the extents that valued the dues owed to the crown and that commuted most of them into cash payments was a painful experience. Not a few Welshmen emerged from it feeling victimized. Among the petitions presented to the prince of Wales in 1305, complaints about the fraudulence and injuriousness of the ex-

13. *BPR*, 3:410.
14. When in the late fifteenth century Siôn Eos was executed after having killed a man in a brawl in the lordship of Chirk, the poet Dafydd ab Edmwnd was moved to denounce the heartless law that demanded an eye for an eye: "O men, why isn't it better, / if one is killed, not to kill two? . . . / Even if body paid for body / compensation would be better for the soul. . . / I hate the churlish law / of the Chirk lordship; it took a nightingale away" (Gwyn Williams, *Welsh Poems*, p. 74).

tents figured prominently. In reply to these grievances, Prince Edward appointed a panel of five men to examine and amend the surveys.[15]

This commission, however, put an end neither to the alleged abuses nor to complaints about them. For example, in 1308 the free tenants of the Merionethshire commote of Ystumanner sent a petition to the government. They acknowledged that before the conquest they had been obliged to roof the houses of the prince's maerdref in Ystumanner. Crown agents had valued this service, together with certain other dues, at 20s. Unfortunately the maerdref had subsequently burned to the ground. Roger de Eccleshall, sheriff of Merioneth, had thereupon ordered them to rebuild it. They had refused, arguing that all their obligations for labor service were discharged by the annual payment of 20s. Eccleshall's reaction had been repeatedly to "vex" Ystumanner's freemen on this issue.[16]

As the vicissitudes of the bondmen of Penrhosllugwy in Anglesey illustrate, disputes about the legitimacy of the sums recorded in the Edwardian extents could drag on for years. The men of Penrhosllugwy appear to have been victims of slipshod administrative practices. When the dues of the villagers of Anglesey were surveyed after the conquest, Edward I appointed Master Richard Abingdon and Llywelyn, prior of the Dominican convent of Bangor, to compile Penrhosllugwy's extent. Master Richard, acting alone, imposed on the township's bondmen a global cash due of about £20. Sometime after Master Richard's visit, Friar Llywelyn surveyed the vill a second time. When the various local extents were consolidated into a single document, the sums in these two separate surveys were accidentally added together. The villagers therefore found themselves compelled to pay an extra £20 a year. When they petitioned Prince Edward on this matter in 1305, the prince and his council ordered William de Sutton, then justice of North Wales, to investigate. Sutton concluded that the bondmen's complaints were justified and ordered that the demand for the excess rent be respited. There the matter rested until John de Sapy became sheriff of Anglesey in 1312 and promptly renewed the demand for the extra rent. The men of Penrhosllugwy had therefore once again to approach Edward, now king. Edward ordered a second investigation. This new inquest also failed to resolve the dispute, for the villeins

15. RC, pp. 213–14.
16. Cal. Anc. Pets., p. 325. For other complaints about the assessment of rent, see RC, p. 217; Cal. Anc. Corr., p. 106; CCR, 1307–13, p. 284.

of Penrhosllugwy were once again seeking redress in 1322. Yet another inquest was ordered, which again found in favor of the villagers. The collectors of the king's revenues in Gwynedd were tightfisted men, however, and in 1325 the men of Penrhosllugwy were still importuning the king about their rent.[17]

Although the cash dues imposed on the people of Gwynedd constituted an important source of revenue for the crown, they were not enough for the new rulers. Royal agents were constantly on the lookout for renders and dues that the extentors might have missed during the original surveys. For example, Thomas de Esthall, chamberlain of North Wales, in his account for the year 1304–5 noted that unvalued dues worth over £170 had been discovered since the last extent.[18]

The crown also constantly engaged in manipulations designed to increase its income. The reletting of escheated land, for example, offered an opportunity to raise rents.[19] The sheriff's account for the county of Caernarfon for the year 1303–4 provides a clue as to how lucrative these transactions could be. In that year, the sheriff accounted not only for the normal £483 14s. 1³/4d. of the county's extended value, but also for another £60 2s. 6¹/4d. of various rents and dues that had not been included in the original extent. These increments were equal to 12.4 percent of the county's initial value.[20]

It is possible that the Welsh sense of grievance over the commutation of dues and services into cash payments declined with the passage of time. But there were other economic matters that never ceased to disturb them. Chief among these was the grip of the English boroughs on the country's commercial life. The regulations requiring everyone living within a prescribed distance of the boroughs to transact his commercial dealings in their markets were highly unpopular. Welsh recalcitrance and ill-will on this matter provoked a number of petitions from angry English burgesses. For example, the burgesses of Beaumaris reported in 1305 that the people of the three Anglesey commotes adjoining their town were obliged to trade in their market. This, however, the natives refused to do. Instead they were taking their

17. For documents concerning this dispute, see Seebohm, *Tribal System*, appendix Ac, pp. 29–31; *Cal. Anc. Pets.*, pp. 260–63; *Cal. Inq. Misc.*, vol. 2, no. 563; *CCR*, 1323–27, p. 304; Natalie Fryde, ed., *Welsh Entries*, no. 563. The dispute is discussed in Carr, *Medieval Anglesey*, pp. 135–38.

18. Lewis, "Account," pp. 257–58.

19. For some examples, see *RC*, pp. 5, 23, 52.

20. Waters, "Account," pp. 143, 147.

goods to Newborough, where they could deal with ethnically Welsh burgesses. Early in the fourteenth century the citizens of Conwy informed the royal council that they were dependent for their livelihood on the trade of the Welsh "and if anything was taken from them [that is, the Welsh], they held it for extortion and the greatest wrong that had ever been put upon them, since such custom had never been levied in those parts. For which reason they ceased coming with their chattels." In the 1330s the burgesses of Beaumaris were complaining once again that the Welsh were avoiding the town and holding their own markets in the countryside.[21]

The suspicion and hostility of the peasant for the slippery townsman was in this case exacerbated by the fact that boroughs were often bastions of English privilege. There were Welshmen dwelling in the towns; indeed, some were predominantly Welsh in character. But in the castellated boroughs, the linchpins of English military dominance, efforts were made to restrict Welsh settlement and to keep the natives in a position of inferiority. Ordinances were issued barring Welshmen from living in the English towns.[22] Similarly, the English burgesses claimed for themselves the right to be tried on pleas of the crown by juries composed solely of their fellow countrymen.[23] The existence of these privileged enclaves of aliens was so galling that the men of Tegeingl in 1378 organized a subsidy among themselves to petition for an end to the burgesses' privileges.[24]

The requisitioning of supplies for the castles and the practice of purveyance also aroused discontent. In 1305 the people of Gwynedd complained to Edward of Caernarfon that they were being unfairly compelled to cart material for the construction of his castles, manors, and mills. They also alleged that they were being forced to sell their goods involuntarily to the king's bailiffs for the maintenance of the fortresses. This last grievance remained a point of contention throughout the century. In 1308 or 1309, the freemen of North Wales again protested to Edward, who was now king, that they were being required to sell their goods to stock his castles. In 1360 a new genera-

21. RC, p. 223; Cal. Anc. Pets., p. 469. See also BPR, 3:486. The quotation is from Cal. Anc. Pets., p. 312.
22. RC, pp. 131–32. See also Cal. Anc. Pets., p. 172.
23. If they were deprived of this privilege, so they claimed in a petition to the Black Prince, "there would not. . . be any Englishman in Wales alive within a short time." Cal. Anc. Pets., p. 440.
24. Davies, Lordship, p. 317.

tion of free tenants was complaining to yet another English king, Edward III, about this same matter.[25]

Another economic grievance that pitted Welshman against Englishman involved access to the local pastures and forests. In an economy so dependent on pastoralism, these resources were of paramount importance. Therefore the effort by the new English masters to establish the preeminence of their rights over woods and wastes provoked no small measure of debate and dispute. This issue seems to have been particularly vexing in the county of Flint and in the new Marcher lordships.[26] In 1292 an inquiry into the conduct of the bailiffs on the estates of the late Queen Eleanor gathered a crop of complaints concerning forest rights. Welshmen from Hope and Estyn claimed that the queen's bailiff had cleared some twenty to sixty acres of new arable in their forest of "Swardewode" and rented these assarts to various people, most of whom seem to have been ethnically English. Forty-nine inhabitants of Bangor Is-Coed in Flintshire claimed that they had been deprived of their liberties in certain woods, pastures, and wastes. Owain ap Gronw of Hampton charged that he and his tenants had been disseised of their rights in four different woods.[27] The men of Maelor Saesneg in Flintshire also claimed that they had lost their customary rights and had seen their animals impounded by the queen's agents.[28] The efforts of the Marcher lords of northeast Wales to assert their dominance over woods and wastes provoked similar complaints.[29] In the Principality of North Wales, pasture access seems not to have been such a burning question. But the assertion of ultimate royal lordship over all woods and wastes created some discontent. Both the bishop of Bangor and the abbot of Bardsey were moved to complain about the difficulties royal agents caused their tenants concerning traditional rights of pasture.

The use of Wales by the crown as a source of military manpower also antagonized large segments of Welsh society. As we have seen, one of the causes of the rebellion of 1294–95 was the raising of troops for a campaign in Gascony. Although subsequent demands for money and men for the king's wars did not produce open rebellion, they were

25. *RC*, p. 213; *Cal. Anc. Pets.*, p. 115; *WTL*, 1:299.
26. See Davies, *Lordship*, pp. 120–27.
27. Just. Itin. 1/1149, ms. 2, 6, 5d.
28. Natalie Fryde, "Royal Inquiry," p. 371.
29. See, for example, complaints from Dyffryn Clwyd (*Cal. Anc. Pets.*, pp. 168–69) and Chirk (*Cal. Inq. Misc.*, vol. 2, no. 1203).

nevertheless unpopular. Only a few weeks after Edward III's victory at Crécy in 1346, justices were at work in Anglesey imposing penalties on Welsh villagers for failing to contribute to the military effort. Nineteen villages in the commote of Talybolion and ten in Twrcelyn were amerced for not paying their share of "army money." The village of Bodafon was penalized for not appearing at the arraying of troops at Conwy. Finally, the people of Penrhosllugwy were mulcted for not finding their share of the cost of the army's draft horses.[30]

The administrative correspondence of Edward the Black Prince, lord of Wales from 1343 until 1376, reveals the difficulties that English ministers in Gwynedd could experience in raising troops. In 1345 Roger Trumwyn, lieutenant to the justice, reported numerous problems in recruiting the 250 spearmen and archers required by the prince. In May troops raised in Caernarfonshire and Anglesey had assembled at Conwy. But the levies from Merioneth had refused to enter the town or take their wages. They remained at the Conwy ferry, "nor would they in any way be intendent to the mandates of the prince or of his justice." A year later John Weston informed the prince that the hundred spearmen he had mustered at Conwy had been dissatisfied with the wages promised them.[31]

There is nothing unique to Gwynedd about these social and political tensions. All across western Europe in the late thirteenth and early fourteenth centuries, such matters as taxation, rent, access to wood and pasture, the regulation of trade, and the levying of military service were matters of lively debate. What distinguishes Gwynedd is the fact that all these issues pitted Welshmen against Englishmen. The discontent of peasants with their landlords here often found Welsh peasants opposed to English lords. The unhappiness occasioned by the demands of the increasingly organized and needy political entities of the high middle ages here pitted Welsh taxpayers and conscripts against English tax collectors and military recruiters. The growing tension between urban and rural sectors of the economy here envenomed the relations of Welsh countrymen and English burgesses. All of the strains and stresses of late medieval society in western Europe were exacerbated in Gwynedd by an already deeply felt ethnic antipathy.

30. G. Peredur Jones, ed., "Anglesey Court Rolls, 1346," pp. 34–38.
31. *Cal. Anc. Corr.*, p. 235. The quotation is from ibid., p. 247. For other examples of difficulties encountered in raising Welsh troops in the 1340s and 1350s, see *BPR*, 1:9, 49, 52–53; 3:215.

The Welsh Squirearchy and the English Regime

In addition to those aspects of English rule that offended and antagonized virtually every inhabitant of Gwynedd, the English also specifically thwarted and frustrated certain politically important elements. By the end of the fourteenth century, the English had antagonized significant sections of the Welsh squirearchy and clergy. The reasons for the discontent of the Welsh squirearchy are easy enough to imagine.[32] The political world of the English kingdom was largely closed to men of Welsh birth. Within Gwynedd itself the ambitions of the squires were often frustrated. Although Welshmen staffed the lower ranks of the English government in the principality and in the Marcher lordships, they were kept away from the real levers of power. Welsh squires also found that the English often hindered their efforts to increase the size of their landed patrimonies. Repeated bids to have traditional rules concerning the alienation and inheritance of land modified so that estates might be more easily constructed and more effectively protected against partition among multiple heirs were largely ignored by the royal government. It was not until the late fourteenth and fifteenth centuries that large landed estates began to come into existence in Wales, and then many were in the hands of English families from the plantation boroughs. Even where native Welsh families succeeded in consolidating and defending coherent blocks of land, their estates cut a poor figure compared to those of the English landlord class.[33]

The Welsh Clergy and the English Regime

The Welsh clergy also found their ambitions frustrated. Although some Welsh churchmen had favored Edward I in his wars with Prince Llywelyn, they soon discovered that the English king and his

---

32. On the participation of the Welsh gentry in Glyndŵr's rising, see R. R. Davies, "Owain Glyn Dŵr."

33. Davies, *Conquest,* pp. 428–30, 433; Pierce, "Landlords," pp. 373–74. The very wealthiest of the Welsh gentry in the early fifteenth century do not seem to have had incomes that exceeded £200 a year. Owain Glyndŵr's estates seem to have been worth a little less than this figure, while those of Gwilym ap Gruffudd ap Gwilym, one of the few other Welsh squires whose income is known even approximately, estimated the value of his estates at £112 in 1413. (See Davies, "Owain Glyn Dŵr," pp. 153, 155.)

successors could be even more exacting masters than the native princes. Shortly after the conquest, Bishop Anian of Bangor was moved to protest to the king about the oppressive conduct of his agents.[34] The hands of the king's minions were also laid heavily on the regular clergy. Despite privileges granted them by both Llywelyn ap Gruffydd and Edward I, the monks of Aberconwy in the early fourteenth century were harassed over their right to build mills, alter the flow of streams, and receive whomever they wished into their order. They were also, in violation of their privileges, asked to provide pensions to former royal servants.[35]

Perhaps more important than this bullying by English ministers was the fact that the Welsh clergy found itself cut off from access to high church office. From the middle of the fourteenth century, Welsh cathedral chapters essentially lost the right to elect their bishops. In effect the king, the prince of Wales, and the pope cooperated in appointing bishops to Welsh sees. Most of these appointees were men who had made their careers in royal service. As the century progressed, the chances of a Welshman securing high office declined. Before 1347 most of the bishops of Saint David's had been men who were either Welsh by birth or who had had close associations with the diocese. For the century and a half after 1347, only two bishops of Saint David's had any connection with the see before their appointment. Of the sixteen men who were made bishops in Wales between 1372 and 1400, only one was a Welshman.[36] Some English bishops in Wales had no great love for their flocks. Thomas Ringstead, bishop of Bangor from 1357 to 1366, left £100 in his will to his cathedral provided that his successor in the see was not a Welshman. Similarly, Welshmen were barred from receiving any of the money he left to support poor scholars at Oxford or Cambridge universities.[37]

Not only was the Welsh episcopal bench increasingly staffed by royal favorites who were strangers to the country, the ranks of cathedral canons were also filled by royal appointees. At Saint David's forty king's clerks were appointed to prebends between 1343 and 1400. Most of these men had had no prior connections with the diocese. Similarly, few if any of the provosts of the collegiate church of

34. Glanmor Williams, *Welsh Church*, pp. 56–57; *Cal. Anc. Pets.*, pp. 464–65.
35. Hays, *Aberconway*, pp. 87–92.
36. Williams, *Welsh Church*, pp. 122, 127–28; and *Owen Glendower*, p. 15.
37. Davies, *Conquest*, pp. 439–40.

Caergybi in Anglesey seem to have been Welsh or to have had any prior connections with Wales. Even the less profitable maerdref churches often found their way into the hands of Englishmen. Of the twenty presentations made to the livings in the maerdrefi of Aberffro, Llan-faes, Rhosyr, and Penrhosllugwy between 1308 and 1340, only one was of a Welshman.[38] Ironically, the progressive closing of higher office to ambitious Welshmen came about at precisely the same time that Welsh clergymen, who were attending English universities in growing numbers, were becoming better educated and more talented.[39]

Given the fact that the plums of ecclesiastical preferment were reserved for English royal servants, it is not surprising that large numbers of clergymen supported Owain Glyndŵr. A list of Anglesey inhabitants who submitted to the king in 1406 indicates that perhaps as many as forty-five members of the local clergy joined the rebellion. From the very beginning of the revolt, the dean of the cathedral of Saint Asaph was a supporter. David Daron, the archdeacon of Bangor, was also active in the rebellion. Welsh clerics at Oxford were greatly agitated by news of the revolt, and many are said to have gone home to join the rebels. Among Owain's chief advisers were such clergymen as Gruffydd Young, his chancellor; and John Trefor II, bishop of Bangor.[40]

The Role of the English Regime in Facilitating the Organization of Welsh Resistance

A century of English rule had thus served to unite many Welshmen in a common antipathy to their foreign masters. The Welsh political elite, both clerical and lay, found its interests systematically thwarted by the English. The judicial, institutional, and economic changes introduced into Gwynedd made virtually all native social groups feel injured by some aspect of the English regime. Accordingly, when rebellion came in the first years of the fifteenth century, it enjoyed widespread support among all ranks of the population. A document drawn up in 1406 lists those inhabitants of Anglesey who had

38. Williams, *Welsh Church*, p. 137; Carr, *Medieval Anglesey*, pp. 279–82.
39. Hays, "Welsh Students," pp. 326–27.
40. Carr, *Medieval Anglesey*, p. 322; Williams, *Welsh Church*, pp. 219–22; and *Owen Glendower*, pp. 45–46.

submitted to the crown and agreed to pay fines. It lets us estimate the dimensions of support for Glyndŵr. The names of 2,121 individuals were enrolled by crown agents; this group probably represents a sizable portion of the adult, active population of the county.[41]

But foreign domination did more than merely give Welshmen common grievances. English rule was not only a process of exploitation, it was a process of education. By forcing the Welsh of the Principality of North Wales to adopt English governing institutions, the English kings gave native life an institutional and political cohesion it had previously lacked. In doing so they helped lay the basis for a relatively effective resistance to their own regime. The Welsh who rebelled in the first years of the fifteenth century had for over a century been participants, albeit marginal ones, in the English political system. The lessons they had learned from their masters served them well during the years of rebellion.

For example, Glyndŵr and his allies, in their efforts to mobilize support for the rebellion, borrowed one of the most distinctive innovations of the late medieval English polity, the parliament. In 1404, at the height of his power, Glyndŵr presided over such an assembly at Machynlleth. Later that same year he held a second parliament at Harlech. Finally, in March 1406 the rebels held a major conclave at Pennal to discuss the transferral of the country's ecclesiastical obedience from the Roman pope to his Avignonese rival.[42]

It also seems that the Welsh made good use of their long experience of war in English-led armies. To be sure, Glyndŵr and his followers adopted the ancient expedient of retreating before invaders into the hills, safe bastions from which they could harass stragglers and baggage trains. But the Welsh revealed that they were now better masters of conventional warfare than they had been a century before. In the course of the rebellion, Glyndŵr and his allies achieved several important victories. In 1402 they captured Reginald Grey, one of the most important Marcher lords; they also won a victory over a mixed English and Welsh force at Bryn Glas in Radnorshire. This last success delivered into their hands the enemy commander, Edmund Mortimer, another Marcher magnate. The rebels also proved that they had mas-

41. This list is printed in Glyn Roberts, "Anglesey Submissions," pp. 39–61. See the discussion in Carr, *Medieval Anglesey*, pp. 321–22.
42. Lloyd, *Owen Glendower*, pp. 82, 101, 119.

tered the techniques needed to capture at least some of the great fortresses that dominated their country. Conwy castle was seized in 1401. In 1402 both Harlech and Aberystwyth were taken. The great southern castle of Carmarthen was captured twice, in 1403 and again in 1405. In 1403 a rash of English strongholds fell to the Welsh, among them Llanstephan, Dryslwyn, New Castle Emlyn, Carreg Cennen, and Cardiff.[43]

The Welsh experience in the English polity had also familiarized them with the rules and players of the political game in England and elsewhere in western Europe. The rebels were therefore in a better position to seek allies abroad and to exploit the internal weaknesses and divisions of their enemies. Given the long experience of Welsh troops in France and the presence there of Welsh exiles, it is not surprising that the rebels entered into negotiations with the Valois monarchy. In the autumn of 1403 a French fleet cruised Carmarthen Bay. With the aid of this force, Glyndŵr pushed a vigorous, although unsuccessful, siege of Caernarfon castle. In the summer of 1405 a French army landed at Milford Haven. With its assistance Glyndŵr captured Carmarthen and Cardigan castles and led an eastward push that brought his forces close to the English town of Worcester.[44]

The long Welsh apprenticeship in English politics allowed them to exploit the discontent aroused by the deposition of Richard II and the seizure of the throne by Henry IV. Edmund Mortimer, whom Glyndŵr took prisoner at Bryn Glas, eventually became one of his allies. He also found allies in the powerful Percy family. In February 1405 the Percy earl of Northumberland, Mortimer, and Glyndŵr agreed to the so-called Tripartite Indenture, which envisaged mutual cooperation against Henry IV and provided for the division of the English kingdom among the confederates.[45] On a more humble and definitely less fanciful level, alliance with the Percies secured for the rebels the active assistance of their client, Thomas Barneby, who was receiver of both the county of Anglesey and the castle of Beaumaris.[46]

43. Williams, *Owen Glendower*, pp. 34–35. Beaumaris may also have fallen to the Welsh; Carr, *Medieval Anglesey*, pp. 244, 320–21.

44. Lloyd, *Owen Glendower*, pp. 101–6. Some Scottish troops also helped with the siege of Beaumaris; Carr, *Medieval Anglesey*, p. 244.

45. Lloyd, *Owen Glendower*, pp. 93–95. Wylie, *History*, 2:378–81, and Kirby, *Henry IV*, pp. 218–19, date the agreement to 1406.

46. Ralph A. Griffiths, "Glyn Dŵr Rebellion," pp. 154–56.

Ultimately, of course, Glyndŵr's rebellion failed. His allies, both English and French, proved either weak or undependable. The rebels were not strong enough to stand alone against the English and those Welshmen who remained loyal to the crown. After 1405 the tide ran steadily against Owain and his allies. By 1408 most of southern Wales was again under royal control. Although Glyndŵr held out in the north, his support steadily eroded. By the end of 1411 Henry IV felt confident enough to issue a general pardon to all his Welsh subjects with the exception of Glyndŵr himself. In June 1413 Glyndŵr's wife and some of his children and grandchildren were captured. In 1415 the king empowered Sir Gilbert Talbot to negotiate with the rebel and restore him to royal grace. After 1416 Glyndŵr disappears from the records.

This long rebellion in the first decades of the fifteenth century illustrates the paradoxical effects of English rule in Gwynedd. On the one hand, the new regime was sufficiently thorough and efficient to keep the Welsh mostly quiet for over a century. On the other hand, that same thoroughness and efficiency antagonized and alienated almost all economic, social, and political groups in native society. It thus guaranteed that, when rebellion finally came, it met with widespread support. English rule, which remade Gwynedd in the course of the fourteenth century, also provided the Welsh with the very tools they needed to resist their foreign masters. The century-long schooling that the Welsh received in English patterns of political behavior made the rebels of the early fifteenth century formidable opponents of the regime that had spawned them.

Languedoc

The French, in the early days of their domination, had to contend with a number of uprisings in Languedoc. With their alien tongue, their alien customs, and their championship of a persecuting and tithe-collecting church, they were not universally popular figures in the Midi. For a time the zealous adherents of Catharism presented some military problems for the French. Driven out of the lowlands of Languedoc, the Cathars and their sympathizers took refuge in the Pyrenees. But following the capture of the heretic strongholds of Montségur (1244) and Quéribus (1255), Catharism ceased to constitute an organized, military threat to French rule. Henceforth the heresy was merely an underground religious sect, hounded by an increasingly effective inquisition until it died out in the first decades of the fourteenth century.

Early Resistance to French Rule

During the early years of French domination, discontent with the royal regime remained high among sectors of the nobility. Raimond VII of Toulouse chafed at the amputation of property and authority he was compelled to accept in 1229. Other local lords longed to recover the estates they had lost during the crusades. And the zealous, resolute, and often brutal behavior of the king's administrators did little to make the change of mastery in the south more palatable. The result was two major rebellions. In 1240 Raimond Trencavel, the disinherited son of the former viscount of Carcassonne, led a group of exiles in an uprising. Despite some early successes, the rebels failed to capture the French citadel in the cité of Carcassonne, and their rebellion collapsed. In 1242 Raimond VII, who had held aloof in 1240, joined a number of other Languedocian lords, the count of La Marche, and the king of England in an alliance against Louis IX. But when Louis defeated La Marche and the English king, the Languedocians hastened to submit to the royal will.

The failure of these revolts marked the end of anything resembling serious resistance to French rule. In large part this was due to the conciliatory policies pursued by Louis IX. Local urban consulates were generally treated favorably by his government. Louis also proved receptive to the complaints voiced about the conduct of his officials. The investigations conducted by his enquêteurs did much to dampen discontent and assuage outraged sensibilities. Louis also managed to reach a degree of accommodation with many of those Languedocian nobles who had rebelled against his government (see chapter 4). Thanks to this conciliatory policy, Languedoc was not full of a disinherited, resentful, and seditious native aristocracy. Although individual aristocrats were on occasion to contemplate rebellion, never after 1242 did the entire nobility or even a major segment of it rise up against the northerners.

This does not mean that Languedocians sank into an inert passivity after the middle of the thirteenth century. The documents produced by the royal administration reveal that in the course of its work, it frequently encountered determined, indeed violent, opposition. The long dispute with the bishops of Albi about royal jurisdiction in that city, a dispute attended by riots and assaults on the king's servants, has already been described. Other examples are easy to come by. In 1320 the Parlement of Paris recorded a dramatic defiance of royal authority. Bernard de Trenqueleon had arrested Durand Cantacorp of Toulouse and relieved him of the money he was transporting from Condom to Toulouse. Three times Trenqueleon was summoned to answer for his deed in the court of the seneschal of Toulouse. Each time he failed to appear. When the seneschal's agents tried to seize Bernard's castra of Corronsac and Vic-Fezensac the inhabitants turned out in arms, crying after the king's servants, "Kill them! Down with the rascals and thieves. We know neither king nor queen."[47] Another act of defiance occurred in 1322 when the bayle and men of Mèze in the sénéchaussée of Carcassonne attacked the farm of Bernard Guilhem and carried off his animals. When a royal sergeant was despatched to recover the beasts, the bayle summoned his neighbors, threatened the sergeant with violence, and arrested Bernard Guilhem. Similarly, in the early 1320s Peire de Grimoard barred the Tarn river near Villebrumier and began demanding tolls from all wayfarers. The seneschal of Toulouse ordered the castellan, bayle, and other officials of Buzet to dismantle this illegal toll station. But when they attempted to do so, they were set upon by Peire and his men, beaten, and thrown into the Tarn.[48]

Too much importance should not be attached to incidents such as these. They reveal that the king's agents did not always find it easy to carry out their duties. But these affairs do not reveal any longing for an end to French rule on the part of Languedocians. The Languedocians who abused, insulted, assaulted, and arrested royal servants were not small-time guerrillas, longing for the days of southern independence. They were not seeking to overthrow the royal regime but merely to keep the king's rights within what they thought were reasonable and legitimate bounds. If we look beyond this petty, chronic haggling over the extent of royal authority, we find little to suggest that Languedocians ever seriously contemplated expelling the French. This does not

47. Boutaric, ed., *Actes*, vol. 2, nos. 6111–12. The identification of the two castra as Corronsac (Haute-Garonne) and Vic-Fezensac (Gers) is tentative.

48. Boutaric, ed., *Actes*, vol. 2, nos. 6999, 7383. For another example of an assault on a royal official carrying out his duties, see ibid., vol. 2, no. 7922.

mean that some people in the region did not hatch plots against the regime. But these schemes involved only small groups of men. None of the conspiracies succeeded in mobilizing large segments of the Languedocian population in united opposition to the French kings. As a result none posed a serious threat to their dominance. To illustrate this point, I will briefly describe what appear to be some of the more significant manifestations of discontent with the rule of the kings from the north.

The Revolt of Roger Bernard of Foix

Count Roger Bernard III of Foix, a belligerent and bellicose seigneur, caused the French administration considerable difficulty. In the late 1260s and early 1270s several issues troubled his relations with the French court, among them the endlessly vexing question of the pariage of Pamiers.[49]

The issue that brought open warfare in 1272 was Roger Bernard's involvement in a feud between Géraud V, count of Armagnac, and Géraud de Casaubon. The count of Armagnac claimed that Casaubon held the castle of Sompuy in the diocese of Auch from him as a fief. Casaubon maintained that he held from the king of France. In a skirmish the count of Armagnac's brother was killed. To avenge his death, Armagnac enlisted the aid of Roger Bernard. Casaubon sought protection from the French, surrendering Sompuy into the custody of the seneschal of Toulouse. This did not prevent the two counts from capturing the castle, massacring its garrison, and ravaging Géraud's lands. This disregard of his authority galvanized Philip III into action. He summoned Géraud d'Armagnac and Roger Bernard to appear before the Parlement in Paris. Armagnac obeyed, but Roger Bernard did not. To deal with the count, Philip set about raising an army.

Roger Bernard put Foix into a state of defense and attacked the seneschal of Toulouse, Eustache de Beaumarchais. Eustache responded by subduing the northern part of the county of Foix. By the beginning of June 1272 Philip III and his army reached Languedoc. Roger Bernard appealed for aid to King Jayme of Aragon, from whom he claimed to hold the southern half of his county as a fief. Jayme tried

49. J.-M. Vidal, "Bernard Saisset," pp. 431–38. See also *HL*, vol. 9, 12 (n. 2), for Roger Bernard's dispute with the count of Ampurias, a case in which the latter appealed to the French for justice.

to negotiate a settlement with Philip, but failed. The French proceeded to invest the castle of Foix, perched on its rock at the confluence of the Ariège and Arget rivers. The siege progressed well and Roger Bernard soon surrendered. Carted off to prison in Carcassonne, he remained in custody for more than a year.[50]

The Conspiracy of the Viscount of Narbonne

The counts of Foix were not the only members of the local aristocracy to give the French difficulty. In 1282 the government discovered a plot by the viscount of Narbonne and some of his family to cooperate with the king of Castile in driving out the French.[51] This alliance apparently went back to 1276. At that time agents of Alfonso X approached Viscount Aymeri IV and his brothers Amauri and Guilhem about forming a pact against the French king. In the spring of 1277 the brothers swore to aid the king of Castile against all others, including Philip III of France.

This alliance, however, had no practical effect. Aymeri and his brothers never sought to act on their agreement with the Castilians. As a meaningful threat to French dominance in Languedoc, the conspiracy was an utter failure. Indeed, several clients of the viscount's family regarded the alliance as ridiculous. Jean de Portal, a bourgeois of Narbonne and one of the familiars of Aymeri's brother Amauri, told his master that the agreement with Alfonso was an act of folly and that no one in the region would answer the call to rebellion against the king of France. The opinion of Viscount Aymeri's notary, Guilhem Catala, was that the pact with Castile amounted to nothing less than the ruin and disherison of his master and his family.[52]

Nothing might ever have come of this plot had not the viscount's brother, Amauri, decided to reveal it. In the late spring of 1282, he denounced his brother. Philip III arrested Aymeri and seized his lordship. The investigation of the viscount's alleged treason, however, proved inconclusive. No copy of the agreement with Alfonso could be found. And it seems that the government was not overly impressed by

---

50. My description of this war is based on *HL*, 9:12–21; 10: *Notes*, 9–13; Guillaume de Puylaurens, *Chronique*, pp. 202–7; Langlois, *Règne*, pp. 59–63.

51. My description of this plot is based on the account in Auguste Molinier, "Trahison," pp. 409–24. See also *HL*, 10: *Preuves*, cols. 180–84.

52. Molinier, "Trahison," pp. 413, 420.

the gravity of the affair. In September 1284 Aymeri received a full pardon; his brother Amauri was banished to the holy land.[53] A year later the viscount took part in Philip's expedition against Aragon and behaved with notable loyalty.

The Affair of Bernard Saisset, Bishop of Pamiers

The secular ruling elite was not the sole source of worry for the French government. Although the church hierarchy had supported Simon de Montfort and the Capetians in the Albigensian crusades, the prelates were among the more inveterate opponents of the expansion of royal authority when it did not serve their interests. The determined opposition to royal claims by many of the bishops of the region has already been touched on. This dogged opposition to the growth of monarchical authority within church lordships never resulted, however, in a permanent alienation of the loyalty of the local prelates. There may, however, have been one exception to this pattern, Bernard Saisset, the cantankerous bishop of Pamiers.

Saisset, who had been abbot of Saint-Antonin of Pamiers, became the first bishop of the new see of Pamiers when it was split off from Toulouse in 1295.[54] A determined and bellicose individual, Saisset by 1300 had behind him a long history of quarrels with his neighbors. On the one hand, there were his differences with the bishop of Toulouse over the delimitation of the borders of his new diocese. On the other, there was the interminable dispute with the count of Foix over the pariage of Pamiers. This had just completed a particularly violent phase. In 1295 the royal garrison that had occupied Pamiers for several years had withdrawn. This had ushered in a confused period of raids, sieges, murder, and arson as Count Roger Bernard III tried to enforce his claims. Through all of this Philip IV did little to assist Saisset. A compromise between the bishop and the count was finally arranged through the arbitration, not of the French king, but of the lord of Mirepoix.

Saisset thus had little reason to feel much gratitude to the Capetians. Whether he plotted treason against Philip IV, however, is diffi-

53. Régné, *Amauri II*, pp. 98–99.
54. My description of the affair of Bishop Saisset is based on Vidal, "Bernard Saisset," pp. 177–98, 371–89.

cult to say. Nevertheless, by the spring of 1301 his conduct had become suspect to the royal court, and enquêteurs were dispatched to investigate. Saisset's old enemies were more than willing to paint a black picture of the bishop's conduct. The enquêteurs sequestered his property, seized his papers and castles, and brought the bishop himself north to answer to the king.

Saisset was eventually accused of several misdeeds. He was reported to have said that Louis IX had told him that the French kingdom would perish in the third generation, that is, in the time of the current king, Louis's grandson. It was also claimed that he had defamed Philip, saying that the king was a bastard and a counterfeiter who behaved like a statue or an owl, doing nothing but stare at men. Furthermore, the bishop was said to have called the French the enemies of the people of Languedoc, doing them nothing but ill. Most important, he was accused of plotting treason against the king, suggesting to both the count of Foix and the count of Comminges that they drive the French out and seize the county of Toulouse for themselves.

One is probably justified in doubting the truth of many of these accusations. The procedure against Saisset has all the hallmarks of the other "judicial" processes launched by Philip and his entourage against those whom they wished to destroy. It was characterized by the same secret interrogation of witnesses, the same liberal application of torture, the same disregard for normal judicial process, and the same use of fantastic allegations of heresy and moral depravity.[55] Saisset may have thought Philip IV no more useful than an owl and may even have reflected on how pleasant life would be without the French, but he probably never plotted treason.

Corroboration for this view is provided by the subsequent behavior of Philip and his councillors. The procedure against Saisset embroiled the king with Pope Boniface VIII in a series of events that eventually resulted in an assault on the pontiff at Anagni. As this greater quarrel developed, Philip's minions lost interest in Saisset. The bishop was released from custody relatively quickly and by the autumn of 1302 was in Rome. By late 1305 he had returned to his diocese. There he was allowed to live out the rest of his life unmolested by the royal government.

55. Ibid., pp. 371–79.

The Treason of Carcassonne

Saisset's treason may have been no more than a figment of the imagination of a number of royal councillors. But at the same time that Saisset was entangled in Philip IV's toils, a more serious plot to get rid of the French was being hatched in the bourg of Carcassonne. This was the consequence of a complex series of events that pitted important elements of the population of Languedoc against the Dominican inquisitors and, finally, the king of France.

Carcassonne, in addition to being the capital of one of the royal sénéchaussées and an episcopal see, was from 1255 headquarters for one of the permanent Dominican inquisitorial tribunals. In the last half of the thirteenth century this organization gave many of the bourg's inhabitants a difficult time. The extent to which the Carcassonnais were involved in heresy is not clear. Over the years, however, the inquisitors developed a body of evidence that in their eyes implicated many of the townsmen. In the 1280s the Carcassonnais began organizing against the inquisitors. Proclaiming their innocence and the inquisitors' malevolence, they appealed variously to king and pope for protection.[56]

In the mid-1290s the resistance began to turn violent. In 1295 the inquisitor Nicholas d'Abbeville was driven from the pulpit and stoned through the streets when he tried to preach. Other Dominicans were assaulted, and the entire order was boycotted by the townspeople.[57] In 1296 an attempt by the inquisitors to arrest several suspects who had taken refuge in the local Franciscan convent set off a riot.[58] For a time King Philip IV showed himself willing to temper the authority of the inquisition, but his support proved short-lived.[59] Pope Boniface VIII was also deaf to the entreaties of the Carcassonnais.[60]

With neither the king nor the pope willing to protect the Carcassonnais, the inquisitors were able to grind them down. By 1299 Nicholas

---

56. Guiraud, *Histoire*, 2:295–302; Mahul, ed., *Cartulaire*, 5:635–36, 638–43; Doat, vol. 26, fols. 153v, 215v–16v, 250r–57v, 261v–64r, 266r–67r; vol. 27, fol. 236v; vol. 28, fols. 166v–70r; vol. 30, fols. 93r–93v, 97v; *HL*, 9:336; J.-M. Vidal, *Jean Galand*, pp. 39–43. See also Lebois, "Complot," pp. 159–63.

57. Lea, *Inquisition*, 2:68–69; Gui, *De fundatione*, p. 102; Doat, vol. 30, fol. 94r.

58. BN, Ms. Lat. 4270, fols. 231r–32v, 238r–38v.

59. Lea, *Inquisition*, 2:65–67; *HL*, 10: *Preuves*, cols. 274–75.

60. BN, Ms. Lat. 4270, fols. 119v–20r.

d'Abbeville had brought his enemies to the point of surrender. In October the bourg's consuls and the inquisitors negotiated a settlement.[61] The exact terms of this agreement were, however, kept secret. In a few years they were to become the subject of considerable controversy and not a little fear.

As d'Abbeville negotiated with the people of Carcassonne, events were transpiring in Albi that were to give the Carcassonnais new allies in their struggle. The bishop of Albi, Bernard de Castanet, was at loggerheads with the subjects of his diocese.[62] His difficulties with the people of Albi may have prompted his decision to begin a heresy investigation late in 1299. Setting up his own inquisitorial tribunal with assistance from the Dominicans of Carcassonne, he arrested over forty suspects, seventeen of whom had been town consuls between 1280 and 1298. With the help of Nicholas d'Abbeville, Castanet tried and condemned twenty-four Albigeois.[63] These men were removed from Albi and lodged in the inquisitorial prison in Carcassonne.

It was widely believed in Albi that the condemned were innocent and had been forced to confess through the vigorous application of torture. The Albigeois found a spokesman in the Franciscan Bernard Délicieux, a long-time critic of the inquisitors. In the autumn of 1301, Délicieux and a delegation of Albigeois journeyed north to present their complaints to Philip IV. Their petition persuaded the king to order restraints on the behavior of the inquisitors and to seize the temporalities of the see of Albi.[64] The condemned Albigeois, however, remained in the inquisitors' prison. The king also refused to accede to Délicieux's demand that members of the Franciscan order be placed on the inquisitorial tribunals.

In the following years the conflict between the Carcassonnais and the inquisitors heated up. In the summer of 1303, Délicieux, taking advantage of the visit of a royal enquêteur, Jean de Picquigny, managed to secure a copy of the 1299 agreement between the consuls and the inquisitors. The interpretation that the friar put on this document was a very dark one. By its terms, so he claimed, the consuls had admitted that they and all the people of the bourg had aided and

61. Doat, vol. 32, fols. 283r–88r, 299r–308r.
62. My description of Castanet's inquisitorial work is based on Biget, "Procès," pp. 273–341.
63. The records of this investigation have been published in Davis, ed., *Inquisition*.
64. Compayré, *Etudes*, pp. 239–40; Lea, *Inquisition*, 2:79–80; Dmitrewski, "Bernard Délicieux," p. 208; *HL*, 10: *Preuves*, cols. 379–84.

abetted heresy. This meant that if the inquisitors thereafter proceeded against any of the bourg's inhabitants, they could treat them as relapsed heretics and consign them to death by burning. Bernard communicated his views to the Carcassonnais in an inflammatory sermon. An attempt by the incumbent inquisitor, Geoffroy d'Ablis, to provide a more palatable exegesis of the terms of the 1299 agreement only succeeded in touching off a riot.[65]

The bourg was now in a virtual state of insurrection. The townsmen forced the king's enquêteur to remove the condemned Albigeois from the inquisitors' prison and lodge them in the royal citadel. The Dominicans were boycotted, their convent stoned, and their sympathizers among the townsmen assaulted. Royal officials in the cité dared not venture out from the safety of its walls for fear of being disarmed by the townsmen.[66] At Christmas 1303, King Philip arrived in Languedoc. His tour through the province, however, did little to calm the situation. Philip's old enemy, Boniface VIII, had died the previous October. With a new pope on the throne, and a Dominican one at that, the king was less disposed to curry favor with the inquisitors' opponents. At Toulouse Philip entertained complaints about the conduct of Bernard de Castanet and the inquisitors. The actions he took, however, failed to satisfy the demands of their opponents. From Toulouse the king went to Carcassonne. His visit there was a signal failure. He refused to see the condemned Albigeois lodged in the royal citadel. He also quarreled publicly with Elie Patrice, the leader of the bourg's militia.[67]

Philip's behavior convinced Délicieux, Patrice, and others that they could hope for no further protection or aid in their struggle with the inquisitors. They decided that it was time to find a new lord who could protect them. Overtures were therefore made to Ferrand, the son of King Jayme of Majorca. When he proved receptive, the consuls of the bourg decided to call on him to supplant Philip as lord of Carcassonne. Délicieux was given the task of transmitting the offer to Ferrand.[68]

---

65. BN, Ms. Lat. 4270, fols. 135r, 160r–61r, 194r–94v, 199r–99v, 206v, 211r–213r, 224v, 287r–87v.
66. BN, Ms. Lat. 4270, fols. 49r–49v, 59r–59v, 155v–56r, 221v–22v, 271v, 281v, 291r; Doat, vol. 64, fols. 320r–23v; Gui, *De fundatione*, p. 104.
67. BN, Ms. Lat. 4270, fols. 74v, 233r–33v, 226r–26v.
68. BN, Ms. Lat. 4270, fols. 195r–96v, 284r, 294r–96r, 113r–14r, 76r–78r, 219r, 250v–51r, 204r–7v, 219v.

Délicieux located Ferrand at his father's court near Perpignan. The Franciscan's presence aroused King Jayme's suspicions. During a stormy interview in which the enraged king struck his son and pulled clumps of hair out of his scalp, Jayme discovered the purpose of Délicieux's visit. The king promptly ordered the friar out of his kingdom.[69] Carcassonne's experiment in treason had failed almost before it had begun.

Retribution was not long in coming. Word of the conspiracy soon reached the royal court. A number of the bourg's citizens were tried and found guilty of plotting against Philip; several went to the gallows. The bourg was deprived of its consulate and was saddled with a fine of 60,000l.t.[70]

The Difficulties of Organizing
Opposition to the Royal Regime

A consideration of the details of these affairs suggests some generalizations. The most striking feature of all these conspiracies was their futility. The count of Foix's defiance of Philip III in 1272 necessitated a major response by the king's government, but it did not pose a serious threat to its authority in Languedoc. Languedocians did not hasten to join the count in his rebellion. Indeed many of the local nobles served under the king's banner. The count himself cannot be said to have resisted in a determined manner. He may have been willing to brawl with the seneschal of Toulouse, but once Philip III arrived with his army, he hastened to strike a deal with his suzerain. The other affairs we have considered were even less serious. Some indeed seem more fitting for comic opera than for the stage of history.

The protracted efforts of the people of Carcassonne to restrain the inquisitors or to eject a king who would not protect them produced no positive results. The paternal wrath of the king of Majorca put an end to their schemes in a single afternoon. Even if Prince Ferrand had been allowed by his father to assume the lordship of Carcassonne, one is

---

69. BN, Ms. Lat. 4270, fols. 197v–98r; Finke, ed., *Acta aragonensia,* 3:131–34.
70. Mahul, ed., *Cartulaire,* vol. 6, pt. 1, pp. 10–11; *HL,* 9:277–80; 10: *Preuves,* cols. 461–63; Hauréaux, *Bernard Délicieux,* pp. 126–28; Gui, *De fundatione,* p. 105; Doat, vol. 64, fols. 47r–47v. As for Délicieux, he was arrested by the king but eventually set free. However, in 1319 he fell victim to his old enemies, the inquisitors, and was condemned for heresy. Ultimately he died in prison.

probably justified in doubting that he could have had much success in asserting his mastery of the city. All that this particular scheme achieved was to send several of the bourg's consuls to the gallows. The other plots were even less significant. Although the viscount of Narbonne entered an agreement with the king of Castile directed against the king of France, he never took any action that we know of to implement the provisions of the alliance. When the French began their investigation of his conduct, he meekly surrendered into their hands. As for the affair of Bernard Saisset of Pamiers, it is doubtful if his treason consisted of anything more formidable than the exasperated muttering of an old, disgruntled bishop.

It is clear that in the late thirteenth and early fourteenth centuries the French never had to deal with a resistance movement that marshaled the support of a wide spectrum of the people of Languedoc. Not only did would-be rebels in the Midi find it difficult to recruit allies among their fellow Languedocians, the resistance movements we have examined often aroused vehement opposition within the region itself. Virtually every would-be rebel had his native enemies who preferred dealing with the French. In the case of Bernard Saisset, if he did indeed approach the counts of Foix and Comminges about driving the French out of the Midi, these men proved willing to testify against him to the French. Bernard was also denounced by Pierre de la Chapelle-Taillefer, the bishop of Toulouse, who had had his share of disagreements with Saisset over the parishes and revenues that were to be subtracted from his control to provide the endowment of the new see of Pamiers.[71]

Aymeri, viscount of Narbonne, was also surrounded by enemies. Although his brother Amauri had joined him in his alliance with Alfonso X of Castile, it was he who denounced the viscount to the French. For this disloyalty Amauri had strong motivation. It seems that when the brothers' father died in 1270, he left a sizable portion of his inheritance to Amauri. Aymeri, however, managed to set aside the will and force his younger brother to accept a more modest property settlement. Amauri was therefore glad to see his brother suffer discomfiture at royal hands.[72] Numbered among the viscount's local enemies there were also the townsmen of Narbonne. The consuls, in

71. Vidal, "Bernard Saisset," pp. 178–79.
72. *HL*, 8: cols. 1728–31; 9:61; Molinier, "Trahison," pp. 410, 414.

an attempt to reduce Aymeri's authority, had turned to the king's government for help, claiming that they owed their allegiance to the king in his capacity as duke of Narbonne. The viguier of Béziers had taken the consuls under royal protection, an act that in 1280 caused Aymeri to complain to the king's justices.[73] Narbonne therefore harbored not a few men who hoped to see the destruction of their lord. As one of these told Guilhem Catala, the viscount's notary, "If Aymeri does not lose his land as a result of the denunciation that his brother has gone to make against him to the king, we will make such revelations as will surely bring about the viscount's dispossession."[74]

The difficulties that Bernard Délicieux and the Carcassonnais experienced in trying to recruit allies clearly reveal how internal Languedocian rivalries prevented any resistance movement from creating a strong base of opposition to outsiders, whether those outsiders were inquisitors or the king of France. One problem faced by Délicieux and his allies was the fact that many people in Languedoc did not share their negative opinion of the inquisition and its activities. As Bernard himself realized, there were many men who had relatives and friends among the Dominicans and were therefore reluctant to join a movement against them. More important, perhaps, the cause that Délicieux and his friends defended was suspect in the eyes of many. Although the Cathar heresy continued to have its adepts in the south of France well into the fourteenth century, the days when a significant fraction of the population was sympathetic to the heretics were over. And, despite the assertion by Délicieux and his allies that the men imprisoned by Castanet and Nicholas d'Abbeville were innocent, many believed that they were in fact guilty and that the inquisitors had acted properly. When the consuls of Alet were asked to contribute money to the anti-inquisitorial association organized by Bernard, they replied that they could find no fault with the conduct of the inquisitors.[75]

Délicieux's efforts to construct a broadly based coalition against the inquisitors and later against the king were also hampered by the intense conflicts that divided the towns of Languedoc. Bernard was successful in enlisting the bulk of the population of the bourg of

73. *HL*, 9:73. During the summer of 1282 the two brothers were also supporting different factions among the quarreling townsmen; ibid., 10: *Preuves*, cols. 180–81.
74. Molinier, "Trahison," p. 422.
75. BN, Ms. Lat. 4270, fols. 302r, 227r–28v.

Carcassonne against the inquisitors. But to do this he had to sow dissension in the town. What influenced the Carcassonnais against the inquisition was Bernard's fiery sermon on the dire consequences of the 1299 agreement. The immediate result of the friar's oratory was a riot in which the houses of several of the men who had been consuls in 1299 were destroyed. This drove some of them into exile and, seemingly, into the arms of the inquisitors.[76]

The chronic conflicts that pitted urban rich against urban poor also hampered the anti-inquisitorial party's search for allies. In those towns where the consuls favored the idea of joining the alliance, the poor often showed themselves hostile. This hostility stemmed not so much from Catholic bigotry as from resentment against the taxes levied to defray the expenses of the campaign against the inquisitors. For example, Délicieux's efforts to raise money in Cordes, Rabastens, and Lapourouquial aroused opposition. Certain factions insisted that any money raised should be used only for the good of the towns themselves. Even at Albi the consuls' attempts to fund their exertions on behalf of their imprisoned citizens met with resistance; compulsion had to be employed to make the recalcitrant pay up. At Limoux, on the other hand, it seems that the poor favored Délicieux while the rich opposed him. When the town consuls proved unwilling to take any action against either the king or the inquisitors, the friar's response was to liken them to ignorant pigs and to appeal over their heads to the town's poor. These, he claimed, lacking the connections and influence of the rich, would not be able to protect themselves from the inquisitors. The poor of Limoux apparently took Bernard's words to heart; his visit was followed by rioting.[77]

If Délicieux and his friends among the Carcassonnais found it difficult to recruit allies against the inquisitors, they found it even more difficult to win support for their scheme to call in Ferrand. An invitation to the consuls of Albi to join them in treason was immediately rebuffed. Even in Carcassonne itself the plan met with opposition. Some of the bourg's consuls denounced the idea of betraying the king; they had to be expelled from the meeting at which the decision was made to offer the lordship of Carcassonne to Ferrand.[78] It was accordingly only a tiny group of conspirators, not even representative of the

76. BN, Ms. Lat. 4270, fols. 199r–99v, 213r, 223v–24r, 281v, 286v–87v.
77. BN, Ms. Lat. 4270, fols. 243r–43v, 266r, 212v, 265v, 301r–2r.
78. BN, Ms. Lat. 4270, fols. 78r–79r, 205r, 207v, 219r.

entire political elite of the bourg, that launched itself on the path of treason.

A consideration of the way in which resistance to French rule was hampered by social and political cleavages leads to another conclusion. Most of the plots directed against the king's government in the second half of the century grew more out of internal quarrels between Languedocians than out of dissatisfaction with the royal regime. Revolt against the king was contemplated largely because he was perceived to be either an ally of an internal opponent or a useless patron and protector. The roots of the war between the king of France and the count of Foix lay in the dispute between the count of Armagnac and Géraud de Casaubon. Roger Bernard of Foix only became involved in this quarrel as an ally of Armagnac, and the king only because Casaubon called on him for protection. In the case of Bernard Saisset, it seems that the bishop's pique over the way in which his former ally, the king of France, had deserted him in his struggles with the count of Foix led him to utter the words, treasonable or not, that brought down on him the wrath of Philip IV. Although we cannot be as definite about what impelled the viscount of Narbonne to enter into an alliance with the king of Castile, it would be reasonable to assume that Aymeri's disputes with the townsmen of Narbonne, disputes in which the burgesses turned to the royal government for aid, had something to do with his decision. Finally, it is clear that the consuls of the bourg of Carcassonne felt compelled to renounce their allegiance to the king of France only when it became apparent that Philip IV would never adequately protect them against the inquisitors.[79]

The evidence in the preceding pages should make it clear why the French never had to deal with a resistance movement as massive as the English encountered in the rebellion of Owain Glyndŵr. French policy in Languedoc did not succeed in simultaneously offending several important political and economic groups, thus giving large numbers of men a common feeling of grievance against the regime. The effort of the French kings to conciliate even the most dissatisfied of the secular nobility coupled with their generally respectful attitude toward the privileges of the urban consulates did much to dampen discontent. Above all, royal government did little to cause Languedocians to put aside their own internal differences in favor of a common opposition

79. BN, Ms. Lat. 4270, fols. 195v–96r, 204v, 219r.

to the French. As we have seen in the previous chapter, French rule itself often did much to exacerbate the preexisting tensions. Languedocians were too divided against one another to unite in opposition to royal overlordship. Indeed, for many in Languedoc the king and his servants appeared to be useful allies in their struggles with their local enemies. Many of the anti-French plots of the last half of the thirteenth century therefore grew out of the internal divisions of Languedoc. For most of the would-be rebels their real enemies— whether rivals for power among the local aristocracy, a grasping town consulate, a tyrannous bishop, or the new and terrifying inquisition— were located within Languedoc. It was only when the king's government inclined toward one contestant that the other party contemplated the drastic step of expelling the royal government. As a result the rebels and plotters of late thirteenth-century Languedoc found it difficult to recruit allies from within the region. Their fellows were either indifferent to their designs or actively hostile. Accordingly all efforts at rebellion against the French were dismal failures. Although some of them may have given the French king and his agents some troubled nights' sleep, none ever constituted a significant threat to the continuation of French dominance in Languedoc.

Conclusion

In this chapter we have examined a significant difference in the behavior of Gwynedd and Languedoc under outside rule. In Gwynedd a century of relative quiet after the English conquest preceded a massive uprising. In Languedoc, on the other hand, the establishment of the French regime was accompanied by constant turbulence. The agents of royal authority were frequently and often successfully challenged. Yet there were, after the early 1240s, no major rebellions against the new regime.

In part this contrast was a consequence of the very different effectiveness of the French and English royal governments. English rule in Gwynedd Uwch Conwy was, by the standards of the fourteenth century, strong governance. The new Principality of North Wales was covered with a network of fortresses supported by colonies of Englishmen. English techniques of local government were also imported into the country. In short, the English after 1283 set up a system of control and coercion that was far more thorough than anything the country had previously known. At the same time the native ruling elites went into a long period of decline. It was therefore not surprising that this part of northern Wales was not openly rebellious after the failure of the rebellion of 1294 and 1295.

The very thoroughness of English rule, however, helped lay the groundwork for the uprising of the early fifteenth century. The English antagonized the elites of Welsh society, both secular and ecclesiastic. The operations of the governing institutions and the economic policies put in place by the new regime also gave virtually every social group in northwest Wales a set of common grievances. Finally, English rule provided parts of Gwynedd with an institutional and political unity it never had in the days of its independence. During this first century of outside rule many Welshmen received training in new forms of military and political behavior. The Wales that rose against Henry IV in 1400 was thus a more unified and coherent entity than the Gwynedd that had confronted Henry III and Edward I in the thirteenth century.

In Languedoc, however, French rule was much less thorough. The French may have been dominant in Languedoc, but they were not masters of the country in the same sense that the English were of Gwynedd. Royal agents found their authority constantly challenged and curtailed. In a way this very weakness of French rule was its strength. Although the royal regime had many enemies, it was never so strong as to convince all the politically significant elements in the region that their interests would be best served by its elimination. Political and social divisions ran so deep that, for every potential enemy of French power, there was a potential supporter who saw in the king a useful ally. French rule in Languedoc was therefore marked by turbulence. But significant conflicts in Languedoc usually set one native against another. Few individuals were moved to challenge openly the continuation of the French regime, and those who did never constituted a serious threat to it.

Factors other than the relative strength of outside rule, however, were involved in shaping the behavior of Languedoc and Gwynedd. The establishment of French dominance in Languedoc entailed no major changes in local social and economic arrangements. In Gwynedd, however, the English conquest meant that at least part of the country was subjected to a species of forced "modernization" that transformed many aspects of local life, thereby generating new sources of political and social tension. Under English rule the Welsh found themselves dragged into a more complex world. A country that had known little specialization of political roles received within a few years a new, powerful, and foreign ruling class. A country with a relatively undeveloped commercial life rapidly acquired an urban infrastructure and a burgess class equipped with important privileges. Welshmen were compelled to participate in a new web of social relationships, one that was highly asymmetric in nature, marked by great differences in the distribution of wealth and authority. That this situation laid the foundations for a major explosion is not surprising.

In Languedoc, however, the imposition of French rule had no such profound, transforming effects. By the early thirteenth century Languedoc had attained a relatively advanced stage of development. When the Albigensian crusades began, the region already possessed a complex and differentiated set of social structures. Its development, with its strongly asymmetrical distribution of wealth and power, produced a series of conflicts that set rich against poor, townsman against countryman, the strong against the weak. In all these respects Languedoc was not much different from northern France. Accordingly, the coming of French rule did not imply a profound upheaval in Languedocian social arrangements. The incorporation of Languedoc into the French royal polity was a process of coordination, not one of transformation. All the conflicts between rich and poor, townsman and peasant, ruler and ruled—which in Gwynedd pitted Englishman against Welshman—in Languedoc pitted Languedocian against Languedocian. This left the French with the opportunity often to play a mediating role.

In effect, the incorporation of our two regions into larger polities had led to the development in Gwynedd of a greater contradiction between state and society than in Languedoc. This difference manifested itself in several ways. First, there was a wider diffusion of political authority through Languedocian than Welsh society. In Languedoc indigenous organizations remained endowed with much real power. Members of the native ruling elite continued after the conquest, as before, to produce authoritative decisions regulating important aspects of local life. As a result, Languedocian political life did not revolve exclusively around the royal government. In Gwynedd, however, local social organizations were shorn of almost all the authority they had possessed. Most political authority and decision making were concentrated in the hands of English outlanders, whether agents of the king or of the new Marcher magnates.

Second, the people of Gwynedd and Languedoc experienced very different success in influencing the policies of their outside masters. In Gwynedd, where the powers of direction and coercion were largely monopolized by the crown or by English Marcher lords, the Welsh had little influence in the setting of either royal or Marcher policy. Confined for the most part to the lesser ranks of the new administrations, they were largely restricted to implementing decisions arrived at by Englishmen. In Languedoc the situation was very different. Even though not all aspects of Languedocian life hinged on the decisions of the French kings, the people of Languedoc had an important role in shaping those decisions. Recruited in large numbers into the royal government and regularly consulted in formal assemblies, Languedocians had more opportunity to influence the formulation of royal policy.

Finally, the fiscal burden of the state mechanism proved far more difficult to bear in Gwynedd than in Languedoc. The economy of Languedoc was fairly productive by medieval standards, while that of Gwynedd was not. The surplus that the outside political directors could appropriate for their own uses was undoubtedly smaller in Gwynedd. The demands made on the Welsh economic surplus were, however, very heavy. For the task of extracting tribute from Gwynedd the English were able to employ a relatively developed set of fiscal mechanisms. In Languedoc the agents of the French king did not possess as finished a set of fiscal devices. Furthermore, Welshmen were much less capable than Languedocians of defending themselves against the demands of their rulers. All told, the state mechanism that the Principality of North Wales received in the wake of its conquest was more imperative, more elaborate, and more expensive than could be easily supported by its social and economic institutions. In Languedoc, however, there was no such disparity between the political institutions introduced by the French and local resources. In essence, Languedoc could afford its royal government; Gwynedd could not.

Thus, French rule in Languedoc, which was relatively weak and inexpensive and did not imply radical changes in local social and economic arrangements, failed to arouse any widespread, concerted resistance. The south of France may have been turbulent, but this turbulence never seriously threatened the domination of the royal agents from the north. English rule in Gwynedd, however, was expensive, strong, and transforming. It thus mobilized against itself widespread discontent, out of which there eventually emerged the important challenge to the English regime that was the rebellion of Owain Glyndŵr.

Conclusion

This conclusion is divided into two parts. In the first I pull together what the comparison of Languedoc and Gwynedd under outside rule has to tell us about the process of political incorporation in the central middle ages. In the second I discuss a few of the larger questions about the nature of the state and the political process on which this book casts some light.

In summarizing what this book reveals about the political incorporation process in medieval Europe, I want first to discuss those features that were common to both Gwynedd and Languedoc. First, and most striking, is the fact that neither the French nor the English monarchy was able fully to integrate and digest its newly acquired territory. Both Gwynedd and Languedoc remained institutionally and politically distinct from the core areas of the French and English monarchies. The legal systems of both regions continued to retain peculiarities that distinguished them from England or northern France. Even the new Principality of North Wales, which was given a government modeled closely on that of England itself, was not completely integrated into the English kingdom. Constitutionally and legally it remained separate from England until the early sixteenth century. In the first generations of their rule, neither the French nor the English created institutions common to all their newly acquired territories. Even Gwynedd—which had a tradition, although only a relatively short-lived one, of rule by a common dynasty—was not treated as an organic whole by the English; instead part of it was incorporated into the royal Principality of North Wales, and part used to form new Marcher lordships.

Just as the encapsulation of our two regions into larger polities was not accompanied by the construction of an institutional framework common throughout the newly enlarged polity, so it was not part of any nation-building program. Gwynedd and Languedoc became members of larger organizations, but their masters from outside did little to foster among the people of these two regions the idea that they belonged to a common political community with the outsiders. Little effort was made by the rulers to spread the burdens and benefits of the political community equally among all sectors of the population. The costs and rewards of royal government were unequally distributed throughout both polities, a factor that inhibited the development of any feeling of community with the outside rulers.[1]

Neither the French nor the English sought to socialize their new subjects into a "national" culture. Welshmen and Languedocians retained their own languages and their own literary and cultural traditions. No effort was made to impose either French or English culture on the peoples of Gwynedd and Languedoc. The English may have been provoked by the Glyndŵr rebellion to legislate against Welsh bards and other "vagabonds" and to contemplate the destruction of the Welsh language, but they made no systematic efforts to eradicate or remake Welsh culture as a whole.[2] Indeed, the fourteenth century saw Welsh literature flourish, with many accomplished poets active and with learned Welshmen endeavoring to collect Welsh literature and law. The seductions of Welsh literature were so strong that some Welsh poets even attracted the patronage of ethnically English lords.[3] Welshmen may have sought to absorb English culture by attending English schools and by taking service in the households of English magnates, but they did so on their own initiative, not as part of any consciously formulated English policy of cultural imperialism.

1. On the importance of policies of equitable resource mobilization and income redistribution in building a sense of national community, see Ardant, "Financial Policy," pp. 232–36.

2. Glanmor Williams, *Recovery*, p. 10.

3. R. R. Davies, *Conquest*, pp. 418–19; Parry, *History of Welsh Literature*, pp. 127–63; Williams, *Recovery*, p. 99.

In Languedoc a determined and ultimately successful effort was made to stamp out the Cathar heresy; but the goal here was not to make Languedocians conform to "French" culture but rather to the norms of the supranational Catholic church. Although it is tempting to claim that the thirteenth century saw a decline in Occitan literature from the major achievements of the twelfth century, the period after the Albigensian crusades nevertheless witnessed a number of noteworthy productions in poetry and prose.[4] Although twentieth-century readers may not be as impressed by late medieval Occitan literature as they are by earlier works, Languedocians themselves remained interested in their own language and literature, with, for example, the people of Toulouse in the first half of the fourteenth century establishing a *Consistori del Gai Saber* to conduct an annual poetry contest.[5]

Another similarity in the way Gwynedd and Languedoc were integrated is the fact that neither set of outside authorities fashioned a new set of governing techniques specifically designed to deal with the unique characteristics of their new subjects. In their new territories, both the French and the English monarchies employed their traditional institutions. The French took over many indigenous Languedocian institutions. Where they introduced novel administrative mechanisms, they contented themselves with using the same techniques found north of the Loire river. Although the English pursued a dual policy in Gwynedd, creating new Marcher lordships in the east while fashioning the western districts of the country into the Principality of North Wales, both policies followed established precedent. The new lordships of the northeast—with their extensive political privileges and in some cases their administrative divisions, Welshries and Englishries— were replicas of the older lordships of the middle and southern border, whose histories went back to the last half of the eleventh century. In the Principality of North Wales, the crown deployed roughly the same institutions of local governance known in England itself.

We also see similarities in the ways in which the French and English sought to exploit the economic resources of their new subjects. In essence, the economic policies of both monarchies were primarily concerned not with affecting the underlying structures of the economies of Gwynedd and Languedoc but with extracting, through vari-

4. Camproux, *Histoire*, pp. 47–63.
5. Wolff, ed., *Histoire du Languedoc*, pp. 226–27; Miremont and Monestier, *Littérature d'oc*, pp. 203–7.

ous forms of tribute exaction, some of the surplus produced within those economies. Little effort was made to increase local production; virtually none was devoted to promoting new forms of production. Royal investment in both Languedoc and Gwynedd was directed primarily to increasing the government's means of coercion, and hence its extractive capacity, rather than to increasing production. We should also note that this behavior did not constitute an innovation in either Gwynedd or Languedoc. Before the coming of outside rule, the local dominant classes had also relied primarily on extraeconomic coercion to transfer to themselves part of the economic surplus generated by direct producers.

Those interventions in the local economy that were not concerned with direct, extraeconomic surplus extraction were designed to affect not the sphere of production but the sphere of circulation. In Gwynedd the English planted a series of towns and endowed them with trading monopolies. In Languedoc the French monarchy at times acted to restrict exports from the region. But such manipulations of exchange relations had little impact on the basic processes or relations of production in the economies of either Languedoc or Gwynedd.

This primacy of political, extraeconomic forms of resource extraction probably helps explain the relatively conservative approach of both outside regimes to the questions of landholding and law. Since tribute extraction did not entail direct intervention in processes of production, neither monarchy needed to alter patterns of landholding to make them suitable for a new scheme of production relations. For the same reason, the system of legal rules that underpinned traditional forms of property holding did not have to be revised. Legal change was thus primarily a matter of institutions, not rules, as both the English and French monarchies deployed a network of courts in their new territories. In Gwynedd, the English, finding local norms morally offensive, overhauled criminal law. But both monarchies left the body of rules governing the holding and transmission of land largely unchanged.

These similarities are not surprising. They fit nicely into the framework of medieval political and social behavior. For example, the fact that the English and French primarily relied on extraeconomic forms of resource mobilization is what we would expect. In almost all of the social formations of western Europe in the middle ages, this was the primary mechanism by which the dominant classes extracted surplus from the producing but subordinate classes. Everywhere lords—kings as well as nonroyal members of the dominant classes—supported themselves by using their political powers of coercion to force peasants to surrender part of what they won from the soil.[6] If the French and English relied on this form of surplus extraction at home, it is not surprising that they continued to do so in their new territories.

The inability or unwillingness of outside rulers to integrate fully their new subjects into a unified polity or to engage in anything that looks like nation-building is also to be expected. The English and French kings did not rule over the sort of unified, unitary polities whose structures provided a set of clear guidelines for incorporating new communities. Powers of legitimate coercion and control were not concentrated in royal hands but were widely diffused throughout society. Even the most developed governing mechanisms possessed by kings were relatively rudimentary. One can hardly say that even the most determined royal government had successfully penetrated its society in the sense that it had set up a unified, rational field administration for resource mobilization, the creation of public order, and the coordination of collective efforts. No royal government had devised mechanisms by which to give all elements of the population a degree of participation in its workings; nor had any monarchy established institutions, such as universal schooling, through which its subjects could be socialized to identify with the state.

Kings thus confronted not a planar social field of citizens each formally equal with respect to the law and the state, but a highly unequal array of subjects, some individual, some corporate, each possessed of varying rights and duties vis-à-vis the state and some endowed with their own legitimate right to wield coercive authority. This was, of course, less true of England than of France. The historians of England make much of the great degree of political integration that the English kingdom had achieved, but it must be remembered that England appears "well integrated" only when compared to other kingdoms of the day. England contained within its borders large areas, such as the Welsh March, where the king's writ did not run and where the normal infrastructure of royal local government did not exist. In a very real sense there was in both England and France no unified "core" into which Gwynedd and Languedoc could be integrated.

6. Anderson, *Passages*, pp. 147–48.

Similarly, there was no "national" community into which new subjects could be assimilated. The states of medieval Europe were, as J. R. Strayer has aptly put it, "mosaic" entities. Gwynedd and Languedoc simply were new pieces of the jigsaw puzzles that made up the kingdoms of England and France.

Despite their similarities, the incorporation of Gwynedd and Languedoc was also marked by contrasts. Probably the most immediately striking difference between Gwynedd (or at least those parts incorporated into the Principality of North Wales) and Languedoc was the much greater degree of penetration of local society achieved by the English monarchy. In Languedoc many of the political structures—town corporations, lordships lay and ecclesiastical—that had come into existence before the Albigensian crusades survived the imposition of Capetian overlordship. Indeed some of these political entities consolidated their internal organization and expanded their authority under royal hegemony. Although the royal government deployed a network of governing institutions in the region, these had to fit themselves into and around those produced by the local political system. In many important respects political authority remained in local hands in Languedoc.

In Gwynedd, however, almost no significant native concentrations of political authority survived the wars of conquest in the 1270s, 1280s, and 1290s. Once the English had destroyed the house of Llywelyn ap Gruffydd, they did not have to contend with any significant local power centers. Welsh social organizations could thus be safely stripped of much of whatever authority they possessed. All significant political power came to rest in English hands, whether Marcher or royal. In the new Principality of North Wales, the crown was able to deploy uniformly throughout the region a form of government modeled almost exactly on that of England, but enjoying a greater monopoly of power and authority than in England itself.

The regimes imposed by outsiders differed in their abilities to mobilize the resources of their subjects. In Gwynedd the destruction of indigenous power centers allowed the English to demand, and apparently receive, a much larger portion of the local economy's surplus than the native rulers had been able to appropriate. In Languedoc the continued vitality of local political organizations meant that Languedocians were able to restrain the demands of the Capetian kings. Indeed, if one cares to speculate, one can argue that English fiscal demands in Gwynedd were so heavy that they may have contributed to the economic dislocation apparent in the fourteenth century; royal French fiscal demands, however, seem not to have had much, if any, negative impact on the economy of Languedoc.

The political practices of the people of Gwynedd and Languedoc were also differently affected by their incorporation into larger polities. Those members of the lesser political elite of Gwynedd who survived the conquest were forced into a marginalized position. Not only were they excluded from posts of importance in England, they found it difficult to secure important appointments in the new government of their own country. Members of the Languedocian elites— possessed of greater wealth and political authority and with access to the resources offered by political and social organizations outside the kingdom of France—not only played an important role in governing their own land but also managed to make their presence felt on the kingdom-wide political scene.

Patterns of internal conflict in our two incorporated societies were also differently affected by outside rule. The English, by destroying the state-building ambitions of the princes of Gwynedd, put an end to the most fertile source of significant political conflict within Welsh society. In Languedoc the assertion of royal overlordship did not have such an impact. With local social formations retaining important degrees of political authority and with royal servants either unable or unwilling to put an end to local squabbles, Capetian government failed to end significant political and social strife within the ranks of its Languedocian subjects.

The English monopoly of authority in Gwynedd succeeded in creating a situation in which almost all major political and social conflicts pitted Englishmen against Welshmen. The English pursued policies that eventually offended virtually every social group in northern Wales. Simultaneously, the innovations introduced into Gwynedd by the English helped provide a political infrastructure around which opposition could coalesce. The result was a major rebellion slightly over a century after the assertion of English lordship. The French monarchy, since it exercised much less thorough control over Languedoc, never succeeded in simultaneously antagonizing a large cross section of local society. Significant social and political conflict in the region thus tended to pit Languedocians against one another, rather than against the royal government. Thus after the 1240s, although there was much small-scale resistance to royal authority, there was no widespread uprising in Languedoc.

In essence, outside rule in Gwynedd meant that the Welsh were reduced to a status of colonial dependency.[7] Endowed with governing institutions that were the product not of Welsh but of English history, with its traditional ruling elite destroyed or marginalized and subjected to a much more rigorous regime of resource exploitation than it had previously known, Gwynedd after 1283 was a subordinate appendage of the English kingdom. Languedoc did not know such a fate. Instead the country simply became another of the regional societies over which the Parisian monarchy claimed hegemony.

This "variation-finding" aspect of the comparison between Gwynedd and Languedoc produces what is probably the most interesting conclusion of this essay. The feudal state structures that emerged in northwestern Europe may have borne a strong resemblance to one another, but they did not interact in a uniform way with the regions that were subject to them. The social structures of the areas that came under the control of kings and their servants played a significant role in determining the nature of the interactions between rulers and subjects. The patterns we have observed in Languedoc were possibly the most common ones. At least they bear some resemblance to what other scholars have discovered in areas such as Normandy, Valencia, and Pescia. But the fate of Gwynedd stands as a reminder that quite divergent patterns of adaptation were possible.

The crucial intervening variable in explaining these differences seems to be the degree to which political authority was institutionalized in Gwynedd and Languedoc before the imposition of outside rule. Before the assertion of outside rule, it appears that Languedoc had created a denser internal framework of political organization. On the one hand, certain members of the aristocracy, both lay and ecclesiastical, had advanced fairly far down the road toward the creation of coherent lordships. No ruling house dominated the entire region, but the power of such magnates as the counts of Toulouse and Foix, the viscounts of Carcassonne, and the lords of towns like Narbonne was

---

7. This conclusion has been apparent to Welsh historians for some time. See R. R. Davies, "Colonial Wales," pp. 13–21.

growing. Other social classes had also managed to fashion for themselves a measure of institutionalized political power, of which the most imposing example was the self-governing towns of the region.

In independent Gwynedd, however, political authority seems to have been relatively less institutionalized and coherent. The princes of Aberffro made much progress during the thirteenth century toward creating a territorial principality, but on the eve of the English conquest their lordship still remained relatively new, and their authority was resented and contested by many of their subjects. In contrast to the situation in Languedoc, other social organizations had failed to find a strongly institutionalized expression for the authority they possessed. There was in Gwynedd nothing comparable to the self-governing towns of Languedoc. The local bishops and abbots, although rich in Welsh terms, were few in number. The kinship groups that were so important to Welsh social life lacked much in the way of formal organization or coercive authority. Welsh villages were not nearly as large, organized, and powerful as were the castra of Languedoc.

One is tempted to link this differing degree of political development to the distinctive natures of the economies of our two regions. Certainly Gwynedd's economy offered a smaller surplus with which to construct a powerful lordship than did Languedoc's. However—as neo-Marxist students of politics, who have been eager to grasp the ways in which economic and political structures determine one another, have pointed out—it is mistaken to posit a neat, unambiguous, and deterministic relationship between economics and politics. Before we can provide an adequate analysis of the nature of the link between economic and political structures, we need additional comparative studies of political practice in the different regions of medieval Europe.

The examination of Gwynedd and Languedoc under outside rule does, however, lend some support to those who feel that the use of the Marxist concept of a feudal mode of production can make a positive contribution to the study of medieval society. Key to the concept of the feudal mode of production is the fact that the dominant classes support themselves through extraeconomic means of coercion, that is, through means that are above all *political* in nature. Although the concept of a feudal mode of production is not without problems, it does point to the crucial role played by politics in understanding medieval society.[8] As we have seen from our comparison, politics, far from being the epiphenomenon that some social historians would claim it to be, is of crucial importance in understanding medieval social and economic development. I do not mean to say that in medieval Europe the political realm enjoyed absolute autonomy with respect to other social structures and that medieval politicians had an unusual capacity to shape social and economic structures as they chose. Indeed, much of this book has been concerned to show how preexisting social and economic structures shaped the nature of the regimes created in Gwynedd and Languedoc. We should not treat the realm of politics as necessarily determinant or dominant in medieval societies, but we should bear in mind that politics played a key role in the reproduction of medieval social relations. Social structure and political behavior were locked together in a mutually conditioning relationship, an analysis of which ought to be an important task for students of medieval history.

At the beginning of this book, I advanced as a working hypothesis the thesis that in the middle ages local communities, when incorporated into larger political entities, would be expected to retain most of their indigenous political institutions and that local political life would continue to be practiced in accordance with traditional norms. The material I have assembled suggests that this hypothesis cannot be accepted, at least in an unmodified form. Whereas the experience of Languedoc under outside rule tends to confirm the hypothesis, that of Gwynedd tends to disprove it.

8. The primary problem with the Marxist concept of feudalism is the fact that virtually all noncapitalist modes of production postulated by Marxists are characterized by the dominance of extraeconomic means of surplus appropriation. It thus becomes very difficult to make a meaningful distinction between such supposedly different modes of production as feudalism, slavery, and the "Asiatic" mode of production. Some scholars deal with this problem by arguing that the feudal mode of production is but a local example of a larger, "tributary mode of production." (For an example of this approach, see Wolf, *Europe*, pp. 79–82.) However, this procedure—which lumps together such seemingly diverse social formations as medieval Europe, ancient Egypt, early modern China, and the New World empires of the Incas and the Aztecs—does not seem particularly useful. For a critique, produced by Marxists of a structuralist bent, of the traditional notions about the feudal mode of production and an effort to construct an alternative Marxist concept of this mode, see Hindess and Hirst, *Pre-Capitalist Modes of Production*, pp. 221–59.

In light of these findings, it would seem appropriate to revise the hypothesis as follows: When a society such as Languedoc—with a relatively diversified and productive economy, a relatively wealthy aristocracy, and a relatively developed array of political organizations— is incorporated into a monarchically led polity like that of Capetian France, then that newly encapsulated society will retain much of its indigenous political institutions and traditions of political behavior. However, when a society such as that of Gwynedd—with its less productive economy, its less differentiated and asymmetrical social system, and its less developed institutions of coercive governance—is incorporated into a feudal monarchy like that of England, it will experience important changes in the way in which it conducts its political life. Nevertheless, it will not be completely integrated into the engulfing polity and all its traditional political institutions "normalized" to make them conform to those of the new, outside rulers.

This statement is not so much a conclusion as it is a new working hypothesis. On the basis of a mere two case sample, one cannot expect to make a valid generalization that applies to all of Europe in the thirteenth and fourteenth centuries. Moreover, my rephrased hypothesis does not take into account the fact that we can find in medieval Europe many examples of failed political incorporation. The union of the three crowns of Norway, Sweden, and Denmark in the late middle ages ultimately disintegrated. In Britain, although the English endeavored to establish control over Scotland and Ireland, they did not thoroughly conquer either area. Despite a major military effort at the end of the thirteenth and the beginning of the fourteenth centuries, the English failed to conquer Scotland. In Ireland, although the Anglo-Norman lords who entered the country in the late twelfth century initially enjoyed much success, overrunning much of the country, in the fourteenth century the Irish rolled back the English and confined their effective power to only part of the island. The reasons why some efforts at state-building succeeded and why some failed need to be investigated. In the case of Scotland, one could argue that the kingdom had succeeded in creating too tough an institutional framework to allow the English to overrun it. One can argue that Ireland was too remote from the core areas of English power and too poor to warrant the major effort that would have been necessary to reduce it to obedience. But this is mere speculation, and we need additional comparative studies of both failed and successful efforts at political incorporation if we are to understand the dynamics of the medieval state system.

This is not the place to attempt an analysis of the medieval political system as a totality. But I would like to suggest how my research may help us conceptualize the study of medieval politics. The material assembled here at least prompts a cautious approach to much of the conventional wisdom about the nature of medieval politics.

What has been the dominant organizing concept employed by most students of medieval politics? The answer seems to be a species of "modernization" paradigm. This is especially true of administrative historians. For them the history of the medieval state often involves the movement of medieval kingdoms toward the structures of the modern state, with its centralization of authority and its array of differentiated, complex, autonomous, coherent, and adaptable political institutions.

The ultimate inspiration for this line of argumentation seems to be the work of the sociologist Max Weber. For Weber the gradual drift toward a greater "rationalization" of human affairs, intellectual as well as political and economic, was central to his conception of history.[9] In the realm of politics and administration, Weber felt that the inherent technical superiority of bureaucratic organization over other forms was one of the central facts of the sociology of politics.[10]

These ideas have inspired much writing on medieval politics. J. R. Strayer has summarized this line of reasoning in his *On the Medieval Origins of the Modern State* (1970). In this book Strayer writes as though European political history is in essence the story of how the modern state struggled to attain its true form, which, although immanent in the medieval and early modern periods, was not fully realized. Strayer begins by defining the state as equivalent to that which we find in twentieth-century industrialized societies.[11] Essential to a state are "impersonal, relatively permanent political institutions, . . . which al-

9. Gerth and Mills, eds., *From Max Weber*, p. 51.
10. Weber, *Economy and Society*, 2:973.
11. Strayer does find the task of defining the state a difficult one. In one place he is forced to take refuge in a formulation that seems to smack of mystification, asserting that "a state exists chiefly in the hearts and minds of its people." (*Medieval Origins*, p. 5.) This formulation reduces politics and the state to mere intersubjectivity. The state and the other coercive and ideological structures of a society, however, are concrete realities, existing apart from the individual consciousness of those who are subject, at times unwillingly, to them. What Strayer here is discussing is what most political scientists refer to as legitimacy, or what Gramscians might call hegemony. Many states are legitimate, but as any late twentieth-century person should realize there are many viable and enduring states that are not accorded much legitimacy by their citizens.

low a certain degree of specialization in political affairs and thus increase the efficiency of the political process, institutions which strengthen the sense of political identity of the group." The superior efficiency, rationality, and integrative capacity of these institutions explain their success. Not only do the masters of such institutions ultimately triumph on the political scene, but their triumph is conducive to the good of society as a whole.[12] As Strayer succinctly puts it, "the state gave greater peace and security, more opportunity for the good life, than loose associations of communities."[13]

Although much medieval administrative and political history can be fit into such an interpretive mold, the material we have considered points up some shortcomings in this approach. Interpretations such as Strayer's tend to assume that political and administrative developments are self-generating and unfold according to an inbuilt logic in which simple, "irrational" ways of doing things are progressively replaced by more complex, specialized, "rational," and efficient mechanisms. What such an approach tends to overlook is the dialectical interaction of social structures and political forms. A consideration of such interactions lies at the heart of much modern political analysis.[14]

Medieval administrative historians have not been completely oblivious to the fact that social arrangements condition political developments. But they tend to handle the dialectical relationship between the two in a mechanical fashion. The model of the interaction between political and social development usually presented is a relatively simple one of challenge and response, that is, new tasks summon forth the appropriate bureaucratic and administrative responses. Several historians, for example, have argued that the territorial expansion of medieval monarchies necessitated administrative innovation.[15] Others have

12. Ibid, pp. 6—7. Strayer thus fits into the liberal tradition of political thought that sees the state as a mechanism for realizing the common good of society as a whole. On this tradition of political analysis, see Carnoy, *State*, pp. 11–43.

13. Strayer, *Medieval Origins*, p. 10. Interestingly, Strayer makes no mention of violence, a key element in Weber's concept of the state, which Weber regarded as "a human community that (successfully) claims the *monopoly of the legitimate use of physical force* within a given territory." (Gerth and Mills, eds., *From Max Weber*, p. 78.)

14. For a summary of Marxist discussion of this subject, see Carnoy, *State*. For a discussion of the same issue from a non-Marxist perspective, see Easton, *Framework*, pp. 59–75.

15. See, for example, Fawtier, *Capetian Kings*, p. 180; and Painter, *Feudal Monarchies*, pp. 32–33. See also Richardson and Sayles, *Governance*, p. 157.

argued that the rise of a money economy required the streamlining of the procedures of accounting and revenue management.[16] There is much to recommend this line of reasoning.

Such arguments, however, ultimately confront some intractable difficulties. One is the problem of accounting for those occasions when a challenge failed to evoke the necessary response. As Strayer notes, precisely such a situation arose in fourteenth-century France, when the monarchy, which had previously been fertile in institutional innovations, failed to deal adequately with the great challenges presented by economic decline, demographic collapse, and chronic war. Explaining this phenomenon involves Strayer in an unpersuasive argument concerning bureaucratic inertia and the personal shortcomings of royal servants.[17]

If nothing else, the material in this book suggests that such a simple challenge-and-response model needs to be amplified. Social and economic conditions did not simply present challenges for medieval administrators. They also set the parameters within which those administrators operated. Existing social and economic relations constrained the ways in which medieval political institutions could develop. The economic, political, and social structures that existed in independent Gwynedd and Languedoc help explain the fact that the regimes that took shape in these areas differed in important ways.

Our evidence also reveals that efforts to interpret the growth of more organized and centralized polities as conducive to the good of a society as a whole are not very satisfactory. If there was any place in northwestern Europe that came close to having something that looks like a modern state, where coercive authority was concentrated in the hands of a state elite that enjoyed a great deal of autonomy in its relations with local society, it was the Principality of North Wales. Yet it does not seem that this unified political system did much, at least in the eyes of many of its Welsh subjects, to give greater "opportunity for the good life." Whether or not one accepts the suggestion made earlier that English rule may have contributed to economic dislocation in Gwynedd, it is clear that enough Welshmen found the political system under which they lived inimical to their interests to make possible the protracted uprising of the early fifteenth century. The building up of

16. Lyon, *Constitutional History*, p. 390.
17. Strayer, *Medieval Origins*, pp. 72–77, 88, 92.

large-scale political organizations did not automatically produce some universal social good. It benefited some groups and harmed others.

Students of state-building in early modern Europe have long been aware that it was a conflict-ridden process. As Charles Tilly puts it, early modern state-builders "had to tear or dissolve large parts of the web [of existing political relations], and to face furious resistance as they did so."[18] We would do well to remember that the medieval process of the concentration of political authority was destructive as well as constructive, and its end result was not necessarily conducive to the well-being of society as a whole.

This is hardly a surprising conclusion. Societies are complex entities composed of various social groups, the interests of which are often necessarily antagonistic. The state plays an integrative function in holding these disparate groups together, but it is not a neutral arbiter floating above the battleground of competing interests. We do not need studies that explore how (or worse, presume that) the growth of medieval political institutions promoted some nebulous social good. Instead we need to ask which social groups under what conditions benefited or suffered from the construction of large-scale polities in the central middle ages and how these groups' efforts to defend their interests shaped further political developments.

If one of the larger implications of this study is that the modernization paradigm of medieval political development favored by many historians is overly simplistic, another is that our conceptions of medieval political history have often been too elitist. For the most part medieval political history is written as though the only actors on the stage of politics are kings, nobles, and prelates. Some medievalists indeed have displayed a tendency to exaggerate the creative and determining role of kingship.[19] Divorced from the social and political milieu in which they operated, kings are often made to appear as all-creating geniuses heroically shaping their plastic and nearly passive realms. As Robert Fawtier puts it in his brief survey of the Capetian dynasty, "the . . . achievements [of the Capetians], territorial, politi-

---

18. Tilly, "Reflections," p. 25.

19. See, for example, Bryce Lyon's remark in his survey of the constitutional history of England that "Underlying all cultures, however primitive, has ever been the concept of the leader." (*Constitutional History*, p. 36.)

cal, administrative, and their acceptance by the French people, were the vital advances along the road towards the creation of France."[20]

I do not mean to denigrate the importance of kings and their governments in medieval political history. But I do want to point out that in writing the political history of medieval Europe, we have probably exaggerated their role and that of their governments. This is, of course, not a novel observation. Susan Reynolds has recently criticized the practitioners of medieval political history for underestimating the extent and the significance of lay political activity; she has argued that our frame of reference should be expanded to take into account the collective activity of communities such as towns and villages rather than focusing narrowly on the vertical bonds that united kings and their subjects.[21]

The results of the present investigation lend some force to her argument. Any conception of medieval politics that regards it as primarily the affair of a narrow elite is overly simplified. The practice of politics was not the exclusive domain of the dominant classes. Our examination of the political encapsulation of Gwynedd and Languedoc has required a discussion of almost every social group in our two societies—aristocrats and churchmen great and small, townsmen rich and poor, and the peasant masses. All social classes were involved in the medieval political process, although now it may be difficult for us to perceive the modalities of their participation. Historians should turn aside from their heavy emphasis on the affairs of rulers and their agents and begin to analyze the ways in which the members of all the social classes of medieval Europe represented their interests on the political level of their societies.[22]

The material here also serves as a corrective to a tendency, noticeable in the work of some scholars, to discount the importance of political history in premodern Europe. With the growth of social history and the increasing interest in various structural interpretations of the societies of premodern Europe, there has been a tendency to displace the study of politics into an increasingly marginalized position.

20. Fawtier, *Capetian Kings*, p. 216.
21. Reynolds, *Kingdoms and Communities*, pp. 1–4, 9. One of the most thorough investigations of the political life of villagers is in Bourin-Derruau, *Villages médiévaux en Bas-Languedoc*, especially 2:145–202, 285–332.
22. For one attempt to do this, see Given, "Factional Politics," pp. 233–50.

One of the most eminent of these social historians, Fernand Braudel, is prone to reduce politics to the status of an epiphenomenon. As Braudel argues, there are different types of historical "time" and hence different types of history. One is a "history whose passage is almost imperceptible, that of man in relationship to his environment, a history in which all change is slow, a history of constant repetition, ever-recurring cycles." A second type of historical time is marked with "slow but perceptible rhythms." This is the realm of social history, "the history of groups and groupings." Finally, there is traditional history, "history, one might say, on the scale not of man, but of individual men," "a history of brief, rapid, nervous fluctuations." Given such a scheme, it is hard to resist the temptation to turn the slowly evolving planes of history into deep structures that, in Braudel's words, "resist the course of history and therefore determine its flow."[23] Viewed from this perspective, the realm of politics can be made to seem an almost meaningless shadow play, "surface disturbances, crests of foam that the tides of history carry on their strong backs."[24]

I would hope that anyone who has read these pages would see that politics in medieval Europe was not a mere epiphenomenon. Political history and social history should not be split apart. They should be pulled back together and their dialectical interaction examined. The social structures of Languedoc and Gwynedd did much to determine the nature of the regimes they received after the end of their political autonomy. Under the proper conditions, political arrangements could have dramatic and far-reaching consequences for at least one of our encapsulated societies. One can err by overstressing the freedom of the directors of political institutions to do as they please; but one can also err by regarding political behavior as simply the totally determined product of underlying social structures. Neither society nor politics is the automatic expression of the other. What we need to do is to unravel the complex connections between the two and thus understand the laws of motion that explain the combined development of all aspects of a society—social, political, economic, and ideological.

Some of the most commonly propagated notions about the nature

---

23. Braudel, "History," p. 154.
24. Braudel, *Mediterranean*, 1:20–21. See also Le Roy Ladurie, "Histoire immobile," p. 29.

of politics in the middle ages thus are inadequate in characterizing or explaining the phenomena we have examined in Gwynedd and Languedoc. Criticism, however, is always easy. But what can we do to help reorient the study of political history in new, and, one hopes, more profitable directions? In the rest of this section I will mention briefly some of the interpretive concepts that have recently been debated by contemporary social scientists and suggest how such concepts can help us clarify medieval politics.

One of the great problems in medieval political history is the issue of conflict. Those scholars who subscribe to various common-good interpretations of the medieval state, who see the increase in size of medieval polities and the concentration of authority as conducive to the good of society as a whole, often find it difficult to incorporate conflict and dissent into their analyses. If the expansion of royal rule brings in its train the good things of life, conflict—especially the dissent sparked by royal state-building—becomes a puzzling, indeed annoying, problem. Conflict is thus often treated not as an inherent feature of a specific political system but as something pathological, a sign that something has gone wrong with the political system, or as an aberration that has no significant impact on real politics.[25] Marxists, of course, have always been interested in conflict, since many conceive of class conflict as the motor of history. One can find in the literature many accounts of the class interests that motivated particular social and political conflicts.[26]

Most such accounts can be regarded as examples of a frustration-aggression theory of conflict. Such theories are a form of psychologism in that they assume that, in the words of Charles Tilly, "the central things to be explained by a theory of revolution [or political conflict] are why, when, and how large numbers of individual men become discontented."[27] My description of the origins of the Glyndŵr uprising, with its discussion of how the English regime frustrated the desires of most social groups in Gwynedd, is an example of such an argument. Such descriptions of political conflict assign a definite and limited role to the state as one *actor* among others in the arena of

25. For examples of talented historians displaying difficulty accounting for political conflict, see Powicke, *King Henry III*, p. 342, and Dobson, *Peasants' Revolt*, p. 27.

26. See, for example, Hilton, *Bondmen Made Free*, pp. 113–19.

27. Tilly, "Does Modernization Breed Revolution?" pp. 431–32. See also Tilly, *From Mobilization to Revolution*, pp. 16–24.

politics. Some may interpret the state as acting to defend the interests of a particular class or class fraction; some may argue that the state is capable of acting to further its own interests independent of those of any social class. But all such interpretations agree in treating the state as one actor among others.

This is not, however, the only role that a state can play in the dynamics of intrasocietal conflict. Recently political scientists have moved away from examining the state as an actor in the arena of political conflict and begun to analyze the ways in which different states *structure* political conflict. This approach seeks to understand how the state unintentionally influences the ways in which different political actors struggle with and against one another.[28] Central to this line of interpretation is the idea that conflict flows not out of stresses, strains, and disjunctures in the political or social process but directly out of a society's central political processes.[29]

This concept of the state—not as a political actor, but as a structure that shapes the arena of political conflict—has an immediate relevance to the fates of Gwynedd and Languedoc under outside rule. My discussion of rebellion in Wales and Languedoc in chapter 8 can be read as an effort to explain an important quantitative difference in the nature of resistance to outside rule. It can also be read as a demonstration that the state regimes set up by outsiders played a different role in structuring conflict within these two societies. In Languedoc, the state—that is, the government of the Capetian kings—played a relatively marginal role in local conflict. The important political, social, and ideological issues that agitated Languedocian society tended to pit local people against one another. Since coercive authority was widely diffused throughout the region, there was not a single arena in which these conflicts were fought out. The Capetian government provided only one conflict arena among others. The institutions of governance that contending parties in Languedoc sought to control or influence were often local in nature. In Gwynedd, however, the concentration of authority brought about as a result of the English conquest meant that there was only a single political arena, that provided by the English and their institutions of governance.

By borrowing the language of the systems analysts, we can say the

28. Skocpol, "Bringing the State Back In," p. 21.
29. Tilly, "Does Modernization Breed Revolution?" p. 436.

same thing in a slightly different way. These scholars conceive of a political system as a perpetual conversion system. It takes in from its environment both support and demands that it act on certain issues; some of these demands are converted by the authorities into outputs, that is, into binding decisions. To avoid overload, however, the political system must be able to regulate and reduce the flow of demands. Not every want expressed in a political system's environment can or should be converted into a demand on the system, and not every demand can or should produce an authoritative output. Political systems thus have gatekeeping mechanisms to control the process by which wants are turned into demands requiring a response from the authorities.[30]

Using these terms, we can argue that in Languedoc there were many gatekeeping mechanisms that limited the number of demands made on the French authorities. Most of these mechanisms seem to have been structural, that is, the product of the configuration of social and political power within the Languedocian environment itself rather than an aspect of the institutions of the royal government. The reduction of demands by these gatekeeping mechanisms limited the number and nature of the crown's outputs. This restricted its ability to intervene effectively in Languedocian affairs; but it also limited the chance that any of the regime's outputs would offend important actors in its environment and result in the reduction of support. In Gwynedd there seem to have been fewer gatekeeping mechanisms. A larger array of demands were made on the English authorities. We could argue that this resulted in system overload, the generation of insufficient and unsatisfactory outputs, ending ultimately in the explosive reduction of support that was Glyndŵr's rebellion.

One need not care especially for the rather mechanistic language of systems analysis to realize that the concept of gatekeeping is an important one. We need to understand under what conditions social issues in medieval Europe were "politicized," that is, transformed into matters in which people demanded a resolution at the level of the state. Misled by the belief that "political society" was confined to the ranks of the aristocracy, we have not yet even posed this question in a meaningful fashion.

Linked to the notion that states unintentionally structure political

30. Easton, *Systems Analysis*, pp. 29–33, 85–99, 351.

conflict into certain patterns is the idea that states play a large role in determining the political capacity of classes or other broad collectivities. Theda Skocpol has argued that, although class tensions are present in all societies, the political expression of these tensions is not automatic. This depends on the capacities that classes have for achieving self-consciousness and organizing themselves. These capacities in turn often depend on the ways in which states structure their societies' political arenas.[31]

This idea can be applied to our data from Gwynedd and Languedoc. In Languedoc, the advent of Capetian rule certainly increased the political capacity of at least one important collectivity, the bishops of the local church. The Albigensian crusades, by weakening the authority of much of the local nobility, allowed the bishops to expand greatly their political authority. The peasantry may also have been able to benefit from the shock experienced by the local nobles; at least it is in the aftermath of the wars that we find many villages equipped with the self-governing institutions of the consulate. The situation is less clear in Gwynedd. Here the "demobilizing" aspects of the English regime, that is, its near total extirpation of the upper strata of the native ruling elite, are most apparent. But there are aspects of outside rule that may have helped increase the political capacities of local classes. The Welsh gentry, although excluded from access to high positions in royal and Marcher administrations and in the church, were involved in the middle and lower levels of the new administrative apparatuses introduced by the English. The influence they thus acquired, the alliances they formed, and the skills they learned in service to their new masters may have helped them more effectively press their claims against the English. Similarly, the fact that the English fastened collective responsibilities on commotes and villages may have given these entities a coherence and capacity for independent action that they had previously lacked. Many medievalists have implicitly dealt with the way in which particular states mobilized or demobilized certain classes. But the question of how the structures of medieval states affected the political capacities of social collectivities has not been explicitly formulated and given adequate analytic attention.

Another concept of contemporary political science that is potentially fruitful in the field of medieval history is that of the "autonomy

31. Skocpol, "Bringing the State Back In," p. 25.

of the state." This question of the state's relative autonomy is an issue that has recently been intensely debated, especially in the context of modern capitalist societies.[32] Two issues seem to be involved here: the extent to which states can become social actors in their own rights, endowed with their own interests apart from those of any particular social class within their societies; and the capacity of the state to act contrary to the wishes of those classes that are socially and economically dominant within the polity. Even Marxists, who have usually been firmly committed to what have been termed "society-centered" explanations of political behavior, have recognized that in certain conditions states enjoy a degree of "relative autonomy" with respect to even the economically dominant classes. Like non-Marxists, they have been interested in the conditions that produce this relative autonomy; they have also asked whether this relative autonomy has a function in preserving the dominance of the capitalist classes and the capital accumulation process.[33]

The question of the relative autonomy of medieval states has seldom been posed directly. On the one hand, there are grounds for thinking that medieval states, at least in the kingdoms of northwestern Europe, might have a high degree of autonomy. Royal governments were in important respects the private property of kings. Royal servants were the king's personal agents, freely chosen by him and answerable only to him. They thus may have had an unusually high capacity to act contrary to the interests of the politically and economically dominant classes within those kingdoms.

On the other hand, there are reasons to believe that state autonomy was relatively limited. States were headed by kings who were definitely members of a particular social class, that of the land-owning aristocracy. Like all other aristocrats, their economic well-being depended on their capacity to extract surplus from the peasants living on their estates. They thus shared the interests of the dominant class in a direct and personal fashion. Moreover, they were bound to other members of the aristocracy by many personal ties, including those of vassalage and marriage. They participated in an aristocratic culture that was largely closed to members of other classes. Finally, their governments were staffed primarily by members of the aristocracy.

32. Skocpol, *States and Social Revolutions*, pp. 24–33.
33. See Krasner, "Approaches," pp. 230–40; Carnoy, *State*, pp. 54–55, 108–9, 200–202; Poulantzas, *Political Power*, pp. 255–321.

Our analysis of Gwynedd and Languedoc under outside rule, however, has shown that the degree of autonomy enjoyed by medieval
states could vary widely. The autonomy of the Capetian state in Languedoc was relatively limited. It did not enjoy a monopoly of coercive
authority in the region; important positions in its administrative
organs were often held by local men; and the loyalty of these administrators was often divided. In Gwynedd, however, the state system set
up by the English had a much greater degree of autonomy. Coercive
authority was, in medieval terms, highly concentrated, important
positions in the local administration were largely reserved for Englishmen, and ethnic animosity kept English administrators from coming
to feel much solidarity with those they governed. I have suggested that
the differing degrees of autonomy enjoyed by the state systems in
Languedoc and Gwynedd can be linked to the degree to which political authority had been concentrated and institutionalized before the
assertion of outside rule. Other cases, however, need to be explored
before we can be certain that this hypothesis holds across western
Europe as a whole.

The question of the "functionality" of the "relative autonomy of the
state" in medieval Europe has barely been addressed, in this or other
works. One could argue that the relative lack of autonomy of the
Capetian state was a factor in explaining the relative lack of hostility
to it within Languedoc. The Capetian state may have had limited
means of intervening in local affairs, and it may have been unable to
police effectively internal conflict in Languedoc, but it did not present
itself in an alienated and alienating guise to its Languedocian subjects.
In Gwynedd, however, the greater autonomy enjoyed by the English
state system seems to have been a major cause of the Glyndŵr rebellion. The relative monopoly of coercive authority enjoyed by the
English in Gwynedd and their capacity to intervene actively in local
affairs made the role of the state a central and controversial item on
the agenda of North Welsh politics.

In the feudal states of medieval Europe, we may thus see an inverse
correlation between state autonomy and political stability. From the
point of view of political stability, a high degree of state autonomy,
together with its concomitantly greater capacity for effective intervention in the affairs of civil society, may have been dysfunctional. A high
degree of state autonomy may have been linked to more intense internal conflict. A low degree of state autonomy may have meant a re-

duced capacity for effective state intervention, but it also decreased opportunities for the state to collide with important social groups. However, this statement can be no more than a hypothesis awaiting further exploration.

A discussion of the "functionality" of the state's relative autonomy brings us inevitably to a consideration of the relationship of political power and the state to the economic underpinnings of society. This question is probably best addressed within a Marxist framework, since Marxists have provided the most acute analysis of the relation of politics and the economy.

In the construction and the maintenance of capitalist social relations, the role of the state is fairly clear-cut. In the transition from feudalism to capitalism, the state used its coercive authority to break apart the preexisting social and economic constraints that hampered the full development of capitalist social relations. In the fully developed capitalist societies of the nineteenth and twentieth centuries, the state has played several important roles in maintaining capitalist production. In the constant struggle in which capitalists necessarily find themselves engaged to increase productivity and expand their markets, the state plays an important role. Within individual polities states undertake such important tasks as providing "social capital" (a trained labor force, means of transport and communication, etc.) and in assuming the social costs of capitalist production (social welfare measures such as unemployment insurance, environmental cleanup, etc.).[34] In the international arena, the state uses its diplomatic and military means to help its entrepreneurs in the struggle to control the flows of capital, labor, and profit within the world economy.

In turning to medieval Europe, the problem of the role of the state and politics in maintaining and promoting the structures of the economy is much more problematic. The common Marxist interpretation of feudalism emphasizes the pivotal role of extraeconomic coercion in the extraction by the aristocracy of economic surplus from the hands of the peasantry. Only after the peasants had produced a surplus did the seigneurial class requisition a portion of it. Lords did engage in their own economic production, but on a relatively small scale. And, unlike the activity of capitalists, their involvement in direct production was not central to the economy as a whole.

34. See O'Connor, *Fiscal Crisis.*

In effect, medieval lords were unnecessary to the medieval production process. The peasants could have gotten along perfectly well without them. The seigneurial class was thus purely parasitical, living off part of a surplus it played no role in creating. The same could be said of the feudal states of northwestern Europe. These made no investment in social capital; instead they spent their revenues on conspicuous display, the creation of patronage networks, and on warfare, which entailed the organized destruction of the means of production. To carry this line of reasoning out to its end, one could argue that too great success by lords and states in extracting surplus could be deleterious to the economy. If peasants were forced to surrender too much of what they produced, they might have to reduce the portions of their revenue intended for direct consumption or for the replacement of the minimum equipment needed for a further production cycle. Carried to an extreme, overly successful surplus extraction could push the peasant economy into difficulty as too many resources were channeled into tribute payments.

J. R. Maddicott and Guy Bois have suggested that such mechanisms were at work in late-medieval England and Normandy.[35] Increasing demands for tribute, whether from individual lords or from the state, helped push the peasant economy into the protracted crises of the late middle ages. The evidence accumulated in this book supports such an interpretation. The Capetian regime in Languedoc was relatively less successful than the English regime in Gwynedd at extracting surplus. Capetian rule was thus compatible for several generations with economic progress in the south of France. In Gwynedd, however, the burden of English financial demands may have been so high as to help send the economy into a period of decline.

Our evidence thus supports neo-Marxist arguments, of the sort advanced above, about the impact of political institutions on the feudal economy. However, it should be clear that the question is far more complex than it appears at first glance. First, peasants can respond to increased demands for tribute in a variety of ways. In some cases, they may try to reduce consumption and reinvestment in their farms. In other circumstances, they may try to become more efficient and produce a larger surplus, much of it destined for the marketplace.[36]

---

35. Maddicott, *English Peasantry*, pp. 3–5, 74–75; Bois, *Crisis*, pp. 401–7.
36. On the strategies peasants may follow, see Wolf, *Peasants*, pp. 15–17.

Peasants in some areas, such as Gwynedd, may have responded to increased demands for tribute by reducing consumption and reinvestment. But in some areas of thirteenth-century England, some, at least, seem to have turned increasingly to production for the market.[37] Instead of a priori reasoning about how peasants might respond to increased tribute demands, we need to know what strategies different peasant groups pursued and what conditions determined their choices.

Second, one could argue that the seigneurial class was not simply a parasitical group but that it had a definite role to play in the economic reproduction of society. The contribution of lords to economic development was occasionally direct, as in the construction of such useful things as mills and irrigation systems. Some may also have contributed indirectly, by creating the political environment necessary for the operation of the complex and communally regulated agrarian practices of the common-field villages that have been so intensively studied by English social historians. Similarly, states could act to defend economic interests. In this book we have encountered the French monarchy acting, at least for a time, to defend the interests of Languedocian merchants. Just as we need to know more about the strategies peasants could pursue, so we need to pay more attention to the variety of roles that medieval lords and states could play in the economy, as well as to the factors that determined those roles. The Marxists may be correct in emphasizing the role of politics in the medieval economy, but such an observation raises as many questions as it answers, questions that medievalists would do well to explore.

We began this book with a relatively straight-forward question about how Gwynedd and Languedoc were integrated into larger polities. We end, not with a simple and conclusive answer, but with new and more perplexing questions, not only about the incorporation of local communities but about the nature of the medieval political system as a whole. I do not pretend that I have provided answers, even provisional ones, for most of these questions. But asking them is the first step toward a new and more profound understanding of politics and society in medieval Europe.

37. Biddick, "Missing Links," pp. 277–98.

Bibliography

I have not attempted to create an exhaustive bibliography of either Welsh or Languedocian history in the thirteenth and fourteenth centuries. The following is merely a finding list for titles cited in the notes to this book.

MANUSCRIPTS

Archives Municipales d'Albi (Albi):
    Series FF   Miscellaneous legal documents

Archives Municipales de Cordes (Albi):
    Series FF   Miscellaneous legal documents

Archivio Segreto Vaticano (Vatican City):
    Collectorie 404   Investigation of Bishop Bernard de Castanet

Bibliothèque Nationale (Paris):
    Collection Doat   Miscellaneous documents relating to Languedoc
    Ms. Lat. 4270   Heresy trial of Bernard Délicieux

Public Record Office (London):
    Justices Itinerant 1   Eyre Rolls, Assize Rolls, Etc.
    Special Collections 2   Court Rolls
    Special Collections 6   Ministers' and Receivers' Accounts

PRINTED WORKS

Works that are primarily editions of original documents or that contain important collections of documents are marked with an asterisk.

Abadal i de Vinyals, Ramon. "A Propos de la 'domination' de la maison comtale barcelonaise sur le Midi français." *Ann. Midi* 76 (1964): 315–45.

Allègre, Victor. "La Vie économique d'Albi et de la région albigeoise au XIVe siècle." *Revue du Tarn* 3d ser. 87 (1977): 329–49.

Althusser, Louis, and Etienne Balibar. *Reading Capital*. London, 1970.

Anderson, Perry. *Lineages of the Absolutist State*. London, 1979.

———. *Passages from Antiquity to Feudalism*. London, 1974.

André, René. "Un Nîmois exemplaire au moyen âge: Pierre Scatisse." *Mémoires de l'Académie de Nîmes* 7th ser. 60 (1977–79): 122–50.

Ardant, Gabriel. "Financial Policy and Economic Infrastructure of Modern States and Nations." In Tilly, ed., *The Formation of National States in Western Europe*, pp. 164–242.

Auriac, Eugène d'. *Histoire de l'ancienne cathédrale et des évêques d'Alby, depuis les premiers temps connus jusqu'à la fondation de la nouvelle église Sainte-Cécile*. Paris, 1858.

Baldwin, John W. "La Décennie décisive: Les Années 1190–1203 dans le règne de Philippe Auguste." *Revue Historique* 266 (1981): 311–37.

———. "L'Entourage de Philippe Auguste et la famille royale." In *La France de Philippe Auguste*, pp. 59–73.

———. *The Government of Philip Augustus: Foundations of French Royal Power in the Middle Ages*. Berkeley, Calif., 1986.

Bardon, Achille. *L'Exploitation du bassin houiller d'Alès sous l'Ancien Régime*. Nîmes, 1898.

———. *Histoire de la ville d'Alais de 1250 à 1340*. Nîmes, 1894.

Barrow, G. W. S. *Robert Bruce and the Community of the Realm of Scotland*. 2d ed. Edinburgh, 1976.

Belperron, Pierre. *La Croisade contre les Albigeois et l'union du Languedoc à la France (1209–49)*. Paris, 1942.

Berthe, Maurice. *Le Comté de Bigorre: Un Milieu rural au bas moyen âge*. Paris, 1976.

*Beugnot, A. A., ed. *Les Olim*. 3 vols. Paris, 1839–48.

Biddick, Kathleen. "Missing Links: Taxable Wealth, Markets, and Stratification among Medieval English Peasants." *Journal of Interdisciplinary History* 18 (1987): 277–98.

Biget, Jean-Louis. "Un Procès d'inquisition à Albi en 1300." *CF* 6 (1971): 273–341.

———. "La Restitution des dimes par les laïcs dans le diocèse d'Albi à la fin du XIIIe siècle: Contribution à l'étude des revenus de l'évêché et du chapitre de la cathédrale." *CF* 7 (1972): 211–83.

Bisson, Thomas N. *Assemblies and Representation in Languedoc in the Thirteenth Century*. Princeton, N.J., 1964.

———. "Coinages and Royal Monetary Policy in Languedoc during the Reign of Saint Louis." In Bisson, *Medieval France*, pp. 393–419.

———. *Medieval France and Her Pyrenean Neighbours: Studies in Early Institutional History*. London, 1989.

———. "Mediterranean Territorial Power in the Twelfth Century." *Proceedings of the American Philosophical Society* 123 (1979): 143–50.

———. "Negotiations for Taxes under Alfonse of Poitiers." In *Studies Presented to* the International Commission for the History of Representative and Parliamentary Institutions, no. 31 (1965): 77–101.

——. "The Organized Peace in Southern France and Catalonia." In Bisson, *Medieval France*, pp. 215–36.

Bloch, Marc. "A Contribution Towards a Comparative History of European Societies." In Bloch, *Land and Work in Medieval Europe: Selected Papers by Marc Bloch*, pp. 44–81. Trans. J. E. Anderson. New York, 1969.

Bois, Guy. *The Crisis of Feudalism: Economy and Society in Eastern Normandy, c. 1300–1550.* Cambridge, 1984.

Bonnassie, Pierre. *La Catalogne du milieu du Xe à la fin du XIe siècle: Croissance et mutation d'une société.* 2 vols. Toulouse, 1975–76.

——. "Du Rhône à Galice: Genèse et modalités du régime féodale." In *Structures féodales et féodalisme dans l'occident méditerranéen (Xe–XIIIe siècles): Bilan et perspectives de recherches*, pp. 17–44. Paris, 1980.

Bonnaud-Delamare, R. "La Légende des associations de la paix en Rouergue et en Languedoc au début du XIIIe siècle (1170–1229)." *Bulletin Philologique et Historique du Comité des Travaux Historiques et Scientifiques* (1936–37): 47–78.

Borrelli de Serres, Léon-Louis. *Recherches sur divers services publiques du XIIIe au XIVe siècle.* 3 vols. Paris, 1895–1909.

Bourin-Derruau, Monique. *Villages médiévaux en Bas-Languedoc: Genèse d'une sociabilité, Xe-XIVe siècle.* 2 vols. Paris, 1987.

Boutaric, Edgard. *La France sous Philippe le Bel.* Paris, 1861.

——. *Saint Louis et Alfonse de Poitiers.* Paris, 1870.

*——, ed. *Actes du Parlement de Paris: Première série—de l'an 1254 à l'an 1328.* 2 vols. Paris, 1863–67.

*——, ed. "Notices et extraits de documents inédits relatifs à l'histoire de France sous Philippe le Bel." *Notices et extraits des manuscripts de la Bibliothèque Impériale et autres bibliothèques* 20, pt. 2 (1852): 83–237.

Bowen, E. G., ed. *Wales: A Physical, Historical, and Regional Geography.* London, 1957.

*Bowen, Ivor, ed. *The Statutes of Wales.* London, 1908.

Braudel, Fernand. "History and the Social Sciences: The Long Term." *Social Sciences Information* 9, no. 1 (1970): 145–74.

——. *The Mediterranean and the Mediterranean World in the Age of Philip II.* Trans. Sian Reynolds. 2 vols. New York, 1972.

Brenner, Robert. "The Agrarian Roots of European Capitalism." In T. H. Aston and C. H. E. Philpin, eds., *The Brenner Debate: Agrarian Class Structure and Economic Development in Pre-Industrial Europe*, pp. 213–327. London, 1985.

Brinton, Crane. *The Anatomy of Revolution.* New York, 1952.

Brown, Judith C. *In the Shadow of Florence: Provincial Society in Renaissance Pescia.* New York, 1982.

Burns, Robert Ignatius. *Islam under the Crusaders: Colonial Survival in the Thirteenth-Century Kingdom of Valencia.* Princeton, N. J., 1973.

——. *Medieval Colonialism: Postcrusade Exploitation of Islamic Valencia.* Princeton, N.J., 1975.

Butler, Lawrence. "The Evolution of Towns: Planted Towns after 1066." In M. W.

Barley, ed., *The Plans and Topography of Medieval Towns in England and Wales*, pp. 32–48. London, 1976.

*Cabié, Edmond, ed. *Droits et possessions du comte de Toulouse dans l'Albigeois au milieu du XIIIe siècle*. Paris, 1900.

Campbell, Gerard J., Jr. "Clerical Immunities in France during the Reign of Philip III." *Speculum* 39 (1964): 404–24.

Camproux, Charles. *Histoire de la littérature occitane*. Paris, 1953.

Carnoy, Martin. *The State and Political Theory*. Princeton, N.J., 1984.

Carr, Anthony D. "An Aristocracy in Decline: The Native Welsh Lords after the Edwardian Conquest." *WHR* 5 (1970–71): 103–29.

——. "The Barons of Edeyrnion, 1282–1485." *Journal of the Merioneth Historical and Record Society* 4 (1963–64): 187–93, 289–301.

——. "The Making of the Mostyns: The Genesis of a Landed Family." *Transactions of the Honourable Society of Cymmrodorion* (1979): 137–57.

——. *Medieval Anglesey*. Llangefni, 1982.

——. "Medieval Dinmael." *Transactions of the Denbighshire Historical Society* 13 (1964): 9–21.

——. "Medieval Gloddaith." *Transactions of the Caernarvonshire Historical Society* 38 (1977): 7–32.

——. "Rhys ap Roppert." *Transactions of the Denbighshire Historical Society* 25 (1976): 155–70.

*——. "Some Edeyrnion and Dinmael Documents." *BBCS* 21 (1964–66): 242–49.

——. "A Welsh Knight in the Hundred Years' War: Sir Gregory Sais." *THSC* (1977): 40–53.

——. "Welshmen and the Hundred Years' War." *WHR* 4 (1968): 21–46.

Castaing-Sicard, Mireille. *Monnaies féodales et circulation monétaire en Languedoc (Xe-XIIIe siècles)*. Toulouse, 1961.

Castaldo, André. *Seigneurs, villes et pouvoir royal en Languedoc: Le Consulat médiéval d'Agde (XIIIe-XIVe siècles)*. Paris, 1974.

*Castillon, H. *Histoire du comté de Foix, depuis les temps anciens jusqu'à nos jours*. 2 vols. Toulouse, 1852.

Cazelles, Raymond. *La Société politique et la crise de la royauté sous Philippe de Valois*. Paris, 1958.

Chague, Marie-Martine. "Contribution à l'étude du recrutement des agents royaux en Languedoc aux XIVe et XVe siècles." In *France du Nord et France du Midi*, pp. 359–78.

Chevalier, Michel. *La Vie humaine dans les Pyrénées ariégeoises*. Paris, 1956.

Cheyette, Fredric L. "The 'Sale' of Carcassonne to the Counts of Barcelona (1067–70) and the Rise of the Trencavels." *Speculum* 63 (1988): 826–64.

Chotzen, T. M. "Yvain de Galles in Alsace-Lorraine and in Switzerland." *BBCS* 4 (1928): 231–40.

*Clancy, Joseph P., ed. *Medieval Welsh Lyrics*. London, 1965.

Clignet, Remi. "A Critical Evaluation of Concomitant Variation Studies." In Naroll and Cohen, eds., *A Handbook of Method in Cultural Anthropology*, pp. 597–619.

Combes, Jean. "Les Foires en Languedoc au moyen âge." *AESC* 13 (1958): 231–59.

——. "Montpellier et les foires de Champagne." In *France du Nord et France du Midi*, pp. 381–428.

*Compayré, Clément. *Etudes historiques et documents inédits sur l'Albigeois, le Castrais et l'ancien diocèse de Lavaur*. Albi, 1841.

Contamine, Philippe. *Guerre, état et société à la fin du moyen âge: Etudes sur les armées des rois de France, 1337–1494*. Paris, 1972.

Craig, John. *The Mint: A History of the London Mint from A.D. 287 to 1948*. Cambridge, 1953.

Curie Seimbres, A. *Essai sur les villes fondées dans le sud-ouest de la France aux XIIIe et XIVe siècles sous le nom générique des bastides*. Toulouse, 1880.

Davies, Elwyn. "*Hendre* and *Hafod* in Denbighshire." *Transactions of the Denbighshire Historical Society* 26 (1977): 49–72.

Davies, James Conway. "Felony in Edwardian Wales." *THSC* (1916–17): 145–96.

*——, ed. *The Welsh Assize Roll, 1277–84 (Assize Roll, no. 1147)*. Cardiff, 1940.

Davies, R. R. "Buchedd a Moes y Cymry." *WHR* 12 (1984–85): 155–79.

——. "Colonial Wales." *Past and Present* 65 (1974): 2–23.

——. *Conquest, Coexistence, and Change: Wales, 1063–1415*. Oxford, 1987.

——. *Lordship and Society in the March of Wales, 1282–1400*. Oxford, 1978.

——. "Owain Glyn Dŵr and the Welsh Squirearchy." *THSC* (1968): 150–69.

——. "Race Relations in Post-Conquest Wales: Confrontation and Compromise." *THSC* (1974–75): 32–56.

——. "The Survival of the Blood-Feud in Medieval Wales." *History* 54 (1969): 338–57.

——. "The Twilight of Welsh Law." *History* 51 (1966): 143–64.

Davies, Wendy. "Land and Power in Early Medieval Wales." *Past and Present* 81 (1978): 2–23.

——. *Wales in the Early Middle Ages*. Leicester, 1982.

*Davis, Georgene W., ed. *The Inquisition at Albi, 1299–1300: Text of Register and Analysis*. New York, 1948.

Delcambre, Etienne. "Le Paréage du Puy." *BEC* 92 (1931): 121–69, 285–344.

Denholm-Young, Noel. "Feudal Society in the Thirteenth Century: The Knights." In Denholm-Young, *Collected Papers of N. Denholm-Young*, pp. 83–94. Cardiff, 1969.

Depeyrot, Georges. "Le Trésor de Toulouse et le numéraire féodal aux XIIe et XIIIe siècles." *Ann. Midi* 94 (1982): 125–49.

*Devic, Claude, and Joseph Vaissète. *Histoire générale de Languedoc*. Ed. Auguste Molinier. 16 vols. Toulouse, 1872–1904.

Dictionary of National Biography. Ed. Leslie Stephen et al. 66 vols. Oxford, 1885–1901.

Dictionary of Welsh Biography down to 1940. Ed. J. E. Lloyd et al. London, 1959.

Dictionnaire de biographie française. Ed. J. Balteau et al. 15 vols. Paris, 1933–82.

*Dmitrewski, Michel de. "Fr. Bernard Délicieux, O.F.M., sa lutte contre l'inquisition de Carcassonne et d'Albi, son procès, 1297–1319." *Archivum Franciscanum Historicum* 17 (1924): 183–218, 313–37, 457–88; 18 (1925): 3–32.

Dobson, R. B. *The Peasants' Revolt of 1381*. 2d ed. London, 1980.

Dognon, Paul. *Les Institutions politiques et administratives du pays de Languedoc du XIIIe siècle aux guerres de religion*. Toulouse, 1895.

Donkin, R. A. *The Cistercians: Studies in the Geography of Medieval England and Wales*. Toronto, 1978.

Dossat, Yves. *Les Crises de l'inquisition toulousaine au XIIIe siècle (1233-73)*. Bordeaux, 1959.

——. "Les Divisions administratives de l'Agenais à l'époque d'Alphonse de Poitiers." *Bulletin Philologique et Historique (jusqu'à 1715) du Comité des Travaux Historiques et Scientifiques* (1951–52): 303–17.

——. "Gui Foucois, enquêteur-réformateur, archevêque et pape (Clément IV)." *CF* 7 (1972): 23–57.

——. "Le Massacre d'Avignonet." *CF* 6 (1971): 343–50.

——. "Restauration du domaine du roi par Eustache de Beaumarchais, sénéchal de Toulousain et d'Albigeois." In *France du Nord et France du Midi*, pp. 261–324.

*——, ed. *Saisimentum comitatus tholosani*. Paris, 1966.

Douais, Célestin. "Guillaume Garric, de Carcassonne, professeur de droit, et le tribunal de l'inquisition (1285–1329)." *Ann. Midi* 10 (1898): 7–45.

*Dufau de Maluquer, A. de. "Le Pays de Foix sous Gaston Phoebus: Rôle des feux du comté de Foix en 1390." *Bulletin de la Société des Sciences, Lettres et Arts de Pau* 2d ser. 28 (1898–99): 1–280.

Dumas, Françoise. "La Monnaie dans le royaume au temps de Philippe-Auguste." In *La France de Philippe Auguste*, pp. 541–72.

Dupont, André. "L'Evolution sociale du consulat nîmois du milieu du XIIIe au milieu du XIVe siècle." *Ann. Midi* 72 (1960): 287–308.

——. "L'Exploitation du sel sur les étangs du Languedoc, IXe-XIIIe siècles." *Ann. Midi* 70 (1958): 7–25.

Duvernoy, Jean. "Pierre Autier." *Cahiers d'Etudes Cathares* 2d ser. 47 (1970): 9–49.

*——, ed. *Le Registre d'inquisition de Jacques Fournier, évêque de Pamiers (1318–25)*. 3 vols. Toulouse, 1965.

Easton, David. *A Framework for Political Analysis*. Englewood Cliffs, N.J., 1965.

——. *The Political System: An Inquiry into the State of Political Science*. 2d ed. New York, 1971.

——. *A Systems Analysis of Political Life*. Chicago, 1979.

Eckstein, Harry. "On the 'Science' of the State." *Daedalus* 108, no. 4 (1979): 1–20.

Edwards, J. G. "Edward I's Castle-Building in Wales." *Proceedings of the British Academy* 32 (1946): 15–81.

——. *The Principality of Wales, 1267–1967: A Study in Constitutional History*. Denbigh, 1969.

——. "Sir Gruffydd Llwyd." *English Historical Review* 30 (1915): 589–601.

*——, ed. *Calendar of Ancient Correspondence Concerning Wales*. Cardiff, 1935.

*——, ed. *Littere Wallie, Preserved in Liber A in the Public Record Office*. Cardiff, 1940.

Ellis, T. P. "The English Element in the Perfeddwlad." *Y Cymmrodor* 35 (1925): 187–99.

——. *Welsh Tribal Law and Custom in the Middle Ages.* 2 vols. Oxford, 1926.

*——, ed. *The First Extent of Bromfield and Yale, A.D. 1315.* London, 1924.

Emanuel, Hywel David. "Studies in the Welsh Laws." In Elwyn Davies, ed., *Celtic Studies in Wales,* pp. 71–100. Cardiff, 1963.

*——, ed. *The Latin Texts of the Welsh Laws.* Cardiff, 1967.

Emery, Richard Wilder. *Heresy and Inquisition in Narbonne.* New York, 1941.

Evans, D. L. "Some Notes on the History of the Principality of Wales in the Time of the Black Prince (1343–76)." *THSC* (1925–26): 25–110.

——. "Walter de Mauny, Sheriff of Merioneth, 1332–72." *Journal of the Merioneth Historical and Record Society* 4 (1963): 194–203.

*——, ed. *Flintshire Ministers' Accounts, 1328–53.* Flintshire Historical Society, Record Series, vol. 2, 1929.

Evans, Peter B., Dietrich Rueschemeyer, and Theda Skocpol, eds. *Bringing the State Back In.* Cambridge, 1985.

Farmer, D. L. "Some Grain Price Movements in Thirteenth-Century England." *Economic History Review* 2d ser. 10 (1957–58): 207–20.

Favier, Jean. *Philippe le Bel.* Paris, 1978.

Fawtier, Robert. *The Capetian Kings of France: Monarchy and Nation, 987–1328.* London, 1960.

*——, and François Maillard, eds. *Comptes royaux (1285–1314).* 3 vols. Paris, 1953–56.

*—— et al., eds. *Registres du Trésor des Chartes.* 3 vols. Paris, 1958–78.

*Finke, Heinrich, ed. *Acta aragonensia: Quellen zur deutschen, italienischen, französischen, spanischen, zur Kirchen- und Kulturgeschichte aus der diplomatischen Korrespondenz Jaymes II. (1291–1327).* 3 vols. Berlin, 1908–22.

Fossier, Robert. *La Terre et les hommes en Picardie jusqu'à la fin du XIIIe siècle.* 2 vols. Paris, 1968.

*Fournier, Pierre-Fr., and Pascal Guébin, eds. *Enquêtes administratives d'Alfonse de Poitiers, arrêts de son parlement tenu à Toulouse et textes annexes, 1249–71.* Paris, 1959.

La France de Philippe Auguste: Le Temps des mutations. Paris, 1982.

France du Nord et France du Midi: Contacts et influences réciproques. Actes du 96e Congrès National des Sociétés Savantes. Toulouse, 1971. Section de Philologie et d'Histoire jusqu'à 1610, vol. 1.

Friedlander, Alan Ralph. "The Administration of the Seneschalsy of Carcassonne: Personnel and Structure of Royal Provincial Government in France, 1226–1320." Ph.D. dissertation, University of California, Berkeley, 1982.

——. "Les Agents du roi face aux crises de l'hérésie en Languedoc, vers 1250–vers 1350." *CF* 20 (1985): 199–220.

——. "Les Sergents royaux du Languedoc sous Philippe le Bel." *Ann. Midi* 96 (1984): 235–51.

*Fryde, E. B., ed. *Book of Prests of the King's Wardrobe for 1294–5: Presented to John Goronwy Edwards.* Oxford, 1962.

Fryde, Natalie. "A Royal Inquiry into Abuses: Queen Eleanor's Ministers in North-East Wales, 1291–92." *WHR* 5 (1970–71): 366–76.

——. *The Tyranny and Fall of Edward II, 1321–26.* Cambridge, 1979.

——. "Welsh Troops in the Scottish Campaign of 1322." *BBCS* 26 (1974–76): 82–89.

*——, ed. *List of Welsh Entries in the Memoranda Rolls, 1282–1343.* Cardiff, 1974.

Gavrilovitch, Michel. *Etude sur le Traité de Paris de 1259, entre Louis IX, roi de France, et Henry III, roi d'Angleterre.* Paris, 1899.

*Gaydon, A. T., ed. *The Taxation of 1297: A Translation of the Local Rolls of Assessment for Barford, Biggleswade, and Flitt Hundreds, and for Bedford, Dunstable, Leighton Buzzard, and Luton.* Publications of the Bedfordshire Historical Record Society, vol. 39, 1959.

Gellner, Ernest. "The Stakes in Anthropology." *American Scholar* 57 (1988): 17–30.

*Gerald of Wales. *The Journey through Wales and the Description of Wales.* Trans. Lewis Thorpe. Harmondsworth, 1978.

*——. *Opera.* Ed. J. S. Brewer, James F. Dimock, and George F. Warner. 8 vols. London, 1861–91.

Gerth, H. H., and C. Wright Mills, eds. *From Max Weber: Essays in Sociology.* New York, 1946.

Gilles, Henri. "Le Clergé méridional entre le roi et l'église." *CF* 7 (1972): 393–417.

——. "Les *Doctores tholosani* et la ville d'Albi." In *Mélanges Roger Aubenas.* Université de Montpellier I, Recueil de Mémoires et Travaux Publiés par la Société d'Histoire du Droit et des Institutions des Anciens Pays de Droit Ecrit, fascicule 9, 1974, pp. 313–42.

Giordanengo, Guido. "La Féodalité." In Jean Favier, ed., *La France médiévale,* pp. 183–99. Paris, 1983.

Given, James. "The Economic Consequences of the English Conquest of Gwynedd." *Speculum* 64 (1989): 11–45.

——. "Factional Politics in a Medieval Society: A Case Study from Fourteenth-Century Foix." *Journal of Medieval History* 14 (1988): 233–50.

——. "The Inquisitors of Languedoc and the Medieval Technology of Power." *American Historical Review* 94 (1989): 336–59.

Given-Wilson, Chris. *The English Nobility in the Late Middle Ages: The Fourteenth-Century Political Community.* London, 1987.

Godelier, Maurice. "The Object and Method of Economic Anthropology." In David Seddon, ed., *Relations of Production: Marxist Approaches to Economic Anthropology,* pp. 49–126. London, 1978.

Gouron, André. "Diffusion des consulats méridionaux et expansion du droit romain aux XIIe et XIIIe siècles." *BEC* 121 (1963): 26–76.

——, and J. Hilaire. "Les 'Sceaux' rigoreux du Midi de la France." *Recueil de Mémoires et Travaux Publiés par la Société d'Histoire du Droit et des Institutions des Anciens Pays de Droit Ecrit,* fascicule 4, no. 1 (1958): 41–77.

Great Britain. Land Utilization Survey. *The Land of Britain.* Ed. L. Dudley Stamp. 92 parts. London, 1937–46.

*Great Britain. Public Record Office. *Calendar of Inquisitions Miscellaneous (Chancery).* 7 vols. London, 1916–68.

*——. *Calendar of the Charter Rolls Preserved in the Public Record Office.* 6 vols. London, 1903–27.

*——. *Calendar of the Close Rolls Preserved in the Public Record Office: Edward I.* 5 vols. London, 1900–1908.

*———. *Calendar of the Close Rolls Preserved in the Public Record Office: Edward II.* 4 vols. London, 1892–98.

*———. *Calendar of the Close Rolls Preserved in the Public Record Office: Edward III.* 14 vols. London, 1896–1913.

*———. *Calendar of the Fine Rolls Preserved in the Public Record Office.* 22 vols. London, 1911–62.

*———. *Calendar of the Patent Rolls Preserved in the Public Record Office: Edward II.* 5 vols. London, 1894–1904.

*———. *Calendar of the Patent Rolls Preserved in the Public Record Office: Edward III.* 16 vols. 1891–1916.

*———. *Calendar of Various Chancery Rolls: Supplementary Close Rolls, Welsh Rolls, Scutage Rolls, A.D. 1277–1326.* London, 1912.

———. *List of Sheriffs for England and Wales, from the Earliest Times to A.D. 1831.* Reprint ed. New York, 1963.

*———. *Register of Edward the Black Prince.* 4 vols. London, 1930–33.

*Great Britain. Record Commission. *Ancient Laws and Institutes of Wales.* Ed. Aneurin Owen. London, 1841.

*———. *Registrum vulgariter nuncupatum "The Record of Caernarvon."* Ed. Henry Ellis. London, 1838.

*———. *Rotuli Parliamentorum.* 6 vols. London, 1767–77.

Griffe, Elie. *Les Débuts de l'aventure cathare en Languedoc, 1140–90.* Paris, 1969.

———. *Le Languedoc cathare au temps de la croisade (1209–29).* Paris, 1973.

———. *Le Languedoc cathare de 1190 à 1210.* Paris, 1971.

———. *Le Languedoc cathare et l'inquisition (1229–1329).* Paris, 1980.

*Griffiths, John. "Early Accounts Relating to North Wales, Temp. Edward I." *BBCS* 14 (1950–52): 235–41, 302–12; 15 (1952–54): 126–56; 16 (1954–56): 109–33.

*———. "Two Early Ministers' Accounts for North Wales." *BBCS* 9 (1937–39): 50–70.

Griffiths, Quentin. "New Men among the Lay Counselors of Saint Louis' Parlement." *Mediaeval Studies* 32 (1970): 234–72.

Griffiths, Ralph A. "The Glyn Dŵr Rebellion in North Wales through the Eyes of an Englishman." *BBCS* 22 (1966–68): 151–68.

———. *The Principality of Wales in the Later Middle Ages: The Structure and Personnel of Government.* Vol. 1: *South Wales, 1277–1536.* Cardiff, 1972.

———. *The Reign of King Henry VI: The Exercise of Royal Authority, 1422–61.* Berkeley, Calif., 1981.

———. "The Revolt of Llywelyn Bren, 1316." *Glamorgan Historian* 2 (1965): 186–96.

———. "The Revolt of Rhys ap Maredudd, 1287–88." *WHR* 3 (1966–67): 121–43.

———, ed. *Boroughs of Mediaeval Wales.* Cardiff, 1978.

*Gui, Bernard. *De fundatione et prioribus conventuum provinciarum Tolosanae et Provinciae Ordinis Praedicatorum.* Ed. by P. A. Amargier. Monumenta Ordinis Fratrum Praedicatorum, vol. 24, 1961.

*Guillaume de Puylaurens. *Chronique: Chronica magistri Guillelmi de Podio Laurentii.* Ed. and trans. Jean Duvernoy. Paris, 1976.

Guillemain, Bernard. *La Cour pontificale d'Avignon (1309–76): Etude d'une société.* Paris, 1962.

———. "Les Français du Midi à la cour pontificale d'Avignon." *Ann. Midi* 74 (1962): 29–38.

———, and Catherine Martin. "Les Elections épiscopales de la province de Narbonne entre 1249 et 1317." *CF* 7 (1972): 107–13.

———, and Catherine Martin. "Origines sociales, intellectuelles et ecclésiastiques des évêques de la province de Narbonne entre 1249 et 1317." *CF* 7 (1972): 91–106.

Guiraud, Jean. *Histoire de l'inquisition au moyen âge.* 2 vols. Paris, 1935–38.

Harriss, G. L. *King, Parliament, and Public Finance in Medieval England.* Oxford, 1975.

*Hauréau, B. *Bernard Délicieux et l'inquisition albigeoise (1300–20).* Paris, 1877.

*Haydon, Frank Scott, ed. *Eulogium historiarum.* 3 vols. London, 1858–63.

Hays, Rhŷs W. *The History of the Abbey of Aberconway, 1186–1537.* Cardiff, 1963.

———. "Welsh Students at Oxford and Cambridge Universities in the Middle Ages." *WHR* 4 (1968–69): 325–61.

Henneman, John Bell. "Nobility, Privilege, and Fiscal Politics in Late Medieval France." *French Historical Studies* 13 (1983): 1–17.

Hewitt, H. J. *The Black Prince's Expedition of 1355–57.* Manchester, 1958.

———. *The Organisation of War under Edward III, 1338–62.* Manchester, 1966.

Higounet, Charles. *Le Comté de Comminges, de ses origines à son annexion à la couronne.* 2 vols. Toulouse, 1949.

———. "Un Grand chapitre de l'histoire du XIIe siècle: La Rivalité des maisons de Toulouse et de Barcelone pour la prépondérance méridionale." In *Mélanges d'histoire du moyen âge dédiés à la mémoire de Louis Halphen,* pp. 313–22.

———. "Le Groupe aristocratique en Aquitaine et en Gascogne (fin Xe-début XIIe siècle)." *Ann. Midi* 80 (1968): 563–71.

———. "Mouvements de population dans le Midi de la France du XIe au XVe siècle d'après les noms de personne et de lieu." *AESC* 8 (1953): 1–24.

———. "Pour l'histoire de l'occupation du sol et du peuplement de la France du sud-ouest, du XIe au XIVe siecle." In Charles Higounet, *Paysages et villages neufs du moyen âge,* pp. 373–97. Bordeaux, 1975.

———. "Problèmes du Midi au temps de Philippe Auguste." In *La France de Philippe Auguste,* pp. 311–20.

Hilton, R. H. *Bondmen Made Free: Medieval Peasant Movements and the English Rising of 1381.* London, 1973.

———. *A Medieval Society: The West Midlands at the End of the Thirteenth Century.* London, 1966.

Hindess, Barry, and Paul Q. Hirst. *Pre-Capitalist Modes of Production.* London, 1975.

Hollister, C. Warren, and John W. Baldwin. "The Rise of Administrative Kingship: Henry I and Philip Augustus." *American Historical Review* 83 (1978): 867–905.

Holt, J. C. *Magna Carta.* Cambridge, 1965.

Holtzmann, Robert. *Wilhelm von Nogaret: Rat und Grossiegelbewahrer Philips des Schönen von Frankreich.* Freiburg i.B., 1898.

Hughes, R. Elfyn, Jane Lutman, A. G. Thomson, and J. Dale. "A Review of the Density and Ratio of Sheep and Cattle in Medieval Gwynedd, with Particular Reference to the Uplands." *Journal of the Merioneth Historical and Record Society* 7 (1973–76): 373–83.

Jack, R. Ian. "The Cloth Industry in Medieval Wales." *WHR* 10 (1980–81): 443–60.

——. "Fulling Mills in Wales and the March before 1547." *Archaeologia Cambrensis* 130 (1981): 70–130.

——. *Medieval Wales*. London, 1972.

——. "Ruthin." In Ralph A. Griffiths, ed., *Boroughs of Mediaeval Wales*, pp. 244–61.

Jenkins, Dafydd. "Law and Government in Wales before the Act of Union." In Dafydd Jerkins, ed., *Celtic Law Papers, Introductory to Welsh Medieval Law and Government*, pp. 23–48. Brussels, 1973.

Jewell, Helen M. *English Local Administration in the Middle Ages*. Newton Abbot, 1972.

*Jones, G. Peredur, ed. "Anglesey Court Rolls, 1346." *Transactions of the Anglesey Antiquarian Society and Field Club* (1930): 33–49; (1932): 42–49; (1933): 44–49.

*——, ed. *The Extent of Chirkland (1391–93)*. London, 1933.

*——, and Hugh Owen, eds. *Caernarvon Court Rolls, 1361–1402*. Caernarfon, 1951.

Jones, Glanville R. J. "The Defenses of Gwynedd in the Thirteenth Century." *Transactions of the Caernarvonshire Historical Society* 30 (1969): 29–43.

——. "The Distribution of Bond Settlements in North-West Wales." *WHR* 2 (1964–65): 19–36.

——. "Field Systems of North Wales." In Alan R. H. Baker and Robin A. Butlin, eds., *Studies of Field Systems in the British Isles*, pp. 430–79. Cambridge, 1973.

——. "Post-Roman Wales." In H. P. R. Finberg, ed., *The Agrarian History of England and Wales*. Vol. 1, pt. 2: *A.D. 43–1042*, pp. 279–382. Cambridge, 1972.

——. "Rural Settlement in Anglesey." In S. R. Eyre and G. R. J. Jones, eds., *Geography as Human Ecology: Methodology by Example*, pp. 199–230. New York, 1966.

——. "Rural Settlement in Ireland and Western Britain." *Advancement of Science* 15 (1959): 338–42.

——. "The Tribal System in Wales: A Re-Assessment in the Light of Settlement Studies." *WHR* 1 (1960–63): 111–32.

Kirby, J. L. *Henry IV of England*. London, 1970.

Köbben, André F. "Comparativists and Non-Comparativists in Anthropology." In Naroll and Cohen, eds., *A Handbook of Method in Cultural Anthropology*, pp. 581–96.

Kosminsky, E. A. *Studies in the Agrarian History of England in the Thirteenth Century*. Oxford, 1956.

Krasner, Stephen D. "Approaches to the State: Alternative Conceptions and Historical Dynamics." *Comparative Politics* 16 (1984): 223–46.

Lacger, Louis de. "Bernard de Castanet, évêque d'Albi (1276–1308)." *Bulletin de Littérature Ecclésiastique* 55 (1954): 193–220.

Langlois, Ch.-V. "Pons d'Aumelas." *BEC* 52 (1891): 259–64.
——. *Le Règne de Philippe III le Hardi.* Paris, 1887.
*——. "Rouleaux d'arrêts de la cour du roi au XIIIe siècle." *BEC* 48 (1887): 177–208.
Latour, Philippe de. "Les Dramatiques trente premières années du Comte Bernard VI de Comminges et la formation de l'axe Foix-Béarn (1241–71): Regard sur la crise des Pyrénées centrales au milieu du XIIIe siècle." *Revue de Comminges, Pyrénées Centrales* 91 (1978): 181–88, 319–27, 449–59; 92 (1979): 33–44.
*Laurière, Eusèbe-Jacob de, et al., eds. *Ordonnances des roys de France de la troisième race.* 22 vols. Paris, 1723–1849.
Lea, Henry Charles. *A History of the Inquisition of the Middle Ages.* 3 vols. New York, 1922.
Lebois, Michèle. "Le Complot des Carcassonnais contre l'inquisition (1283–85)." In *Carcassonne et sa région.* Actes des XLIe et XXIVe Congrès d'Etudes Régionales Tenus par la Fédération Historique du Languedoc Méditerranéen et du Roussillon et par la Fédération Historique des Sociétés Académiques et Savantes de Languedoc-Pyrénées-Gascogne, 17–19 mai 1968, pp. 159–63.
*Léonard, Emile-G., ed. *Catalogue des actes de Raymond V de Toulouse.* Nîmes, 1932.
Le Roy Ladurie, Emmanuel. *Histoire de Languedoc.* 3d ed. Paris, 1974.
——. "L'Histoire immobile." In Emmanuel Le Roy Ladurie, *Le Territoire de l'historien,* 2:7–34. 2 vols. Paris, 1973–78.
——. *Les Paysans du Languedoc.* 2d ed. 2 vols. Paris, 1966.
Lewis, Archibald R. *The Development of Southern French and Catalan Society, 718–1050.* Austin, 1965.
*Lewis, Edward A. "The Account Roll of the Chamberlain of the Principality of North Wales from Michaelmas 1304 to Michaelmas 1305." *BBCS* 1 (1921–23): 256–75.
——. "A Contribution to the Commercial History of Mediaeval Wales." *Y Cymmrodor* 24 (1913): 86–188.
——. "The Decay of Tribalism in North Wales." *THSC* (1902–3): 1–75.
——. "The Development of Industry and Commerce in Wales during the Middle Ages." *Transactions of the Royal Historical Society* new ser. 17 (1903): 121–73.
——. *The Mediaeval Boroughs of Snowdonia.* London, 1912.
Lewis, Norman Bache. "The English Forces in Flanders, August-November 1297." In R. W. Hunt et al., eds., *Studies in Medieval History Presented to Frederick Maurice Powicke,* pp. 310–18. Oxford, 1948.
Lewis, Timothy. "A Bibliography of the Laws of Hywel Dda." *Aberystwyth Studies* 10 (1928): 151–82.
Llobet, Gabriel de. *Foix médiéval: Recherches d'histoire urbaine.* Foix, n.d.
Lloyd, J. E. "The Death of Llewelyn ap Gruffydd," *BBCS* 5 (1929–31): 349–53.
——. *A History of Wales: From the Earliest Times to the Edwardian Conquest.* 2d ed. 2 vols. London, 1912.
——. "Law and Lawyers among the Ancient Welsh." *Transactions of the Liverpool Welsh National Society,* 6th session (1890–91): 96–113.
——. *Owen Glendower.* Oxford, 1931.
Lodge, Eleanor C. *Gascony under English Rule.* London, 1926.

Longnon, Auguste. *La Formation de l'unité française.* Paris, 1922.

Lot, Ferdinand. *L'Art militaire et les armées au moyen âge, en Europe et dans le Proche Orient.* 2 vols. Paris, 1946.

――. "L'Etat des paroisses et des feux de 1328." *BEC* 90 (1929): 51–107, 256–315.

――, and Robert Fawtier. *Histoire des institutions françaises au moyen âge.* 3 vols. Paris, 1957–62.

Lyon, Bryce. *A Constitutional and Legal History of Medieval England.* 2d ed. New York, 1980.

Madaule, Jacques. *The Albigensian Crusade: An Historical Essay.* New York, 1967.

Maddicott, J. R. *The English Peasantry and the Demands of the Crown, 1294–1341.* Past and Present, supplement 1, 1975.

Magnou-Nortier, Elisabeth. "A Propos de la villa et du manse dans les sources méridionales du haut moyen âge." *Ann. Midi* 96 (1984): 85–91.

――. *La Société laïque et l'église dans la province de Narbonne: (Zone cispyrénéene) de la fin du VIIIe à la fin du XIe siècle.* Toulouse, 1974.

*Mahul, M., ed. *Cartulaire et archives des communs de l'ancien diocèse et de l'arrondissement administratif de Carcassonne.* 6 vols. Paris, 1857–82.

Maillard, François. "A Propos d'un ouvrage récent: Notes sur quelques officiers royaux du Languedoc vers 1280–1335." In *France du Nord et France du Midi,* pp. 325–58.

Maitland, F. W., and F. Pollock. *The History of English Law before the Time of Edward I.* 2 vols. 2d ed., reissued. Cambridge, 1968.

Martin, Catherine. "L'Episcopat de la province ecclésiastique de Narbonne, de la mort du comte de Toulouse Raymond VII à la création de la province ecclésiastique de Toulouse (27 septembre 1249–25 juin 1317): Esquisse sociologique." In *Pays de Langue d'Oc, histoire et dialectologie.* Actes du 96e Congrès National des Sociétés Savantes. Toulouse, 1971. Section de Philologie et d'Histoire jusqu'à 1610, vol. 2, pp. 153–93.

Martin, Ernest. *Histoire de la ville de Lodève, depuis ses origines jusqu'à la Revolution.* 2 vols. Montpellier, 1900.

Marx, Karl. *The Eighteenth Brumaire of Louis Bonaparte.* New York, 1963.

――. "On the Jewish Question." In *The Marx-Engels Reader,* pp. 26–52.

――, and Friedrich Engels. "The Manifesto of the Communist Party." In *The Marx-Engels Reader,* pp. 469–500.

――, and Friedrich Engels. *The Marx-Engels Reader.* Ed. by Robert C. Tucker. 2d ed. New York, 1978.

Mélanges d'histoire du moyen âge dédiés à la mémoire de Louis Halphen. Paris, 1951.

*Ménard, Léon. *Histoire civile, ecclésiastique, et littéraire de la ville de Nîmes.* 7 vols. Nîmes, 1873–75.

*Michel, Robert. *L'Administration royale dans la sénéchaussée de Beaucaire au temps de saint Louis.* Paris, 1910.

*Mignon, Robert. *Inventaire d'anciens comptes royaux dressé par Robert Mignon sous le règne de Philippe de Valois.* Ed. Ch.-V. Langlois. Paris, 1899.

Mills, Mabel. "Exchequer Agenda and Estimate of Revenue, Easter Term 1284." *English Historical Review* 40 (1925): 229–34.

Miremont, Pierre, and Jean Monestier. *La Littérature d'oc: Des Troubadours aux Félibres*. Périgueux, 1983.

Mitchell, B. R. *Abstract of British Historical Statistics*. Cambridge, 1962.

*Molinier, Auguste. "La Commune de Toulouse et Philippe III." In *HL*, 10:147–62.

———. "Etude sur l'administration de Louis IX et Alfonse de Poitiers (1226–71)." In *HL*, 7:462–570.

———. "Etude sur l'administration féodale dans le Languedoc (900–1250)." In *HL*, 7:132–213.

———. "Etude sur les démêlés entre l'évêque d'Albi et la cour de France au treizième siècle." In *HL*, 7:284–95.

———. "De Quelques registres du Trésor des Chartes relatifs au Midi de la France." In *HL*, 7:260–74.

———. "Trahison du vicomte de Narbonne, Aymeri (1276–84)." In *HL*, 10: Notes, pp. 409–24.

*———, ed. *Catalogue des actes de Simon et Amauri de Montfort*. Paris, 1874.

*———, ed. *Correspondance administrative d'Alfonse de Poitiers*. 2 vols. Paris, 1894–1900.

Molinier, Charles. *L'Inquisition dans le Midi de la France au XIIIe et au XIVe siècle: Etude sur les sources de son histoire*. Paris, 1880.

Morgan, Richard. "The Barony of Powys, 1275–1360." *WHR* 10 (1980): 1–42.

Morris, John E. *Bannockburn*. Cambridge, 1914.

———. *The Welsh Wars of Edward I: A Contribution to Mediaeval Military History, Based on Original Documents*. Oxford, 1901.

Morris, William Alfred. *The Early English County Court*. Berkeley, Calif., 1926.

Mundy, John Hine. *Liberty and Political Power in Toulouse, 1050–1230*. New York, 1954.

*———. *The Repression of Catharism at Toulouse: The Royal Diploma of 1279*. Toronto, 1985.

Munro, J. H. "Wool-Price Schedules and the Qualities of English Wools in the Later Middle Ages, c. 1270–1499." *Textile History* 9 (1978): 118–69.

Musset, Lucien. "Quelques problèmes posés par l'annexion de la Normandie au domaine royal français." In *La France de Philippe Auguste*, pp. 291–307.

Naroll, Raoul, and Ronald Cohen, eds. *A Handbook of Method in Cultural Anthropology*. Reprint ed. New York, 1973.

———. "Some Thoughts on Comparative Method in Cultural Anthropology." In Hubert M. Blalock, Jr., and Ann. B. Blalock, eds., *Methodology in Social Research*, pp. 236–77. New York, 1968.

Nettl, J. P. "The State as a Conceptual Variable." *World Politics* 20 (1968): 559–92.

Nortier, Michel, and John W. Baldwin. "Contributions à l'étude des finances de Philippe Auguste." *BEC* 138 (1980): 5–33.

O'Connor, James. *The Fiscal Crisis of the State*. New York, 1973.

Oldenbourg, Zoé. *Le Bûcher de Montségur: 16 mars 1244*. Paris, 1959.

Ourliac, Paul. "La Féodalité méridionale." In *Les Pays de la Méditerrannée occidentale au moyen âge: Etudes et recherches*, pp. 7–11. Paris, 1983.

———. "L'Hommage servile dans la région toulousaine." In *Melanges d'histoire du moyen âge dédiés a la mémoire de Louis Halphen*, pp. 551–56.

———. "Le Pays de la Selve à la fin du XIIe siècle." *Ann. Midi* 80 (1968): 581–92.

——. "Réalité ou imaginaire: La Féodalité toulousaine." In *Religion, société, et politique: Mélanges en hommage à Jacques Ellul*, pp. 331–44. Paris, 1983.

——. "Le Servage dans la région toulousaine." In X Congresso Internazionale di Scienze Storiche, Roma, 4–11 Settembre 1955, *Relazioni*. Vol. 7: *Riassunti delle Comunicazioni*, pp. 191–93.

——. "Les Villages de la région toulousaine au XIIe siècle." *AESC* 4 (1949): 268–77.

Owen, David Huw. "Denbigh." In Ralph A. Griffiths, ed., *Boroughs of Mediaeval Wales*, pp. 164–87.

——. "The Englishry of Denbigh: An English Colony in Medieval Wales." *THSC* (1974): 57–76.

——. "The Lordship of Denbigh, 1282–1485." Ph.D. dissertation, University of Wales, 1967.

Owen, Edward. "Owain Lawgoch—Yeuvain de Galles." *THSC* (1899–1900): 6–105.

Painter, Sidney. *The Rise of Feudal Monarchies*. Ithaca, N.Y., 1951.

*Pales-Gobilliard, ed. *L'Inquisiteur Geoffroy d'Ablis et les cathares du comté de Foix (1308–9)*. Paris, 1984.

Palmer, Robert C. *The County Courts of Medieval England, 1150–1350*. Princeton, N.J., 1982.

Parry, Thomas. *A History of Welsh Literature*. Oxford, 1962.

Partak, Joëlle. "Structures foncières et prélevement seigneurial dans un terroir du Lauragais: Caignac dans la seconde moitié du XIIIe siècle." *Ann. Midi* 97 (1985): 5–24.

*Peckham, John. *Registrum epistolarum*. Ed. Charles Trice Martin. 3 vols. London, 1882–85.

Pegues, Franklin J. *The Lawyers of the Last Capetians*. Princeton, N.J., 1962.

*Pelhisson, Guillaume. *Chronique*. Trans. Jean Duvernoy. Toulouse, 1958.

Pélissier, E. "La Lutte des classes à Foix au XIVe siècle." *Bulletin Périodique de la Société Ariégeoise des Sciences, Lettres et Arts et de la Société des Etudes du Cousserans* 14 (1914–16): 96–103.

Pierce, T. Jones. "Aber Gwyn Gregin." *Transactions of the Caernarvonshire Historical Society* 23 (1962): 37–43.

——. "The Age of the Princes." In Pierce, *Medieval Welsh Society*, pp. 19–38.

——. "Ancient Meirionydd." *Journal of the Merioneth Historical and Record Society* 1 (1949–51): 12–20.

——. "A Caernarvonshire Manorial Borough: Studies in the Medieval History of Pwllheli." In Pierce, *Medieval Welsh Society*, pp. 127–93.

——. "The Growth of Commutation in Gwynedd during the Thirteenth Century." In Pierce, *Medieval Welsh Society*, pp. 103–25.

——. "Landlords in Wales: The Nobility and Gentry." In Joan Thirsk, ed., *The Agrarian History of England and Wales*. Vol. 4: *1500–1640*, pp. 357–81. Cambridge, 1967.

——. "The Laws of Wales—The Kindred and the Bloodfeud." In Pierce, *Medieval Welsh Society*, pp. 289–308.

*——. "A Lleyn Lay Subsidy Account." *BBCS* 5 (1929–31): 54–71.

——. "Medieval Settlement in Anglesey." In Pierce, *Medieval Welsh Society*, pp. 251–87.

——. *Medieval Welsh Society: Selected Essays*. Cardiff, 1972.

——. "A Note on Ancient Welsh Measures of Land." *Archaeologia Cambrensis* 97 (1943): 195–204.

*——. "Two Early Caernarvonshire Accounts." *BBCS* 5 (1929–31): 142–55.

Poulantzas, Nicos. *Political Power and Social Classes*. London, 1973.

Powicke, F. M. *King Henry III and the Lord Edward: The Community of the Realm in the Thirteenth Century*. 2 vols. Oxford, 1947.

Pratt, Derek. "Wrexham's Medieval Market." *Transactions of the Denbighshire Historical Society* 15 (1966): 8–14.

Prestwich, Michael. *War, Politics, and Finance under Edward I*. London, 1972.

Prince, A. E. "The Strength of English Armies in the Reign of Edward III." *English Historical Review* 46 (1931): 353–71.

*Ramière de Fortanier, Charles. *Chartes de franchises de Lauragais*. Toul, 1939.

Ramsay, James H. *A History of the Revenues of the Kings of England, 1066–1399*. 2 vols. Oxford, 1925.

Recueil des historiens des Gaules et de la France. Ed. Martin Bouquet et al. 24 vols. Paris, 1738–1904.

*Rees, William, ed. *Calendar of Ancient Petitions Relating to Wales*. Cardiff, 1975.

——. *Industry before the Industrial Revolution*. 2 vols. Cardiff, 1968.

Régné, Jean. *Amauri II, vicomte de Narbonne (1260?–1328): Sa Jeunesse et ses expéditions, son gouvernement–son administration*. Narbonne, 1910.

Reyerson, Kathryn L. "Le Rôle de Montpellier dans le commerce des draps de laine avant 1350." *Ann. Midi* 94 (1982): 17–40.

Reynolds, Susan. *Kingdoms and Communities in Western Europe, 900–1300*. Oxford, 1984.

*Richards, Melville, trans. *The Laws of Hywel Dda: (The Book of Blegywryd)*. Liverpool, 1954.

Richardson, H. G., and G. O. Sayles. *The Governance of Mediaeval England from the Conquest to Magna Carta*. Edinburgh, 1963.

*Rishanger, William. *Chronica et annales, regnantibus Henrico tertio et Edwardo primo, A.D. 1251–1307*. Ed. Henry Thomas Riley. London, 1865.

Roberts, Brynley F. "Un o lawysgrifau Hopcyn ap Tomos o Ynys Dawy." *BBCS* 22 (1966–68): 223–28.

*Roberts, Glyn. "The Anglesey Submissions of 1406." *BBCS* 15 (1952–54): 39–61.

——. *Aspects of Welsh History*. Cardiff, 1969.

——. "The Dominican Friary of Bangor." In Glyn Roberts, *Aspects of Welsh History*, pp. 215–39.

——. "Wales and England: Antipathy and Sympathy, 1282–1485." *WHR* 1 (1960–63): 375–96.

——. " 'Wyrion Eden': The Anglesey Descendants of Ednyfed Fychan in the Fourteenth Century." In Glyn Roberts, *Aspects of Welsh History*, pp. 179–214.

Roderick, A. J., ed. *Wales through the Ages*. Vol. 1. Aberystwyth, 1959.

Rogers, James E. Thorold. *A History of Agriculture and Prices in England: From the Year after the Oxford Parliament (1259) to the Commencement of the Continental War (1793)*. 7 vols. Oxford, 1866–1902.

Rogozinski, Jan. *Power, Caste, and Law: Social Conflict in Fourteenth-Century Montpellier*. Cambridge, Mass., 1982.

* "Roll of Fealty and Presentments on the Accession of Edward the Black Prince to the Principality of Wales: Ministers' Accounts, Early Series, 16 and 17 Edw. III, No. 16." *Archaeologia Cambrensis, Original Documents* 1 (1877): cxlviii-clxxv.

Romestan, Guy. "La Gabelle des draps en Languedoc (1318–33)." In *Hommage à André Dupont: Etudes médiévales languedociennes*, pp. 196–237. Montpellier, 1974.

Saint-Blanquat, Odon de. "Comment se sont crées les bastides du Sud-Ouest de la France." *AESC* 4 (1949): 278–89.

Sayous, André-E., and Jean Combes. "Les Commerçants et les capitalistes de Montpellier aux XIIIe et XIVe siècles." *Revue Historique* 188–89 (1940): 341–77.

*Seebohm, Frederick. *The Tribal System in Wales*. 2d ed. London, 1904.

Sivéry, Gérard. "Le Mécontentement dans le royaume de France et les enquêtes de Saint Louis." *Revue Historique* 269 (1983): 3–24.

——. *Saint Louis et son siècle*. Paris, 1983.

Skocpol, Theda. "Bringing the State Back In: Strategies of Analysis in Current Research." In Peter B. Evans et al., eds., *Bringing the State Back In*, pp. 3–37.

——. *States and Social Revolutions: A Comparative Analysis of France, Russia, and China*. Cambridge, 1979.

Smith, J. Beverley. "Dynastic Succession in Medieval Wales." *BBCS* 33 (1986): 199–232.

——. "Edward II and the Allegiance of Wales." *WHR* 8 (1976–77): 139–71.

——. "Gruffydd Llwyd and the Celtic Alliance, 1315–18." *BBCS* 26 (1974–76): 463–78.

——. *Llywelyn ap Gruffudd, Tywysog Cymru*. Cardiff, 1986.

——. "The Middle March in the Thirteenth Century." *BBCS* 24 (1970–72): 77–93.

——. "The Rebellion of Llywelyn Bren." In T. B. Pugh, ed., *Glamorgan County History: Volume III, the Middle Ages*, pp. 72–86. Cardiff, 1971.

*Smith, Llinos Beverley. "The *Gravamina* of the Community of Gwynedd against Llywelyn ap Gruffudd." *BBCS* 31 (1984): 158–76.

Spufford, Peter. *Handbook of Medieval Exchange*. Royal Historical Society Guides and Handbooks, no. 13, 1986.

Stepan, Alfred. *The State and Society: Peru in Comparative Perspective*. Princeton, N.J., 1978.

Stephenson, David. *The Governance of Gwynedd*. Cardiff, 1984.

——. "The Politics of Powys Wenwynwyn in the Thirteenth Century." *Cambridge Medieval Celtic Studies* 7 (1984): 39–61.

Strayer, Joseph R. *The Albigensian Crusades*. New York, 1971.

——. "Consent to Taxation under Philip the Fair." In Joseph R. Strayer and Charles Taylor, *Studies in Early French Taxation*, pp. 1–105. Cambridge, Mass., 1939.

——. *Les Gens du justice du Languedoc sous Philippe le Bel*. Toulouse, 1970.

——. *Medieval Statecraft and the Perspectives of History*. Princeton, N.J., 1971.

——. "Normandy and Languedoc." In Strayer, *Medieval Statecraft and the Perspectives of History*, pp. 44–59.

——. *On the Medieval Origins of the Modern State*. Princeton, N.J., 1970.

——. *The Reign of Philip the Fair.* Princeton, N.J., 1980.

——. "Viscounts and Viguiers under Philip the Fair." In Strayer, *Medieval State-craft and the Perspectives of History*, pp. 213–31.

Stubbs, William. *The Constitutional History of England in Its Origin and Development.* Vol. 2. 4th ed. Oxford, 1897.

*——, ed. *Select Charters and Other Illustrations of English Constitutional History from the Earliest Times to the Reign of Edward the First.* 9th ed. Oxford, 1921.

Sylvester, Dorothy. *The Rural Landscape of the Welsh Borderland: A Study in Historical Geography.* London, 1969.

*Teulet, Alexandre et al., eds. *Layettes du Trésor des Chartes.* 5 vols. Paris, 1863–1902.

Thomas, Colin. "Peasant Agriculture in Medieval Gwynedd: An Interpretation of the Documentary Evidence." *Folk Life* 13 (1975): 24–37.

——. "Thirteenth-Century Farm Economies in North Wales." *Agricultural History Review* 16 (1968): 1–14.

Thomas, David, ed. *Wales: A New Study.* Newton Abbot, 1977.

Thomas, Louis. "La Vie privée de Guillaume de Nogaret." *Ann. Midi* 16 (1904): 161–207.

Tilly, Charles. *Big Structures, Large Processes, Huge Comparisons.* New York, 1984.

——. "Does Modernization Breed Revolution?" *Comparative Politics* 5 (1973): 425–47.

——. *From Mobilization to Revolution.* Reading, Mass., 1978.

——. "Reflections on the History of European State-Making." In Tilly, ed., *The Formation of National States*, pp. 3–83.

——. "Western State-Making and Theories of Political Transformation." In Tilly, ed., *The Formation of National States*, pp. 601–38.

——, ed. *The Formation of National States in Western Europe.* Princeton, N.J., 1975.

Timbal, Pierre. *Un Conflit d'annexion au moyen âge: L'Application de la coutume de Paris au pays d'Albigeois.* Toulouse, 1950.

Titus, C. H. "A Nomenclature in Political Science." *American Political Science Review* 25 (1931): 45–60.

Tout, Thomas Frederick. "The Captivity and Death of Edward of Carnarvon." In T. F. Tout, *The Collected Papers*, 3:145–90. 3 vols. Manchester, 1932–34.

——. *Chapters in the Administrative History of Medieval England.* 6 vols. Manchester, 1928–37.

——, and Dorothy M. Broome. "A National Balance Sheet for 1362–3, with Documents Subsidiary Thereto." *English Historical Review* 39 (1924): 404–19.

Trabut-Cussac, J. P. *L'Administration anglaise en Gascogne sous Henry III et Edouard I de 1254 à 1307.* Geneva, 1972.

Tucoo-Chala, Pierre. *Gaston Fébus et la vicomté de Béarn, 1343–91.* Bordeaux, 1960.

——. *Gaston Fébus: Un Grand prince d'Occident au XIVe siècle.* Pau, 1976.

Vidal, Henri. "Les Mariages dans la famille des Guillems, seigneurs de

Montpellier." *Revue Historique de Droit Français et Etranger* 62 (1984): 231–45.

Vidal, J.-M. "Bernard Saisset, évêque de Pamiers (1232–1311)." *Revue des Sciences Religieuses* 5 (1925): 416–38, 565–90; 6 (1926): 50–77, 177–98, 371–93.

*———. *Un Inquisiteur jugé par ses 'victimes': Jean Galand et les Carcassonnais (1285–86)*. Paris, 1903.

*Vinogradoff, Paul, and Frank Morgan, eds. *Survey of the Honour of Denbigh, 1334*. London, 1914.

Wakefield, Walter L. *Heresy, Crusade, and Inquisition in Southern France, 1100–1250*. Berkeley, Calif., 1974.

Walker, Williston. *On the Increase of Royal Power in France under Philip Augustus, 1179–1223*. Leipzig, 1888.

*Waters, W. H. "Account of the Sheriff of Caernarvon for 1303–4." *BBCS* 7 (1933–35): 143–53.

*———. "Documents Relating to the Office of Escheator for North Wales for the Year 1309–10." *BBCS* 6 (1931–33): 360–68.

———. *The Edwardian Settlement of North Wales in Its Administrative and Legal Aspects (1284–1343)*. Cardiff, 1935.

Weber, Max. *Economy and Society: An Outline of Interpretive Sociology*. Ed. Guenther Roth and Claus Wittich. 2 vols. Berkeley, Calif., 1968.

*Wiliam, Aled Rhys. *Llyfr Iorwerth: A Critical Text of the Venedotian Code of Medieval Welsh Law, Mainly from Cotton MS. Titus Dii*. Cardiff, 1960.

Willard, James Field. *Parliamentary Taxes on Personal Property, 1290 to 1334: A Study in Mediaeval English Financial Administration*. Cambridge, Mass., 1934.

Williams, Glanmor. *Owen Glendower*. Oxford, 1966.

———. *Recovery, Reorientation, and Reformation: Wales, c. 1415–1642*. Oxford, 1987.

———. *The Welsh Church from Conquest to Reformation*. 2d ed. Cardiff, 1976.

*Williams, Gwyn. *An Introduction to Welsh Poetry: From the Beginnings to the Sixteenth Century*. London, n.d.

*———, trans. *Welsh Poems: Sixth Century to 1600*. Berkeley, Calif., 1974.

Williams, W. R. *The Parliamentary History of the Principality of Wales*. Brecknock, 1895.

*Williams ab Ithel, John, ed. *Annales Cambriae*. London, 1860.

Williams-Jones, Keith. "Caernarvon." In Ralph A. Griffiths, ed., *Boroughs of Mediaeval Wales*, pp. 72–101.

*———, ed. *The Merioneth Lay Subsidy Roll, 1292–3*. Cardiff, 1976.

Wolf, Eric R. *Europe and the People without History*. Berkeley, Calif., 1982.

———. *Peasants*. Englewood Cliffs, N.J., 1966.

Wolff, Philippe. "Achats d'armes pour Philippe le Bel dans la région toulousaine." In Wolff, *Regards*, pp. 395–402.

———. *Commerces et marchands de Toulouse (vers 1350-vers 1450)*. Paris, 1954.

———. "La Draperie en Languedoc du XIIe au début du XVIIe siècle." In Wolff, *Regards*, pp. 437–70.

*———. *Les 'Estimes' toulousains des XIVe et XVe siècles*. Toulouse, 1956.

——. "Une Famille du XIIIe au XVIe siècle: Les Ysalguier de Toulouse." In Wolff, *Regards*, pp. 233–57.
——. *Histoire de Toulouse*. Toulouse, 1958.
——. "Les Luttes sociales dans les villes du Midi français du XIIIe au XVe siècle." In Wolff, *Regards*, pp. 77–89.
——. "La Noblesse toulousaine: Essai sur son histoire médiévale." In Wolff, *Regards*, pp. 213–31.
——. "Réflexions sur l'histoire médiévale de Carcassonne." In Wolff, *Regards*, pp. 425–36.
——. "Réflexions sur l'histoire médiévale de Montauban." In Wolff, *Regards*, pp. 333–45.
——. *Regards sur le Midi médiéval*. Toulouse, 1978.
——, ed. *Histoire du Languedoc*. Toulouse, 1967.
Wood, Charles T. "The Return of Medieval Politics." *American Historical Review* 94 (1989): 391–404.
Wylie, J. *History of England under Henry IV*. 4 vols. London, 1884–98.
*Wynne, John. *History of the Gwedir Family*. London, 1770.

Index

Library of Congress Cataloging-in-Publication Data

Given, James Buchanan.
   State and society in medieval Europe : Gwynedd and
Languedoc under outside rule / James Given.
      p. cm. — (The Wilder House series in politics, history, and
culture)
   Includes bibliographical references (p.).
   ISBN 0-8014-2439-9 (alk. paper) — ISBN 0-8014-9774-4 (pbk: alk. paper)
    1. Languedoc (France—Politics and government. 2. Gwynedd
(Wales)—Politics and government. I. Title. II. Series.
JN2433.L36A44 1990
942.9'202—dc20

90-31274